Defending Human Rights in Russia

Sergei Kovalyov is a central figure in the struggle for human rights in Russia. He was a leading Soviet biologist and, in the 1970s after becoming active in dissident circles, was arrested by the KGB, tried, imprisoned and subjected to internal exile. After his release, he continued to work for human rights, eventually becoming chairman of the Supreme Soviet Human Rights Committee and chairman of the Presidential Human Rights Commission. He rose to become Russia's first Human Rights Commissioner under President Yeltsin, in which he was extremely influential in framing human rights provisions in post-Communist Russia. He subsequently took President Yeltsin to task for the tragic war in the southern republic of Chechnya, eventually resigning in protest. This book, by tracing Kovalyov's political career, shows his attempts to shape a new human rights culture in Russia in the late Soviet and post-Soviet era.

Emma Gilligan received a PhD from the University of Melbourne, Australia, in 2002. She spent five years in Moscow, researching for this book and working for The Andrei Sakharov Foundation. She is currently a post-doctoral fellow with the History Department at the University of Chicago, working on a book on human rights and Chechnya.

BASEES/RoutledgeCurzon Series on Russian and East European Studies

Series editor: Richard Sakwa, *(Department of Politics and International Relations, University of Kent)*,

Editorial Committee:
George Blazyca, (Centre for Contemporary European Studies, University of Paisley), Terry Cox, *(Department of Government, University of Strathclyde),* Rosalind Marsh, *(Department of European Studies and Modern Languages, University of Bath),* David Moon, *(Department of History, University of Strathclyde),* Hilary Pilkington, *(Centre for Russian and East European Studies, University of Birmingham),* Stephen White, *(Department of Politics, University of Glasgow)*

This series is published on behalf of BASEES (the British Association for Slavonic and East European Studies). The series comprises original, high-quality, research-level work by both new and established scholars on all aspects of Russian, Soviet, post-Soviet and East European Studies in humanities and social science subjects.

Defending Human Rights in Russia

Sergei Kovalyov, Dissident and
Human Rights Commissioner,
1969–2003

Emma Gilligan

RoutledgeCurzon
Taylor & Francis Group

LONDON AND NEW YORK

First published 2004
by RoutledgeCurzon
11 New Fetter Lane, London EC4P 4EE

Simultaneously published in the USA and Canada
by RoutledgeCurzon
29 West 35th Street, New York, NY 10001

RoutledgeCurzon is an imprint of the Taylor & Francis Group

© 2004 Emma Gilligan

Typeset in Times by Taylor & Francis Books Ltd
Printed and bound in Great Britain by TJ International Ltd, Padstow,
Cornwall

British Library Cataloguing in Publication Data
A catalogue record for this book is available from the British Library

Library of Congress Cataloging-in-Publication Data
A catalog record for this book has been requested

ISBN 0–415–32369–X

For my Mother

Contents

Illustrations

Acknowledgments

I wish to acknowledge the help and kindness of many individuals displayed over the course of the past five years. To Robert Horvath and Edward Kline who, in the daunting initial stages of my research in Moscow and New York, provided endless encouragement, intellectual inspiration and enthusiasm for my chosen topic. I am extremely grateful to Sergei Kovalyov's chief aid, Lydia Ivanovna Siomina, whose commitment to honesty and the hard truth saved this book from any romantic musings; and to her colleagues at the Presidential Human Rights Commission, Sergei Sirotkin and Mikhail Arutyunov, who offered their time and important knowledge of events in the Russian Duma. To Oleg Orlov, Director of Memorial's Human Rights Centre, for his kindness, information and great insight into Sergei Kovalyov's character; to Alexander Daniel, Head of Memorial's History of the Dissident Movement Project, for stimulating conversations; and to Associate Professor Stephen Wheatcroft of the University of Melbourne, for insightful comments on drafts and support with travel grants and funding. I am grateful to Tatyana Bakhmina of Memorial's archive in Moscow for gathering the illustrations, and to the University of Melbourne for financial support while preparing the final manuscript. Thanks also to Sheila Fitzpatrick for inviting me to the University of Chicago as a post-doctoral fellow and providing me with the time to finish this manuscript. I am grateful to my good friends Anne Farrelly, Philip Grant, Geoff Wilkes and Erna Thomas. And finally, to my mother, Helen Gilligan, and my sister, Therese Grant, whose tireless encouragement and emotional support saw me through some of those darker days in Moscow.

Introduction

We must overcome some of the old 'antipathies' of the Russia intellectual – for example, his disgust for compromises ... not all compromises are 'dishonest'.

Sergei Kovalyov[1]

In September 1969, Sergei Adamovich Kovalyov reluctantly left his friends and colleagues at Moscow State University. The thirty-nine-year-old biologist, author of over eighty academic articles and head of the laboratory on mathematical methodology, had just been forced to resign for his active participation in the Soviet Union's first non-government human rights organization, the *Initiative Group for the Defence of Human Rights*. His resignation from the Soviet Union's most prestigious university marked the end of a successful scientific career and the beginning of a public life as one of the world's most prominent human rights advocates.

Twenty-one years later, in March 1990, Kovalyov entered the world of Soviet politics. In an attempt to exert influence over the legislative process, he became Chairman of the RSFSR Supreme Soviet's Human Rights Committee, Russia's first Human Rights Commissioner and a prominent international diplomat as Russia's representative to the United Nations Human Rights Commission. Yet the problems in this transition were more complex than might have been predicted. Kovalyov was cast into political life on the eve of the collapse of the Soviet Union with little experience, either political or managerial. And although he managed to institute substantial mechanisms for the protection of human rights in Russia, his central concern with civil and political rights did not fit well with the majority of his parliamentary deputies. He was ousted from the post of Commissioner just over a year after his appointment, and he resigned in despair from the Presidential Human Rights Commission in the wake of Russia's drawn-out attack on the republic of Chechnya in the winter of 1994.

This book is about one man's struggle for fundamental human rights in Russia. It is about his determination and courage in an era of collapsing traditions. It contains several interrelated themes. The theme of cooperation between Russian human rights activists and the state, the struggle to build a human rights culture, and the human story of Sergei Kovalyov's public career. In choosing Sergei Kovalyov as the focus of this book I have sought to show not only his successes and failures, but to explore a problem which radiates outwards from his experience in government. Kovalyov was not the only dissident who defied the conventions of his peers in order to gain leverage over government policy. Many human rights defenders across the former Soviet Union entered government structures. Many became disillusioned, trying to reconcile their principles with the political reality. Many endured unforeseen personal compromises and contradictions while working in a period of collapsing traditions. What were the circumstances that contributed to the problems faced by Kovalyov and his colleagues? How did the political struggles in the State Duma, the inadequate human rights culture and the concern for economic well-being over civil and political rights influence their struggle for human rights mechanisms in the post-Soviet era?

Sergei Kovalyov was always a vocal critic of his country when he felt it violated fundamental human rights. His open criticisms began in 1959 when he appealed to the Dean of Moscow State University to change the curriculum. Together with two others he co-authored the first published article in *Nauka i Zhizn'* refuting Lysenko's theory of genetics. He turned next to the *Initiative Group for the Defence of Human Rights*, an open organization established in 1969 that sought to monitor human rights violations in the Soviet Union. By the time he was barred from Moscow State University he had already defended his doctorate (*Kandidate Nauk*) and was about to become the editor of *The Chronicle of Current Events*, the Soviet Union's leading *samizdat* journal. During *perestroika*, he criticised the Gorbachev regime for its failure to adopt international human rights standards. In the Supreme Soviet from 1990 to 1993, he criticised legislation not in accordance with international law. His criticisms of the Chechen war were acknowledged in the Western world with the prestigious Nuremberg International Human Rights Award, the Council of Europe's Human Rights Award and the League of Nations Human Rights Prize. He was nominated for the Nobel Peace Prize and within his own country named *Man of the Year* by the Russian daily, *Izvestiya*.

Arrested in 1973 for his role as editor of the *Chronicle*, Kovalyov spent seven years in prisons and labour camps. In 1984 he returned from exile in Magadan to the city of Kalinin, until he was finally permitted to resettle in Moscow in 1987. Aged fifty-four, he had missed fifteen years of research in his specialized area of neurophysiology and remained reluctant to return to his previous career. Not having foreseen the changes that arrived with Gorbachev's rule, he nevertheless quickly took advantage of the new opportunities furnished by *perestroika*. In the beginning he remained close to dissident circles and helped found the *Press Klub Glasnost*. By the winter of 1987 he had helped to organize the first major human rights seminar in preparation for the 1991 Moscow CSCE Conference. Soon he became active in the burgeoning democratic movement that was later to unite under the political bloc, Democratic Russia.

Kovalyov respects the traditions of classical liberalism as founded in Western countries – respect for individual rights and political liberty. He maintained that his understanding of liberalism was informed more by his own experiences than through a formal study of liberal theory. At the age of forty he had experienced the wrenching of freedom from his own life and believed that, despite the isolation of the dissident milieu of the 1960s, many activists managed to respect all the most important components of liberal philosophy, especially a commitment to the rule of law. Countering all those who maintained that Russia needed strong authoritarian rule in its transition to democracy, he insisted that Russia had to live and experience democracy in order to truly understand it.

But the what and how of Russia's transformation were questions to which Kovalyov only gradually worked out answers. It began in 1970 when the physicists Andrei Sakharov, Valery Chalidze and Andrei Tverdokhlebov formed the Moscow Human Rights Committee and appealed to the Soviet regime for cooperation between human rights activists and the state on the question of human rights. Kovalyov sympathised with those who favoured dialogue with the regime. His position was by no means submissive, informed by his belief in the necessity of compromise, a tradition he felt his intellectual predecessors had been incapable of. While his view may do some injustice to his precursors, his attitude was profoundly influenced by the excesses of the October Revolution of 1917. There was by no means a linear evolution towards this view. At times he expressed his disgust with politics and its polemics, what he saw as the flagrant dishonesty and self-interest of politicians, but he also strongly believed that the despotism of the Soviet state could not be countered by the intellectual elite's rejection of it. By 1989 he felt even more convinced that their task was to take the path of peaceful dialogue in the quest for human rights reform.

The profoundly moralizing climate of the dissident milieu of the 1960s continued to encircle Kovalyov's decisions deep into his political career. The tenets of the movement in which many activists had answered only for themselves turned Kovalyov's decision to enter Russian politics in March 1990 into a moral debate on cooperation between human rights activists and the state. While he respected his contemporaries and encouraged their role in Russia's nascent civil society, his own view of moral responsibility was not always accorded the same respect.

His belief in cooperation at last received expression in the first Human Rights Committee of the Supreme Soviet. Many of his personal ambitions were borne out in these years, especially his long-standing view that new and amended legislation was one of the first key steps to changing the Soviet Union's human rights record. With the help of his colleagues he facilitated a series of legislative initiatives, beginning with draft laws on states of emergency, the penal system, the law on the Human Rights Commissioner and ending with a comprehensive report on human rights violations in the Russian Federation; these were some of the most striking achievements of this period.

As a universalist, Kovalyov rejects the idea of the sovereignty of states when it comes to human rights violations. He deeply admires Western democratic political orders and throughout his career he constantly deployed the United Nations Universal Declaration of Human Rights in his defence. A Western democracy in Russia, however, was inconceivable without a liberal constitution, and for that reason he worked conscientiously on the human rights provisions of the 1993 Constitution to enshrine the inalienable rights of the individual as the supreme value. Charting a democratic course also meant that the Russian population had to have means to redress state violations. Removing the complaint point from the offices of the Procurator and forming an independent body in the tradition of the Swedish Ombudsman became for Kovalyov a conscious mission.

Many of the failures of the Human Rights Committee can be explained by the exigencies of the moment. There were few attitudes that Kovalyov shared with the nationalist Duma majority. While trying to settle the plight of Russians in Moldavia or travelling to prison camps across Russia, he also had to face the speaker of the Russian parliament, Ruslan Khasbulatov, whom he characterized as intelligent but dangerously ambitious. While the rivalry between Yeltsin and Khasbulatov brewed, Kovalyov showed his allegiance to Yeltsin, a position he was to adopt again during the dissolution of the parliament in October 1993.

While many democrats drifted out of Democratic Russia after the catastrophic elections of 1993, Kovalyov's position became increasingly complicated. After the dissolution of the parliament, Yeltsin asked him to chair the Presidential Human Rights Commission, *pri prezidenti*. Within a year, relations between the President and Kovalyov were strained; for Yeltsin, the self-proclaimed human rights advocate, the day of reckoning came in November 1994 when he ordered the attack on the breakaway republic of Chechnya.

Kovalyov spoke out against the Chechen war with a moral urgency that few could rival. In *Literaturnaya Gazeta*, he joined his contemporaries and signed a collective statement condemning the attack as an "act of terrorism against the Chechen people."[2] He could not support the view that Chechnya posed a threat to Russia's security, and he returned from Grozny visibly shaken and shocked at what he had witnessed in the republic's capital. Braving the patriotic maelstrom, he insisted on peace in Chechnya and defended his appeal to international opinion. He returned repeatedly to the southern republic where he continued to monitor human rights violations, exposing the attack on the village of Samashki and helping to resolve the hostage crisis in Budyonnovsk. He was disturbed most acutely by the way Yeltsin invoked human rights discourse to whitewash and legitimate the atrocities.

Through all the tumult of these years, Kovalyov remained prey to doubts about Russia's democratic future. He claimed that he had never been certain of how effective his efforts would be and he despised the ceremonial patriotism that he saw everywhere in post-Soviet Russia. His anxieties were reinforced when President Vladimir Putin reignited the Chechen war in September 1999, the cruelty of which he understood to be disguised behind the global campaign against terrorism. There was disappointment but no shock in the shift in the politics of his country. While in New York in March 1996, he turned his attention even more forcefully to international support and argued for a supernational organ where individuals instead of states would be protected.

Sergei Kovalyov united features that were both positive and negative in a parliamentary leader. His strength of will, great moral courage and capacity for work were clearly assets in a challenging political sphere. He was well respected by his colleagues for his honesty and integrity, his admirable ideals and his indifference to ambition or prestige. Russians in the Baltic States and Chechens in Grozny appreciated his racial and religious tolerance, and his claims to relevance were always modest. Yet Kovalyov frequently lacked political instinct. He was inclined to drop everything at the expense of all else when an issue arose that he cared strongly about, he found it difficult to trust those he did not know and bridge the personal and professional gap between himself and state bureaucrats. His judgement on issues like the Phoenix school was questionable. His failure to leave the political party, Russia's Choice, once appointed Russia's first Human Rights Commissioner, has been criticised.

For the radical democrats, Kovalyov's unwillingness to support lustration laws or de-communization only reinforced the root of their dilemma. As the shallowness of Russia's transition grew increasingly clear, Kovalyov continued to support the view that the purging of the administration or criminal liability for the crimes of the Soviet era would only protract the reform process. He did not fail to acknowledge the logic of his opponents' argument, and the reality of the first Chechen war led to a certain degree of self-reflection on his part. Would such a process have averted the inordinate and arbitrary violence? Despite the consequences, he remained circumspect. For Kovalyov, implicating individuals would only have exonerated Soviet society at large of responsibility. His critics attacked his belief in "collective responsibility" as a hollow notion incompatible with the reality of the Soviet era.

Kovalyov became less conciliatory and increasingly tired of the political battles he had to fight in the Duma. His independent cast of mind and vocal criticisms were often viewed as political liabilities. Yet several of his colleagues felt that his return to classical dissidence after a powerful letter of resignation to Yeltsin in 1997 was an irretrievable loss to the struggle to implement human rights mechanisms in Russia. Kovalyov was frequently and unfairly compared to his friend, Andrei Sakharov, in which he was cast as the physicist's spiritual successor, a comparison that he himself seemed to grow progressively irritated by.

When I began this study in June 1995 in Moscow, Sergei Kovalyov was in the midst of negotiating the release of over one hundred people during the hostage crisis in the Stavropol city of Budyonnovsk. The disquiet that circled around him in this period said something much deeper and unsettling about the state of Russian politics. More fundamentally, it provoked my interest in trying to trace the history of his struggle to institutionalize human rights mechanisms in post-Soviet Russia, and his defence of rights, in and outside the parliament; to piece together an untold story that would offer an interesting insight into the complex challenges, physical and psychological, that Russia faced in the first five years after the collapse of the USSR.

Since the collapse of the Soviet Union the weight of Western attention has been focused on market reform, the rise of the oligarchs and the court struggles between Yeltsin and his opposition. Recent publications, like Lawrence Klein and Marshall Pomer's *The New Russia: Transition Gone Awry*, Ander's Aslund and Martha Brill Olcott's collection, *Russia after Communism*, and Stephen White's *Russia's New Politics* make no mention of Sergei Kovalyov. His defence of human rights and his quest for human rights mechanisms has been largely ignored. Serious interest in his political activity began in earnest during the first Chechen war, but there has been no full-scale study of his struggle for human rights, either before or after the collapse of the Soviet Union. In his homeland, notable attention has been paid him in the Russian press and, with Alexander Daniel, Kovalyov set about writing his autobiography in 1995 which has been published in German by Rowolt Press. In 1999, Kovalyov's new initiative, The Human Rights Institute, published a collection of his speeches and essays, entitled *Sergei Kovalyov: The Pragmatics of Political Idealism* (*Sergei Kovalyov: Pragmatika Politicheskogo Idealizma*).

Collating information for this study was complicated by a number of issues. This book is largely based on information from the Human Rights Committee of the Supreme Soviet and the Presidential Human Rights Commission. The fire in Moscow's White House in October 1993 completely destroyed the Human Rights Committee archive, but documents were made available by Kovalyov's assistant, Lydia Siomina, and the Director of Memorial's Human Rights Centre, Oleg Orlov; and from the private archive of the President of The Andrei Sakharov Foundation (USA) and the Russian–American Human Rights Project Group, Edward Kline. Many of the most important insights of this book are derived from interviews with members of the Human Rights Committee and the Presidential Human Rights Commission, conducted from 1995 to 1999. Several members were interviewed up to three times. The interviews are important primary sources that offer valuable facts, otherwise unattainable, and personal insight into major events. They significantly enhanced my own awareness of the complexity of events and the divisions and frustrations within the human rights community. They gave me a deeper insight into the individual personalities striving for human rights reform as views on cooperation and post-Soviet politics were openly shared.

This study also greatly benefited from access to Kovalyov's *Memoirs* which were made available by Edward Kline. The *Memoirs* were extremely helpful when trying to understand Kovalyov's attitude to key events. They are limited by the fact that they were written with the assistance of Alexander Daniel and bear the marks of a ghostwriter. Mr Kline's personal archive in New York provided invaluable material on the work of the Russian–American Human Rights Project group and the personal correspondence between Mr Kline, Kovalyov and his aide, Lydia Siomina over the turbulent periods of the August coup of 1991 and the firing on the White House in 1993.

This study has also relied on Russian newspaper articles, journals and unpublished materials made available by the library of Memorial and The Andrei Sakharov Archive, Museum and Public Centre, particularly correspondence between Sakharov and Kovalyov, the transcripts of the trial of the Communist Party, and earlier *samizdat* material. Certain documents were also made available by the State Archives of the Russian Federation (GARF).

The methodology used in this book does have certain limitations. The original information provided in this study, especially through interviews, is often coloured by subjective opinions and should be treated with the caution accorded all interviews. The fire in the Human Rights Committee Archive in 1993 has left parts of this story with fragmented information and, despite great efforts, these gaps were difficult to overcome. This book does not engage in arguments with other Western or Russian scholars on Russia's compliance with international human rights laws or engage in arguments regarding key political events, nor does it concentrate on social and economic rights. It does not seek to analyse the degree to which the Human Rights Movement laid the foundations for *perestroika* or the emergence of the democratic movement. It attempts to show parts of a story from inside Russia and seeks to analyse the conflicts, paradoxes and dilemmas faced by Kovalyov in the changing circumstances of the post-Soviet era. Given the contemporaneity of these events, this book makes no claim to be definitive. On many issues it remains at best a starting point for future scholars who may recast much of what I have written.

Divided into six chapters, this book is largely descriptive with a preference for the narrative mode of exposition, with an emphasis on individuals and events. Chapter 1 examines Kovalyov's participation in the Soviet Human Rights Movement in the 1960s and 1970s in Moscow up until the time of his arrest in 1974 and his return from internal exile in 1984, and seeks to assess his contribution to the ideals which shaped the movement in this early period. Chapter 2 traces the period from 1984 to 1990 and Kovalyov's role in the *perestroika* period. This chapter attempts to understand the major arguments within dissident circles regarding collaboration between human rights activists and the government. Chapter 3 analyses the work of the Human Rights Committee of the Supreme Soviet (RSFSR) and Kovalyov's participation in the 1992 trial in the Russian Constitutional Court on the banning of the Communist Party. This chapter seeks to illuminate Kovalyov's attempts to amend legislation to conform with international human rights norms and to redefine Russia's image in the West. Chapter 4 examines the work of the

Presidential Human Rights Commission and the struggle for the post of Human Rights Commissioner in the State Duma. Chapter 5 looks at Kovalyov's role in exposing atrocities in the 1994–1996 Chechen war that resulted in his resignation from the Presidential Human Rights Commission. Chapter 6 narrates the history of his career since 1997 and the extremely unsettling times that have followed with the second Chechen war and the rise of Vladimir Putin as Russian President in March 2000.

Many people have worked tirelessly over the past decade to build a human rights culture in Russia along with Kovalyov. It is also the story of his colleagues, Sergei Sirotkin, Oleg Orlov, Lydia Siomina, Mikhail Arutyunov, Boris Zolotukhin, Mikhail Molostvov, Vyacheslav Bakhmin and all the less celebrated figures, experts and volunteers alike, who have shaped this unique era of human rights reform in post-Soviet Russia.

Notes

1   S. Kovalyov, "Without Barricades", *XX Century and Peace*, No. 9 (1988): 44–8.
2   *Literaturnaya Gazeta*, No. 28 (July 12, 1995): 2.

1 *Dissidentstvo*

... a master accustomed to the hypocrisy of dealing with slaves is frightened
by the mere suggestion of a dignified discussion among equals.

Valery Chalidze[1]

In the first two decades after the fall of Nikita Khrushchev, the principal
vehicle of the Soviet Human Rights Movement was the concept of the
integrity of the individual.[2] This led to a revolt against the collectivist principles of the socialist regime, with an emphasis on *glasnost*, human dignity,
freedom of expression and respect for the constitution. This was not a
conceptual framework that grew out of ideas imported from the West.
Indeed, to search for a philosophical and conceptual framework in the early
days of the movement's formation is difficult.[3] For many, its beginnings can
be traced to a simple but remarkably strong intuitive reaction to the moral
ugliness of the Soviet regime. For the majority of the Soviet scientific and
literary intelligentsia – the content of their protest was aesthetic and ethical
rather than political – it was directed against a regime that persisted in perse-
cuting individuals who were struggling to live out their independent lives.

The term *dissidentstvo* is how the spectre of movements within the Soviet
Union came to be characterized by mid-1990. By no means a homogenous
group, the Soviet Human Rights Movement formed only one of the many
movements within the USSR.[4] Right from the beginning, every movement was
preoccupied with its own cause – the *refuseniks* with anti-Semitism and emigration, the Baptists with religious persecution, the Crimean Tartars with
repatriation, the Lithuanian Nationalist Movement with independence. Within
these movements there existed liberals, socialists, communists, anti-communists, nationalists, anarchists, pacifists, artists, writers and scientists. And in this
respect it was, of course, a microcosm of civil society, defined and distinguished
by a plurality of opinions and differences in political leanings, and linked by a
common belief that every individual had the right to freely express his/her
views and defend his/her rights without fear of persecution. These were normal
acts that we have been witnessing in Western societies for decades. It was the
context in which these acts were made, however, that clearly distinguished these
individuals from the conventions of their era.

The Soviet Human Rights Movement emerged as perhaps the most well known of all the movements. Closely aligned to the physicist, Andrei Sakharov, it has been recognized for its remarkable contribution to the distribution of information on human rights violations across the Soviet Union through the *samizdat* text, *The Chronicle of Current Events*. The movement was born out of anxiety for the fate of friends or colleagues against a backdrop of attempts to rehabilitate the Stalin era. The well known trial of writers Andrei Sinyavsky and Yuli Daniel in 1966, tried for the opinions of their fictional characters, embodied the entire scope of what became an absurd nightmare for the many individuals struggling for elemental freedoms over the course of the next twenty-five years.[5] The slogan of human rights became an instrument for the defence of the movement itself, but simultaneously, as its members grew increasingly assured of the righteousness of their position, they began to express concern for individuals victimized by the regime regardless of their connection to the movement. They also began to step outside their own national boundaries and the petitions and open letters once addressed to the Soviet regime and leading political figures began to include appeals to the world community.

The questions to which the human rights movement addressed itself were interpreted by its members as fundamental to the future of the Soviet Union. It is important, therefore, to understand the sincerity with which they first petitioned the Soviet government. Some believed that their demands for fair and open trials, for respect for the law and the constitution, for freedom of expression, were the most convincing non-violent means to address the arbitrary rule of a totalitarian regime, and that their realization lay within the realm of possibility. As the well-known activist Larissa Bogoraz pointed out: "The truth consists of the fact that we appealed to the government structures, having in mind the possibility to collaborate with them if they wanted to listen to us."[6]

The movement itself was divided on the question of a philosophy of action. As it grew in confidence and was confronted by different circumstances, its members were forced to define strategies that would not merely help them avoid arrest, but that would reflect their commitment to certain essential milestones in their work. Their actions were driven by three major factors.[7] The first and foremost was a commitment to non-violence. The second involved the concepts of truth and honesty, and the third was a strong commitment to working from within the laws of the Soviet Union. Their aims varied and were interpreted accordingly – from existential acts of protest to the overthrow of the existing order, to the struggle for political rights, cultural freedom and moral resistance.[8]

The polemic over the precise social, political and cultural components of the Soviet Human Rights Movement began in the middle of the 1980s. Much of it was centred on defining what the movement had been. Kovalyov believed that there had been a clear division within the movement that he divided into two categories – the legalists (*zakonniki*) and the politicals (*politiki*).[9] The legalist strain of the movement, as epitomized in the early days by Alexander Esenin-Volpin and Valery Chalidze, was concerned primarily with defending where possible the integrity and rights of the individual against the arbitrary actions of the regime. "Probably we were naive," recalled Chalidze, "but we were sincere when we called for respect for the constitution, when we said we were not struggling against the authorities, but simply demanding that they respect their own laws ..."[10] The legalists defended individuals regardless of their political views and were concerned more with supporting the individual's right to legal justice and freedom of expression. Nor were they as concerned as the "politicals" with the political system under which they lived so long as the system ceased to systematically violate human rights. The politicals certainly hoped to one day witness the end of the Soviet regime.

Not only did the distinction between these two currents of thought rest in the ultimate goals of either group, but Chalidze went so far as to stress that attempts by the legalists to begin a dialogue with the Soviet authorities were undermined by the politicals. Chalidze criticised the politicals for "violating the ethical principles of the movement" and discouraging support from within the regime. "There was a realisation that we all lived under the same axe and still another that we were so few that it seemed better to try and work together despite our differences. We were wrong."[11]

The first public effort to engage the authorities in collaborative work ended in 1973 with the dissolution of Chalidze's Human Rights Committee. Established in 1970 with Sakharov, Andrei Tverdokhlebov, Alexander Esenin-Volpin and Boris Tsukerman, the founding statement of the Committee had declared its aim to provide "consultative assistance to the organs of government in the establishment and application of guarantees of human rights, carried out on the initiative of the Committee or of interested organs of government." The Committee took as its guide the principles of the Universal Declaration of Human Rights, but recognized the "special characteristics of Soviet law taking into account the ... real difficulties faced by the state in this sphere."[12] Over the course of eighteen months the Committee appealed to the state organs regarding criminal cases, and often wrote to the RSFSR Supreme Soviet pointing out discrepancies in the law and problems with court proceedings. The reaction to the formation of the Committee was diverse. Some questioned why it had embarked on such a futile exercise, others marked it as the birth of political opposition in the USSR and saw in the Committee a potential leader. The most vehement attack was by Alexander Solzhenitsyn: "A strange committee, it was, of course: set up to advise the cannibals (when requested) on the rights of those they were eating alive."[13]

Chalidze was but one of many intellectuals of the 1960s who supported the third way; a way neither revolutionary nor political but one of dialogue with the regime, aimed at encouraging discussion.[14] But as Sakharov grew frustrated with the theoretical and legal underpinnings of the Committee's work, a scepticism Kovalyov also shared, and Chalidze was forced into exile in November 1972, the Committee gradually ceased its activity.

The idea of dialogue was nevertheless kept alive by Andrei Sakharov during the 1970s and 1980s, despite his growing frustration with the depravity of the Soviet regime. He acknowledged repeatedly the simple truth that the Soviet government was the only government they had and he always attempted to keep the channels open.[15] Moreover, the physicist Yuri Orlov, head of the Group to Assist the Implementation of the Helsinki Agreements in the USSR, established in May 1976, appealed to the government in his letter, "Thirteen Questions to Brezhnev" (September 11, 1973) and an open appeal on International Human Rights Day, December 10, 1974. He recalled: "Although we dissidents were absolutely united in our struggle with the Soviet regime, we were far from agreement on the question 'What is to be done?' None of my friends seemed to share my view that political reform could come from the top as a result of our pressure ..."[16]

The idea of cooperation did dwindle over time as the movement grew disillusioned with a regime unable to relinquish its corrupted power.[17] As Bogoraz later pointed out: "the Soviet government showed no interest in listening to us."[18] For the Soviet historian, Roy Medvedev: "There is no DIALOGUE with the authorities as understood in the West and we are a long way from a similar dialogue. If a 'dialogue' does take place with the authorities it more often takes the form of an interrogation."[19] As the Fifth Directorate of the KGB continued to arrest and imprison individuals for openly expressing their opinions, prominent members of the movement began to seriously chronicle human rights violations throughout the Soviet Union, significantly expanding their former agenda of protest letters and petitions. For many this was achieved by working on the *samizdat* text, *The Chronicle of Current Events*: "Our affair was with words," recalled Kovalyov. "Not because political terrorism or calls to revolution were not possible in the Soviet Union, but because the thought itself was repulsive to us ... The 'pure human rights activists' were a small group within the general dissident movement, but we created one informational source, not only uniting all, but even exceeding the limits of the dissident world."[20] What concerned these men and women was not only that they avoid violence, but that they attempt as much as possible under Soviet conditions to remain faithful to their fundamental right to receive and distribute information. Therefore, the concepts of truth and honesty in their portrayal of Soviet reality became their leading motives. For the group who edited the *Chronicle*, Natalaya Gorbanevskaya, Tatyana Velikanova, Tatyana Khodorovich, Anatoly Yakobson, Sergei Kovalyov and others, a commitment to these concepts was born out in every issue of the journal.

This small group of intellectuals in Moscow who distributed information on human rights violations tried to live as freely as possible under Soviet conditions. Their essential contribution to the formation of a civil society in the USSR was their struggle *not* to subject themselves to the intimidation of the Soviet regime. It was a struggle to recover a small measure of individual power from below. It was within this context that Sergei Kovalyov matured and, under the influence of Andrei Sakharov, nurtured his own belief in a transparent and open society and the potential for dialogue with the Soviet regime. These guiding motifs later underpinned his personal human rights philosophy. He could never have anticipated where they would take him.

Childhood and youth

Sergei Adamovich Kovalyov was born in the Ukrainian town of Seredina Buda on March 2, 1930. He entered the world on the eve of the Ukrainian famine. As Stalin consolidated his power with the collectivization campaign of 1929–30, the Ukraine suffered a mass movement of peasants into its sprawling urban centres with the larger cities beset by inadequate housing, overcrowding and growing social tensions.[21] Far from isolated from Stalin's expanding political hegemony, stories of Ukrainian peasants crawling on their hands and knees along the roadside begging for bread were recounted to the young Kovalyov by his mother. They remained vivid images that he carried into adulthood.

In 1932, as the famine progressed, Kovalyov's parents left their small town of Seredina Buda in the Symskaya region, located on the northern frontier close to the Russian border.[22] They moved to Podlipki, a small district just outside Moscow and home of the Soviet Union's Central Artillery Construction Bureau. Later renamed Kaliningrad, the region of Podlipki was quiet and hardworking, dominated by the weapons factories that employed the town's some 30,000 residents.[23]

Born in the Ukraine, Kovalyov's mother, Irena Ivanovna Makarenko, was the daughter of Vasilii Ivanovitch, an engineer and small-time entrepreneur. Recognized in their small town as a well-to-do family, at the age of eighteen Irena Ivanovna was sent to Kiev to study medicine. The young Irena's first chance for intellectual and personal freedom, however, ended in 1919 when she was recalled to care for her sick mother. She never resumed her studies. Kovalyov's father, Adam Adamovich Kovalyov, was born into a religious family in Belorussia who named their sickly son after the biblical Adam when they were certain of his imminent death. He survived nevertheless to pursue an undistinguished education in Belorussia. There, he first occupied a modest position as a middle-level bureaucrat on the railways. In the early 1920s, just after the civil war, he arrived in Seredina Buda from Belorussia where, shortly afterwards, he married Kovalyov's mother.[24]

Kovalyov's parents belonged to a generation of Russians forced into silence over the coming decades as Stalin's purges sent men and women off to camps across the Soviet Union. They tried to instill in their son the practice of silence and acquiescence that grew out of their own fear of a rapidly changing country.[25] Kovalyov's childhood was similar to that of thousands of children who lived in working towns across Russia, yet he and his elder brother, Yuri, understood quite early that in their parents silence was a criticism of the system. He later attributed the death of his childhood spirit as a young Soviet Pioneer to their guarded silence.[26]

Something of the fastidious personality and encyclopaedic approach to problems that would later make Kovalyov a meticulous editor of the most important human rights *samizdat* journal can be seen in an argument with his schoolteacher over Article 125 of the 1936 Soviet Constitution. Article 125 guaranteed freedom of speech, street processions and demonstrations to all Soviet citizens under the condition that they reflect the interests of the workers and peasants. A quarrel arose between Kovalyov and his teacher, Elena Vasil'evna, around the conditions of that freedom. Kovalyov wanted to know who exactly had the right to decide what was in the interests of the workers.[27] Sent to Sergei Sergevitch, the Director of the school, Kovalyov recalled him saying: "Seryozha, we adults have our own difficulties. When you get older you will understand them. Let's agree that today we will only discuss the constitution ... You know the text and I'll arrange for the teacher to examine your knowledge and not to ask you any superfluous questions."[28]

World War Two saw the young Kovalyov's life bound to a dugout trench in the courtyard. He dreamed of joining the partisans if the Germans ever reached Podlipki, and his brother Yuri went off in anticipation of reaching the front, only to be sent back again.[29] In his autobiographical notes, Kovalyov draws particular attention to one aspect of life in Podlipki during the war. This small town reacted against the rise of Russian chauvinism and its accompanying patriotic slogans during this period. He recalled how the people of his town responded: "Everyone wanted to defeat the Germans as quickly as possible, but any kind of patriotic big-talk was considered inappropriate and distasteful – either at home, in the yard or at school."[30] The experience left a lasting impression, one which resonated in his later rejection of the anti-cosmopolitan campaign of 1948 and the virulent attacks on his own patriotism at the height of the first Chechen campaign of 1994–96.

Figure 1.1   Sergei Kovalyov in 1946. 9th Class, aged 16

Source: Memorial Archive, Moscow.

Beyond Kovalyov's scattered insight into the injustices of Soviet society, there was a growing consciousness of human rights as the principles that define the quality and freedom of individual life. He recognized the fatal flaw of Elena Vasil'evna's interpretation of the constitution and the importance of Sergei Sergevitch's face-saving compromise. Above all, he maintains in his *Memoirs* that, like many of his generation, he sensed that "hypocrisy and cruelty" pervaded Soviet society and "whatever social or economic rights did exist, they did little more than serve that hypocrisy."[31] This growing consciousness was born less of intellectual reasoning than a natural intuitive gift which later served as the foundation of many of his decisions. The conflict with Elena Vasil'evna played an important role in his decision to concentrate on the natural sciences. Although he had contemplated a career in law or history, he decided not to pursue this direction. He graduated in 1948 with a silver medal and ventured into the world of science, a realm he knew little about.

Anti-cosmopolitan campaign; Moscow university; Lysenko

Kovalyov's educational destiny, however, suited his needling personality. He was accepted into the Faculty of Physiology at Moscow State University in 1951. He went on to successfully defend his *Kandidat Nauk* in 1959 on *The Electrical Properties of the Myocardial Fibres of a Frog's Heart*. While researching and preparing his thesis, he was employed as a senior research officer in the interdepartmental laboratory of mathematical methodology in biology, where he remained until 1969. Over the next twenty years he produced over sixty internationally recognized scientific publications on neural networks and electrophysiology.[32] For Kovalyov personally, this decade was also a time of important friendships and political awakenings.

In the interim years between his graduation in 1948 and his acceptance into Moscow State University in 1951, Kovalyov enrolled in a medical degree. During this period he was exposed for the first time to the anti-Semitism of the anti-cosmopolitan campaign of 1948 that culminated in the Doctors' Plot of 1952. He vigorously repudiated the racial reading of difference and the narrative of hierarchy that the campaign embraced, and these years consolidated his strong antipathy toward patriotic rhetoric. The ease with which many seemed so ready to assume their own superiority deeply troubled him.

Kovalyov's first independent steps saw him unprotected by the general tolerance of Podlipki. One incident at the Medical Institute No. 1 in Moscow, to which he had transferred in 1950, sorely tested his independence. The Komsomol Executive fabricated a case against a fellow student, Arkady Rogov.[33] The son of a Russian diplomat posted to the United States, Rogov returned to Moscow from America to witness the public humiliation of his father and the financial hardship of his family. He worked night shifts for the ambulance service to supplement their income and studied at the

Institute during the day. Gathered for a general vote organized to dismiss Rogov under claims of incompetence, Kovalyov found himself, along with the rest of the students, raising his hand to expel the young student. He recalled that he immediately regretted his decision and, in what was the first of many such campaigns, he successfully lobbied to ensure that Rogov was able to stay and complete his degree.[34]

Anxious to leave the Institute, Kovalyov entered Moscow State University (MGU) in the autumn of the same year to study his newly-formed interest, physiology. Despite the relative tolerance of MGU, it was not an auspicious time for his discipline. The cult of T. D. Lysenko ruled the universities and research institutes after Lysenko's demagogic victory at the 1948 Congress of the Lenin All-Union Academy of Agricultural Sciences (LAAAS) three years before. For the best part of three decades, Lysenko had managed to convince Stalin and Khrushchev respectively that his innovations could change the face of Russian agriculture. He rejected the chromosome theory of heredity and the theory of mutation on the grounds that genetics was formalistic, bourgeois and essentially a metaphysical science.[35] He won Stalin over with his new theory of a class biology – that inherent differences existed between socialist and capitalist biology and that genetics was a "tool of American imperialism."[36] His political predominance empowered him to dismiss hundreds of well-qualified scientists and biologists,[37] including M. Shmal'gauzen, Professor of Darwinism, and M. Zavadovsky, Professor of Developmental Biology of Moscow University, and replace them with members of his own circle.

Lysenko's popularity in the political sphere did not extend uniformly to the scientific community. There was significant pressure from prominent scientists, which varied in influence and effect, to keep the study of genetics alive.[38] The degree to which his theories touched particular institutions and universities depended largely on the internal forces at work within the faculties themselves.[39] Moscow University wavered over the years, but any real attempt to expose Lysenko's fabrications was curbed by V. N. Stoletov, Professor in Genetics at MGU, RSFSR Minister of Higher Education and open supporter of Lysenko's theories. The voice of the scientific elite was contained for many years by the political interests of the Communist Party and, in the absence of relevant competing literature, Lysenko's scientific notions prevailed.[40]

Kovalyov entered the physiology department in 1951. He was taught by Mikhail Yudelnov, who later supervised his dissertation, and by Nikolai Nuberg.[41] He soon joined the science collective run by the well-known mathematician Professor Izrail Moiseevitch Gelfand. Kovalyov's work on the electrophysiology of myocardial tissue was of pioneering significance for biology and he was among the first biologists in the world to work on cellular interaction and its role in the behaviour of non-excitable cellular systems.[42] In these early years, he remained critical of the university's curriculum that continued to be based on theories Lysenko had borrowed from the horticulturist Ivan Michurin.

Fortunately, Kovalyov's growing frustration with MGU coincided with the death of Joseph Stalin in 1953. Inspired and emboldened by Khrushchev's denunciation of the former leader, he and a group of graduates, young researchers and laboratory assistants appealed to the Dean to cease the teaching of Michurinist theory at the university. Despite Lysenko's dismissal from the LAAAS in 1955, students were still being taught that his was the only progressive theory of genetics and other trends were excluded as bourgeois or pseudo-science.[43] The students gathered at Kovalyov's apartment in Podlipki in 1956 to draft the letter. They appealed to the Dean:

> We young scientists believe that scientific thought must be freed from any form of dogma, it must be grounded in facts and worked out in the course of free and open discussion. Those who are presently reading genetics in the biology faculty of Moscow State University are being given the impression by scholars that there is only one school in genetics and all the rest in the world are either reactionary, formal or based on a falsified science.[44]

In conclusion, they requested that their lectures be based on something other than articles from the 1948 issue of *Pravda*, the year of Lysenko's victory at the Congress.[45] Signed by approximately eighty people,[46] the letter was intercepted before the authors had posted it and made its way to the local Party Bureau at Moscow University.[47] The signatories were called in for questioning and asked who had prompted them to write the letter. Several professors under suspicion at the time were named. A row erupted at a meeting of the Young Communist League where several of Lysenko's loyalists angrily objected to the students' criticism, exemplifying the growing generational rifts of the time. Kovalyov recalled a professor announcing: "So you want to be taught some other genetics, do you? Probably you should also be taught the Bible as part of a course on scientific atheism?" Kovalyov stood up and answered: "If you want to instruct us in scientific atheism, it would not be wrong at all to give us an idea of what the Bible is."[48]

Kovalyov left the Komsomol after the department began calling the students' parents into the university. As the pressure continued, the majority of the signatories fell back into the demands of the old curriculum, while some ten students, including Kovalyov, remained adamant to see the curriculum changed. In the Spring of 1957 he was called into the personnel department and interrogated by the KGB regarding the letter. In an effort to intimidate him they inquired about the health of his two-year-old son, Vanya.[49] He described his meetings as frightening encounters:

> The KGB wanted me to report to them about my conversations with foreigners studying in the department and with other young people in general ... We also discussed the letter, of course. The usual who-why-and-how business. Nothing came of it. I was reluctant to cooperate, and they left me in peace.[50]

Figure 1.2   Sergei Kovalyov in 1955. A graduate student in the department of
            biophysics, Moscow State University

Source: Memorial Archive, Moscow.

Seven years later, in October 1964, Khrushchev stepped down as Party
leader, and one of the important changes that coincided with his fall was the
demise of Lysenko. In June 1964, Lysenko's colleague, candidate member
Nikolai Nuzhdin, failed to be elected a full member of the Academy of
Sciences after a public attack by the prominent physicist, Andrei Sakharov.[51]
Over time, the Party and leading scientists began to assess the widespread
damage that Lysenko's theories had inflicted on biology to the detriment of
the Russian countryside.[52] Kovalyov's regular hunting trips had brought him
face to face with the deteriorating Russian landscape and he had often
discussed his concerns with friends at the laboratory. His experiences with
his friend and teacher, Mikhail Yudelnov, in the northern regions of
Yaroslavl and Vologda played a significant role in his growing criticism of
the regime. He had listened to stories by peasants about collectivization and
had observed the poverty of the collective farm; he began to understand it
as a crime inflicted on the nation initiated by Stalin and his circle.

In October 1964, Nikolai Nikolaevich Semenov, the renowned physicist,
Nobel laureate and vice-president of the Academy of Sciences, approached
Kovalyov, Lev Chailakhian and Misha Berkinblit. He asked if they would be

prepared to write an article for the daily broadsheet, *Pravda*, repudiating Lysenko and his methods under the guise of an attack on formal genetics.[53] The young scientists gathered at Semenov's apartment over the winter of 1964 and completed the article within three months. A journalist and philosopher were contracted, the former to work on the style and the latter to ensure that the article was furnished with the appropriate Marxist viewpoint. Semenov was not only attempting to undermine Lysenko's theories, but he wanted to undercut the ideological roots on which Lysenko sustained his position. He succeeded in achieving this by attributing Marxist support to a new theory of genetics.[54] The significance of this article was not that the scientific community was unaware of the damage of Lysenko's theories, but rather that Semenov had been given official permission to publish an article in the most-widely distributed central party organ. The editors of *Pravda* received it, but it failed to appear on the appointed date. During a state function at the Kremlin, Semenov was allegedly encouraged to publish it in the popular science journal, *Nauka i Zhizn'* (Science & Life).[55] Within a month, *Nauka i Zhizn'* accepted the article and it was printed on February 1, 1965 under the title "A Few Questions on the Sociology of Science."[56] Kovalyov likened the response to its publication to that of an exploding bomb.[57]

After his first confrontation with the KGB in 1957, Kovalyov's life had taken a more peaceful course. He found himself set apart from the burgeoning ethos of the period and he sought solace in his research in the lead-up to the defence of his *Kandidate Nauk* in 1964. Later, he would reveal a certain confusion about his place in the "thaw" years, confessing that he did not feel ready for a public struggle and he harboured serious doubts about the effectiveness of letter-writing campaigns and protests. Not long after the events at Moscow University he expressed his feelings to his close friend and colleague, Alexander Lavut: "I'm going to practise science. At least that is honest work. I don't want to throw bombs and I can't see any other way of struggling against the regime."[58]

Unlike the young poets who gathered at the statue of Vladimir Mayakovsky in 1958, Kovalyov did not belong to the literary period that signaled the beginning of Soviet *samizdat*.[59] The literary period and its accompanying youth culture was epitomized by the twenty-year-old Vladimir Bukovsky and the founders of the *samizdat* journals, Alexander Ginzburg (*Syntax*,) Yuri Galanskov (*Phoenix 66*), Vladimir Osipov (*Boomerang*) and Edward Kuznetsov. The role of the poets and writers in dismantling some of the old political legitimacies cannot be underestimated. It by no means provided a political solution to the problem of a totalitarian regime, but it inspired a *glasnost* that would later contribute to its downfall. Beginning with the publication of Vladimir Pomerantsev's "On Sincerity in Literature" (1953), Valentin Ovechkin's *The Collective Farm & other Short Stories* (1953), Ilya Ehrenburg's *The Thaw* (1954), Dudintsev's *Not by Bread Alone* (1956), Alexander Solzhenitsyn's *One Day in the Life of Ivan Denisovich* (1962) and Pasternak's *Doctor Zhivago* (1965),[60] the poets contributed to the awakening of a new generation. Indeed, the future Soviet Human Rights Movement may have been inconceivable without the youthful restlessness and courage of the young poets who advanced the quest for intellectual autonomy and lay the groundwork for a network of dissent. It was precisely their claim to a public space that prefigured the struggle for the civil arena later undertaken by the human rights movement.

Importantly for the future human rights activists, the poetry meetings provided a forum for the philosopher and mathematician, Alexander Esenin-Volpin (1925–) to deliver his "Strategy on Legality."[61] This meticulous philosopher of logic introduced the young poets to the language of Soviet law and furnished them with a vocabulary and context that sought to frame a restless intuition. The simple genius of Esenin-Volpin was that he consistently underlined the significance of accepting the language of the law at face value, and not its Soviet interpretation.[62] Like many of his contemporaries, he had personally experienced the arbitrary cruelty of the Soviet government as early as 1949 with his forced incarceration in a psychiatric hospital. But he refused to pay tribute to the law's superficial function or allow it to sink into an obsolete collection of slogans. For Esenin-Volpin, it had to become their primary weapon. His strategy would eventually shape the movement's public struggle.

The liberalism of Kovalyov in these early years is difficult to define. In short, it stood for freedom of expression and freedom of information. He never directed his energies towards political questions, and the views which eventually shaped his life were still largely undefined and inchoate. For most of the period prior to 1964, his cautious public activities did not differ greatly from those of the many thousands growing up in the era of the Soviet Union's spiritual emancipation. Along with his contemporaries, he tested the limits by writing and signing protest letters, reading *samizdat*, and he expressed in private *kompanii* his concern over the anti-cosmopolitan campaign and the Soviet Union's invasion of Hungary in 1956. More importantly, he listened to the shared memories of the GULag survivors.

Yet Kovalyov was never so deeply engaged in public activity as to neglect his research. He was stimulated by his own studies at Moscow University and, after 1959, his work with the Gelfand laboratory consumed most of his time and energy. He formed many important and long-lasting friendships during his ten years as the youngest researcher within the collective and, with this newly-discovered circle of friends that socialized together at the university and at home, his environment was not only intellectually satisfying, but personally fulfilling. It was at the laboratory that he met his second wife, Ludmilla Iur'evna Boitseva (1940–), a senior laboratory assistant. Together they had a daughter, Varvara.[63]

To those of Kovalyov's generation, the thaw years presented exceptionally complex problems – how could they invigorate and reform old institutions unwilling to yield any power? At the age of twenty-seven, Kovalyov continued to measure his public actions in terms of visible success and, since he could not detect any notable initiatives on the part of the regime to genuinely reform Soviet society, he grew increasingly despondent and retreated further into his work at the laboratory. By his own reckoning he began to doubt whether the system could be reformed without violence, so entrenched as it was in a tradition of lawlessness.[64] But he would not fight the crude legal sensibilities of the regime with its own weapons, and his own unequivocal rejection of violence placed him in an ambivalent position. As a child of the post-revolutionary years and World War Two he continued to equate radical change with violence. He clung to this notion for nine years.

New circles

The short period which ran from 1966 to 1968 may justly be called the turning point of Sergei Kovalyov's early career. Having completed his dissertation in 1964, he was now a full-fledged scholar. After sixteen years as a student, he had a promising career ahead. But what should have been the beginning of a rewarding and stable era of his life, proved otherwise. The intellectual freedom he had carved out for himself in the Gelfand laboratory was compromised by his deepening engagement in the concerns of Soviet life. Increasingly drawn away from his research, much of the confused ambivalence he had come to feel up until 1966 gradually diminished. He discovered a new circle of friends, fashioning the tactics that would later define his public action for the next twenty-five years.

The year 1966, that began with the renowned trial of writers Andrei Sinyavsky and Yuli Daniel, marked the beginning of the Soviet Human Rights Movement.[65] The thaw period was visibly shaken by the arrest of the two writers and attracted the unprecedented contempt of Moscow's scientific and cultural elite. The intellectual community was daunted by the regime's attempt to try Sinyavsky and Daniel's fictional characters as part of Brezhnev's new strategy to reign in the *glasnost* of the Khrushchev era: a gesture that significantly changed the political landscape. As Vladimir Bukovsky recalled of the protest movement: "There were more people, there was more publicity and the people came from higher up the social scale; professors, academicians, writers – not to be compared with the striplings of the early 1960s."[66]

Kovalyov carefully followed the events surrounding the trial.[67] Like many others he quickly fathomed that the charges against Sinyavsky and Daniel formed part of an offensive by conservative forces within the party to rehabilitate Stalin. An article appeared in *Pravda* a week prior to the arrest of the writers that warned against the continued use of the term "cult of the personality" coined by Khrushchev to signal the end of the Stalin era.[68] Coercive pressure was also used to eliminate mention of the purges from the press,[69] while Professor Sergei Trapeznikov, Head of the Central Committee of the Department of Science and Education, described the Stalin era "as one of the most brilliant in the history of the Party and the Soviet state."[70]

This was followed, shortly after, by attempts to falsify the war period with a new, multi-volume, *History of the Second World War* that not only concealed essential historical facts, but grossly exaggerated Stalin's leadership role in the war.[71]

Esenin-Volpin organized a demonstration in protest against the arrest of Sinyavsky and Daniel on Constitution Day, December 5, 1965. He distributed a "Civic Appeal" in which he called on Soviet citizens to attend the demonstration.[72] "In the past illegal acts of the government cost the lives of millions of Soviet citizens," he wrote. "It is easier to sacrifice one day of peace than to suffer the consequences of unchecked arbitrary authority for years to come ... You are invited to a public meeting on December 5 at six o'clock in the evening at Pushkin Square near the statue of the poet ..."[73] Kovalyov joined his contemporaries in expressing his outrage at the disregard for legal procedure and equality before the law. He helped draft a protest letter to the USSR Presidium of the Supreme Soviet shortly after the verdict was announced: "We, the undersigned have learnt about the outcome of the trial of writers Sinyavsky and Daniel from the paper. It seems to us that the verdict of the Supreme Court of the RSFSR has flouted the law and put the rights and freedoms of the citizen guaranteed by the Constitution under threat. We appeal for your intervention."[74]

The period following the verdict both paralysed the energy of many of the supporters of the thaw, and galvanized the determination of the rights defenders. It was the slogans that appeared on the placards during Esenin-Volpin's demonstration in December that caught Kovalyov's attention. The slogans called for an "Open trial for Sinyavsky and Daniel" and "Respect for the Soviet Constitution."[75] Esenin-Volpin was not advocating the downfall of the regime, he was committed to legal procedure and he reproached the regime for its flagrant manipulation of the law for its own ends in defiance of the Constitution. Kovalyov found the idea of the subordination of the realm of politics and ideology to fundamental human rights a compelling one. He was attracted, above all, to the methods of the burgeoning legalist strain of the movement as epitomized by Esenin-Volpin's *samizdat* articles and practical treatises on interrogation: "Documents on Judicial Practice from the Interrogation Protocol" (*Dokumenti Iuridicheskoi Praktiki iz Protokola Doprosa*, 1967), "Duty or Obligation?" (*Dolg ili Obyazannost'?*, 1970), and "Legal Instruction" (*Iuridicheskaya Pamyatka*, 1973). Although under no illusion about the reality of Soviet life, Kovalyov had finally discovered a way within the limits of the law to pressure the Soviet government to accept responsibility for its actions. Reform was not sought in the idealized form of revolution or political theories, but in the essential connection between the rule of law and individual rights and liberties.

Kovalyov's self-discovery was influenced and ran parallel to that of many of his peers. Two of the most outstanding legalists of the post-Stalin era were Esenin-Volpin and the physicist Valery Chalidze (1938–).[76] Often referred to as the "prince", Chalidze was a passionate and knowledgeable expert on Soviet law whose personal influence on the movement grew in the late 1960s.[77] Chalidze's Moscow apartment was a gathering point for many activists who sought his knowledge of criminal and procedural codes. Renowned for receiving guests from his sofabed, handing out advice and reinforcing the importance of the rule of law for Soviet society,[78] Chalidze did his best to promote his ideas through his own texts, writing a series of books and educational booklets, and editing a *samizdat* journal. Part of his plan was to raise public consciousness on the question of rights and legality. In Chalidze's *samizdat* text, *Problems of Society*, he and Esenin-Volpin sought to enlighten their readers on legal questions.[79] The work of Chalidze embodied the conviction that the Soviet Union's liberation depended more on public education about rights than a change of government.[80] The link between gradualism and education was the essence of his long-term plan for the Soviet Union, and wherever possible he tried to find a synthesis between his vision and its execution.

Renowned for his conservatism, Chalidze's approach was often described as pedantic. He was patient, but subtle and persistent, and his views grew from an appreciation of the importance of gradualism as opposed to revolution; the twentieth century made so bloody by radical reform instilled in him the importance of working from within the established laws of the state: "Certain basic axioms were clearly defined from the beginning of my involvement," stressed Chalidze, "the first being observance of existing laws. This principle requires me to refrain from breaking any laws but does not prevent my criticism of these laws nor disagreement with the official legal and ideological doctrine of communism."[81]

Accepting the political reality of the Soviet Union, Chalidze tried to encourage other activists to work from within the laws of the state.[82] His passion for the law was shared by other rights defenders, including Kovalyov who sympathized, although sometimes sceptically, with the methods espoused by Chalidze.[83] Undeterred by the subordination of the legal system to ideology, Chalidze tried to motivate rights defenders to exercise a rigorous and critical approach to domestic and international law in the hope of curbing the government's arbitrary power and keeping a check on "official hypocrisy."[84] It was important in Chalidze's view that, when human rights activists appealed to the authorities, they aligned themselves with something more than moral outrage. If they knew the law they were better prepared to defend themselves or others.

Chalidze embodied in words many of Kovalyov's instinctual feelings. But Kovalyov diverged from Chalidze on a number of significant issues. Chalidze stressed how important their actions were as examples to others. He recommended that they promote the notion of individual rights through appealing to individual interests. If the average Soviet citizen could learn to defend their individual interests whether they be religious, national or economic, Chalidze believed that they would slowly begin to integrate an understanding of the law into their everyday existence.[85] Kovalyov disagreed. He tried not to interpret his actions as examples to others – which he believed was enforcing a hierarchy of behaviour. He strongly believed that his actions were a result of personal decisions which others were not bound to follow. In retrospect he stressed that his involvement with the defence of human rights grew in the first instance out of his own personal desire to live free of the restrictions imposed by the regime.[86] "I do not want to serve either as an example or as a reproach," he argued.[87]

Kovalyov shared many traits characteristic of an enlightenment thinker. He valued moral practice over abstract theology. His morality was founded on a rational philosophy that stemmed from a scientific worldview, and he shared the enlightenment practice of questioning authority; intellectual, religious, social and political. Unlike his contemporary, Alexander Solzhenitsyn, he did not give precedence to the "eternal" over the "temporal". His views certainly fell under the writer's category of "rationalistic humanism" with their emphasis on the role of positive law. For Solzhenitsyn, however, whenever "the tissue of life is woven of legalistic relationships, this creates an atmosphere of spiritual mediocrity that paralyzes man's noblest impulses". He professed that "law is our attempt to embody in rules a part of that moral sphere which is above us".[88]

Kovalyov did not alienate the notions of natural and moral law from his worldview. Indeed Kant was his favorite philosopher. Nor did he disagree with Solzhenitsyn's quest to "encourage the inner, the moral, the healthy development of the people."[89] He just did not share the writer's belief that religion should serve as the source of moral law. The notion of the "absolute", of a spiritual presence outside of rational thought, was perhaps more difficult for him to embrace. He admitted many years later, however, that he could not banish mystery from the world completely, nor interpret the world as rational and intelligible through and through, and he became a self-confessed agnostic. "My faith is closer to Eisenstein and Sakharov," he recalled; "there is 'something'. If there was a cataclysm, I don't believe that our collective memory would be wiped out entirely."[90]

For Kovalyov, the period after the trial of Sinyavsky and Daniel was a time when the tempo of his life sharply accelerated. As it turned out, the trial of the writers was but the first of many that drew his attention over the next seven years. In his *Memoirs*, he observed that the most significant trial for him personally was that of Pavel Litvinov, physicist and son of Maxim Litvinov, Foreign Minister and Ambassador to the United States between 1930 and 1939.[91] Acquainted with Litvinov from university,[92] Kovalyov sympathized with the young physicist, who was among those who bravely demonstrated on Red Square in protest at the Soviet Union's violent suppression of events in the former Czechoslovakia.[93]

Kovalyov himself had placed many of his personal hopes in Alexander Dubcek's reforms, and joined his contemporaries in the autumn of 1968 at Moscow's Municipal Court as a sign of moral support for the demonstrators. There he met for the first time the Red Army General and human rights activist, Pyotr Grigorenko, recently released after a period of forced

incarceration in a psychiatric asylum.[94] Kovalyov attributes great significance to the friendship he formed with Grigorenko, and the General was
equally impressed with the young biologist and his long-time friend,
Alexander Lavut.[95] This new circle was soon to replace Kovalyov's friends at
the university. He recalled:

> And so I fell into a new circle.... Victor Krasin, economist, former pris-
> oner of the Stalinist era ... called it the "democratic movement". But
> can one honestly call it a movement? There was no program, no
> ideology, or structure. It was a group of friends united in essence by
> only one thing: an active dislike for official lies and a preparedness to
> publicly and openly protest the arbitrary violation of the law.[96]

It was the physicist Andrei Sakharov, however, who influenced Kovalyov
most profoundly.[97] They first met during the spring of 1970 at Valery
Chalidze's apartment, and although they met irregularly, they formed a close
friendship.[98] "For a long time" recalled Kovalyov, "Sakharov cherished the
hope that the Soviet authorities would decide to reform themselves."[99] And it
was Sakharov's untiring perseverance, his willingness to engage in constructive dialogue, his linking of human rights to universal peace and support for
the "small rebellions" that lay "the foundations for a chain reaction, for the
self-liberation of Soviet society", that most moved Kovalyov.[100] Nine years
his junior, Kovalyov shared much in common with the physicist, in both character and worldview; a conservative approach to reform, acknowledgement
of but refusal to accept the historical reality, and a modest manner backed by
a strong will. Certainly Sakharov's well known 1968 essay, *Reflections on
Progress, Peaceful Co-existence and Intellectual Freedom*, set Sakharov apart
from his contemporaries and influenced Kovalyov. It was exactly the
weighing of Sakharov's moral commitment with his strategic attempts to
convince Soviet leaders to reform domestic policy that shaped his powerful
impact. It was these values that Kovalyov continued to espouse long after
Sakharov's death and the eventual collapse of the Soviet Union in 1991.

Kovalyov had at last found both emotional and intellectual grounds for
his growing commitment to human rights.[101] He responded first from a
sense of solidarity and loyalty with his friends and colleagues, then from
anger, and finally it became a matter of reconciling his actions with his
conscience, until he was committed to helping those victimized by the
regime.[102] By his own reckoning, it was the circumstances that compelled
him to respond. It was not until later that his decisions were taken more
deliberately and consciously.[103] There is a strong sense, however, that
Kovalyov's actions were more often than not spontaneous, a trait which
seemed to be deeply rooted in his personality. This trait would later incite
some of his most courageous and moral stands, and at other times it would
force him to sublimate long-term goals to the urgency of the moment.

Kovalyov had distanced himself from the thaw generation when he felt he had to, but he now appeared to possess the self-confidence to speak his mind. In some ways his scientific career had laid a firm foundation for his future and fed that need in him, generated by his research to seek out the truth. He had known intellectual freedom in the laboratory in so far as his research was concerned, and he had taken his independence seriously. It is not surprising, therefore, that he took the intellectual independence of his contemporaries seriously also. He later claimed that scientists could not "reconcile themselves to the thought that there is no freedom to question or freedom to find answers".[104]

Even if Kovalyov had once harboured doubts about the effectiveness of his appeals and letter-writing campaigns, he was no longer concerned solely with the practical outcome of his actions. He found in his growing consciousness of the importance of the rule of law for Soviet society that long-sought-after approach to the problem of human rights violations. The importance of the law as the central tool of any free and democratic society shaped his thinking for the next thirty years, and later formed the central motif of his political agenda. To an extent it also satisfied that tenaciously "practical" bent of his mind.

His protests became for him, therefore, a personal expression of principles rather than a political act. The impulse to bring about actual and immediate social reform was replaced by the need to bear witness to the injustices of the regime and to offer moral and practical support to its victims. Kovalyov does not mention in his notes the conviction hitherto fixed in his mind linking change to violence. He was now thirty-seven, surrounded by people who shared similar concerns and no longer alone in his public activity. Nor did he appear concerned that he may have a future founded on minimal concessions wrung from the Soviet regime. And at issue, of course, were his career and his future. He did not dwell upon what might be the future consequences of present action.

The initiative group and resignation

In later years, Kovalyov's friend and colleague Oleg Orlov described Kovalyov's personality as "hair splitting".[105] Over the course of the next five years, Kovalyov became more absolute, a sterner advocate of the rights of the individual and a more committed rights campaigner. The signing of protest letters no longer completely satisfied him and, as he grew increasingly aware of the extent and breadth of human rights violations across the Soviet Union, he became to an extent radicalized. The year 1969 marked the beginning of the most productive period of his public career. He became a co-founding member of the first independent human rights organization in the Soviet Union, and the principles that defined his career – respect for the law, non-violence, freedom of expression and access to and freedom to circulate information – were firmly consolidated during this period.

The coming years were not to be without their own problems, however. The schisms within the Soviet Human Rights Movement on questions of strategy were often too divisive to rectify. The demands of working with people of different ideological and philosophical persuasions quickly became apparent. He was forced to face new challenges and make new decisions. One of the first and most important of those decisions was linked to moving away from individual action to forming a human rights organization.

In late 1968, Ivan Yakhimovich, philologist, chairman of a collective farm in Latvia and member of the CPSU, wrote a letter to the Communist Party. He expressed his concern for the fate of the arrested human rights activists Alexander Ginzburg and Yuri Galanskov. "It is stupid to see in them the enemies of Soviet power," wrote Yakhimovich to chief of ideological matters Mikhail Andreevitch Suslov, "and more than stupid to let them rot in prisons and to mock them. For the party, such a line is equivalent to self-strangulation ... Ideas cannot be murdered with bullets, prisons or exile. He who does not understand this is no politician, no Marxist."[106] Yakhimovich was a self-proclaimed and dedicated communist, which explains his decision to write to Suslov, the then formidable influence over *Agitprop*. The letter itself was widely publicized and Yakhimovich was expelled from the Communist Party, arrested and later committed to a psychiatric hospital without trial.[107] The arrest of the Latvian attracted the sympathy of General Pyotr Grigorenko and instigated a discussion among activists on the possibility of forming a working group to defend Yakhimovich.[108]

The idea of a working group was Grigorenko's brainchild. First discussed at a gathering in the General's apartment in the spring of 1969, the participants were of two minds concerning the structure of the group. Grigorenko argued single-mindedly for drawing together the efforts of a "group of courageous people to organize protests against illegal arrests."[109] Grigorenko's idea was informed by two central propositions; in the first instance he was driven by his concern for Yakhimovich. But he also anticipated the need for human rights activists to coordinate their activity and create a group that would act jointly and issue common declarations.[110] He believed that their appeals would exert more influence if they were representative of an organization.

Looking back, Kovalyov observed that the discussion at this first gathering turned out to be "long and stormy".[111] Indeed, the divisions that characterized this first meeting set the tone for the future of the group. The editor and literary critic Anatoly Yakobson was present with his wife Maya Ulanovskaya. Kovalyov observed that Maya took issue with Grigorenko's proposal and argued that they should target their appeals to society through *samizdat* and Western radio broadcasts, rather than to the government. Maya also believed that the group would ideally serve as the foundation for a future political party. She herself had been arrested in 1951 for involvement in the organization "Union of Struggle for the Revolutionary Cause".[112] Grigorenko's reaction to

Maya Ulanovskaya in his *Memoirs* is highly critical and he described her behaviour as the "hysterics of a half-conscious person".[113] Kovalyov observed that Grigorenko's assessment was "malicious" and "unjust", particularly his suggestion that she "incited" the security forces.[114]

Kovalyov remained silent throughout the arguments. By his own reckoning, he fluctuated between supporting and rejecting the establishment of a working group. He was attracted to the concept of an organization. He saw it as a challenge which in itself constituted a realization of the rights and freedoms of the individual and the freedom of association written in the Soviet Constitution.[115] Where Kovalyov did differ significantly from his friend Grigorenko was on the question of the group's structure and agenda. He argued that its main task had to be the research and analysis of human rights issues in the Soviet Union, and believed that it had to balance its public activity with scholarly work to provide the group with an on-going agenda.[116] He believed that an organization had to have another purpose other than the signing of letters of protest.[117]

Kovalyov also recognized the problems associated with the transition from individual action to joint work. Decisions that stemmed from personal choices to those that entailed responsibility for others and inevitably some degree of compromise removed a certain level of independence. He was concerned that the very existence of individual acts that had defined the movement and were in themselves a protest against official Soviet collectivism were under threat with their decision.[118] He shared the general concern that entering into any formal organization may well be misconstrued as a political act. Like his friend Boris Shragin, philosopher and frequent contributor to *samizdat*, he agreed that the movement was "still involved in a vicious circle whose exit [was] not ideological but existential".[119] Kovalyov and Velikanova were also concerned about the ability of other interested individuals, especially Pyotr Yakir and Viktor Krasin, to refrain from provocative gestures that might unduly provoke the Soviet authorities. According to Yakobson, this was the reason why Kovalyov had previously refused to vote.[120]

The General's friends continued to struggle for a unanimous decision until Grigorenko was arrested for a second time in Tashkent on May 7, 1969. They agreed to compile a report on political repression and other violations of human rights in the Soviet Union and address it to the United Nations with their individual signatures. On May 20, 1969 Kovalyov with Velikanova, Lavut, Yakobson, Grisha Podyapolskii, Khodorovich, Natalya Gorbanyevskaya, Anatoly Emmanuilovich Levitin and Yuri Maltsev met at Yakir's apartment to discuss the report. Shortly after, Yakir and Krasin arrived at the apartment and presented a text to the activists. It soon became apparent that Yakir had actually passed on the text to the foreign press and a United Nations representative that morning without consulting the others. He had signed the letter *The Initiative Group for the Defence of Human Rights in the USSR*.[121] All fifteen individuals were now unwitting members of a new public organization.[122]

Yakir and Krasin's move was by no means an empty gesture. Their decision incited an outburst by the others who understood the ramifications for
themselves, both domestically and internationally. Within days it would be
in newspapers across the world and within their own country it would be
used as a pretext for their arrest.[123] A resolution was immediately drafted
that outlined the regulations of the Initiative Group. The most important
result was that each member was accorded the right to decide whether they
would sign a protest letter, document or appeal. Each document would be
signed under the name of the Initiative Group, but the document would
only reflect the views of those who had given their individual signatures.[124]

The letter was significant as the first letter sent to the United Nations by
a public non-government organization in the Soviet Union. Yakir and
Krasin appealed to the United Nations thus:

> We are appealing to the UN because we have received no answer to the
> many protests and appeals which we have sent over the course of several
> years to high government and court institutions. Our hopes of being
> heard and our hopes that the authorities would desist from the lawless-
> ness that we have persistently pointed out have been disappointed.[125]

Over the course of 1969, the Initiative Group sent four letters to the
United Nations. In each instance, it appealed for recognition and assistance
with the human rights problems in the Soviet Union. In its second letter, on
August 20, 1969, the anniversary of the suppression of liberal forces in
Czechoslovakia, it expressed its solidarity with the Czechoslovak people
aspiring to socialism with a human face.[126] All its letters to the United
Nations remained unanswered. In its third letter, on September 26, it
declared that "[t]he silence of an organization of international law unties the
hands of those who will be inspired to further persecutions".[127] Meanwhile,
the United Nations Secretary General, U Thant, gave instructions to the
UN's fifty information centres worldwide that they were not to accept any
petitions from individuals.[128]

Kovalyov felt keenly the silence that followed the letters he sent to the
Soviet authorities and he must have felt the silence from the West also. He
later observed that he was criticised by friends who disagreed with his decision
to appeal overseas.[129] The decision to take the argument outside the Soviet
Union and request that the United Nations intercede on behalf of Soviet
society was an important step. As an organization, committed to exposing
human rights violations, they were putting the problem of human rights in the
Soviet Union on the international stage. They drew public attention to urgent
problems, the persecution of participants in nationalist movements, of religious believers, Jews and Crimean Tartars, and the abuse of psychiatric
medicine.[130] By 1970, however, the UN General Assembly issued a
"Declaration on Principles of International Law concerning Friendly
Relations and Cooperation among States" which stated: "No state or group of

states has the right to intervene, directly or indirectly, for any reason whatsoever, in the internal or external affairs of any other State."[131] A convenient
document for the USSR, but untimely for those human rights activists
appealing to the world community. The movement strongly contested the
Soviet Union's position on state sovereignty over human rights.

In this atmosphere of apparent indifference, however, the Europeans were
undertaking a campaign that would eventually chip away at the prevailing
discourse of state sovereignty. On March 17, 1969 at the Warsaw Pact
Summit in Budapest, 35 participating European states issued the Budapest
Declaration outlining three fundamental areas of discussion for a forthcoming Conference on Security and Cooperation in Europe (CSCE). These
were: "renunciation of the threat of the use of force in relations with countries of Europe, expansion of trade, economic, scientific, technological and
cultural relations and the formation of a permanent multilateral mechanism
for peace and security in Europe."[132] The Soviet Union was extremely
anxious to secure political recognition of its post-war borders in the wake of
the Prague Spring. The Europeans used this to lever "respect for human
rights and fundamental freedoms" as an essential provision of future relations between European states.[133] The negotiation process with regard to the
CSCE conference and the inclusion of human rights on the agenda lasted
more than two years.[134] The final result was the Helsinki Final Act of 1975.

The spontaneous decision by Yakir to issue the statement to the UN
appeared to set an ominous precedent for the Initiative Group. They were
riddled by internal divisions that circled around the still unresolved arguments on the nature of the group. Yakobson observed that "[t]here were
always differences among us and we never had complete confidence in each
other".[135] Anatoly Levitin-Krasnov (1916–), writer and religious philosopher, expressed in his *Memoirs* that the arguments of 1970–71 centred on
contacts several Initiative Group members had formed with NTS, the
Popular Labour Alliance.[136] An émigré organization based in Frankfurt,
NTS promoted the downfall of the Soviet Union through its associated periodicals, *Grani* and *Posev*, that reprinted *samizdat* texts including *The
Chronicle of Current Events*. Some members believed that NTS could help
them receive information from Western countries and distribute *samizdat*.[137]

For Kovalyov, avoiding links with NTS was extremely important. The
authorities used those links to discredit the Human Rights Movement and
frequently accused NTS of being a front organization for America's
Central Intelligence Agency.[138] Anatoli Yakobson left the Initiative Group
after he and Levitin-Krasnov allegedly passed on documents to an NTS
courier. Kovalyov and Lavut also threatened to leave.[139] Yakobson is enig-
matic about this contact with NTS in his *Memoirs*, most likely to protect
those who were still living in the Soviet Union; Kovalyov does not mention
it at all.

The debates surrounding the creation of the Initiative Group and its
agenda illustrate vividly Kovalyov's attitude to his human rights activity. He

did not want the group to carry any political messages, however subliminal, and he dwelt on the need to avoid provocative gestures. Levitin-Krasnov, on the other hand, wanted the group to be the centre of a democratic movement and he described Kovalyov as his "constant, untiring opponent."[140] Above all, Kovalyov wanted the Initiative Group to be a traditional human rights organization, and in this he was not alone. Tatyana Velikanova (1932–2002), mathematician and future co-editor with Kovalyov of *The Chronicle of Current Events*, was strongly opposed to Krasnov's suggestion and expressed her indignation that the group might become an organizational centre for a democratic movement.[141] Kovalyov was also supported by Tanya Khodorovich, a future colleague on the *Chronicle*, and his close friend Alexander Lavut.

For Kovalyov, there was no discernible alternative to the group's future. He was acutely aware that the movement was comprised of too many personalities, too many opinions and ideological differences to form a serious political agenda, as witnessed by earlier discussions.[142] But more importantly, he always interpreted the human rights movement as a group of individuals expressing their "moral incompatibility" with the regime. It was the moral force of the principles themselves that they had to rely upon to gradually reform the Soviet government."[143]

Kovalyov divided the Soviet Human Rights Movement into two currents of thought: the legalists (*zakkoniki*) and the politicals (*politiki*).[144] The neatness of this distinction perhaps simplifies the complex of thought that characterized this period, but Kovalyov often refrained from abstractions and philosophizing when reflecting on the movement. He never attached himself to an idealized conception of the Soviet intelligentsia and accepted that every person simply wanted to live freely and independently under conditions that made this almost impossible. In his *Memoirs* he makes a conscious effort to avoid belittling others by attributing their differences to the spirit and conditions of the times. But at the same time, he stubbornly insisted on his own point of view and his support for any individual or cause was always conditional. As one perceptive Russian journalist noted many years later, his "gentleness [was] fitted with a steel rod."[145]

In making these distinctions, Kovalyov did not seek to undermine the legitimacy of either group, but sought to provide a framework to reflect on the differences that motivated individual action. The legalist strain was concerned primarily with defending the integrity and the rights of the individual. In agreement with Chalidze, Kovalyov proposed that the legalists cared less about the political system they lived under so long as that structure ceased to systematically violate human rights. The legal strain of the movement differed considerably in its aims from those of the politicals, the ultimate aim of which was the collapse of the regime.

Indeed, neither Chalidze nor Kovalyov specified individual names in their categories – but one can surmise that, among the politicals, they included Viktor Krasin, Pyotr Yakir, Vladimir Bukovsky, Valeriya Novodvorskaya and Alexander Podrabinek. When one compares the personal experiences of the more radical activists, notably Yakir and Bukovsky as compared to Kovalyov, Sakharov or Chalidze, the differences in tactics are explainable. Bukovsky was arrested six times, the first time at the age of 21, whereupon he endured cruel spells in psychiatric hospitals and prisons.[146] "That humiliating sense of being unfree," he recalled, "that sense of outrage I had experienced when outsiders attempted to dispose of my life, had cut me to the quick and I was eager to fight back as energetically as I could."[147] Bukovsky vowed to spend his time, when out of prison, exposing the system in any way possible. Similarly, Viktor Yakir, the son of the purged Army Commander Ion Yakir, was taken away at the age of 15 to a prison in the southern oblast of Astrakhan near the Volga River. There, as a young boy, he experienced physical torture, witnessed acts of suicide and innocent individuals being led away to be shot.[148]

The first-hand experience of the brutality of the prison regime in the Soviet Union for these two young men shaped their actions in later life and instilled a sense of urgency in their actions. They had little to lose, sure of their inevitable return to prison, maddened by the wrenching of their individual freedom. Activists like Bukovsky felt a sense of responsibility to the common men and women who suffered under the injustices of the system, defenceless and ignorant of their rights. They felt compelled to move beyond such a cautious and tactical position.

The legalists, Kovalyov and Chalidze, entered the movement later in their lives, with established and successful careers as scientists. They were in their late thirties, cautious, without personal experience of prison life and convinced that democratic reform would never take shape quickly in the Soviet Union. They were not inclined, like Valeriya Novodvorskaya, to throw leaflets from the theatre balcony at the Palace of Congress calling for revolution from the "Moscow Resistance Group."[149] Or declare, as Novodvorskaya did: "It always seemed to me that it had to be 'one or the other'. Either them or us. Either freedom or slavery. Either Communists or anti-Communists. Either the KGB or the possibility to publish this small book."[150] It is arguable, however, whether indeed it was not precisely the dramatic acts of the politicals that urged the movement on. For later, as the human rights defenders suffered increased repression, activists like Sakharov and Kovalyov began to make their own dramatic gestures in long, life-threatening hunger strikes.

Unlike Chalidze, Kovalyov believed that it was both important and desirable that these two currents of thought had played a role in Soviet dissident history.[151] By his own reckoning the intentions of the politicals were as "pure" as those of the legalists in their struggle for human rights.[152] He never sought to demonstrate conclusively that they were right and the others wrong, only that the actions of the politicals ran counter to the legalists' natural inclination to seek a cautious balance between reform and the conditions under which they lived. The knowledge of revolution in shaping Soviet history, and the memory of the purges, were a potent factor that considerably influenced their decision-making. It was not until *perestroika*, however, when the first real opportunity for cooperation with the Soviet authorities arose, that the division between the two strains of thought became publicly decisive. The division itself would later be bitterly questioned by prominent human rights activist Alexander Podrabinek.

Despite its debates, the Initiative Group still managed to devise an outline for the group that culminated in its first anniversary statement: "As a matter of principle the Initiative Group refrains from making any political statements whatsoever. Now, as in the past, it considers its primary duty to be the defence of human rights in the country."[153] It is noteworthy that, at the time of this statement, Levitin-Krasnov had been arrested. Moreover, just after the first anniversary statement, a letter appeared in *samizdat*, "Notes on the Democratic Movement" by Andrei Slavin, in which the author called for "the creation of a conspiratorial organization capable of winning mass support" and criticised the Initiative Group for not taking upon itself this task.[154]

The Initiative Group of 1969 set the agenda for a generation by forming a public organization. For all of its shortcomings, it represented an important stage in the history of the Soviet Human Rights Movement and established a precedent for all the committees and organizations that followed. It was also a healthy sign of a reanimated society in which debate thrived. It illustrated that the Soviet Union could have a public forum in which views were able to be expressed. And finally, its public nature opened it up for external support and later acted as an important gathering point for material for *The Chronicle of Current Events*.

Kovalyov's initial proposal of studying and analysing human rights was never taken up by the group. Its achievements were rather nebulous when weighed against the volume of letters and information gathered by Chalidze's Human Rights Committee of 1970. It took the authorities six months to form a case against the Initiative Group. The internal divisions that gripped the group were accompanied by external repression, explaining the great lapses between letters over the course of the next seven years. From 1970, the majority of its protest letters related to the repression of its own members and, by 1972, eight of its fifteen members had been arrested.[155] In 1969, Natalya Gorbanevskaya was arrested and confined to a psychiatric hospital, as were Yuri Maltsev and Victor Borisov. Levitin-Krasnov was arrested and held under "preventative detention" for eleven months, and then re-arrested on May 8, 1971. The Crimean Tartar activist Mustafa Dzhemilev was sentenced to three years. Genrikh Altunyan was arrested in Kharkov in July, and Victor Krasin was sentenced to five years of exile in December. At the beginning of 1972, Leonid Plyushch was placed in a psychiatric hospital. By the middle of 1972, Pyotr Yakir and Victor Krasin were arrested, and practically every member of the group had been searched. By the end of 1972, the only members at liberty were Kovalyov, Lavut, Velikanova, Khodorovich, Podyapolsky and Yakobson.

Not long after the group had formed in May of 1969, Kovalyov travelled to the Far East on a scientific expedition. On his return in September, he found that six members of the Initiative Group had already been called in for questioning by the KGB. During his absence his own fate at the university was being decided. The secretary of the ideological department of the Moscow Komsomol was sent to Moscow University to seek out "two aliens".[156] Presenting a short speech, she drew particular attention to the activities of Kovalyov and his friend and colleague Alexander Lavut.[157] Before the situation deteriorated and members of the faculty were forced to vote for or against his dismissal, Gelfand urged Kovalyov to resign. Kovalyov observed that Gelfand was also torn. He appreciated the importance of Kovalyov's research and the fact that the young biologist had been with him since the laboratory was first established. But despite the increasingly uncomfortable situation over the course of October, Kovalyov refused to leave of his own accord. He stressed to Gelfand that it was "unlawful to remove a person on account of his personal views".[158] This was the Soviet Union of the 1970s and Kovalyov could not rely on his colleagues to support him. He maintained that he began to feel troubled by the situation he had unwittingly forced on them. "I lived among people for whom a general negative attitude toward official dogma was normal," recalled Kovalyov. "But for these people, social problems were never the focus of their lives."[159] He finally conceded that they should not be threatened with the end of their experiments because of his personal choices.[160] He resigned in November.

For Kovalyov, the year 1969 was a sustained lesson in the price he would be forced to pay for his actions. Not only was he losing a lifetime of research work, he was threatened with an uncertain future which may well have seen him arrested for "parasitism" if he failed to find other work. Within a year of his resignation from Moscow University, he had secured a new position as senior researcher in an experimental fish hatchery in Kalinin. From there he continued to write articles and broadened his research to trace a method of using chemical mutation agents in the breeding of fish.[161] This employment was arranged for him by the biologist Vitaly Rekubratsky, who was married to Andrei Sakharov's cousin, Katya Sakharov.[162]

The Chronicle of Current Events

In his Memoirs, Kovalyov describes his time as editor of *The Chronicle of Current Events* (*Khronika Tekushchykh sobytiya*) as the most rewarding time of his early dissident career.[163] For him personally it gave shape to all that was positive about his human rights work, and he finally succeeded in drawing together his talents as a scientist and his strong commitment to rights into a comprehensive human rights bulletin. What he sought, he insisted over and over again, was a bulletin, free of emotional attacks on the regime or political debate and defined by its objectivity.[164] And in keeping with many of his values, the issues of the *Chronicle* that appeared between the spring of 1972 and the winter of 1974 were a direct result of his commitment to the impartial presentation of information, and their success can be attributed largely to his influence and hard work. The consequence of all this, of course, was that the *Chronicle* has since become the most respected historical source to document human rights violations in the Soviet Union during this period.

Long before Kovalyov started as editor, the style of the *Chronicle* was shaped by its founder, the poet and philologist Natalya Gorbanevskaya. On her arrest in 1969, Gorbanevskaya was succeeded by Anatoly Yakobson, literary critic, author of the treatise on Alexander Blok, *The End of A Tragedy*, and one of Kovalyov's closest friends. By 1972, Yakobson was threatened with arrest and was considering emigration to Israel. Tatyana Velikanova was concerned that, after three years as editor, Yakobson was exhausted by his responsibility for the journal which, given its secrecy, was a demanding and exacting commitment. She was concerned for the future of the *Chronicle*, and in the spring of 1972 she asked Kovalyov to take on the editorial role.[165]

The readiness with which Kovalyov accepted the position perhaps best illustrates how resolute he had become. His contacts with the journal since 1969 had been sporadic and irregular, confined to the transfer of information on the Lithuanian Nationalist-Religious Movement. But during this period he had also formed close friendships with Velikanova and Yakobson, people who had shared his vision for the Initiative Group, and this may well have influenced his decision. But by his own reckoning, *The Chronicle of Current Events* was the quintessence of the movement, and he had his own ambitions regarding its future.[166] The nucleus of the new editorial board consisted of Kovalyov, Velikanova and Khodorovich; Kovalyov as chief editor, Velikanova as the administrator responsible for collating material and organizing apartments for meetings, and Khodorovich who regularly passed on information.[167]

Meanwhile other events were unfolding in Moscow. Kovalyov's decision to edit the *Chronicle* was accompanied shortly afterwards by the arrest of Yakir in June and Krasin three months later.[168] The result was that, while under the pressure of investigation by KGB General Yaroslav V. Karpov, Yakir and Krasin gave damaging depositions on the *Chronicle* and on members of the Initiative Group.[169] They appeared on Soviet television where they urged their fellow activists to stop the publication of the *Chronicle* and threatened that, for every issue published after the broadcast, there would be an arrest.[170] The Initiative Group was similarly criticised. According to Kovalyov there were disputes among the members, notably with Podyapolsky and Levitin-Krasnov regarding how they should respond to the public reproof. Podyapolsky and Levitin-Krasnov argued for a statement condemning the depositions as an act of betrayal and a sign of disloyalty.[171] Characteristic of Kovalyov's tolerance and his distinct ability to see that the question of Yakir and Krasin's depositions went beyond the narrow frame of betrayal into the greater one of power, he argued that to condemn those who had been "broken" by the inhuman process of investigation was inappropriate. He wanted, above all, to object to the methods adopted by the authorities that forced people to subject themselves, their ideals and their contemporaries to a criterion externally imposed, the foundation of which was isolation and fear.[172]

How this dispute was resolved is unclear, but a compromise seems to have been drawn. The Initiative Group issued a statement declaring that Yakir and Krasin had made "false statements". It argued that it had "never sought to discredit the social system or the government", and objected only to those actions which would be considered "inadmissible under any system and any government".[173] The declaration also included an objection to the inhumane methods of interrogation adopted by the KGB.[174]

This was the last statement of the Initiative Group until 1974. The *Chronicle* had also suspended publication with Issue 27, dated October 15, 1972. Set against this apprehensive atmosphere, they decided to prepare three retrospective issues in order to cover the period interrupted by the interrogations.[175] The situation was not improved by the arrest in January 1973 of Irina Belogorodskaya, the first victim of the recent threat.[176] On the fringe of the movement, occasionally assisting with typed manuscripts for the journal, Belogorodskaya's arrest forced yet another ethical dilemma on Kovalyov and his colleagues.

The objective of the authorities was twofold. On the one hand they sought to hold the editors to ransom, to indirectly make hostages of them. On the other hand they perhaps hoped that the ultimatum might prove to be a divisive issue for the movement. On both accounts they were wrong. Certainly Kovalyov and the other members of the group felt their predicament keenly, but they refused to submit to a threat tantamount to blackmail. Their main task was to prolong the publication of the *Chronicle*, and the first measure they took to partially resolve this problem was a statement in the introduction to Issue 28 in 1973. The declaration stated that a decision had been made to resume the publication of the journal, since the editorial board found the ultimatum imposed on them by the security forces to be "incompatible" with "justice, morality and human dignity".[177]

Between them, they decided on a second measure that was significantly more profound. They agreed that they would circulate a declaration to accompany the *Chronicle*, acknowledging their personal responsibility for its dissemination. This was the first time in the history of the *Chronicle* that its editors linked their names to the *samizdat* text. They hoped to place the authorities in a predicament that would make it increasingly difficult to implicate others. In May 1974, Kovalyov, Velikanova and Khodorovich met with foreign correspondents and passed out the issues, Nos 28, 29 and 30. The declaration that accompanied the journal stated: "Despite the repeated assertion of the KGB and Soviet courts, we do not consider *The Chronicle of Current Events* to be an illegal or slanderous publication. We regard it as our duty to promote its widest possible circulation. We are convinced that accurate information about violations of elementary human rights in the Soviet Union should be available to all who are interested."[178] This was a startling and courageous decision. It made a forcible contrast to the previously anonymous activity that characterized the compilation of the *Chronicle* and its distribution. It was also testimony to the openness that increasingly defined all of Kovalyov's public activity.

Despite events, Kovalyov still managed to collate and verify material for the *Chronicle*. On the whole his approach was encyclopaedic, and the chronicling of trials, arrests, searches and other violations was notably scholarly with a fine attention to detail. Over the course of three years, Kovalyov introduced three new sections into the *Chronicle*. These included *Events in Lithuania*, *Events in the Ukraine* and *Events in Georgia*. The repression of intellectuals struggling to preserve their national culture became a dominant theme in these three sections. The first section, *Events in Lithuania*, grew out of his acquaintance with Arimantis Raskanis, a young postgraduate linked to the Lithuanian National-Religious movement. With the Catholic Church at the centre of this struggle, the quest for a national revival in Lithuania eventually played a leading role in the republic's independence in 1991. Kovalyov was first acquainted with Raskanis at the Medical Institute, and later through the Gelfand laboratory where they regularly exchanged *samizdat*.[179] At around the same time that Kovalyov decided to edit the *Chronicle*, the Lithuanian Catholic Church, inspired by the example of their Soviet neighbours, began to publish their own journal, the *Chronicle of the Lithuanian Catholic Church*, news from which later formed the basis for Kovalyov's new section. Through Raskanis, Kovalyov was also introduced to Petras Plumpa, who twenty years later became Chairman of an independent Lithuanian KGB. Together they organized the transfer of information to the West. The section *Events in the Ukraine* similarly chronicled the repression of Ukrainian intellectuals fighting for the restoration of their culture.[180] Kovalyov linked with the Georgians through the philologist Zviad Gamsakhurdia, later to become the first President of Georgia and an organizer of the underground publication of Solzhenitsyn's *Gulag Archipelago*.

Kovalyov admired the accuracy with which the Lithuanians approached their work. He began to feel that the quest for human rights was a lonely journey in the Soviet Union without a unified struggle for something akin to national independence. His relations with the Lithuanian movement clinched his view that, in order for the concept of human rights to move the majority, the driving force had to be something greater than isolated individuals struggling to live freely.[181] Despite the sobering realization that the Soviet Union was not united in its cause, he did not shrink from his work with the journal. He carried his responsibility for the *Chronicle* to great lengths, in a manner that was at once determined and pedantic.

Kovalyov's ambitions for the *Chronicle* illustrate vividly one of his most important and controversial views on Soviet society. Beyond their importance as historical records, for Kovalyov personally the *Chronicle* was a sustained argument against a polemic that he believed dominated dissident circles and towards which he felt a strong antipathy. In retrospect a distinction can be drawn between the editorial style that shaped Gorbanevskaya's approach to the journal and the objective methods that began with Yakobson and were later instilled by Kovalyov.[182] Many years later, Kovalyov would argue that Gorbanevskaya's style was driven by a particular view of Soviet reality that encouraged the simple concept of a dual society. While the authorities represented the enemy located on one side of the equation, the people represented the victimized and existed on the other. Kovalyov argued against an overly abstract conception of Soviet life, a simple line between "us and them", which made the task of laying blame shamelessly simple. Not only was this interpretation counterproductive, but in his own words it was "too good for Soviet society. We have to acknowledge a worse variant. This is a sick society ... what has happened to us and what is happening now – is our common misfortune and guilt."[183]

Kovalyov's deepest conviction was that every individual shared responsibility for both the past and the future of the Soviet Union. This conviction of shared guilt, which was one of his deepest, was also the most controversial and incited attacks by other human rights activists later in his career. Interpretations of history played a significant role in shaping his thought. He insisted that the 1917 Russian Revolution did not constitute a radical break with the Russian past, but a continuation between past history and their own time. In this respect he broke radically from Solzhenitsyn's view that the 1917 Revolution constituted a radical schism in Russian history and insisted that states, above all, are not abstract concepts that exist outside the individual, but are constituted by individuals who participate willingly in their construction.

For him, the system had successfully refashioned Soviet society in its image. He knew that many expressed their discontent with the system in private, but he understood that the regime shared, if not merely the confidence, then the fear of the masses. If it had not, its existence would have crumbled. "Totalitarianism is not only government pressure over society," he recalled. "It consists also of a society who displays a readiness to submit itself to that violence and even assist state terror."[184] For Kovalyov, the system had effectively established a relationship of trust between the state and the individual.

> ... this trust is akin to the faith a child has in an adult. Apart from the meagre material blessings and comparative spiritual comfort, it is exactly this kind of trust that guarantees a totalitarian state and liberates the individual from civil responsibility. Is a child expected to bear responsibility for the actions of an adult? Therefore, in a totalitarian society, the state answers for everything, including the weather ... We are used to relating to the state as some external force that we either

despise or worship from childhood – but for whose actions we take no responsibility. And just like a three year old child who does not need civil rights, we also do not need them.[185]

For Kovalyov, the absence of private property and initiative had led to a miserable deadlock in Soviet society. He argued that the state ownership of property in which every citizen was a hired worker of the "one landlord, the government" had forced Soviet society to engage in corruption, stealing, carelessness and a disregard for rights that had reached unprecedented levels of customary law.

It angered him that his society had lost the tools with which to measure its moral decline, or the courage to speak out against its subjection to an inexorable system. "The doctor was always more important than the patient," he argued. "The trader was more important than the consumer, the clerk more important than the client and the policeman more important than the pedestrian."[186] The readiness of society to accept the predominance of the state bureaucracy and its inability to move beyond its paternalistic expectations remained a lifelong theme for Kovalyov, a topic that shaped some of his most poignant and bitter speeches.

Kovalyov grew increasingly radical during the course of 1972. He wrote to Yuri Andropov, Chairman of the KGB, requesting the return of his copy of Solzhenitsyn's *Gulag Archipelago*.[187] In 1972, the year that Solzhenitsyn's "experiment in literary investigation" first began to circulate in *samizdat*, Kovalyov had lent his copy to a colleague at the fish hatchery, Valery Maresin. When photocopying the book, one of Maresin's co-workers took the text and reported it to the authorities. During interrogation, Maresin was pressured to disclose the name of its owner but refused to indict Kovalyov. Kovalyov wrote to Andropov, stating that he was the owner of Solzhenitsyn's *Gulag Archipelago*. "You know better than I that this book is based on historical facts and contains neither lies nor slander ... I demand that you return this book which belongs to me. This demand is founded on the natural and obvious right of every individual to have their own personal library which they should not have to hide from their friends."[188] The letter was not well-received, and several days later he found it outside his back door, dirty and crumpled.[189]

Apart from engaging in his work with the journal, Kovalyov remained committed to giving practical help to individuals. In 1970, Simas Kudirka jumped onto the US Coast Guard cutter *Vigilant*, seeking asylum in America. The US Coast Guard returned him to a Soviet ship, whereupon he was sentenced to ten years hard labour in a Soviet prison. Kudirka's mother, Marija Sulskis, was an American citizen, born in Brooklyn and raised in Russia. To establish her citizenship claims to ensure the release of her son and her own exile, she had to reach the US Embassy in Moscow. After a failed attempt to get past the militia and KGB prohibiting access to the Embassy, Sulskis appealed to Sakharov.

Figure 1.3   From left, Evgeny Rybkin, Arii Mizyakin and Sergei Kovalyov, 1974, the summer before his arrest

Source: Memorial Archive, Moscow.

Sakharov wrote to the embassy announcing that Sergei Kovalyov would be standing in for Mrs Sulskis to establish her citizenship claims. Kovalyov, however, was picked up by the KGB and detained when he attempted to enter the building. He refused to hand over Mrs Sulskis's papers.[190] He organized a spontaneous press conference in May 1974 to report that the Soviet authorities were violating the regulations of the US–Soviet Consular Convention that guaranteed Soviet citizens free access to the consulate.[191] In late May 1974, he accompanied Mrs Sulskis to the consulate where she confirmed her citizenship. Later that year she and her son left for America.[192]

By November 1974, Kovalyov and ten others, including Andrei Tverdokhlebov, Valentin Turchin and Yuri Orlov, succeeded in registering a Moscow group of Amnesty International. For over a year they struggled to register themselves with Amnesty's International Secretariat, who displayed great caution in including the activists and granted them "group" rather than full status, with no permission to send their representatives abroad to Amnesty Congresses.[193] They took on three cases in Bangladesh, Spain and Yugoslavia, following the Amnesty tradition of writing letters expressing concern over the fate of political prisoners.

On October 30, 1974, Kovalyov, Velikanova, Khodorovich and Lavut organized a press conference to commemorate the first "Day of the Soviet Political Prisoner". The fate of prisoners and the need for prison reform were to become leading concerns in Kovalyov's career, and the conference was seen as a way to educate people on the conditions of detainment for political prisoners in the USSR. As they pressed ahead with Issue 33 of the *Chronicle* that they hoped to launch on the same day in October, they worked energetically on organizing the information coming in from prison camps across the Soviet Union.[194] The October conference was held in Andrei Sakharov's apartment, packed with foreign correspondents crammed into rooms and down the hallway.[195] To strengthen their protest, prisoners incarcerated in Mordovian and Perm Prison camps announced mass hunger strikes of one or two days, demanding that the status of political prisoner be recognized in the Soviet Union. The press conference was presided over by Sakharov, and Kovalyov handed information to foreign correspondents, most of which had been smuggled from labour camps. The day to commemorate the Soviet Political Prisoner was Kovalyov's last public appearance before his arrest.

The trial

The year 1974 established Kovalyov's reputation as a rights defender, but in the history of the biologist it was both an end and a beginning. This productive year ended abruptly in December with his arrest, and the following decade was defined by isolation, struggle and ill health. When Kovalyov reflected on these years he avoids lingering on their significance for him personally. He wryly remarked many years later that he was grateful to the court for granting him "the opportunity to reflect over the course of ten years".[196] But one of the most startling aspects of Kovalyov's life over this period was that he returned from exile in 1984 with his values intact. What did change were his views on the Soviet system. As his knowledge of the human rights situation in Russia deepened, and with the wrenching of freedom from his own life, he was firmly convinced of the insidious nature of a system that appeared unwilling to change and considered itself free to impose cruel suffering on its citizens.

On the morning of December 23, Velikanova phoned to inform Kovalyov that Khodorovich's apartment was being searched. While still on the telephone, Kovalyov heard his own doorbell ring and, certain that it must be the KGB, he delayed opening the door until he had explained to Velikanova what was going on. By his own reckoning he was prepared for his arrest, but as for the search, his briefcase stood in the entrance, and down the hall the bookcases were crammed with documents, *samizdat*, pamphlets and any number of texts.[197] During the twelve-hour search, the security forces collected more than enough material to implicate him for his direct involvement with *The Chronicle of Current Events*. They took with them statements and letters written by political prisoners, the beginnings of Issue 34, a copy of *The Chronicle of the Lithuanian Catholic Church*, 43 photographs, a list of 135 Lithuanian political prisoners, a copy of the *Gulag Archipelago*, stenogrammes of trials, Valery Chalidze's *To Defend These Rights*, personal letters and notebooks.[198] He later lamented that he had not thought of throwing it all over the balcony.[199]

He explained to his investigator, Anatoly Trofimov, that he refused to participate in the interrogation on the grounds that the security forces had failed to abide by the laws pertaining to searches.[200] He was released, and summoned to return the following day. They held onto his passport.

The next day, he sat in the waiting room at Lubyanka for an hour. According to his *Memoirs*, he left after telling the duty officer that he refused to wait. "You have to wait," replied the officer seriously. "From your point of view I have to wait. But from my point of view I do not. It is chaos here and I have things to do." Two days later Trofimov called and asked him to drop by to pick up his passport and have a "little ten minute chat".[201]

With the long line of arrests of friends and colleagues preceding him, Kovalyov set about putting his things in order.[202] But despite the numerous arrests and trials of others he had documented in the *Chronicle*, it was now his own freedom at stake. The night before his arrest, he visited Sakharov and his wife, Elena Bonner. Sakharov recalled the visit:

> We sat in the kitchen, Kovalyov in his usual spot with his back to the balcony door. We talked about all sorts of things, the mood switching back and forth from half-joking to serious, even philosophical. We all felt that this might be our last conversation with him for a long time. Around midnight, he asked for some paper. He was worried about the threatening letter we'd received a few days earlier from the *Russian Christian Party* (as usual, he was more concerned about others than about himself). He tried to draft a statement; dissatisfied with his first attempts, he kept on making changes. It was after two a.m. when he finally got up and said: "All right then, I'll be going, I have some things to do at home." We saw him to the door and embraced him.[203]

The next day, December 27, Kovalyov went to Lubyanka to collect his passport. He was immediately arrested under Article 70 (anti-Soviet agitation and propaganda)[204] and taken to Lefortovo, the central investigation bureau and KGB prison.[205] The following morning, he was abruptly moved from his cell to an airplane that took him to Vilnius. The pretext used for moving Kovalyov from Moscow to the Lithuanian capital was that three copies of *The Chronicle of the Lithuanian Catholic Church* had been found in his apartment. The authorities were evidently troubled about the reaction his trial would arouse, in both Moscow and the West. By moving the trial to a destination where foreign journalists were not accredited, they could at least minimize its coverage. The official reason mentioned much later was that Kovalyov had allied himself with Lithuanian nationalists, supposed Nazi collaborators of World War Two[206]

The attempt to diffuse the general outcry was made in vain. As soon as news of Kovalyov's arrest reached Sakharov, he responded immediately with an international appeal:

I appeal to Sergei Kovalyov's colleagues – the biologists of all countries. I appeal to Amnesty International, of which Kovalyov is a member; all his activities have been in accordance with the spirit of the organization. I appeal to the International League for the Rights of Man. I appeal to everyone who prizes goodness, integrity and intellectual freedom. I call for an international campaign for the release of Sergei Kovalyov.[207]

On December 30, the Initiative Group issued a statement:

We who know Kovalyov, a man of great mind and heart, cannot accept this act of arbitrary injustice ... Sergei Kovalyov has openly spoken out in defence of a great many unjustly persecuted people; he has defended legality, free speech, humanitarianism. Today, he himself is in need of support. We call on all those who agree with us to come to his support.[208]

Outside the Soviet Union, the reaction was equally as strong. The Federation of American Scientists set up a "Committee in Defence of Sergei Kovalyov". They appealed to Anatoly Dobrynin, the Soviet Ambassador to the United States, in a letter signed by 92 biologists, all members of the National Academy of Sciences, for clemency or amnesty for Kovalyov.[209] The department of Neurobiology and Behavior at Cornell University invited Kovalyov to come to the United States as a visiting scholar,[210] a gesture later supported by the American House of Representatives at the 94th Congress, who urged the President in the spirit of *détente* to pressure the USSR to allow Kovalyov to accept the post.[211] Academics from Leiden University in Holland appealed to V. Kotelnikov, the acting President of the Soviet Academy of Sciences, asking him to take action on behalf of Kovalyov and Tverdokhlebov. "To our dismay we have found out from colleagues and members of the Academy that Kovalyov and Tverdokhlebov have been denied freedom of speech," they wrote. "We fear that their arrest may have a serious impact on the development of scientific contacts between the Soviet Union and other countries."[212]

It would be hard to exaggerate the attempts made by the investigators to hinder Kovalyov's defence. The pre-trial investigation took just under a year and the zeal with which they gathered information and witnesses was striking. Kovalyov was accused of the following: signing appeals on the anniversary of the occupation of Czechoslovakia (1969), in defence of Bukovsky (1971), on Krasin and Yakir (1973), on the exile of Solzhenitsyn (1974), to the UN on the Crimean Tartars (1974), in defence of Khaustov (1974), for his participation in the press conference on October 30, for transmitting abroad information on Soviet camps which was classified in the indictment as "defamatory information", for resuming the publication of the *Chronicle*, for compiling, editing and sending abroad numbers 28–34, circulating the *Gulag Archipelago* and possessing three issues of *The Chronicle of the Lithuanian Catholic Church*.[213]

Kovalyov explained to his investigator, Anatoly Aleksandrovich Istomin of the Perm KGB, that his arrest violated Soviet law and the Constitution of the USSR which permitted freedom of thought.[214] On these grounds he refused to participate in the pre-trial preparations and handed Istomin a statement outlining the reasons for his decision.[215] When reflecting on this period, Kovalyov recalled that Istomin's line of questioning centred around two issues. One concerned the question of the "political activity" of the dissident movement. The second concerned the question as to whether dissident activity actually helped or hindered the process of democratization in the Soviet Union.[216] Kovalyov recalled much later:

> I often recall conversations I had with the KGB when they tried to persuade me: "Sergei Adamovich, you are such a champion of democracy. But, you know that you and all the others are to blame for the fact that we live in a society without freedom. We want democracy, but the conditions are not taking shape because of you. If you were quiet, this democracy would happen far quicker ..."[217]

In Moscow, Investigator Istomin also interrogated Kovalyov's colleague, A. Maresin. He was told that Kovalyov was responsible for establishing an "anti-Soviet" group at the fish hatchery. Other activists interrogated were Valery Turchin, Irina Belogorodskaya, Podyapolsky, Velikanova, Landa and Kovalyov's wife, Ludmilla Boitseva.[218]

It is not exactly clear when Istomin shifted his line of questioning to a discussion of the *Chronicle*. Clearly, his intention was to gather enough information to prove that there were factual errors in the journal that amounted to a defamatory and slanderous undermining of the Soviet State. Kovalyov did not accept that the *Chronicle* was a "slanderous publication" or that he had participated in criminal activity. He decided on further reflection to engage the investigators in a discussion of the documented information they were struggling to prove was false.[219] He sought to prove that the mistakes in the journal were not fabricated or intentionally defamatory, but were genuine mistakes resulting from the conditions he was forced to work under as editor. What was worse for him was his inability to communicate. While the authorities traversed the country gathering information, he was confined to a prison cell in Vilnius. This, he recalled many years later, was one of the more frightening aspects of his detention period.[220]

Appreciating the need for a strong defence counsel who would reflect his personal values and beliefs, Kovalyov's attempts to find such a counsel were hindered by a number of factors, both personal and external. In August 1975, as the Soviet Union finally committed itself to the Helsinki Final Act after two-and-a-half years of negotiation, and published the principles on the front page of *Izvestiya*, Kovalyov sought to enlist the help of well known rights defence lawyers Sofya Kallistratova and Dina Kaminskaya. They personally agreed to represent him, but his wife received a reply from the President of the

Presidium who explained that both lawyers were overburdened with work and would be unable to stand for the defence without an official permit in a case concerning Article 70 of the Criminal Code outside of Moscow.[221] According to Kovalyov's subsequent lawyer, the volume of work taken on by lawyers, even in the Soviet Union, was a personal decision.[222]

Over the course of the next three months, repeated attempts were made by Kovalyov's friends to organize defence counsel. In an open letter to Amnesty International and the International Commission of Jurists, Sakharov appealed on behalf of Kovalyov and Tverdokhlebov. He noted that the charges laid against Kovalyov included his membership in Amnesty, and he called on both organizations to "send their observers and qualified lawyers, who will be independent of the Soviet authorities to the trials of Kovalyov and Tverdokhlebov, so that they can take part in the trials and help to ensure that the accused are afforded their full right to a defence."[223] On October 21, Velikanova, Lavut and Orlov also appealed to Amnesty International, the International Committee of Human Rights in Paris and the International Association of Democratic Lawyers, demanding that the "discriminatory ban" on Kovalyov's right to choose his own lawyer be lifted. They also invited foreign lawyers to participate.[224]

Despite all attempts, Ludmilla Boitseva was forced to find a lawyer outside of Moscow. She hired A. Rozhansky, a prominent lawyer from Leningrad. From the outset, Kovalyov's relations with Rozhansky were strained by the lawyer's suggestion that they concede that *The Chronicle of Current Events* was an anti-Soviet publication.[225] This was the one point Kovalyov categorically refused to accept: "The publication cannot be qualified in this way," he responded. "I'm accused of undermining the prestige of the Soviet state and discrediting its social order. But I only revealed the truth about the violation of the law. Prestige is not something that can be maintained through omission of facts."[226] He decided to defend himself, in protest against the authority's illegal suppression of his right to choose his own lawyer. The pre-trial investigation ended shortly afterwards, on September 27, 1975.[227] In one of those disturbing ironies, Kovalyov heard shortly after that the Amnesty campaign he had worked on for the release of the political prisoners in Spain and Bangladesh had been successful.[228]

The President of the Presidium, in a letter to Kovalyov's wife, declared that only close relatives would be allowed to attend her husband's trial.[229] Predicting problems with his friend's trial, Sakharov appealed to L.N. Smirnov, Chairman of the USSR Supreme Court, on October 6, asking him to grant an open trial to Kovalyov in order that his friends, representatives of the international press and Amnesty International could gain entry. He received no reply to his letter.[230]

On September 4, Valentin Turchin, Chairman of the Soviet Amnesty International Group, also issued a declaration: "I ask the leaders and citizens of countries which were signatories to the Helsinki agreements to demand from the Soviet government that the trials of Kovalyov and

Tverdokhlebov be open to the public and, in particular, to foreign journalists and observers from Amnesty International.[231]

There were problems for Kovalyov's friends who sought to travel to Vilnius for the trial. In Moscow, Velikanova, Khodorovich and Landa were detained on their way to Belorusskaya Railway Station. They were released after the departure of the train to Vilnius, but throughout Kovalyov's three-day trial they were constantly followed. In Vilnius, A. Terleckas, V. Petkus and V. Smolkin were detained at the station as they waited for the train to arrive from Moscow. The *Chronicle* also reported that several Lithuanian Jews who had been denied emigration visas were told that their applications would be approved if they stayed away from the courtroom.[232]

Kovalyov was detained for another two-and-a-half months before his trial, bringing his time in detention to just less than one year. The trial began on December 9, 1975 in the Lithuanian Supreme Court, and lasted for three days. The presiding judge was Mikhail Ignotas who, in February, 1976, received an honorary diploma of the Supreme Court for his successful handling of the Kovalyov case.[233]

Kovalyov's trial spectacularly dramatized the Soviet Union's non-observance of the human rights the authorities had pledged to comply with four months before when it signed the Final Act in Helsinki. The Soviets finally agreed to commit to Principle VII: Respect for human rights and fundamental freedoms, including the freedom of thought, conscience, religion or belief that sought "to promote and encourage the effective exercise of civil, political, economic, social, cultural and other rights and freedoms all of which derive from the inherent dignity of the human person and are essential for his free and full development", in exchange for Principle II: Inviolability of frontiers, Principle IV: Territorial integrity of States and Principle VI: Non-intervention in internal affairs.[234] The Helsinki Final Act was a statement of political intent based on consensus with no institutional framework until 1990. The Soviet government nevertheless distributed 20 million copies of the Act across the Union and awarded every representative of the Soviet delegation an Order of Lenin to celebrate a diplomatic victory that ratified its post-war borders.[235] The 35 participating states agreed to meet in Belgrade in October 1977 for a follow-up meeting to discuss ratification of all the agreed principles.

Within two years of the signing of the Final Act, the Soviet leadership began to understand that significant pressure was being exerted by the European governments and non-government agencies around Principle VII. It had hoped, in the tradition of the Universal Declaration of Human Rights, that the participating states would not strictly monitor compliance with the Act. If indeed pressure was mounted, it knew it could always argue within the central and highly criticised paradox of the Final Act – the simultaneous respect for human rights and non-intervention in internal affairs. On the opening day of Kovalyov's trial, Brezhnev delivered a speech in Warsaw at the Seventh Congress of the Polish Communist Party, in which he alluded to the growing pressure. He insisted:

We stand for consistently filling with life the concrete points of the [Helsinki] conference's Final Act. I would like also to emphasise that it is very important to see and comprehend the importance of this document as a whole, in its entirety, without succumbing to the temptation to tear separate chunks out of it which some regard as tactically more convenient to them.[236]

It was a freezing winter day on December 9 when Kovalyov's trial opened in Vilnius. Those who had managed to reach the capital stood in the lobby of the Supreme Court. Virtually every possible means was taken to stop information coming out of the courtroom and reaching friends. Only people with special passes were admitted. Brief scuffles broke out as the guards kept Kovalyov's friends back from the door and harassed people in the crowd as they waited for updates from his family. Only his son, Ivan, and his wife, Ludmilla Boitseva, were permitted entry. The curtains were drawn across the windows.[237]

At the opening of the trial, Sakharov passed a statement to Judge Ignotas. He declared that since he had committed some of the alleged crimes for which Kovalyov was on trial, he should also be charged.[238] Over the course of the three-day trial Sakharov tried repeatedly to enter the courtroom, shouting: "My voice must be heard in there, I have the right to shout."[239] And Kovalyov himself was denied the right to call any of his own personal witnesses. Witnesses for the prosecution numbered twenty-two.[240] Psychiatrists from the Serbsky Institute and Dr. L.A. Lyubarskaya of Dnepropetrovsk Special Psychiatric Hospital were called to testify that psychiatric methods were not used for repressive methods and to testify that the case of Leonid Plyushch, documented in Issue 30 of *The Chronicle of Current Events*, had been inaccurately reported. When Kovalyov questioned Lyubarskaya about the exact nature of Plyushch's illness, she responded that a medical explanation would be too complex for the courtroom to understand. When he asked her to elaborate, the question was overruled. Dr A.A. Kozhemyakina was also called as a witness for the prosecution regarding Grigorenko's release from a psychiatric hospital. When Kovalyov tried to prove that Grigorenko's discharge was linked to a court decision and not to his mental health, he was told not to ask such questions and was again overruled.[241] Krasin's depositions given during his arrest were used as evidence, but Kovalyov could not call Krasin as a witness.[242] This set the pattern for the entire trial.[243]

At the recess on the second day, Kovalyov's witnesses left the courtroom with a spoken promise from the guard in charge that they would be allowed to return after the recess.[244] When they tried to re-enter shortly after, they were forcibly pushed back from the doors. Yuri Orlov, Mikhail Litvinov and Valery Turchin were detained for several hours and Ludmilla Boitseva was the only person allowed in.[245] Kovalyov returned to the courtroom to find his witnesses missing and in anger stated: 'I refuse to speak in front of this herd of swine!" Marked by a caustic tone otherwise quite uncharacteristic of him, he demanded to be removed from the courtroom.

While being taken away, he called to his family, "My deep love to you all and those who are outside the door and in Moscow. Warmest greetings to Andrei Dmitrievich."[246] Kovalyov refused to participate in the trial and a recess was called until December 11. In an accompanying statement he declared: "the fact is that infringement of the law has now become so customary in judicial procedure in cases of this sort that a tendency has arisen to regard it as inevitable. I shall not alter my demands."[247] He apologized for the expressions he had used earlier, but his demands were nevertheless ignored. The most distressing aspect was that he was denied the opportunity to address the court in his final statement. The final word was given to the prosecution:

> The Soviet government is indifferent to the opinions of a person, if he only keeps them to himself and does not commit criminal acts. In the discourses on freedom in the documents which [Kovalyov] has signed, one theme is clearly apparent: to impose on the Soviet people the bourgeois concept of freedom, an attempt to present freedom as independent of society.[248]

The court announced the verdict in absentia – seven years' strict-regime camp and three years of internal exile. For Kovalyov, the additional sentence of internal exile was completely unexpected.[249]

Kovalyov's trial was given greater resonance across the world by the presence in Vilnius of Andrei Sakharov. While Sakharov's wife Elena Bonner read the Nobel Peace Prize speech for her husband in Oslo, Sakharov stood outside the Supreme Court in Lithuania struggling for the second time to get into the closed courtroom. Indeed, the trial may have been deliberately arranged for this date to ensure that Sakharov was not in Moscow speaking to foreign journalists. In his speech for the 1975 Noble Peace Prize, he wrote:

> I was unable to participate personally in today's ceremony. I thank my friends who live abroad and who honoured me by being my guests here. I had also invited my friends from my own country – Valentin Turchin, Yuri Orlov and two of the noblest defenders of the cause of justice, legality, honour and honesty, Sergei Kovalyov and Andrei Tverdokhlebov, both of whom are at present in jail awaiting trial ... I beg you to kindly consider them my official guests.[250]

The resonance of Sakharov's speech persuaded 46 Nobel laureates to appeal to the United Nations proposing that the world organization exert more pressure on member states to fulfil its obligations to the Universal Declaration of Human Rights.[251] In late December, Sakharov returned to Moscow from Vilnius, depressed by the outcome of Kovalyov's trial.[252] He immediately called a press conference in which he announced: "The trial was unashamedly unlawful – there was no openness, no summing up by each side, no defence by the accused or final statement." He insisted that the sentence be annulled.[253]

The Soviet authorities entered the debate in vigorous fashion in January, 1976. *New Times* published an interview with Alexander Sukharev, Deputy Minister of Justice, under the title, "Human Rights in the Soviet Union – Putting the Record Straight". The criticisms voiced by Sakharov in Oslo and the accusations of injustice and unfair treatment that circulated around Kovalyov's trial were categorically denied by the Soviet authorities.[254] Sukharev's polemics were designed to reach a broader audience, explaining the choice of an English/Russian language publication. In a conscious gesture, the Deputy Minister systematically refuted the criticisms waged against the regime by the human rights community – of illegality, of the persecution of persons on the basis of their political and religious views, and finally that the Soviet Union failed to fulfil its obligations under International Covenants and other conventions. The Western press was routinely characterized by Sukharev as seditious and subversive.[255]

Kovalyov's trial became the focal point of retaliation for the Deputy Minister of Justice. He was anxious to prove that the Soviet authorities had satisfied their obligation to the Helsinki Final Act in its treatment of the case and that Kovalyov was sentenced for his criminal activity, not his documentation of human rights violations. In Sukharev's view, Kovalyov was "not tried for his views, not for his convictions, not for being a 'dissident'.... The court established on the basis of incontrovertible evidence that over the past six years he had systematically engaged in organizational activity aimed at undermining the Soviet system."[256] Predictably, he linked Kovalyov's actions to the Popular Labour Alliance, NTS. When the Federation of American Scientists appealed to the Soviet Embassy to protest the verdict of Kovalyov's trial, they were sent a copy of Sukharev's *New Times* article as a formal reply.[257]

Several months later, the journal *Kommunist* printed an interview with Mikhail Ignotas, member of the Latvian Supreme Court who worked on Kovalyov's case under the headline, "A Slanderer Punished". Ignotas outlined how Kovalyov's allies in the West had convinced him to publish and disseminate "slanderous concoctions".[258]

On December 13, Larisa Bogoraz sent a letter of appeal to Soviet scientists: "Surely you can sense that in making a choice between the fate of Sergei Kovalyov and research on the nucleus of cells, and favouring the latter, you are championing not science, but your own place in it? ... However dismal human experience may be, I cannot believe that there will be no one among you who will dare to defend the honour of science and of Russia, and your own dignity as human beings and as scientists."[259] On January 25, 1976 *The New York Times* published a letter by I. Melchuk, prominent linguist and member of the Soviet Academy of Sciences' Institute of Linguistics. Lamenting that his appeal would not be heard in his own country, Melchuk condemned members of the Soviet Academy of Sciences for becoming "soulless puppets", incapable of supporting Kovalyov and Sakharov.[260] Melchuk's exasperation over the silence of his colleagues was substantiated several months later in a supporting letter by Noam Chomsky.[261]

The outcry was not restricted to Moscow's human rights milieu. One-hundred-and-seventy-nine people from sixteen cities across the Soviet Union, including Crimean Tartars, Lithuanians, Georgians, Ukrainians, Armenians and Jews, signed a letter to protest Kovalyov's sentence:[262]

> In his public activity, which is what he was sentenced for, Kovalyov fights against tyranny and lawlessness and speaks out in defence of people persecuted for their beliefs. As an opponent, in principle, of violence, he fights with words: through verbal protest and wide-ranging, accurate information. He is one of those who publicly declared their responsibility for the distribution of the *Chronicle of Current Events* ... We believe that the age of suicidal and shameful silence in our country will not be repeated ... We demand the revocation of Sergei Kovalyov's sentence![263]

The attention that Kovalyov's sentence attracted is testimony not only to his work on the *Chronicle*, which by Issue 34 had reports from 71 locations, but to the effect he had personally on those he had come into contact with during his time as editor of the journal.[264]

Camp Perm 36 and the ongoing struggle

In his *Memoirs*, Kovalyov openly acknowledged that he found his camp days unexpectedly "ordinary and boring".[265] But this statement may just as easily be underwritten by a comment made not much earlier when he declared: "I think of my camp days with terror".[266] The day-to-day routine of camp life was certainly monotonous, but for Kovalyov it was the freedom of the Camp Administration to publicly humiliate and demean its inmates that he struggled most to overcome.[267] Over the course of the next seven years his relationship with the camp administration was tense, provoked by restrictions placed on his correspondence and family visits.[268] These perpetual restrictions resulted in a succession of hunger strikes that contributed to bouts of serious ill health.

Kovalyov arrived at Camp Perm 36 in the Chusovoi District on January 8, 1976. Perm 36, part of a large complex of forced labour camps for political prisoners and criminal recidivists, was located in the west-central region of the Ural mountains. Set up in 1932 and incorporated into the GULag in 1934, it experienced a revival in the late 1960s. Located in a swamp, the camp was renowned for its constant flow of dirty water. Kovalyov's fellow inmates turned out to be either political prisoners, or Lithuanian and Ukrainian partisans from the Second World War.[269]

The first of what would be many unpleasant experiences for Kovalyov occurred in March, 1976. Within three months of his arrival, he was confined to *Shizo* for ten days for drinking tea on his birthday in the wrong section of the camp.[270] By regulation, prisoners could be confined to *Shizo* for a period of no more than 15 days; there was no bed linen, no books or daily exercise, no meetings, parcels or writing paper. Hot food was served every second day; breakfast was 150 grams of bread and a bowl of thin soup; lunch 200 grams of bread, soup and 5 spoonfuls of kasha every second day. In the evening 100 grams of bread and a piece of fish 30–40 grams. On the next day the prisoner received only 450 grams of bread, 20 grams of salt and a cup of boiling water. In total it was 1350 calories on the first day and 850 on the second.[271]

The camp regulations did not stipulate the temperature of *Shizo*, but Kovalyov was told that it was supposed to be 16 degrees Celsius.[272] The temperature of the punishment cell fell well below 16 degrees, whereupon the cold conditions were used as a form of punishment. Immediately after Kovalyov's release from *Shizo* in April, he was given another sentence of seven days.[273] This habit of repeating the sentence after the initial incarceration was common and could result in a prisoner spending up to 40 days in isolation.

Kovalyov smuggled letters out of prison to the Belgrade CSCE Follow-up Meeting in October 1977 as the participating states planned to monitor implementation of the principles of the Final Act.[274] He also wrote a declaration to the Presidium of the Supreme Soviet on October 3:

> Tomorrow in Belgrade your representatives will begin the normal lying to conceal your crimes. Tomorrow they will again start making accusations against those whom I value. And the day after tomorrow, those who represent us here, not from the outside, but internally, will continue to round up those convicted for their thoughts and words, the new witnesses of your crimes … You haven't the strength to change your path – attempts to conceal crimes never give rise to anything except new crimes. And I will also answer your common crimes and your common lies with the normal *zek* method – with a declaration and a hunger strike.[275]

The CSCE meeting opened in Belgrade on October 4. The Soviet delegation, headed by Yury Vorontsov, was given direct instructions from Moscow to hinder the passage of any final document from Belgrade. In efforts reminiscent of the Soviet delegation instructed to impede the drafting of the Universal Declaration of Human Rights, Vorontsev clashed with the American Ambassador Arthur Goldberg.[276] Throughout the first two weeks, every delegation avoided mentioning individual cases of persecuted individuals, and country names were concealed, despite the masses of material that the 35 participating states had received from non-government organizations.[277] After a bipartisan group of senators and representatives sent a letter to President Carter entitled "Make Human Rights a Central Issue" on October 17, Goldberg was finally given permission to start mentioning individual cases. The result of the meeting was a deadlock, the sole result of which was an agreement to meet again in 1980 in Madrid.[278]

In May 1976, Kovalyov's friend, the physicist Yuri Orlov, established the Group to Assist the Implementation of the Helsinki Agreements in the USSR. As the Initiative Group dissipated, the Moscow Helsinki Group took on a new role in the history of the Soviet Human Rights Movement. Included in the text of the Final Act was a direct appeal to the citizens of signatory countries to assist their governments in implementing the principles. At the initiative of Tolya Shcharansky, Orlov decided to gather and report on human rights violations in the Soviet Union in accordance with Principle VII and Basket III and send the material to the 35 participating states in the spirit of Helsinki. He also saw the Helsinki Accords as a way to "force the authorities into a dialogue with society".[279] On May 12, he gathered his friends and international journalists at Sakharov's apartment and announced that the "Group's aim is to support observance of the humanitarian articles of the Final Act of the Conference on Security and Cooperation in Europe". For some activists, like Landa and Khodorovitch, Orlov's decision to assist the Soviet authorities was again a controversial one. Khorodovitch refused to join: "Whom are you intending to support?" she asked. "Supporting these accords means supporting the Soviet regime. No. I won't participate."[280]

The camp administration discovered drafts of Kovalyov's letters to Belgrade and confined him to the camp prison (*pkt*) for six months.[281] By 1979, he was exhausted by the administration's repeated interference with his correspondence. The camp personnel continually confiscated or censored letters sent to him from family and friends. He was promised a meeting with his family in August, 1978, but this was postponed to October and then later to April, 1979. By June of 1979, members of Kovalyov's family were finally permitted to travel to Perm to visit him, but were denied the meeting on their arrival. The reason given was that he had failed to properly address the Deputy Chief of the Camp Administration.[282]

Kovalyov attempted to organize an appeal against his conviction. Despite a request four years earlier, he still had not received his trial documents. He had met with his lawyer, Elena Reznikova, three times since January of 1976, and on March 1, 1979 Reznikova made the long journey to Perm only to have her bags searched and confiscated. She was permitted only to carry blank paper into the meeting, and left in protest against the camp administration's violation of regulations pertaining to lawyers' visits which stipulated that they were not to be searched or have their documents removed. Kovalyov was told by the camp administration that she had not wanted to meet with him.[283]

By June 12, 1979 Kovalyov decided to send an appeal to the Soviet leader, Leonid Brezhnev. He declared his readiness to begin a hunger strike on June 15 if his demands were not met. In the same letter, he renounced his Soviet citizenship, requesting that the authorities should "no longer consider me a Soviet citizen. If any legal problems or difficulties should arise as a result of this request, I propose that you deprive me of my citizenship for actions incompatible with the title of Soviet citizen in so far as I never strove to accord with this lofty title."[284]

Kovalyov began his hunger strike on June 15. His demands were:

1   Permit visitation rights to family and friends

   a   Remove the blockade on correspondence
   b   No alteration in meeting dates

2   Provide a genuine opportunity to conduct an appeal

   a   The right to hold meetings with a lawyer
   b   The return of all necessary trial documents[285]

During the course of the 27-day hunger strike, Kovalyov's son Ivan received a reply to the letter he had sent in defence of his father. A.S. Pobezhimov of the prosecutor's office responded that none of the complaints outlined in his letter could be substantiated and pointed out in the cruel logic of bureaucratic language that his father's conditions were satisfactory and in accordance with camp regulations. As to the "violation of your father's right to receive and send letters," argued Pobezhimov, "... [t]he Prosecutor's examination of the case did not reveal any violations." In response to Kovalyov's request to renounce his citizenship, he stated that the request was being passed on to the Public Prosecutor, since the law on citizenship was currently undergoing amendment.[286]

Kovalyov continued his hunger strike until he was granted a meeting with Reznikova on July 11. On August 8, he met with his wife, his son Ivan and his daughter Varvara. The victory of his hunger strike, however, was short-lived. By December, the majority of his letters were again being confiscated and, when his son enquired as to the whereabouts of his father's mail, he was told that Kovalyov was not sending any letters.[287] The planned family visit for December 4 was denied him on November 30. The reason given was that he had "intentionally failed to fulfill the [work] norms". He spent another twenty days in *Shizo* as punishment.

Meanwhile, Andrei Sakharov continued to draw attention in the international press and write appeals to Soviet and international leaders on prevailing human rights issues. By the late 1970s, Sakharov was receiving hundreds of letters of complaint that the lawyer Sofia Kallistratova helped him respond to.[288] He also continued his attempts to reach the leadership of the Soviet government, which he had begun with his 1968 essay, *Reflections on Progress, Peaceful Co-existence and Intellectual Freedom*. Sakharov sent a copy of the essay to Brezhnev and followed up with a Memorandum which outlined economic, cultural, legal and foreign-policy concerns that he hoped could serve as an agenda for a meeting with the leader. This was sent on March 5, 1971. After waiting for a reply for a year, he gave the text to foreign correspondents in June of 1972 and repeated: "we seek a dialogue with the country's leadership and a frank and public discussion of problems relating to human rights."[289]

Sakharov himself was exiled to Gorky on January 22, 1980, where he was held for six years with his wife, Elena Bonner, until his return to Moscow on December 23, 1986. Kovalyov's son Ivan was arrested in August 1981 for his work on the supplement to the *Chronicle, Biulleten' V*. Ivan's wife Tanya Osipova was also imprisoned.

Exile

In 1980, Kovalyov was transferred to Chistopol prison, from which he was released in December 1981. Having served his full term of detention, he was still committed to another three years of internal exile. He was met at the airport by his wife and daughter, who had been five years old when he was arrested in 1974. His closest friends were either in exile or had emigrated.

Figure 1.4   Sergei Kovalyov with his wife and daughter, in exile in Kolyma, 1983
Source: Memorial Archive, Moscow.

He was sent to Matrosovo village, some 450 kilometers from Magadan in Eastern Siberia. A landlocked village, the climate was harsh in the winter with temperatures dropping to 50–60 degrees celsius below zero. Just outside the village was a mine and an ore-dressing plant. At the age of fifty-one, with an advanced degree in biology, Kovalyov was employed as a fitter's apprentice with a wage of 56 rubles a month. Within a short time, he managed to find work as a laboratory assistant.[290]

Kovalyov's historical and political thought were intimately connected and grounded in a strong pragmatism. Informed largely by his knowledge of the October Revolution and a general unease with the violent methods that characterized October and its aftermath, he felt strongly that violence of itself denied all attempts at mediation or compromise. For Kovalyov, it resulted in the complete subjugation of one side to the other.[291]

He believed strongly in the law as the central foundation of any successful, civilized society. In general, he avoided abstract concepts pertaining to Russia's national traditions and characteristics. But one area in which he did insist on Russia's inherited national trait was in the area of a poor legal consciousness, or, as he described it, "Russia's cave-dwelling legal consciousness".[292] This commitment to the law grew from a belief that, for Russian citizens to enjoy complete protection from the arbitrariness of the state, the rule of law had to serve as the foundation of Soviet society. His decision to renounce his Soviet citizenship was testimony to the extent of his growing dissatisfaction with the Soviet system. There was a sense that he could no longer partake in the great leap of faith required to imagine that the Soviet Union could reform itself.

But a feeling of guilt and shame for the actions of his government was something Kovalyov carried with him over the years and which developed into an unusual sense of responsibility for Russia's future. The end to which he was prepared to take this feeling of shared responsibility was already clear. He would express his readiness to cooperate, but it was always conditional. And the boundary which he was prepared to cross for his ideals shifted constantly over the years. Circumstances would often compel him to redefine his personal convictions.

Notes

1 V. Chalidze, *The Soviet Human Rights Movement: A Memoir*, New York: American Jewish Committee, 1984, p. 25. See also V. Chalidze, *To Defend these Rights*, New York: Random House, 1974.

2 M. Shatz, *Soviet Dissent in Historical Perspective*, Cambridge: Cambridge University Press, 1980, p. 11.

3 L. Bogoraz, "Printsipi i metodi pravozashchitnoi raboty", *Moskovskaya Khel'sinskaya Gruppa, Sbornik – 1992*, p. 71.

4 There are many terms used to characterize the members of the Dissident Movement: dissidents (*dissidenti*), human rights activists (*pravozashchitniki*), otherwise-thinkers (*inakomislyashie*), non-conformists (*nonkonformisti*) or the democratic

movement (*demdvizhenie*). For the purpose of this book I am using the term human rights activists (*pravozashchitniki*) and the term Soviet Human Rights Movement to depict the small group based fundamentally in and around Moscow in the period from 1968. See L. Bogoraz and A. Daniel, 'V poiskakh nesyshchestuyshchei nayki (Dissidentstvo kak istoricheskaya problema)', *Sovremennaya Rossiya: Vsglyad Iznutri*, Moskva-Bremen: Forschungsstelle Osteuropa an der Universitat Bremen, 1992, pp. 132, 135. See also *Iztoriya, filosofiya, printsipy i metody pravozashchitnoi deyatel'nosti*, Moskva: Rossiiskaya Amerikanskaya proektnaya gruppa po pravam cheloveka, 1995.

5 Opinions differ on when the phenomenon of '*dissidentstvo*' first appeared. See L. Bogoraz and A. Daniel, *op.cit.*, p. 127.

6 Bogoraz, *op.cit.*, p. 73.

7 It was the dissident Boris Shagrin who wrote: "like all international human rights movements, Soviet *dissidentstvo* was reared on anti-fascism. Moreover it emerged in the environment of the collapse of the communist illusion." See 'Sila Dissidentov', *Sintaksis 3*, Vol. 27 (1979): 39.

8 V. Chalidze, *Yavlyaetsya li Dvizhenie Inakomyslyashchikh Faktorom Politicheskogo Razvitiya Sovetskogo Soiuza?*, New York: Khronika Press, 1976, p. 3.

9 S. Kovalyov, 'Pochemy v SSSR net Pravozashchitnoe Dvizhenie', *Vek XX i Mir*, No. 6, (1991): 10.

10 Chalidze, *op.cit.*, p. 7.

11 Chalidze, *op.cit.*, p. 11.

12 For the founding document of the Human Rights Committee, see *The Chronicle of Current Events*, No. 17, December 1970: London: Amnesty International Publications, 1971, pp. 45–7.

13 A. Solzhenitsyn, *The Oak and the Calf*, London: Collins and Harvill Press, 1980, p. 372.

14 A. Daniel, Personal Interview with E. Gilligan, Moscow, June 1998. Henceforth, Daniel (1998).

15 A. Sakharov, *Memoirs*, New York: Knopf, 1990, p. 282. Henceforth, *Memoirs*.

16 Y. Orlov, *Dangerous Thoughts: Memoirs of a Russian Life*, New York: William Morrow and Company, 1991, p. 180. Roy Medvedev's secret *samizdat* journal, *Political Diary*, distributed among party officials was a concealed effort to summon support for reform from within the communist elite and a loyal Marxist framework.

17 Daniel (1998).

18 Bogoraz, *op.cit.*, p. 74.

19 R. Medvedev, "'A Dialogue' dissidentov s vlastynami", *Dvadtsatyi Vek*, London: T.C.D Publications, 1976, p. 8.

20 S. Kovalyov, 'Dissidenti o dissidentstve', *Znamya*, No. 9 (1997): 178–81.

21 G. Liber, *Soviet Nationality Policy, Urban Growth and Identity Change in the Ukrainian SSR 1923–1934*, Cambridge: Cambridge University Press, 1992, pp. 145, 171.

22 S. Kovalyov, *Vospominaniia*, Moscow: unpublished, 1996, p. 3. Henceforth, *Vosp.* The one source on Kovalyov's childhood and youth is his *Memoirs*. Kovalyov began writing them in 1995 with Alexander Daniel, head of Memorial's History of the Dissident Movement project. The manuscript worked on for the purposes of this book contained approximately 140 pages of text relating to Kovalyov's public career. Taped interviews are the main source for these *Memoirs* and are presently held by Memorial's Human Rights Centre in Moscow. A text copy is currently held by Emma Gilligan, Personal Collection in Melbourne, Australia.

23 Kovalyov, *Vosp.*, p. 3.

24 Kovalyov, *Vosp.*, pp. 1–2.

25 S. Kovalyov, 'Neizvestnii Kovalyov', *Evropeets*, No. 6, August 1995, p. 7. Henceforth, *Evropeets*.

26 Kovalyov, *Vosp.*, p. 4.
27 Kovalyov, *Vosp.*, pp. 7–8.
28 Kovalyov, *Vosp.*, p. 8.
29 Kovalyov, *Vosp.*, pp. 5, 6.
30 Kovalyov, *Vosp.*, p. 6.
31 Kovalyov, *Vosp.*, p. 9.
32 J. Stone, 'Letter to The Honorable Alan Cranston, United States Senate from Jeremy Stone, Director, Federation of American Scientists', November 28, 1975, New York: Kline Archive. See also 'Bibliography of Dr Sergei Kovalev', February 12, 1975, New York: Kline Archive.
33 Kovalyov, *Vosp.*, p. 15.
34 Kovalyov, *Vosp.*, p. 16.
35 Z. Medvedev, *The Rise & Fall of T.D. Lysenko*, New York: Columbia University Press, 1969, pp. 20, 22.
36 Medvedev, *op.cit.*, p. 113.
37 Medvedev, *op.cit.*, p. 103.
38 See D. Joravsky, *The Lysenko Affair*, Cambridge, Mass.: Harvard University Press, 1970.
39 Joravsky, *op.cit.*, pp. 110, 158.
40 Medvedev, *op.cit.*, pp. 125, 131.
41 Kovalyov, *Vosp.*, pp. 20–1.
42 "Statement by Dr. Y. Golfand, Moscow, March 21, 1975", *Khronika Press: Information Bulletin*, No. 54, December 30 (1974), p. 3. See also "Kovalev's Contributions to Physiology", *Clearinghouse Report*, December (1981), p. 9.
43 S. Kovalyov, "Sergei Kovalyov's White Book", *New Times*, No. 14, 1990, p. 31. Henceforth, *New Times*.
44 Kovalyov, *Vosp.*, p. 18.
45 See Medvedev, *op.cit.*, for an appraisal of Lysenko's articles in *Pravda*.
46 Kovalyov, *Vosp.*, p. 18.
47 Kovalyov, *New Times*, p. 31.
48 Kovalyov, *New Times*, p. 32.
49 Kovalyov, *Vosp.*, p. 19. His first wife, Elena Viktorovna Tokareva, was the mother of his son, Ivan Kovalyov, who later edited the human rights journal *Biulleten' V.*
50 Kovalyov, *New Times*, p. 32.
51 Sakharov, *Memoirs*, pp. 233–7.
52 Kovalyov, *Vosp.*, p. 22.
53 Kovalyov, *Vosp.*, p. 22.
54 Kovalyov, *Vosp.*, pp. 22–3.
55 Kovalyov, *Vosp.*, p. 23.
56 N. Semonov, "Nekotorye voprosy o sotsiologii nauki", *Nauka i Zhizn*, No. 2 (1965): 16–22.
57 Kovalyov, *Vosp.*, p. 23.
58 Kovalyov, *Evropeets*, p. 7.
59 L. Alekseeva, *Soviet Dissent: Contemporary Movements for National, Religious and Human Rights*, Connecticut: Wesleyan University Press: 1985, p. 13.
60 Alekseeva, *op.cit.*, p. 11.
61 See R. Lisker, "Alexander Yesenin-Volpin", *Ferment*, Vol. 8, No. 6 (1994): 3, 7.
62 A. Daniel', V. Lukashevskii and V. Finn, "Delo Sinyavskogo-Danielya", in *A.S. Esenin-Vol'pin*, Moskva: Rossiiskii gosudarstvennyi gumanitarnyi universitet, 1999, p. 326. See also I. Kirk (ed.), *Profiles in Russian Resistance*, New York: Quadrangle, 1975, p. 119.
63 Arkhiv Samizdat, No. 5942, April, 1987: 2. Unfortunately, we know very little about Kovalyov's personal life, which he does not mention in his *Memoirs* or reflective essays.

64 Kovalyov, *Evropeets*, p. 7.
65 P. Reddaway, *Uncensored Russia: The Human Rights Movement in the Soviet Union*, London: Cape, 1972, p. 61. P. Litvinov, "O dvizhenii za prava cheloveka v SSSR", in *Samosoznanie: Sbornik Statei*, New York: Khronika, 1979, p. 79. Ludmilla Alekseeva marks the beginning of the Soviet Human Rights Movement as the day of the protest demonstration against the trial, December 5, 1965. See *Soviet Dissent: Contemporary Movements for National, Religious and Human Rights*, Connecticut: Wesleyan University Press, 1985, p. 269.
66 V. Bukovsky, *To Build a Castle: My Life as a Dissenter*, New York: Viking Press, p. 353.
67 Kovalyov, *Vosp.*, p. 26.
68 Cited in H. Gelman, *The Brezhnev Politburo and the Decline of Détente*, Ithaca: Cornell University Press, 1984, p. 89.
69 G. Arbatov, *The System: An Insider's Life in Soviet Politics*, New York: Times Books, 1992, p. 149.
70 Cited in J. Dornberg, *Brezhnev: The Masks of Power*, London: Andre Deutsch, 1974, p. 196.
71 Arbatov, *op.cit.*, p. 148.
72 Kovalyov, *Vosp.*, p. 27.
73 Alekseeva, *op.cit.*, p. 275.
74 Kovalyov, *Vosp.*, p. 26.
75 Alekseeva, *op.cit.*, p. 276.
76 See A. Daniel', V. Lukashevskii and V. Finn, *A.S Esenin-Vol'pin*, Moskva: Rossiiskii gosudarstvennyi gumanitarnyi universitet, 1999, p. 326.
77 For Esenin-Volpin, the movement after 1965 was undermined by an emotionalism that he believed compromised his approach. See A. Daniel', V. Lukashevskii and V. Finn, *op.cit.*, pp. 372–9, 380–91, 356–71.
78 See Sakharov, *Memoirs*, p. 314.
79 A total of fifteen volumes of *Problems of Society* were distributed in *samizdat* from 1969.
80 Chalidze, *op.cit.*, p. 3.
81 V. Chalidze, *To Defend These Rights*, New York: Random House, 1974, p. 59. Henceforth, *Defend*.
82 Chalidze, *op.cit.*, p. 4.
83 Daniel (1998).
84 Chalidze, *Defend*, p. 35.
85 Chalidze, *Defend*, p. 36.
86 S. Kovalyov, "Dissidenti o dissidentstve", *Znamya*, No. 9 (1997): 178–81.
87 S. Kovalyov, cited by R. Orlova and L. Kopelev, *My Zhili v Moskve, 1956–1980*, Moskva: Kniga, 1990, p. 249.
88 A. Solzhenitsyn, cited in J. Edward, *Solzhenitsyn: The Moral Vision*, Michigan: William Berdmans Publishing Company, 1980, p. 195.
89 Solzhenitsyn, *op.cit.*, p. 182.
90 "Sergei Kovalyov: Ya "agent" zapadnoi kontsepsii prav cheloveka", *Demoktraticheskii Vybor*, No. 46 (122), November 19–25, 1998, pp. 1–2.
91 Kovalyov, *Vosp.*, pp. 27–8.
92 Daniel (1998).
93 Kovalyov, *Vosp.*, p. 32.
94 M. Meerson-Aksenov and B. Shragin (eds), *The Political, Social and Religious Thought of Russian Samizdat – An Anthology*, Massachusetts: Nordland Company Press, 1977, p. 602. See "Sila Dissidentov", in *Sintaksis*, No. 3, Paris: Syntaxis, 1979: 18–40. See also *Vosp.*, p. 27.
95 P. Grigorenko, *Memoirs*, New York and London: W.W Norton & Company, 1982, p. 336.

96 Kovalyov, *Vosp.*, p. 28.
97 By the late 1960s, Kovalyov had discovered the famous turn-of-the-century anthology *Vekhi (Landmarks)*. Influenced by Bogdan Kistiakovsky's article, 'In Defence of Law: The Intelligentsia and Legal Consciousness', he sought moral support in his liberal predecessors. A well-known lawyer, Kistiakovsky appealed to the radical intelligentsia in the wake of the failed 1905 revolution to revise its approach to reform, and appealed for a liberal politics of compromise, gradualism and the rule of law. He advised the intelligentsia to suppress its passion for moral absolutes and "plunge deeply into its own inner world in order to bring fresh air and health into it. In the course of their inward labour, a genuine legal consciousness must finally awaken in the Russian intelligentsia." *Vekhi (Landmarks)*, Marian Schwartz (trans.), Boris Shragin and Albert Todd (eds), New York: Karz Howard, 1977, p. 95.
98 Sakharov, *Memoirs*, p. 311.
99 S. Kovalyov, "Andrei Sakharov: Otvetstvennost pered razumom", *Izvestiya*, No. 91, May 21, 1998, p. 5.
100 Kovalyov, *ibid.*, p. 5.
101 Kovalyov, *Vosp.*, p. 25. See *New Times*, p. 32.
102 Kovalyov, *New Times*, p. 32.
103 Kovalyov, *New Times*, p. 32.
104 Kovalyov, *Vosp.*, p. 24.
105 O. Orlov, "Missiya Kovalyova na fronte", *Memorial Aspekt*, No. 13, June 1995, p. 2.
106 I. Yakhimovich, "The Duty of a Communist", (October 30, 1964), *In Quest of Justice: Protest & Dissent in the Soviet Union Today*, Abraham Brumberg (ed.), New York: Praeger, 1970, p. 130.
107 Grigorenko, *op.cit.*, p. 385.
108 Kovalyov, *Vosp.*, p. 29.
109 Grigorenko, *op.cit.*, p. 386.
110 A. Yakobson, *Pochva i Sud'ba*, Vilnius–Moscow: Vest, 1992, p. 254. See also A. Lavut, Personal Interview with E. Gilligan, Moscow, June, 1998.
111 Daniel (1998).
112 Kovalyov, *Vosp.*, p. 29.
113 Grigorenko, *op.cit.*, p. 386. See also Nadezhda and Maya Ulanovskaya's Memoirs, *Iztoriya Odnoi Sem'i*, Moscow: Vest VIMO, 1994, pp. 410–27 for an account of these meetings. See also Kovalyov, *Vosp.*, pp. 28–30. Grigorenko later apologized to Maya Ulanovskaya in a letter to her dated August 4, 1970. See M. and N. Ulanovskaya, *op.cit.*, p. 412.
114 Kovalyov, *Vosp.*, p. 29.
115 Kovalyov, *Vosp.*, p. 29.
116 Kovalyov, *Vosp.*, p. 30.
117 Kovalyov, *Vosp.*, p. 30. See also Daniel (1998).
118 Daniel (1998).
119 In 1970, Boris Shragin dedicated his book *Challenge of the Spirit* to Kovalyov, a philosophical treatise on the historical origins of the Soviet Human Rights Movement. Kovalyov's arguments often closely parallel Shragin's. B. Shragin, *Challenge of the Spirit*, New York: Knopf, 1978, p. 183.
120 Yakobson, *op.cit.*, p. 255. M. and N. Ulanovskaya, *op.cit.*, p. 414. Despite deep caution, however, Kovalyov decided to support Grigorenko. See Daniel (1998).
121 Kovalyov, *Vosp.*, p. 49. See also *Put'*, February 25, 1990, p. 6. Although Kovalyov was disappointed in the decision, he accepted that the letter was well-written.
122 Alekseeva, *op.cit.*, p. 291. The members were A. Levitin-Krasnov, L. Plyusch, Y. Maltsev, N. Gorbanevskaya, A.Yakobson, T. Khodorovich, V. Borisov, G. Altunian, M. Dkhemilev, S. Kovalyov, V. Krasin, A. Lavut, G. Podyapolsky, P. Yakir, A. Yakobson and T. Velikanova.

123 See "Soviet Dissidents Petition U.N. by Giving Text to West's Press", *The New York Times*, May 23, 1969, pp. 1, 6. See also "General's son leads appeal to UN by Soviet Group", *The Times*, May 23, 1969, p. 6.

124 Alekseeva, *op.cit.*, p. 291.

125 Alekseeva, *op.cit.*, p. 291.

126 Cited in P. Reddaway, *Uncensored Russia: The Human Rights Movement in the Soviet Union*, London: Jonathan Cape, 1972, p. 107.

127 Alekseeva, *op.cit.*, p. 291.

128 Reddaway, *op.cit.*, p. 153.

129 Kovalyov, *Evropeets*, p. 7.

130 Alekseeva, *op.cit.*, p. 45.

131 Cited in G. Robertson, *Crimes Against Humanity: The Struggle for Global Justice*, London: Penguin, 1999, p. 41.

132 D. Thomas, *The Helsinki Effect: International Norms, Human Rights and the Demise of Communism*, Princeton University Press: Princeton and Oxford, 2001, p. 35.

133 Thomas, *ibid.*, p. 49.

134 Thomas, *ibid.*, p. 49.

135 Yakobson, *op.cit.*, p. 256. See also M. and N. Ulanovskaya, *op.cit.*, p. 415. Lavut (1998).

136 A. Levitin-Krasnov, *Demokraticheskoe Dvizhenie, Vospominaniia Chast IV*, Frankfurt/Main: Possev-Verlag, 1981, p. 405.

137 Lavut (1998).

138 M. Hopkins, *Russia's Underground Press*, New York: Praeger, 1983. p. 34.

139 Levitin-Krasnov, *op.cit.*, pp. 396–7.

140 Levitin-Krasnov, *op.cit.*, p. 401.

141 This version of Velikanova's feelings is by Levitin-Krasnov.

142 Kovalyov, *Vosp.*, p. 36. M. and N. Ulanovskaya, *op.cit.*, pp. 412–13.

143 L. Plyushch, *History's Carnival: a dissident autobiography*, New York: Harcourt Brace Jovanovich, 1979, p. 233.

144 S. Kovalyov, "Pochemy v SSSR net Pravozashchitnoe Dvizhenie", *Vek XX i Mir*, No. 6, (1991): 10. Henceforth, *Vek XX*.

145 M. Pavlova-Silvanskaya, "Kadril' o Sergei Kovalyove", *Novoe Vremya*, August, No. 32, 1995, p. 13.

146 See V. Bukovsky, *To Build a Castle: My Life as a Dissenter*, New York: Viking Press.

147 Bukovsky, *ibid.*, p. 143.

148 P. Yakir, *A Childhood in Prison*, New York: Coward, McCann & Geohagen, Inc., 1973, pp. 11, 31.

149 V. Novodvorskaya, *Po tu storonu otchayaniya*, Moscow: Novosti, 1993, p. 33.

150 Novodvorskaya, *ibid.*, p. 9.

151 Kovalyov, *Vek XX*, p. 10.

152 Kovalyov, *Vek XX*, p. 10. See also, *Vosp.*, pp. 61–3.

153 *The Chronicle of Current Events*, No. 39 (1973): 85. See also *Posev*, No.11, 1970: 8–9.

154 *The Chronicle of Current Events*, No. 16 (1970): 24.

155 Alekseeva, *op.cit.*, p. 292.

156 Kovalyov, *New Times*, p. 33.

157 A. Lavut, Personal Interview with E. Gilligan, Moscow, September, 1997. Henceforth, Lavut (1997).

158 Kovalyov, *Vosp.*, p. 23.

159 Kovalyov, *Vosp.*, p. 24.

160 See also Lavut (1998) for an account of Kovalyov and Lavut's dismissal.

161 "Sergei Kovalyov: Biologist Denied Due Process and Medical Care", *Science: American Association for the Advancement of Science*, Vol. 194, No. 4265, November 5, 1976. See also *Ontogenez* 2, (1971): 512, and *Ontogonez* 3, (1972): 208–11.

162 Sakharov, *Memoirs*, pp. 418–19.

163 Kovlayov, *Vosp.*, p. 41.

164 Kovalyov, *Vosp.*, p. 42.

165 Kovalyov, *Vosp.*, p. 41.

166 Kovalyov, *Vosp.*, p. 49.

167 Kovalyov, *Vosp.*, pp. 41, 50. See also T.Velikanova, Personal Interview with E. Gilligan, Moscow, October 1998. Henceforth, Velikanova (1998).

168 See *The Chronicle of Current Events*, Nos. 29, 30 (1973).

169 V. Belotserkovsky, "Sakharov's Civilisation", *New Times*, May 2003, p. 7.

170 See *The Chronicle of Current Events*, No. 29 (1973): 61. See also M. Landa, "Sergei Kovalyov: fakty biografii", *Pravozashchitnik 2*, April–June 1997: 79–85.

171 Kovalyov, *Vosp.*, p. 49.

172 Kovalyov, *Vosp.*, p. 49.

173 *The Chronicle of Current Events*, No. 30 (1973): 85–6.

174 *Ibid.*

175 Kovalyov, *Vosp.*, p. 50.

176 Belogorodskaya was in the camps for one year. See M. and N. Ulanovskaya, *op.cit.*, p. 420.

177 S. Kovalyov, *The Chronicle of Current Events*, No. 28 (1973): 8.

178 Cited in Andrei Sakharov's *Alarm and Hope*, New York: Knopf, 1978, pp. 9–20. See also *Vosp.*, p. 50. "Clandestine Journal Circulates in Russia Again", *The Times*, May 13, 1974, p. 5. "Return of the Dissidents", *The Times*, May 13, 1974, p. 17.

179 Kovalyov, *Vosp.*, pp. 43–4.

180 *The Chronicle of Current Events*, No. 28 (1973): 28.

181 Kovalyov, *Vosp.*, p. 43.

182 See *Evropeets*, p. 7. See also Mark Hopkins, *Russia's Underground Press: The Chronicle of Current Press*, New York: Praeger, 1983, p. 97. Hopkin attests to the "unprecedented maturity" of the editorial group from Issue 28. See also Lavut (1998).

183 Kovalyov, *Evropeets*, p. 7. See also "Obshaya Vina, Obshaya Otvetstvennost", *Moskovskie Novosti*, No. 5, January 31, 1993, p. 3.

184 S. Kovalyov, "Ulitsa Prav Cheloveka", in *Sergei Kovalyov: Pragmatika Politcheskogo Idealizma*, Moskva: Institut Prav Cheloveka, 1999, p. 17.

185 S. Kovalyov, "Dovorie mezhdu lichnost'iu i gosudarstvom", in *Sergei Kovalyov: Pragmatika Politcheskogo Idealizma*, Moskva: Institut Prav Cheloveka, 1999, p. 57.

186 S. Kovalyov, *Rossiiskaya Gazeta*, December 9, 1993, p. 3.

187 S. Kovalyov, "Pis'mo predsedateliu KGB Y.B. Andropovu v svyazi s iz'yatiem y ego znakomogo t. 2 knigi *Arkhipelag GULag*", October 17, 1978, Moskva: Memorial Archive AC No. 1910, p. 1. See also Kovalyov, *New Times*, p. 33.

188 Kovalyov, *op.cit.*, p. 1.

189 Sakharov, *Memoirs*, p. 419.

190 M. Sulskis, "Letter to the Honorable Gerald Ford: April 22, 1976", New York: Kline Archive, p. 1.

191 Sulskis, *ibid.*, p. 2. See also "Widow's Plea to Flee", *New York Times*, May 10, 1974, p. 1. "Soviet bars U.S. Journey for N.Y.- born Lithuanian", *The Star Ledger*, May, 10, 1974, p. 1.

192 Sulskis, *ibid.*, p. 2.

193 Y. Orlov, *Dangerous Thoughts: Memoirs of a Russian Life*, New York: William Morrow & Company, 1991, p. 176.
194 Kovalyov, *Vosp.*, pp. 50–1.
195 Sakharov, *Memoirs*, p. 417. See also *The New York Times*, October 22, 1974, p. 7.
196 Kovalyov, *New Times*, p. 33.
197 Kovalyov, *Evropeets*, p. 7.
198 *The Chronicle of Current Events*, No. 34 (1978): 2.
199 Kovalyov, *Evropeets*, p. 7.
200 Kovalyov, *Evropeets*, p. 7.
201 Kovalyov, *Vosp.*, p. 56.
202 S. Kovalyov, "Sergei Kovalyov's White Book Part II", *New Times*, No. 15, 1990, p. 35. Henceforth, *New Times II*.
203 Sakharov, *Memoirs*, p. 419.
204 On September 16, 1966, shortly after the Sinyavsky/Daniel trial, the RSFSR Presidium of the Supreme Soviet introduced article 190–1. Not differing radically from Article 70, it was devised specifically to cover those cases awkward to charge under Article 70. The distinct difference was that Article 190–1 included "direct intent to subvert or weaken the Soviet regime". Moreover, article 190–1 was punishable by up to three years. Article 70, under which many human rights activists were charged, was punishable for up to seven years of incaceration and five years of internal exile.
205 "Razgovor s A. Tverdoklebovim", December 28, 1974, Moscow: Memorial Archive AC No. 1911.
206 Interview with M. Ignotas, "Klevetnik Nakazan", *Kommunist*, No. 4 (622) April, (1976): 79–80.
207 *The Chronicle of Current Events*, No. 34 (1978): 27.
208 *The Chronicle of Current Events*, No. 34 (1978): 4.
209 "Letter to His Excellency Anatoli F. Dobrynin from the Committee of the Federation of American Scientists in defense of Sergei Kovalyov", November 28, 1975, New York: Kline Archive.
210 "Russian Joins Faculty: Another Invited", *Cornell Reports*, Vol. 11, No. 1, September, 1976, p. 2.
211 "Resolution 754, 94th Congress, 20th Session House of Representatives, September 17, 1976", New York: Kline Archive.
212 *The Chronicle of Current Events*, No. 38 (1978): 78–9. See also "Letter by Professor L. Bosch of the Biochemistry Department of the State University of Leiden to L. Brezhnev, April 21, 1977", Moscow: Memorial Archive.
213 *Khronika Press: Information Bulletin*, No.57, New York: Khronika Press, 1976, p. 2.
214 Kovalyov, *Vosp.*, p. 52.
215 *Delo Kovalyova*, New York: Khronika Press, p. 27.
216 Kovalyov, *Vosp.*, p. 52.
217 S. Kovalyov, "Tak zhit v takom gosudarstve", *Karta*, 10, New York: Kline Archive, undated, p. 9.
218 *The Chronicle of Current Events*, No. 37 (1978): 19.
219 Kovalyov, *Vosp.*, p. 53.
220 Kovalyov, *Vosp.*, p. 55.
221 S. Kallistratova, *Zapiska Advokata*, Vermont: Khronika Press, 1984, p. 342.
222 A. Rozhansky, "Letter concerning the case of Sergei Adamovich Kovalyov: Jerusalem, June 5, 1976", Translated, Amnesty International, New York: Kline Archive, p. 1.
223 *The Chronicle of Current Events*, No. 38 (1978): 79.
224 *Delo Kovalyova*, New York: Khronika, 1976, p. 17.
225 Rozhansky, *op.cit.*, p. 1.
226 Kovalyov, *New Times II*, p. 36.

227 *The Chronicle of Current Events*, No. 37 (1978): 18.
228 Kovalyov, *New Times II*, p. 34.
229 *The Chronicle of Current Events*, No. 37 (1978): 19.
230 *The Chronicle of Current Events*, No. 38 (1978): 79.
231 *The Chronicle of Current Events*, No. 37 (1978): 57–8.
232 *The Chronicle of Current Events*, No. 37 (1978): 57–58.
233 *The Chronicle of Current Events*, No. 39 (1978): 203.
234 Conference for Security and Co-operation in Europe 1975 Summit, Helsinki, August 1, 1975, Final Act. Available online at : http://www.osce.org/docs/english/1990–1999/summits/helfa75e.htm (accessed March 2003).
235 See Ambassador Yuri Kashlev First Vice-Rector, Diplomatic Academy, Ministry of Foreign Affairs, Moscow. "Soviet Union/Russia in the Helsinki Process", presented to the GCSP/HEI Workshop on the 30th Anniversary of the Launching of the CSCE Process. GCSP, November 25, 2002. Available online at http://www.gcsp.ch/e/news/Kashlev.htm (accessed June 2003).
236 L. Brezhnev, cited in *The New York Times*, December 10, 1975, pp. 1, 20. Brezhnev also presented a report to the 25th Congress of the CPSU on February 24, 1976 condemning the West for distorting "the very substance of the Final Act ..." See D. Thomas, *The Helsinki Effect: International Norms, Human Rights and the Demise of Communism*, Princeton: Princeton University Press, 2001, p. 131.
237 Sakharov, *Memoirs*, pp. 434–7.
238 A. Sakharov, "Soviet Opens Trial of Kovalev, Dissident Biologist", *The New York Times*, December 10, 1975, p. 14.
239 A. Sakharov, "Court Again Bars Sakharov", *The New York Times*, December 12, 1975, p. 14. See also "Zayavlenie v Verkhonnyi sud Litovskoi SSR (s koniei Kovalyovu) s pros'boi vyzvat' v kachestve svidetelya po delu S.A Kovalyova: December 9, 1975", Moscow: The Andrei Sakharov Archives.
240 *Delo Kovalyova*, New York: Khronika, 1976, pp. 27–78.
241 *Ibid.*, p. 27.
242 P. Hofmann, "Émigré says Soviet Abused evidence", *The New York Times*, April 27, 1976, p. 10. Krasin stated that the KGB had made him talk with threats of execution.
243 *Delo Kovalyova*, New York: Khronika, 1976, p. 68.
244 "The Trial of Sergei Kovalyov", Amnesty International, British section, Co-ordinating Group for Prisoners in the USSR, New York, Kline Archive, p. 1. See also *Information Bulletin No. 54*, New York: Khronika Press, 1974.
245 Sakharov, *Memoirs*, p. 436.
246 *The Chronicle of Current Events*, No. 38 (1978) 85.
247 *The Chronicle of Current Events*, No. 38 (1978) 85.
248 Cited in *Science: American Association for the Advancement of Science*, Vol. 194, No. 4265, November 5, (1976): 585–7.
249 Kovalyov, *New Times*, p. 36. See also "Soviet Sentences Dissident to 7 Years in Labor Camp", *The New York Times*, December 13, 1975, p. 7.
250 For the text of this letter, see "Otkrytka S. A Kovalovu v sledstvennyi izolyator g. Vil'niusa s priglazheniem na tseremoniu vrucheniya Nobelevskoi premii mira", November 29, 1975, Moscow: The Andrei Sakharov Archives. See also *The New York Times*, December 11, 1975, p. 10. "Sakharov in Vigil at Friend's Trial", *The New York Times*, December 11, 1975, p. 11. "Excerpts from the Nobel Lecture by Andrei Sakharov on Human Rights Issues", *The New York Times*, December 13, 1975, p. 6.
251 "Soviet Sentences Dissidents to 7 years in Labor Camp", *The New York Times*, December 13, 1975, p. 7.

252 A. Sakharov, "Razgovor po telefonu s Moskvoi", *Rysskaya Mysl'*, January 1, 1975, p. 5.
253 *The Chronicle of Current Events*, No. 38 (1978): 91.
254 A. Sukharev, "Human Rights in the Soviet Union – Putting the Record Straight", *New Times*, No. 1, 1976, pp. 18–22.
255 Sukharev, *ibid.*, p. 21.
256 Sukharev, *ibid.*, p. 21.
257 "Letter to His Excellency Anatoli F. Dobrynin from the Committee of the Federation of American Scientists in defense of Sergei Kovalyov, April 26, 1976", Moskva: Memorial, Arkhiv Samizdat.
258 M. Ignotas, "Klevetnik Nakazan", *Kommunist*, No. 4 (622) April (1976): 79–81.
259 *The Chronicle of Current Events*, No. 39 (1978): 211.
260 I. Melchuk, "Sakharov: World Symbol of Redemption", *The New York Times*, January 25, 1976, p. 1.
261 N. Chomsky, "Ailing in Soviet Prisons", *The New York Times*, November 30, 1976, p. 38.
262 Alekseeva, *op.cit.*, p. 332.
263 *The Chronicle of Current Events*, No. 39 (1978): 212.
264 Alekseeva, *op.cit.*, pp. 332–3.
265 Kovalyov, *Vosp.*, p. 56.
266 Kovalyov, *Evropeets*, p. 8.
267 S. Kovalyov, "Sergei Kovalyov za normalnii put razvitiya blagopoluchnoi strani – kogda ona stanet takoi!", *Put'*, February 25, 1990, pp. 2–3.
268 See *The Chronicle of Current Events*, Nos. 51 (1978), 53 (1978), 55 (1979). See also *Prava Cheloveka: Vesti Iz SSSR*, No. 2 (2–10) (1978): 6; No. 12 (12–22) (1979): 137; No. 18 (18–38) (1980): 368; No. 9 (9–25) (1981): 478.
269 Kovalyov, *Vosp.*, p. 57.
270 *Shizo* is the acronym for a punishment cell located inside an internal prison within the camp.
271 I. Kovalyov, *Istoriya odnoi golodovki: Sergei Kovalyov*, Moscow: Memorial Archive, December, 1979. Henceforth, *Iztoriya*.
272 *Iztoriya*, p. 4.
273 *Iztoriya*, p. 3.
274 S. Kovalyov, "Sergei Kovalyov's White Book Part III", *New Times*, No. 16. 1990: 33. Henceforth, *New Times III*.
275 S. Kovalyov, cited in *Iztoriya*, p. 4.
276 Y. Kashlev, *op.cit.*
277 Thomas, *op.cit.*, p. 145.
278 Thomas, *op.cit.*, p. 148.
279 Orlov, cited in Alekseeva, pp. 336, 337.
280 Orlov, *op.cit.*, p. 189.
281 *New Times III*, p. 32. *Pkt (pomeshchenie kamernogo tipa)* was for longer-term punishment up to a maximum period of six months.
282 I. Kovalyov, *Iztoriya*, pp. 2, 3. See also "Obrashchenie v Mezhdunarodnuiu Amnistiiu, ko vsem litsam i organizatsiyam, ozabochennym sud'boi Sergeya Kovalyova, v svyazi s ocherednym lisheniem ego svidaniya s rodstvennikami", Moscow: The Andrei Sakharov Archive.
283 Kovalyov, *Iztoriya*, p. 3.
284 Kovalyov, *Iztoriya*, p. 4. See also S. Kovalyov, cited in *The Chronicle of Current Events*, No. 53 (1978): 89–90.
285 Kovalyov, *Iztoriya*, p. 6.
286 S. Kovalyov, cited in *Iztoriya*, p. 7.
287 Kovalyov, *Iztoriya*, p. 7.
288 Sakharov, *Memoirs*, p. 536.

289 Sakharov, *Memoirs*, p. 641.
290 Kovalyov, *New Times III*, p. 33.
291 S. Kovalyov, "Without Barricades: Interview with Larisa Bogoraz and Sergei Kovalyov", *Peace & the Twentieth Century*, No. 9, 1988: 47.
292 S. Kovalyov, "Pochemu v SSSR net pravozashchitnogo dvizheniya", *Vek XX i Mir*, No. 6, 1991: 9–11.

2   The dissident *nomenklatura*

> ... the first place is occupied by responsibility. Like independence, this is a
> moral perception. Responsibility for the consequences of our actions.
>
> Sergei Kovalyov[1]

The Soviet Human Rights Movement was unprepared for the rise of
Mikhail Gorbachev. By 1984, the authorities' campaign to suppress the
movement was largely successful. Kovalyov's friends, Andrei Sakharov,
Aleksander Lavut and Tatyana Velikanova, were still in exile, isolated in
towns across the Soviet Union. His son, Ivan and his daughter in law, Tanya
Osipova, were still imprisoned. When Gorbachev became General Secretary
on March 11, 1985, this legacy of political repression cast a long historical
shadow over his future policies of *perestroika* and *glasnost*.

By July of 1986, Gorbachev had publicly outlined his plans for the Soviet
Union. While the roots of *perestroika* may well be explained by the economic
crisis of the 1980s, Gorbachev did not isolate the deteriorating economic situation from the wider social crisis.[2] "Today's *perestroika*," he declared to party
members in Khabarovsk, "comprises not only economic but all other aspects
of the life of society, social relationships, the political system, the
spiritual–ideological sphere, the style and method of work of all the cadres."
By the time of his January 1987 Plenum speech to the Central Committee of
the CPSU, he insisted that "democratization [was] not simply a slogan but the
essence of *perestroika*."[3] This restructuring was to be undertaken from within,
under the guidance of the ruling monopoly of the Communist Party.

Kovalyov was released from Magadan in the winter of 1984. Denied official permission to live in the capital, he moved to Kalinin, 100 kilometers
northwest of Moscow, to work as a night watchman in the town park.[4] He
admitted that he found it difficult to adapt to the changing atmosphere and
shared the general mistrust prevalent in dissident circles regarding
Gorbachev's sincerity.[5] This feeling was made worse by the new leader's
public statements in February 1986 when he told a French journalist for
L'Humanite: "Now, about political prisoners, we don't have any. Likewise,
our citizens are not prosecuted for their beliefs. We don't try people for their
opinions."[6]

In the early period of Gorbachev's rule, a strong distrust for the Human Rights Movement prevailed. Motivated by years of prejudice and a long-held suspicion that the movement was indeed responsible for "creating an anti-Soviet underground in the USSR"[7] financed by Western governments, this distrust was hard to dispel. Kovalyov continued to suffer prejudice and harassment soon after his release from exile. The local administration in Kalinin fabricated a case to dismiss him from his job for "violating work discipline and drinking alcohol",[8] forcing him to find work as a security guard at the local drama theatre on 72 rubles and fifty kopecks a month. Shortly after this, he secured a position as a laboratory assistant, whereupon he frequently returned to his Moscow apartment on 26 Bakiuskikh Komissarov Street to visit his family and friends and to keep abreast of changes. To avoid violating the passport regulations, his visits were limited to seventy-two hours until he acquired a temporary permit to live in Moscow in December 1987.[9]

Kovalyov began to acknowledge the complexity of Gorbachev's undertaking. He recognized that the initiators of reform were displaying a certain degree of courage given the historical moment, and he grew to sympathize with the leader's position and admire his resilience.[10] He stressed that,

Figure 2.1   Sitting: Sergei Kovalyov, his wife Ludmilla Boitseva and their daughter Varya. Standing: Alya Shikhanovich and Lina Zelikhman. Kalinin, on Kovalyov's birthday, March 2, 1985

Source: Memorial Archive, Moscow.

despite the uncertainty of the period and the continued victimization of the movement, Gorbachev's regime marked the end of the fear that had characterized the Soviet era, leaving them with a society "free from the fear of power, a society armed with the freedom of words ... beginning to master the fundamental values of a modern civilization."[11] It was largely this freedom from fear, the opening of the pages of the official press to topics previously discussed in *samizdat*, and the cautious but encouraging steps taken by Gorbachev's government in the area of democratic reform and the rule of law, that convinced Kovalyov to resume his public activity. He believed that the level of freedom for Gorbachev was far less than for those working from below.[12]

For Kovalyov, one of the uniting features of the dissident movement of the 1960s and 1970s had been fear.[13] Its decline under Gorbachev meant that the radical differences in ideas, philosophies and objectives that had once defined the movement gradually moved to the surface. No longer forced to protect each other and the movement in general, the differences turned out to be wide and divisive. For Kovalyov and his former allies, it turned out to be the question of cooperation with the authorities that most divided them, provoking accusations of betrayal, the sacrifice of the moral principles of the movement and collaboration.[14]

Cooperation and political prisoners

For Kovalyov it was the release of Andrei Sakharov from Gorky on December 23, 1986 that marked a major turning point. The physicist's release, however, was overshadowed by the death of the well-known human rights activist Anatoly Marchenko in Chistopol prison, fifteen days earlier on December 8. Emphasizing the discontinuity and cruel lack of discretion of the regime's treatment of political prisoners, it illustrated that Sakharov was still considered a member of the Soviet Union's intellectual elite, while Marchenko was not. This selective pardoning of political prisoners was strongly criticised in a letter entitled "Let Gorbachev Give Us Proof" sent to *Moscow Times* by, among others, Vladimir Bukovsky, Yuri Orlov and Leonid Plyushch.

> ... we cannot help noting that the selective nature of the pardons has been intended to produce a maximum effect at the price of minimal concessions. If the Soviet leaders have truly, as they claim, changed their stand on the human rights issue, if they have decided to renounce suppression as a form of control over free thinking in the Soviet Union, why have they not then pardoned all the prisoners of conscience, instead of making the pleasure last a whole year and freeing in dribs and drabs the most noted of them?[15]

The arguments around cooperation began in 1987 when Sakharov, Bonner and Kovalyov decided to support the government's release of political prisoners on condition that the prisoners sign a statement pledging not to partake in illegal or anti-Soviet activity in the future.[16] Sakharov took the first opportunity on his release to urge Gorbachev "to look one more time at the question of releasing persons convicted for their beliefs. It's a matter of justice. It is vitally important for our country, for international trust, for peace and for you and the success of your programme."[17] Malva Landa and Valeriya Novodvorskaya argued that "for Anatoly Marchenko, the metamorphosis which has occurred recently in the Nobel Peace Prize Laureate [Andrei Sakharov] would be unthinkable."[18] Marchenko's wife, Larissa Bogoraz, and Boris Altshuler reacted strongly to their decision, particularly for encouraging prisoners to accept a pardon over full rehabilitation, freeing the regime from responsibility for its actions and financial compensation.[19] Some activists, like Tatyana Velikanova, Boris Mityashin and Mikhail Kukobaka, refused to sign and were held for another year or more. Reportedly, procurators were sent to labour camps across Russia urging political prisoners to sign the pardon or draft something of their own to ensure their release.[20] The KGB interpreted the pardon as a move that "underlined the humanism of Soviet power".[21]

Kovalyov, Sakharov and Bonner did not want to deny political prisoners the option to return to a relatively normal life, despite the principle at stake. The main question involved determining how many political prisoners remained in labour camps and exile. With no access to official documentation, the exact number still serving terms under articles 70, 190–1, 190–3, 142 and 227 was unknown. They none the less devised an incomplete list of 100 names of prisoners convicted under Article 70 on the basis of unofficial information, and Sakharov handed the list to Gorbachev during a meeting at the Kremlin in January, 1988. Their list, however, was often misused, forcing them to issue a public statement on October 23, 1988:

> It has come to our attention that statements are being circulated to the effect that only a few prisoners remain today in the USSR that can be called political. In this connection, references have been made at various times to Andrei Dmitrievich Sakharov, Lev Mikhailovich Timofeyev, Larisa Iosifovna Bogoraz and Sergei Adamovich Kovalyov as sources of this information…. None of us have ever cited a total number of persons convicted for political motivations, and we never claimed to present complete, exhaustive lists …[22]

In fact, from 1968 to 1986 (with the exception of 1976), 2,468 individuals were convicted under Articles 70 (anti-Soviet agitation and propaganda) and 190–1 (the spreading of deliberate fabrications discrediting the Soviet political and social system) of the Criminal Code.[23] By the beginning of 1987, 288 individuals were still serving sentences.[24] The reaction of the Minister of Justice, Alexander Sukharev, responsible for the *New Times* article supporting Kovalyov's prison sentence in 1975, was testimony to the conflicts that existed in Gorbachev's circle over the question of political prisoners. For Sukharev:

> Our legislation does not know such a term as *corpus delicti* as a political crime. Of course, Article 70 has a political colouring since its purpose is to cut short hostile actions. But this has nothing in common with the allegations of Western propaganda that in the USSR people are arrested for dissent, convictions and criticising the authorities. These allegations are absurd, if not deliberately false ...[25]

The disagreement among members of the human rights movement over the release of political prisoners was merely the beginning of a public debate on the issue of cooperation. For Vladimir Bukovsky: "our movement ended, it broke into those who 'supported Gorbachev' and those who refused to serve as a screen for the General Secretary and his games ... Those who recognized *perestroika* and those who didn't."[26] Alexander Podrabinek, editor of the human rights newspaper *Ekspress Khronika* who soon became Kovalyov's ongoing critic, argued that the "spirit of compromise reigned during *perestroika*.... We are no longer rights defenders, we are *perestroishchiki*."[27] He thought it ironical that they were handing over lists of political prisoners when the government was well aware of the number of prisoners in Soviet labour camps.[28] "Closeness to power is ruinous for human rights activity," he later argued. "A defender of the rights of the individual is always an opponent of the authorities ..."[29] In the December 1988 edition of *Ekspress Khronika*, Kovalyov and his friends were labelled the new "dissident *nomenklatura*".[30]

Kovalyov responded strongly to the accusations in the journal *Twentieth Century and Peace* under editor Gleb Pavlovsky. Despite his own doubts about Gorbachev, he insisted that the human rights movement "had to overcome some of the old 'antipathies' of the Russian intellectual – for example his disgust for compromises.... not all compromises are dishonest. If I agree with something I am ready for conscientious cooperation."[31] The dilemma for Kovalyov was that the kind of moral absolutes that had determined much of their activity in the 1960s and 1970s were not always appropriate as the Soviet regime undertook its transition. They were in the complex position of encouraging the government, exerting pressure and pushing to realize their goals. The government was central to their objective of a law-based state in the USSR and, while Gorbachev was promoting disarmament and international security, they had to use the opportunity to promote their central principle that the observance of human rights was a precondition for international peace.

Kovalyov was encouraged by Gorbachev's words: "Without democracy there can be no rule of law. In turn, democracy cannot exist and develop without the rule of law."[32] Gorbachev's motives mattered less than the opening he had created, which was profound in its consequences. It finally allowed the Soviet human rights community to join the international community to lobby for international law and human rights principles.

For Kovalyov, this meant discouraging political slogans for a multiparty system, the downfall of the CPSU and radical democratization, at least, in the first phase of *perestroika*. His most significant opponent was Valeriya Novodvorskaya. Novodvorskaya established the Democratic Union in May, 1988, the first political party in opposition to the Communist Party. Seeking to establish a democracy in the USSR and a multiparty system with non-violent means, the Democratic Union promoted its programme through its independently published journal, *The Democratic Union Bulletin*. Novodvorskaya's frustration with Kovalyov and those who shared his views reached a climax in her 1988 article, "How Does Political Struggle Differ From Human Rights Activism or are we Sectarians?"[33] "Those who are obedient to the partocracy are obstructing the cause of freedom," she argued. "Human rights activism does not shake the foundation or under-mine the fundamentals, it does not disrupt the habitual world relations." For Novodvorskaya, "political struggle [was] taking human rights activism to its logical end."[34] For Kovalyov it was precisely the struggle for human rights principles supported by international law that could shake the foundation of world relations. It could draw the Soviet Union out of its isolation, a gradu-alist approach to reforming the institutions responsible for enforcing domestic law – a movement, on the most idealistic plane, against sovereignty and for global justice.

In the late 1980s, Kovalyov clung to his belief that the Human Rights Movement had to manoeuvre carefully in the new conditions. He also continued to strongly assert that every Soviet citizen was obliged to acknowledge his or her role in the preservation of the Soviet system and to take upon themselves responsibility for their government's decisions and actions. For those who signed the "Let Gorbachev Give Us Proof" letter, the only way for the Soviet government to gain the trust of its people was if the regime recognized its crimes before the International Court at the Hague or the Court of Human Rights in Strasbourg.[35] For Kovalyov, criminal justice would merely undermine the democratic process. Many would criticise him, and his most staunch critic was Podrabinek:

> You cannot attempt to place moral responsibility for the crimes of the regime and its public defenders on everyone, on the entire intelligentsia, on all equally ... This government was never ours, neither yesterday, nor today and probably will not be ours tomorrow ... The majority of people in our country cannot and must not be held responsible for the crimes of the regime.[36]

This link between his individual life and that of his country and its government is a distinguishing feature of Kovalyov's personality. Regardless of whether one rejects or agrees with his views on guilt and responsibility, they were the basis of many of his individual choices and actions during this period and throughout his entire career. He was by no means a supporter of the Communist system or its accompanying ideological ideals, and it would be misleading to suggest that he in any way saw the system as progressive or humane. He ultimately believed that the quest for the guarantee of human rights was better served by a liberal government with a market economy.[37]

But cooperation with the authorities was a step Kovalyov was willing to take. It was the result of a certain degree of logical conservatism in his politics, closely aligned to his association of radical change with violence. Recalling the violence of the 1917 revolutions, seventy years of Communist rule and all its accompanying psychological damage, he advocated caution and stability. For him, trust between the Soviet regime and society had to be rebuilt without criminal trials through the actions and decisions of the regime itself and pressure from the growing civic organizations.[38] He would do his utmost to support those decisions that fostered respect for individual rights and liberties.

Press Klub Glasnost and the Moscow International Human Rights Seminar

The disagreements on cooperation were witnessed most acutely in the formation of the *Press Klub Glasnost* and The Moscow International Human Rights Seminar of December 1987. On July 7, 1987, Kovalyov, Lev Timofeyev, Father Gleb Yakunin and Larissa Bogoraz formed a civic organization called *Press Klub Glasnost*. The club lasted for little more than two years and was eventually transformed into a revived Moscow Helsinki Group in the autumn of 1989. The immediate aim of the club was to provide a forum for individuals and groups to meet and discuss, openly and critically, the problems facing Soviet society, and for activists to conduct press conferences with Soviet journalists. The founding declaration of the club stated:

> Today, a group of former political prisoners have gathered to announce the creation of the *Press Klub Glasnost,* a new independent association. The goal of our public press club is to provide an avenue for any group or citizen of our country to openly express their views – an opportunity which a significant part of our society whose views do not accord with the officially accepted viewpoint, have been deprived up until now.[39]

The life of *Press Klub Glasnost* may have been short, but its members succeeded in organizing one of the most important human rights seminars of the *perestroika* period. In September 1987 they announced their plans to hold a seminar with the newly-emerging independent civic organizations and representatives of the signatory countries of the Helsinki Final Act. Above all, the organizing committee was seeking to encourage the Soviet government to honour its commitment to the principles of the 1975 Final Act. In an appeal to the international community on September 2, they declared: "We welcome the idea of holding in Moscow an international conference on a wide range of humanitarian problems as proposed by the Soviet delegation to the Vienna meeting of the participating states of the Conference on Security and Cooperation in Europe (CSCE)."[40] The Soviet authorities' interest in holding a conference on human rights issues with the Helsinki nations was in fact first declared by Soviet Foreign Minister Eduard Shevardnadze at the Helsinki Review Conference in Vienna in November 1986.[41] Unlike the clashes that characterized Belgrade, the Head of the Soviet Delegation Yuri Kashlev was encouraged to "strive for a deepening of the Helsinki Process in the spirit of the new political thinking", and to encourage the humanitarian principles of Basket III and a ratification programme.[42] This new political direction resulted in an agreement among states to introduce a new section entitled the "CSCE Human Dimension", to encourage collaboration on the humanitarian principles outlined in Principle VII. It was agreed to convene a conference on the Human Dimension, first in Paris and then in Copenhagen. By the end of the Vienna conference, the Soviet delegation had convinced the participating states to hold the final stage of the Human Dimension Conference in Moscow in 1991.

Kovalyov, Timofeyev and Bogoraz decided to use this opportunity to announce that their seminar would be a preliminary meeting to develop themes for discussion at the conference. Their mandate was expansive: they wanted Hare Krishnas, Pentecostalists and Jewish *refuseniks* to discuss their common struggle for the freedom of religion; Crimean Tartars, Latvians and Armenians to exchange ideas on nationality issues; writers and journalists to discuss problems related to freedom of expression; scientists to discuss international disarmament; academics to discuss social and economic rights; and lawyers to tackle the issue of judicial rights.[43] The second function of the organizing committee was to "establish a climate of trust" between the authorities and the new civil organizations, between Moscow and the world community, the latter of which remained sceptical about holding a human rights conference in Moscow.

This was indeed a radical action for the organizing committee. At the annual International Helsinki Federation meeting in October 1987 they were made an affiliate of the Federation, which gave them access to international groups and organizations in the United States, Europe and Latin America. The International Helsinki Federation was set up in 1982 as a central non-government body to auspice the forty-two Helsinki Committees across the world and assist in monitoring and supporting the work of the non-government sector that grew out of the Final Act.

The working group set about arranging the agenda for the five-day seminar, which they divided into eight working groups. These were:

1   International trust and disarmament
2   Culture and human rights

3   Freedom of speech
4   Freedom of belief
5   Rights of the disabled and other socially dependent groups
6   Human contacts
7   Social and economic rights
8   Judicial guarantees.

Kovalyov was responsible for Working Group 8 on judicial guarantees.

A month prior to the opening of the seminar, the founders forwarded invitations to prominent Soviet public figures, writers, journalists, artists and academics. Stressing the importance of human rights issues for all intellectual and artistic endeavors, they hoped to broaden their support base.[44] They invited Vladimir Oryol, Vice Chairman of the Soviet Peace Committee, who responded publicly in the pages of *Moscow News*:

> We have nothing against taking part in non-official discussions. But what is the point? To come together to find ways for joint solutions to painful problems? Or just to engage in idle talk and hear different opinions? There is no need to gather for discussion on street corners or in kitchens to help the democratic changes in the country. The times are different now.[45]

With no money for the administrative costs of the club, the organizers appealed to the Soviet and international cultural elite to organize a concert to raise money.[46] It did not receive a response. Kovalyov was also intent upon changing the image of human rights activists as radicals in the Soviet press. He was most surprised by the attitude of the new informal organizations.[47] Many harboured deep suspicions of their former activity, seeing them as radicals and incredulous that they were deprived of their freedom just for writing public statements or criticising the regime. For Kovalyov, the young people forming new organizations and making political demands were very different to his own generation. "Compared with us," he wrote, "they are politicians, almost revolutionaries. We were neither.... Our relationship to the law was the core of our democratic movement. To the philosophy of law, to the language of law ..."[48]

The authorities nevertheless continued to sanction perverse measures to suppress the civil initiatives of the human rights community.[49] The prejudice was profoundly deep and, although *perestroika* loosened the roots of that tradition, it did not shift its overwhelming dominance in state structures. Ten days before the opening of the Human Rights seminar, the creation of a new civic organization was announced in the pages of *Izvestiya*,[50] – the Public Commission for International Cooperation on Humanitarian Questions and Human Rights in the USSR. Headed by Fyodor Burlatsky, and better known as the Burlatsky Commission, its mandate was to "strive for the accordance of Soviet legislation with the obligations undertaken by the Helsinki Final

Act and UN Human Rights Documents".[51] Burlatsky was a former political correspondent for *Pravda* and the author of various books on social and economic rights. The Commission worked under the aegis of the Soviet Commission on Security and Cooperation in Europe and the Soviet Peace Fund that claimed to support itself through individual donations.[52]

The sudden appearance of these alleged civic organizations with identical mandates to groups like *Press Klub Glasnost* was more than a coincidence and reflected the self-styled attempt of the regime to imitate the initiatives of the human rights movement. Just like the Soviet Committee for the Defence of Peace, a traditional Party front that positioned itself between Soviet peace activists and their Western counterparts,[53] the Burlatsky Commission attempted to insert itself between international human rights organizations and the movement.[54] Bonner called the commission "a creature of the KGB and the Politburo".[55] Indeed, Westerners often had trouble discerning between government-subsidized organizations and genuine non-government initiatives during *perestroika*. When representatives of the International Helsinki Federation arrived in Moscow for the Human Rights Seminar, Burlatsky invited them to a public lecture, where he explained that the mandate of the public commission was to establish an atmosphere conducive to running the proposed International Human Rights Conference[56] – the exact same mandate proposed by Kovalyov, Bogoraz and Timofeyev.

The Vice-Chairman of the Burlatsky Commission and Director of the All-Union Research Institute of Soviet Legislation was Veniamin Yakovlev. When interviewed, he declared: "The uncalled-for ballyhoo raised around human rights, which distorts the real state of affairs, does not help the democratization process." The emphasis on the word "constructive" in the article's title, "Human Rights – A Constructive Approach" was perhaps meant as an attack on the human rights community and their "unconstructive" approach to human rights violations.[57]

The seminar began on the morning of December 10. The organizers arrived to find the hall they had rented closed. A sign on the door read: "Sanitary Day", and the administration had disappeared. The reasons given for the closure of the three rented halls were faulty plumbing, a planned inspection by the fire department and a cockroach problem. Participants were detained at railway stations and airport terminals.[58] A memorandum from the KGB to the Central Committee on December 28 stated that "measures were implemented to thwart the realization by anti-Soviet elements of the holding of a provocational action ..."[59] The same memorandum concluded that:

> The International section and the Propaganda section of the CC CPSU with the Ministry of Foreign Affairs and the KGB intend to devise additional measures for unmasking the hostile, provocational character of the activity of the organizers and participants of the action and also for the prevention of such actions in the future.[60]

The organizers had foreseen that the authorities might hinder the seminar. They had earlier arranged for eight different apartments scattered across Moscow to be ready to hold the different working sections.[61]

The seminar went ahead and Kovalyov began with a speech on the relationship between the human rights movement and the authorities. The participants in the seminar, however, were unable to reach an agreement on the question of cooperation between the authorities and human rights activists. The extent to which this divided them was witnessed in their decision to issue two separate final resolutions that outlined their differences in approach and beliefs. An important moment in the history of the relations between members of the movement, *Public Defence of the Rights of the Individual, Resolution 1* (Appendix 1) was signed by Kovalyov, Lavut, Bogoraz, Daniel and others, and stated: "We consider it essential to continue persistent attempts to establish a dialogue between the human rights movement in the USSR and the authorities ... we from our side are prepared in all good faith to establish cooperation with the authorities at all levels."[62] *Public Defence of the Rights of the Individual, Resolution 2* (Appendix 2) was devised by Novodvorskaya, who argued that the Soviet regime was incapable of recognizing the very idea of human rights, which made it impossible to cooperate with them: "A political nonviolent struggle with the government of the USSR is essential. The basic demand of our movement is permanent opposition to the government. The demand for a multiparty system in the country."[63] Novodvorskaya attacked Kovalyov in her autobiography, saying that he was against her presenting her report because of its radicalism.[64] Given Kovalyov's caution towards Novodvorskaya, this may well be true.

Despite the internal divisions that plagued the movement in 1987, they managed to outline the major human rights problems in the Soviet Union and to devise new strategies. Kovalyov's working section on "The Juridical Defence of Human Rights" devised a criterion and recommendations on amending legislation (Appendix 3). Among the urgent proposals was to secure the priority of internationally ratified treaties and conventions over domestic Soviet legislation. They called for the signing of the Optional Protocol of the Covenant on Civil and Political Rights, which enabled individuals to lodge complaints with the United Nations Human Rights Commission. They also advocated the Soviet Union's adherence to Convention 105 of the International Labor Organization, the UNESCO conventions on obtaining scientific, education and cultural materials, and the abolition of the death penalty.

On the domestic front, they called for the immediate publication and review of all normative acts; the establishment of a Constitutional Court to review legislation; a new law on the founding of independent publishers; an amended law on demonstrations; the right for all Soviet citizens to access information on the work of government agencies; and a revised procedure for the involuntary hospitalization of persons needing psychiatric care. They also called for the humanization of the penal system; the end of criminal convictions for consenting homosexuals; new legislation on entry and exit from the USSR; the abolition of the *propiska* (the controversial and oppressive registration permit); and a review of Article 72 of the Communications Act.[65]

The group also signed separate documents on the abolition of the death penalty and the proposed withdrawal of Soviet troops from the Czechoslovak Socialist Republic. While Western countries have continued to struggle to enforce the ideals of the 1948 Universal Declaration of Human Rights and the International Covenants of 1976, the Soviet human rights community continued, as they had always done, to take these documents at face value. The basis for Kovalyov's desire for cooperation with the government was to gain direct access to the legislative organs. The seminar certainly helped human rights activists to consolidate their aims, identify trends in human rights violations and strengthen their links with international human rights organizations. It was but one step in a new direction.

The Foundation for the Survival and Development of Humanity

It was Andrei Sakharov's role in the International Foundation for the Survival and Development of Humanity that opened serious domestic opportunities for the human rights community and for Kovalyov personally. In February 1987, Sakharov participated in Gorbachev's international initiative, the Forum for a Nuclear Free World and the Survival of Mankind. This forum attracted over one thousand international figures to Moscow from across the world, from Graham Greene to Gregory Peck, to participate in seven round tables covering international questions ranging from culture to the environment and nuclear disarmament.[66] Despite the discontent his participation evoked amongst some human rights activists, Sakharov worked openly to foster the conditions to formulate a human rights agenda, to seize opportunities for the human rights community and to create a structure in which ideas on human rights could be generated, issues discussed and legislation drafted at the highest level of Soviet politics.[67] Acutely aware that the forum was staged for "propaganda purposes",[68] Sakharov remained committed to an approach based on immediate and actual social reform which helped lay the groundwork for Kovalyov's political agenda.

Sakharov's participation in the forum launched a new era in the history of the movement. His participation played a crucial role in drawing human rights issues into the public arena and bridging that tradition of contempt and suspicion with a modicum of trust. Motivated by a number of factors, economic, ideological and humanitarian, Gorbachev hoped to stimulate the creative and scientific intelligentsia to aid his struggle for peace.[69] His first long-term aim was to reduce the nuclear arsenals of both the United States and the Soviet Union by 50 per cent. It was Sakharov, with his role in the creation of the hydrogen bomb and his later criticisms of the effects of above-ground nuclear testing, who Gorbachev needed to help him convince the international community that he was committed to disarmament. The advantages of Sakharov's participation were twofold; he could appease the international community's ongoing concern over human rights violations, and he could encourage the Russian intellectual elite to support his wider cause. The February forum played a crucial role as a preliminary meeting leading up to the signing of the Intermediate Nuclear Forces Treaty (INF) at the Washington Summit later in 1987.[70]

More importantly for the human rights community was the idea put forward during the forum for the creation of an International Foundation for the Survival and Development of Humanity (IF). This Foundation would encourage multilateral collaboration between scholars and experts from across the globe on issues of international concern.[71] Gorbachev described the Foundation as a "promising and noble idea" which could be "used for open discussion of the threat of nuclear war". The Foundation could encourage research on burning international issues and contribute towards drafting projects on the problems facing humanity.[72]

An international organizing committee was established in order to initiate projects for the Foundation. Behind the creation of the Foundation were Yevgeni Velikhov, vice-president of the Soviet Academy of Sciences, and Jerome Weisner, President Emeritus of the Massachusetts Institute of Technology and former science advisor to US Presidents Kennedy and Johnson.[73] They enlisted the efforts of some thirty international specialists to serve on the Executive Committee, including such notable figures as Frank Von Hippel (Professor of Energy and International Affairs at Princeton University), David McTaggart (Director of Greenpeace International) and Tatyana Zaslavskaya, the well known president of the USSR Sociological Association and economic advisor to Gorbachev. Modelled on the principle of a major grant-making foundation in the United States, the IF sought to act as a non-government organization with offices in the United States, Sweden and the Soviet Union, with its central concerns being international security, environment, development, education, human rights and medicine.[74] Its strategy was to finance working groups and organizations devoted to specific issues that rested within its agenda. Sakharov was invited to join the Foundation's Board of Directors in late 1987. He understood that the IF's agenda, as Velikhov insisted some years later, was "cooperation and influence over Gorbachev as the initiator and guarantor of reforms in the Soviet Union".[75]

Sakharov quickly grew frustrated with the IF's vague and undefined objectives. Twelve months had elapsed since the idea was first discussed, with still no initiative taken on projects. On January 13, 1988 the directors met in Moscow to discuss their agenda for a meeting with Gorbachev in the Kremlin two days later. Sakharov had devised his agenda for the IF so far as the Soviet Union was concerned. He proposed that they speak with Gorbachev on six areas:

1   Reduction in military service;
2   The underground siting of nuclear power plants;

3   A draft agreement to ensure that all scientific research that might contribute to the development of particularly dangerous weapons systems be conducted openly;

4   Legal safeguards for freedom of expression;

5   Legal safeguards to secure for all persons the free choice of country of residence;

6   The humanization of the penal system.[76]

During the meeting Gorbachev stressed the IF's importance as a research body committed to ecology, the scientific–technological revolution, international relations, weapons of mass destruction and their disarmament. He stressed that, although the Foundation was united in its aim of international peace and multilateral collaboration, this could be achieved while remaining "devoted to one's social, ideological and religious choices".[77] Gorbachev emphasized that disarmament was the IF's leading priority.[78] Sakharov, however, used the meeting as an opportunity to discuss continuing human rights violations in the Soviet Union. He passed over the list of 100 political prisoners, and at the same time he called for a reduction in the length of military service. Gorbachev handed the list to the Procurator for consultation.[79]

The idea for a Human Rights Committee under the auspices of the IF was first mentioned in Leningrad in June 1988, during an Executive Committee meeting.[80] Sakharov's ongoing frustration with the foundation's inability to initiate constructive ideas and changes led him to act independently, and he asked Kovalyov to establish a working group to research civil and political rights in the USSR and present a proposal for promoting human rights in the USSR at the next meeting.[81] He also established a Human Rights Committee within the IF, comprised of himself as Chairman, Theodore Hesburgh (Co-chairman), Susan Eisenhower, William Miller and Metropolitan Pitirim. It was decided in June that the first meeting of the Committee would be held in Moscow on September 24 to coincide with the next Executive Committee meeting.

Kovalyov was asked to speak at a small private reception for President Ronald Reagan at the American Embassy in Moscow on May 30. Along with Father Gleb Yakunin and Sergei Grigoryants, he talked briefly about the human rights situation in general. The Soviet press, particularly *Pravda*, attacked Reagan for meeting with dissidents, the "opponents of socialism and *perestroika*" who failed to represent the reality of today's Soviet Union.[82] This was a common criticism aimed at human rights activists – that they were entrenched in the past, unable to cease dragging all the negative questions about Soviet reality to the surface. Kovalyov felt the effects of his speech the following day when he arrived to begin his new job at the Institute for Problems of Information Transmission at the Academy of Sciences. He was told by Professor Ovsiyevich that he had been reprimanded by the Director, Academician Siforov, for employing Kovalyov, particularly after his widely publicized meeting with Reagan. His contract was terminated.[83]

Kovalyov, however, grew busy with the new Human Rights Committee and, professionally, these years opened up new opportunities for him. He took his first trip outside the Soviet Union to Washington DC in November 1988, he built on his knowledge of international human rights law, and he began to draw comparisons between human rights violations in different countries. Sakharov arranged for a meeting with IF representatives, state bureaucrats and human rights defenders to meet in Moscow on September 24, 1988 to discuss the formation of collaborative working groups. By inviting together state representatives like Elena Lukashova, Head of the Human Rights Department of the USSR Institute of State and Law, Professor Vladimir Kartashkin, the then USSR representative to the United Nations, and Soviet human rights activists, Sakharov managed to bring together for the first time individuals from both the government and the human rights community to discuss human rights issues.

Sakharov's position on the creation of working groups was supported by Kovalyov's speech at the meeting. For the first time, Kovalyov appeared as a representative of the human rights community with state representatives. The meeting dramatized the differences between his views and those of the bureaucracy; he was now sharing a table with Vladimir Kartashkin, Doctor of Law, a prominent diplomat who served as the Soviet Union's representative to the United Nations, a role that Kovalyov would later assume. A decade earlier, while Kovalyov was languishing in Camp Perm 36, Kartashkin was criticising the West for supporting dissidents "rejected by their own society".[84] In a series of articles written in the wake of the 1977 Constitution, he celebrated the "Great October Socialist Revolution", declaring that it had "made the greatest contribution to mankind's struggle for rights and freedoms."[85] While criticising the "bourgeois revolutions of America and France", Kartashkin praised the Soviet Union for protecting socioeconomic rights and for guaranteeing "a long list of civil and political rights and freedoms ... Freedom of speech, of the press ... [and] freedom of conscience."[86]

Kovalyov, however, agreed with Kartashkin on the necessity of theoretical studies on human rights and comparative research between countries. He emphasized the central role of the rule of law in the Soviet Union's future, and he highlighted the problem of administrative regulations (*podzakonnie akti*), often unpublished and wielding enormous departmental influence, that often directly contradicted the constitution, other statutes and decrees.[87] Kovalyov proposed that they undertake the following: (a) analysis of the concept of human rights in the Soviet Union; (b) a study of the present conditions of the law and legislative acts; (c) a study of the status of courts and other legal practices; (d) an analysis of the correspondence between Soviet law and international law; and (e) the formulation of proposals.[88]

Lukashova insisted that they concentrate on the right to live, the right to peace and the right to a safe environment.[89] Sakharov rejected Lukashova and Kartashkin's proposal for theoretical and comparative research: "I fear this could lead us to a theoretical dead-end. This type of research should be done in the course of the work, as application of laws is the key." He had hoped that the IF could work with the USSR Institute of State and Law to influence the drafting of legislation on freedom of conscience, reform of the penal system and freedom of movement. Not only did the Institute of State and Law lack influence, but they had no research data to assist the drafting of new legislation.[90]

Sakharov decided that the IF should organize and finance its own working groups on civil rights and penal reform. These groups would be responsible for the research of human rights issues, with the aim of drafting legislation and exerting pressure over the legislative process. He wanted Kovalyov and other human rights activists to lead these projects.[91] His ambitions, however, were frustrated by the concerns of the Executive Committee, who believed that his ideals would politicize the IF and undermine its international character. Weisner argued that their role was *not* to establish working groups on human rights, but to organize screening committees that would accept proposals from organizations outside the IF.[92] The idea most forcefully argued by Sakharov was that this was a crucial turning-point in Soviet history. "We need to help our country move out of the time of decay and move forward," he argued.[93] While Sakharov supported the international character of the foundation, he urged the Executive Committee to recognize that the situation in the Soviet Union was decidedly worse than in the other participating countries. Discussion centred around what the exact function of these working groups would be.

The problem remained for Sakharov to get the Board of Directors in the United States to sanction the working groups. He agreed to go to Washington on November 13, 1988 to discuss the formation of the committees, but insisted that Kovalyov, Larissa Bogoraz, Boris Zolotukhin and Alexander Lavut also attend and be given access to research institutes on human rights. These four people formed the first working group. While in Washington, Velikhov suggested that the Human Rights Committee seek status independent of the IF. The Council of Ministers had signed an unprecedented decree on October 5, 1988 which secured permission for the IF to open an office in Moscow as well as granting it legal status as an independent, non-profit organization with the freedom to publish, fund-raise, employ Soviet citizens, and exempting the foundation's property from confiscation or requisition by the Soviet authorities.[94] The likelihood of the Human Rights Committee ever being registered under such favourable conditions was almost nonexistent.[95]

At the November meeting in Washington, Sakharov insisted that the directors fund three working groups: a Soviet–American working group to examine the protection of civil and political rights in the Soviet Union and the United States; a Soviet–American working group to examine the question of free movement; and a Soviet–American working group to compare conditions of detention of prisoners in Sweden, the USSR and the US.[96] After lengthy discussions, the board agreed to the establishment of the working groups with the final resolution that the groups would combine to form what became known as The Russian–American Human Rights Project Group with 10,000 dollars and 5,000 rubles allocated as starting funds.[97]

The Human Rights Project Group

While Sakharov began to address the questions of a new constitution, a multi-party system and his role in the first Congress of Peoples Deputies, Kovalyov was appointed Chairman of the Russian–American Human Rights Project Group with the mandate to foster legislative and institutional safeguards for the protection of civil and political rights in the USSR.[98] Part of that mandate meant the dissemination and distribution of draft statutes, educational pamphlets and documents to decision-makers, Soviet deputies, libraries and universities. Its approach was to be largely scholarly, but with contemporary problems in view to aid decision-makers and those drafting new legislation.

Kovalyov was keen to publish a Human Rights Bulletin to outline ongoing problems and to analyse the experiences of other countries as an educational booklet to be distributed to Deputies. He was successful in getting a bulletin off the ground – which continues to be published periodically. The Project Group also published briefing papers on the rule of law in modern society, a study on the autonomous status of the Aaland Islands, and a draft statute on States of Emergency.[99]

The law on States of Emergency was certainly a political concern for Kovalyov and his colleagues, especially after Gorbachev's move to the right in October 1989. The human rights community grew concerned about the threat of martial law or a right-wing coup.[100] They also saw that it was becoming impossible to prevent the break-up of the Federal State. Kovalyov and his colleagues worked on a 48-page briefing paper, "With Regard to Legislation Governing States of Emergency", which contained a model law on national emergencies drafted by HRPG members and experts, excerpts from Nicole Questiaux's 1982 UN study on states of siege or emergency, earlier Soviet decrees on the subject, and relevant provisions of French, West German, US, Spanish and Greek laws. The paper was distributed to the deputies.[101]

By the time of the first elections to the Congress of People's Deputies in March 1989, Soviet society was witnessing the growing split between Gorbachev and the democrats.[102] The emerging populist figure, Boris Yeltsin, had received 5 million votes in the March elections.[103] During the first Congress, Sakharov called for the removal of Article 6 from the Soviet Constitution on the leading role of the Communist Party and a market economy, underlined by his split with the Congress to form the Interregional Group along with Boris Yeltsin and other leading 'democrats'.

Kovalyov's full-time involvement in the Human Rights Project group was limited to eighteen months before his own election to the Congress of Peoples Deputies of the Russian Federation the following year. Activists belonging to Memorial, the group dedicated to preserving the memory of the victims of Soviet repression, suggested that he campaign for election, and when he sought the advice of Sakharov on December 11, 1989 the physicist told him that he had to run.[104] The Project Group was to become an important working asset and aid to Kovalyov and his colleagues in the years after the creation of the Supreme Soviet Human Rights Committee. But the successes of 1989 were overshadowed for Kovalyov by the unexpected death of Sakharov three days later on December 14. He was now seen, in many ways, as Andrei Sakharov's spiritual successor. But the new demands placed on him had little in common with those endured by his friend.

By January 1990, Kovalyov's concerns grew increasingly political. With Sakharov's death, the democratic forces moved together to create the umbrella organization, Democratic Russia, whose aim was to defend the ideas of Sakharov.[105] The third stage of Kovalyov's public career began when he joined the organization in January 1990, supporting its democratic agenda, a position he had been cautious and reluctant to lobby for only three years before. But Kovalyov could now see that the emergence of a democratic Russia was possible without widespread violence, and he was emboldened by the civil momentum forming from below.

Notes

1 S. Kovalyov, "Without Barricades", *Peace & the Twentieth Century*, No. 9 (1988): 47.
2 J. Gooding, "Gorbachev and Democracy", *Soviet Studies*, Vol. 42, No. 2, April (1990): 206.
3 M. Gorbachev, cited in Gooding, *op.cit.*, pp. 206, 207.
4 "SSSR Povtornie aresti", *Rysskaya Mysl'*, No. 3607, February 7, 1986, p. 2.
5 S. Kovalyov, L. Bogoraz and V. Goltsin, "Politecheskaya borba ili zashchita prav?", *Perestroika: Glasnost, Demokratiya, Sotsialism – Podrushenie v tryasiny*. Moscow: Progress, 1991, pp. 501–45.
6 M. Gorbachev, *Selected Speeches and Writings*, Moscow: Progress Publishers, 1987, pp. 321–40.
7 Ts.Kh.C.D – Centre for Contemporaray Documentation. F.89, P.18 D.111. N. 2521-Ch, December 26, 1986.
8 See *Prava Cheloveka: Vesti iz SSSR*, No. 9 (9–23), 1986, p. 190. The exact reason for his dismissal is not known to the author.
9 This permit came up for renewal every six months. See M. Landa, "Sergei Kovalyov: fakty biografii'', *Pravozashchitnik 2*, April–June 1997: 78.
10 S. Kovalyov, "Banket dissidentov: perestroika – intelligentsia i politika", *Nezavisimaya Gazeta*, March 16, 1995: 3.
11 *Ibid.*
12 S. Kovalyov, "Without Barricades", *Peace & the Twentieth Century*, No. 51 (1988): 44–8.
13 S. Kovalyov, "Dissidenti o dissidentstve", *Znamya*, No. 9 (1997): 179.
14 S. Kovalyov, "Andrei Sakharov: Otvetstvennost pered razumom", *Izvestiya*, May 21, 1998: 5.

15 V. Bukovsky *et al.*, "Let Gorbachev give us proof", *Moscow News Weekly*, No. 13, 1987, p. 10.

16 A. Podrabinek, "S kem segodniya Akademik Sakharov", *Ekspress Khronika*, September 18, 1988: 1. See also Ts.Kh.C.D – Centre for Contemporary Documentation. F.89, P.18 D.111 N.2521-Ch December 26, 1986, KGB Memorandum to CPSU Central Committee, p. 3.

17 Sakharov, *Memoirs*, p. 616.

18 *Arkhive Samizdat*, A.S 5891, Moscow: Memorial Archive, p. 4.

19 A. Sakharov, *Moscow and Beyond*, New York: Knopf, 1990, p. 6. See also E. Kline, Personal Interview with E. Gilligan, New York: March, 1996.

20 L. Alekseeva, *Nyeformaly: Civil Society in the USSR*, New York: A Helsinki Watch Report, 1990, pp. 3–15.

21 Ts.Kh.C.D – Centre for Contemporaray Documentation. F.89, P.18 D.111 N.2521-Ch December 26, 1986. Memorandum from the KGB to CPSU Central Committee, p. 4.

22 "Statement on Soviet Political Prisoners from Bogoraz, Kovalyov, Sakharov, Timofeev, October 23, 1988", New York: Kline Archive, p. 1. See also *Ekspress Khronika*, October 30, 1988: 1.

23 S. Kovalyov, "Vystuplenie Kovalyova v Konstitustionnom sude", Melbourne: Personal Collection, E. Gilligan. Taped version also available from the Andrei Sakharov Museum and Public Centre, Moscow.

24 Ts.Kh.C.D – Centre for Contemporaray Documentation. F.89, P.18 D.116. KGB Memorandum to the CPSU Central Committee. May 11, 1986, p. 4. See also "Measures to Ensure Human Rights and Fundamental Freedoms are Being Taken in the USSR", *Moscow News*, No. 34 (3282) 1987: 4.

25 A. Sukharev, "We are putting things in order in our juridical house", *Moscow News*, No. 14, 1987: 7.

26 V. Bukovsky, *Moskovskii Protsess*, Paris–Moscow: MIK, 1996, p. 219.

27 A. Podrabinek, *Ekspress Khronika*, No. 51, December 18, 1988: 8–9.

28 A. Podrabinek, "Otvet Borisu Vailu", *Rysskaya Mysl'*, October 28, 1988: 2.

29 A. Podrabinek, *Express Chronicle: English Weekly News Digest*, March 14, 1997: 1.

30 K. Podrabinek, "Zapiski symashedshevo o kolichestve symazshedshikh", *Ekspress Khronika*, No. 51, December 18, 1988: 8–9.

31 S. Kovalyov, "Without Barricades", *XX Century and Peace*, No. 9 (1988): 44–8.

32 Cited in Gooding, *op.cit.*, p. 208.

33 V. Novodvorskaya, "Chem otlichaetsya politichskaya bor'ba ot pravozashchitnoi deyatel'notsi, ili sektanty li my?", *DS Biulleten'*, No. 2–3 (1988): 1. See also V. Novodvorskaya, *Po Tu Storonu otchayaniya*, Moscow: Novosti, 1993, pp. 127–30.

34 V. Novodvorskaya, "Chem otlichaetsya politichskaya bor'ba ot pravozashchitnoi deyatel'notsi, ili sektanty li my?", *DS Biulleten'*, No. 2–3 (1988): 3. See also "Kovalyov vs Novodvorskaya", *New Times*, January 1999: 2–5.

35 V. Bukovsky *et al.*, "Let Gorbachev give us proof," *Moscow News Weekly*, No. 13, 1987: 10.

36 A. Podrabinek, *Ekspress Khronika*, No. 51, December 19, 1988: 8–9 .

37 Kovalyov, *Vosp.*, p. 62.

38 S. Kovalyov, "Obshaya vina, obshaya otvetstvennost", *Moskovskii Novosti*, No. 5, January 31, 1991: 3. See also S. Kovalyov, "Tak zhit v takom gosudarstve", *Karta*, New York: Kline Archive, date unknown, pp. 7–10.

39 *Glasnost 2*, July, (1987): 10.

40 "Appeal: To international and national non-governmental organisations and private citizens interested in the development of the Helsinki Process in the area of Humanitarian Problems and to the governments of the participating states of the Conference on Security and Cooperation in Europe (CSCE)", *Resolutions*

and other documents of the Moscow Independent Seminar on Humanitarian Problems, December 10–15, 1987: A Helsinki Watch Report, August, 1988, Moscow, Memorial Archive, p. 11.

41 "Shevardnadze proposes international conference on humanitarian issues in Moscow", *Radio Liberty*, 421/86, p. 1.

42 See Ambassador Yuri Kashlev, First Vice-Rector, Diplomatic Academy, Ministry of Foreign Affairs, Moscow: "Soviet Union/Russia in the Helsinki Process", presented to the GCSP/HEI Workshop on the 30th Anniversary of the Launching of the CSCE Process. GCSP, November 25, 2002. Available online at http://www.gcsp.ch/e/news/Kashlev.html (accessed June 2003).

43 Resolutions and other documents of the Moscow Independent Seminar on Humanitarian Problems, December 10–15, 1987: A Helsinki Watch Report, p. 12.

44 *Referendum: Zhurnal Nezavisimikh Mnenii*, No. 2, December (1987): 5–7.

45 V. Oryol, cited in "Learning to Communicate", *Moscow News Weekly*, No. 52, 1987: 5.

46 "Obrashchenie o sozdanii funda kluba 'Glasnost'," *Referendum: Zhurnal Nezavisimikh Mnenii*, No. 2, December (1987): 10.

47 S. Kovalyov, "Time to Get Ready for Democracy", *Peace & the Twentieth Century*, No. 10 (1989): 19.

48 *Ibid.*

49 Ts.Kh.C.D – Centre for Contemporaray Documentation. F.89, P.18 D.111. N. 2521-Ch, December 26, 1986. Memorandum of the KGB of the USSR to the Central Committee of the CPSU.

50 *Izvestiya*, November 30, 1987: 1. See also *Moscow News Weekly*, No. 50, 1987: 2.

51 *Radio Liberty*, 10/1988, p. 1.

52 Alekseeva, *op.cit.*, p. 22.

53 Alekseeva, *op.cit.*, p. 11.

54 Alekseeva, *op.cit.*, p. 22.

55 E. Bonner, "A Letter to Boris Nikolayevich Yeltsin", *The New York Review of Books*, Vol. 42, No. 2. February 2, 1995. Available online at www.nybooks.com/articles/2001 (accessed July 2003).

56 *Moscow News Weekly*, No. 50, 1987: 2.

57 *Moscow News Weekly*, No. 50, 1987: 2.

58 *Referendum: Zhurnal Nezavisimikh Mnenii*, No. 2, December (1987): 5–7.

59 Ts.Kh.C.D – Centre for Contemporaray Documentation. F.89, P.18 D.121 N.2594 -Ch December 28, 1987.

60 *Ibid.*

61 *Referendum: Zhurnal Nezavisimikh Mnenii*, No. 2, December (1987): 5–7.

62 "Public Defence of the Rights of the Individual Resolution No. 1", Resolutions and other documents of the Moscow Independent Seminar on Humanitarian Problems, December 10–15, 1987: A Helsinki Watch Report, Moscow: Memorial Archive, August, 1988, p. 11.

63 "Public Defence of the Rights of the Individual Resolution No. 2", Resolutions and other documents of the Moscow Independent Seminar on Humanitarian Problems, December 10–15, 1987: A Helsinki Watch Report, Moscow: Memorial Archive, August, 1988, p. 11.

64 V. Novodvorskaya, *Po Tu Storonu otchayaniya*, Moscow: Novosti, 1993, p. 127.

65 Resolutions and other documents of the Moscow Independent Seminar on Humanitarian Problems, December 10–15, 1987: A Helsinki Watch Report, Moscow: Memorial Archive, August, 1988. See also "O Professional'noi Dobrosovestnosti Yurista", Referendum, No. 5, February 2 (1988): 10–14.

66 "On ways to a Nuclear-Free World", *Moscow News*, No. 9, 1987: 5. "At the Forum and after", *Moscow News*, No. 10, 1987: 7. *The Times*, February 17, 1987: 8. See also *The New York Times*, February 15, 1987: 1.

67 A. Sakharov, *Andrei Sakharov: Mir, Progress i Prava Cheloveka*, Leningrad: Sovetskii Pisatel', 1990, p. 20.
68 A. Sakharov, *Moscow & Beyond*, New York: Knopf, 1990, p. 15.
69 Y. Orlov, *Before & After Glasnost*, New York: American Jewish Committee, 1989, pp. 2, 3 and 7.
70 "Summit Brings Better Ties But No Breakthrough", *Washington Post*, June 2, 1988: A01.
71 E. Kline, "The International Foundation for the Survival and Development of Humanity: An Overview", New York: Kline Archive, 1996, p. 1. Henceforth, *Overview*.
72 M. Gorbachev, "Declaration on The International Foundation for the Survival and Development of Humanity: Draft, 880923 Moscow", New York: Kline Archive, p. 1.
73 Kline, *Overview*, p. 2.
74 "Sovet Ministrov SSSR postanovlenie ot 5 oktybya, 1988 No. 1167 o deyatel'nosti na territorii SSSR mezhdunarodnovo fonda", New York: Kline Archive.
75 E. Velikhov, "Letter to Susan Eisenhower. September 11, 1991", New York: Kline Archive.
76 "Minutes from the Board of Directors Meeting: Moscow January 13, 1988", New York: Kline Archive.
77 M. Gorbachev, *Pravda*, January 15, 1988: 1, 4. See also *Izvestiya*, January 17, 1988: 1.
78 E. Kline, "Narrative Report on the Russian-American Human Rights Group," New York: Kline Archive, p. 2. Henceforth, *Report*.
79 Kline, *Report*, p. 2.
80 "Minutes from the Executive Committee Meeting, Leningrad, June 1988", New York: Kline Archive.
81 Kline, *Report*, p. 2.
82 *Pravda*, No. 152 (25504), May 31, 1988: 2. See also *Izvestiya*, No. 153, June 1, 1988: 2. *Radio Liberty*, No. 236, 1988, p. 12.
83 E. Kline, *Khronika Press: Information Bulletin*, New York: Kline Archive, June, 1988, p. 1. See also "News from Helsinki Watch: Soviet Human Rights Leader Harassed After Reagan Reception," New York: Kline Archive, June 8, 1988.
84 V. Kartashkin, "International Relations and Human Rights", *International Affairs*, August (1977): 30.
85 V. Kartashkin, "Human Rights and the Modern World", *International Affairs*, January (1979): 48.
86 V. Kartashkin, "The Soviet Constitution and Human Rights", *International Affairs*, February (1979): 15.
87 "Minutes from the Human Rights Committee meeting of The International Foundation for the Survival and Development of Humanity, Moscow September 24, 1988," New York: Kline Archive, p. 3. Henceforth, *Minutes*, Sept. 24. See also E. Huskey, "A Framework for the Analysis of Soviet Law", *The Russian Review*, Vol. 50, January (1991): 61–2.
88 *Minutes*, Sept 24, p. 4.
89 *Minutes*, Sept 24, p. 2.
90 A. Sakharov, *Moscow & Beyond*, New York: Knopf, 1989, pp. 43–4, 68–9.
91 Kline, *Report*, p. 3.
92 *Minutes*, Sept, 24, p. 3.
93 *Minutes*, Sept 24, p. 3.
94 "Sovet Ministrov SSSR postanovlenie ot 5 oktybya, 1988 No. 1167 o deyatel'nost na territorii SSSR mezhdunarodnovo fonda," New York: Kline Archive, See also *Izvestiya*, October 23, 1988: 6.

95 E. Kline, Personal Interview with E. Gilligan, New York, March 1996. Henceforth, Kline (1996).
96 Kline (1996).
97 E. Kline, "Planning and General Support Proposal," submitted to the Ford Foundation by the Human Rights Project Group, December 5, 1989, New York: Kline Archive, p. 3. Henceforth, *Proposal.*
98 Kline, *Proposal*, p. 3.
99 Kline, *Proposal*, pp. 4–5.
100 "Time to Get Ready for Democracy," *XX Century and Peace*, No. 10, 1989: 19–21.
101 Kline, *Proposal*, pp. 4–5.
102 J. Dunlop, *The Rise of Russia and the Fall of the Soviet Union*, Princeton: Princeton UP, 1993, 1995, p. 79.
103 Dunlop, *ibid.*, p. 10.
104 "In Moscow, The Dissident Politician: Sergei Kovalyov, Keeping His Promise to Sakharov," *Washington Post*, March 7, 1990: B1.
105 Dunlop, *op.cit.*, p. 90.

3 The Supreme Soviet Human Rights Committee

> It also makes sense to take into account the unique nature of the present moment: a movement of the entire society, including those in power to restructure the government, making the law the foundation of its development. This moment should not be passed over.
>
> Sergei Kovalyov

Election campaign

The year 1990, the year of Kovalyov's election to the Russian Federation's Congress of People's Deputies (CPD RSFSR), was a period when he felt most keenly the pressure to respond to changing circumstances. Sakharov's death steered him into a political career for which he was largely unprepared. He had little in the way of an apprenticeship, no time to learn politics and assess his own strengths and shortcomings before assuming a leader's responsibilities. Personally and with his colleagues he witnessed many lost opportunities in the years between 1990 and 1993, but they also spearheaded great change integral to the building of a human rights culture in Russia. Domestic reform was at last on the agenda with the formation of the Human Rights Committee of the Supreme Soviet. As its chairman and public spokesman, Kovalyov had grounds for hoping that legislation drafted by his Committee might be passed. He was finally given the opportunity to play a direct role in the legislative process and to realize his belief that the law might shape new cultural values in Russia and contribute to the building of a law-abiding state.

The Soviet Union collapsed in August 1991. It sank without significant ceremony or violence. It was not a revolution of the type that defined the 1917 Revolutions, and the result was a confused amalgam of old structures, a critical lack of clarity in the distribution of powers between the legislature and the executive and polarized parliamentary battles that protracted reform.[1] In the tense days of August, Kovalyov shared the trepidation of his colleagues as they waited out the attempted coup in the offices of the Moscow White House. He did not, as one would suspect, regret the demise of the Union and the subsequent rise of the Russian Federation. The transition, however, was neither structurally or psychologically revolutionary and, although Kovalyov heaved a heavy sigh of relief and savoured the new freedoms, the system remained firmly rooted in its traditional habits as he and his contemporaries struggled to consolidate their liberal aspirations.

Kovalyov's move into the world of politics coincided with his acknowledgement that the human rights movement needed to review its agenda to adjust to the new demands of the late *perestroika* period. His frustrations with the movement were made public in June 1990 in his speech at the International Helsinki Federation Meeting in Moscow, and one year later in the publication of his article, "Why There is No Human Rights Movement in the USSR".[2] The article did not appear to arouse much attention among his contemporaries, except from the pages of Alexander Podrabinek's human rights newspaper, *Ekpress Khronika*.[3] Published in the journal *Twentieth Century & Peace*, this article could by no means be compared with some of Kovalyov's later, more reflective and mature writings. He lumped all the reasons for the "deep crisis" in the human rights movement into two pages, with bare explanations and a rhetoric which was often quite characteristic of his style. From Kovalyov's perspective, the split between the legalists (*zakonniki*) and politicals (*politiki*) had reached a crucial point. "The criticism broke out," he argued, "when the legalists began to engage in the new conditions, when they acknowledged the opportunity for themselves of mutual relations with the beloved opponents including even the power structures. So then the accusations began to fall of collaboration and betrayal."[4]

The reasons for the dissonance in the movement ran deeper than the fact that the legalists were willing to cooperate with the regime. Podrabinek took the opportunity to attack Kovalyov over his differentiation between the politicals and the legalists. He accused Kovalyov of devising the categories to justify his decision to enter politics. It is a way of "proving the continuity of their position," argued Podrabinek.[5] For the editor of *Ekspress Khronika* such polarized groups never existed. For Podrabinek, the division lay elsewhere: "in the moral choice between the possibility of collaborating with power, overriding human rights with the help of camps and tanks and the impossibility of collaborating with it." Kovalyov's decision to enter politics and his subsequent relations with the power structures seriously undermined "the possibility of a real opposition based on the moral foundation of the human rights movement, on the ideals of human rights." He concluded by blaming Kovalyov and other recognized activists for "abandoning" the movement.[6]

Despite the shortcomings of Kovalyov's article, it was a forcible reminder of how dramatically the situation for the human rights community had changed during *perestroika*. For Kovalyov, the origins of the problem were clear, and he offered some cogent reasons in support of his claim. Many of the questions which once occupied the movement and functioned as a unifying force were already in the process of being resolved; the struggle for freedom of expression had gained significant ground under *glasnost* and the removal of Articles 70 and 190–1 marked a genuine turning point.[7] Not only had the unifying force for this group dwindled, but Kovalyov believed that many activists were finding it difficult to adjust to an era which no longer acclaimed the heroic gestures that shaped the dissident era at its height.[8] He insisted that "What we once called human rights activism does not exist in this country any more".[9]

Certainly many human rights activists found themselves in a great quandary as to how they should react to the dismantling of repressive controls.[10] Though Kovalyov and Podrabinek differed significantly in their interpretations of how best to secure human rights in Russia, Podrabinek agreed that the movement was in a state of disarray.[11] Considered in conjunction with his speech to the International Helsinki Federation, Kovalyov's article may be read as an attempt to inject new life into the movement and as an argument against an overtly one-sided conception of human rights activity. He found it ironical that the movement turned out to be completely unprepared for positive change and insisted that its struggle required completely new forms of organization. He concluded that it needed more long-term planning, it needed to acknowledge the political realities, to engage in the new problems, and to consolidate a base of human rights activists independent of power who could teach citizens to "build their own future".[12] He himself was beginning to understand some of the problems of practical politics, and wrote:

> Difficulties can also arise because non-government organizations comprise angry people who are not always ready to take into consideration the political reality – i.e., the real difficulties of practical politics. At the same time, however, these organizations are the most sensitive and they are the first to signal disorder in human rights.[13]

Despite the accusations lodged against his personal choices, Kovalyov remained adamant on the importance of civil society as one of the key instruments of democratization. This was no more evident than in his participation in the pro-reform group, Civic Action. On February 4, 1990, Kovalyov stood on a podium and read a declaration from the newly formed Civic Action in a demonstration attended by hundreds of thousands of Muscovites outside Lubyanka. The group had been set up by the Moscow Tribune, Memorial, the Moscow Federation of Voters and others to promote democratic reform and unite democratic reformers into "a single civic movement" calling for a multiparty democracy. Kovalyov declared:

> We exhort all opponents of totalitarianism, whether citizens, public associations, popular fronts, voters' clubs and federations, workers and strike committees or parties, to join this movement. Solidly united in the effort to achieve a civilised civic society, uniting our efforts, we can stave

off a fateful reactionary turn in the destinies of the peoples and ensure the country's peaceful extrication from the crisis and a normal decent life for everyone.[14]

Among its demands Civic Action called for the signing of a federal treaty, the end of the state monopoly over production, the creation of a multiparty system, religious and social pluralism, reform of the army and the removal of the KGB from police work. The movement would become a coordinating centre for "civic resistance" – for rallies, processions, demonstrations "and in extreme cases, for organising political strikes, civic disobedience campaigns and other nonviolent actions."[15]

For Kovalyov, the success of the human rights movement was contingent on two important factors: the building of an independent civil society and the establishment of a state based on the rule of law. His own paramount task from the summer of 1990 was to address the country's legal consciousness. He had always underlined the significance of what he called "Russia's cave dwelling legal consciousness". "Our understanding of legality was drunk from the milk of our mothers," he argued, "and it will be a long and agonising evolution"[16] before Russian citizens realize that the role of the state is to enhance the freedom of the individual and they appreciate the value of a country with a legal infrastructure, capable of protecting their rights as citizens. His solution was to educate society on the rights of the individual over the state and to exert pressure on the government through deputies.[17]

The opportunity to transfer these ideals into realizable demands came with his election to the RSFSR's Congress of People's Deputies in March 1990. In addressing concrete political issues for the first time, Kovalyov began to appreciate the complexities of practical politics. This is evident in his frequent appeals to his peers to take account of the political reality. More importantly, while before he had looked upon his participation in the human rights movement as a personal expression of principles, his entrance into politics dramatically changed his perception of responsibility. He admitted that he could no longer criticise without sharing some responsibility for the outcome. Accountable now to his electorate and later to the country when holding a government post, the period when he could act alone, answerable only to himself, was largely over.[18]

Kovalyov's political career began rather simply. He came to power on the wave of Democratic Russia when he entered its electoral bloc in January, 1990. Ambitious to see democrats elected to the forthcoming elections, the first democratic bloc campaigned hard to secure a voice in the Congress. On January 20, Moscow's Electoral Union and the Interregional Electoral Union organized a conference in the Palace of Youth (*Dvorets Molodezhi*).[19]

During the conference Viktor Sheinis announced the formation of Democratic Russia and set out its demands for the First Congress of People's Deputies. Among its demands was that the Congress recognize the need to work on a democratic constitution, to revoke Article 6 on the leading role of the Communist Party, to implement a democratic law on the press, to give parties and organizations the freedom to assemble.

Kovalyov's campaign was organized by activists of Memorial, headed by Oleg Orlov.[20] After Sakharov's death, Kovalyov was appointed co-chairman of Memorial, the well-known non-government organization committed to researching the history of political repression under the Soviet regime.[21] On the Moscow list of former political prisoners who stood as candidates to the Congress were Kovalyov and Father Gleb Yakunin.[22] Registering Kovalyov's candidature proved to be difficult. With the Electoral Commission firmly in the hands of the Communists, Kovalyov was forced to take one of two options to ensure his registration. Either his campaigners had to organize a public meeting within his proposed electoral district and gather 500 people together to secure his registration. Or they had to find a working collective which was prepared to put forward a democratic candidate as their elected representative. Concerned that there might be attempts to hinder Kovalyov's registration, his campaigners managed not only to gather 500 people at the House of Culture (*Dom Kulturi*) but they secured him a place as a representative with a working collective in a scientific research institute associated with one of Moscow's many Military Industrial Complexes.[23]

Since the new electoral law did not limit the number of candidates standing for election to each constituency, Muscovites were overwhelmed by candidates standing for election to the Congress. The first and most important task for Kovalyov's campaigners was to distinguish Kovalyov from his communist and nationalist opponents. The extent to which the election was dominated by communists became clear directly after the elections when 87.7 per cent of the successful deputies were either full or candidate members of the Communist Party.[24] They managed to separate Kovalyov by promoting his long and close friendship with Sakharov and actively publicizing in his flyers the support of well-known public figures and recognized democrats, Elena Bonner and Boris Yeltsin.[25]

On the day of Sakharov's funeral on December 19, 1989, Arseni Roginsky of Memorial approached Boris Yeltsin, seeking his support for Kovalyov's candidature. It is doubtful whether Yeltsin knew who Kovalyov was, but his aides ensured that support for him was secured within two days of the funeral.[26] Kovalyov, like many, had been impressed by Yeltsin's speech at Sakharov's funeral, but he maintained a healthy scepticism about the future President's career as an apparatchik in Sverdlovsk and his commitment to democracy.[27] He was not to foresee that many years later he would be accused of helping to create "a democratic veil around Yeltsin".[28]

Kovalyov's posters and flyers bore simple slogans. Published in Latvia since access to printers in Russia was virtually impossible in 1990, they read: "Sergei Kovalyov – Democrat", "Human Rights Activist", "Supported by Democratic Russia", "Colleague of Sakharov", "Elena Bonner supports Kovalyov", "Boris Yeltsin supports Kovalyov", and equally important, "Political Prisoner

– seven years in camp, three years exile".[29] Kovalyov believed that his personal history as a political prisoner was useful in persuading the electorate that he was committed to the principles of democracy.[30]

Kovalyov's main opponent in the elections was the nationalist, Sergei Kurginyan. Armenian by birth and a well-known political scientist in Moscow circles, Kurginyan was later connected to the National Salvation Front. Distinguished by a remarkable gift for public speaking, he frequently drew attention to the threat of privatization, the "ethnic cleansing" of the Russian population in the Baltic States, soaring crime and economic turmoil. It was fortunate that Kovalyov was never forced to participate in a televised debate – he was slow and methodical in his speech, with an inclination towards long pauses.[31]

But Kovalyov's shortage of oratorical skills was compensated for by the content of his speeches. He called for the state and economic sovereignty of Russia, he rejected Marxism-Leninism as the official state ideology, he called for the removal of Article 6 of the USSR Constitution, for an end to the KGB's right to carry out political searches, for freedom of activity for all social organizations including political parties and independent trade unions, for freedom of conscience, speech and the press. In the economic sphere he advocated the end of the state's economic monopoly, equal rights for state, collective and private property, and for the opportunity for every individual to obtain land to be passed on to their heirs. He raised the issue of ecological problems. He advocated that expenditure on the army and military should be cut and the savings allocated to social needs. The privileges of the *nomenklatura* should be abolished.[32]

On the eve of the election to the Congress of People's Deputies, Elena Bonner published Andrei Sakharov's statement in support of Kovalyov posthumously. The physicist called on Muscovites to support Sergei Kovalyov in the elections.[33] On March 4 Kovalyov won in the first round, in a four-candidate field with a 53.7 per cent victory, in Chertanovsky District No. 58.[34]

The Supreme Soviet Human Rights Committee

At the first session of the Congress of People's Deputies on May 16 1990, a proposal was launched to establish a Human Rights Committee under the Supreme Soviet. The Committee was the brainchild of Nikolai Arzhannikov, an elected deputy who, before standing for election, served as a police officer with the Leningrad militia for fourteen years.[35] While gathering signatures in support of the Committee, which in the end totalled 250 of the 1,059 deputies, Arzhannikov had already earmarked Kovalyov as the Committee's chairman. Fortunately, among the duties of the congress was the election of the RSFSR Supreme Soviet. During the first congress Kovalyov was nominated to the two-chamber legislature, therefore making him eligible for the post.[36]

Soon after Boris Yeltsin was elected Chairman of the Supreme Soviet of the RSFSR on May 29, he approached Kovalyov and asked him to accept the appointment of Chairman of the Human Rights Committee. At first, Kovalyov flatly refused the offer.[37] He had little administrative expertise or experience as an organizer of large groups of people and he did not seem to want, or wanted only ambivalently, the responsibility and commitment that leadership entailed. Already aged sixty when he was offered the post, he had experienced serious health problems in the past fifteen years of his life. He may have feared that he could not competently combine his obligations as deputy with the responsibilities of chairman of a parliamentary committee. While the reasons which finally compelled him to change his mind are unclear,[38] he certainly understood that the appointment would secure him a platform from which to argue publicly for the principles which had shaped his life. Moreover, a committee of the Supreme Soviet had the right of legislative initiatives, to prepare proposals on the improvement of legislation and to examine draft laws submitted to them for suggestions. Both opportunities were clearly too important to pass over.

Kovalyov's decision to accept the position marked the beginning of a complex relationship between the human rights activist and Russia's first democratically elected President. Yeltsin's nomination of Kovalyov was shrewd; proposing Kovalyov, easily one of the most well-known human rights activists, to be chair of a Committee served to prove Yeltsin's commitment to democratic reform and effectively consolidated his position among the progressive intelligentsia. It also served the additional purpose of inspiring international confidence. It was a decision that Yeltsin may have lived to regret on realizing that Kovalyov would live up to his principled commitment to an open, honest and moral government to the point where the President's actions would also be called into question.

At the first session of the RSFSR Supreme Soviet on June 19, 1990, a decree was adopted establishing eighteen committees, one of which was the Human Rights Committee. Within two weeks, the first objection to the Committee was raised in relation to its membership and chairmanship. Kovalyov insisted that he was only prepared to accept those deputies willing to work solely for the Human Rights Committee, which reduced the initial list of 100 deputies to thirty.[39] From the perspective of several deputies, the committee was prejudiced by a staff made up primarily of deputies from Leningrad and Moscow. Further, the fact that Kovalyov had no formal legal training conspired against him and he was criticised as unqualified. One of the dissenting voices was an unidentified deputy who suggested that Oleg Tiunov, a Perm deputy and Dean of Perm State University with a doctorate in law, should be appointed. Failed attempts were made to force a separate vote on the question of the Chairmanship of the Committee.[40]

Arzhannikov, Sergei Sirotkin and Anatoly Kononov rushed to Kovalyov's defence: "I cannot see any other Chairman of this Committee," declared Kononov, "except Sergei Adamovich Kovalyov. He is one of the most decent people who uses international authority to defend the rights of the citizen. He was concerned with this problem when the concept wasn't even officially recognized."[41] The Supreme Soviet was eventually persuaded and voted for the Committee, headed by Kovalyov in its revised form.

In his first address to the Supreme Soviet, Kovalyov acknowledged that the "circle of questions" on the problem of human rights in the Soviet Union was "extremely wide".[42] He emphasized the urgent matters of the day, the widespread problem of refugees and forced migrants, compensation for the victims of political repression, the appalling condition of the penal system and the armed forces, the *propiska* system (registration of residence) and the urgency to establish an office for a Human Rights Commissioner to handle complaints.[43] One might have expected Kovalyov to have used this opportunity to state plainly the Committee's position on social and economic rights. Though he never made a secret of his views, he neither engaged in a discussion of the schism which had divided liberal democracies from communist regimes – the competitive struggle for the supremacy of social/economic over civil/political rights or vice versa – nor did he address the fact that the Committee would commit itself entirely to promoting and advancing civil and political rights. While the power to decide the composition of the Committee still rested with the Congress, he clearly appreciated the vulnerability of its position.

Several years later, however, he firmly repudiated the notion of collective rights that had constituted the theoretical cornerstone of the Soviet regime for some seventy years.[44] When defending the work of the Committee to the State Duma, he declared: "We have singled out as fundamental the rights of the individual. We believe that political and civil rights are the fundamental basis for the realization of individual rights."[45]

This emphasis was a landmark event. Since the Soviet Union had rejected the predominance of civil/political rights in Western countries over economic/social, and further, the division into "individual" and "collective" rights since 1966, Kovalyov's address had been long awaited. This conceptual dichotomy, as reflected in the two separate covenants, The International Covenant on Civil and Political Rights (ICCPR) and the International Covenant on Economic, Social and Cultural Rights (ICESCR) worked out in San Francisco in 1966, had shaped approaches to human rights worldwide. Kovalyov supported the predominance of civil and political rights as the *fundamental* rights of man. Often referred to as "first generation rights", the Western tradition argued that civil (Art. 1–18: ICCPR) and political (Art. 18, 19, 21, 22, 25: ICCPR) rights were fundamental since they guaranteed the individual protection from the state and provided the foundation for individuals to freely pursue and realize their own talents and capabilities. Collective or "second generation rights" were regarded as aspirations whose realization could vary dependent on the economic wealth of states.

Of equal significance was Kovalyov's successful lobbying with the German delegation at the Third Conference on the Human Dimension of the CSCE in Moscow in September 1991. As co-chairman of the Soviet delegation, he was instrumental in securing the following passage in the final document:

> The participating States emphasize that issues relating to human rights, fundamental freedoms, democracy and the rule of law are of international concern, as respect for these rights and freedoms constitutes one of the foundations of the international order. They categorically and irrevocably declare that the commitments undertaken in the field of the human dimension of the CSCE are matters of direct and legitimate concern to all participating States and do not belong exclusively to the internal affairs of the State concerned.[46]

This was groundbreaking. Despite the waning influence of the CSCE after the collapse of the Union, they secured agreement on conditions for sending missions of experts or rapporteurs to participating states without the corresponding consent of the state[47] – achievements the human rights movement could only have dreamt of ten years before.

By 1993, Kovalyov was in a rather different, less cautious role. His addresses to the Supreme Soviet undoubtedly had vast historical significance, but the great majority of deputies were more intent upon preserving the primacy of social and economic rights as a political tool in the post-Soviet period than they were upon enlightening Russian society on the merits of political and civil freedoms. Undeterred by the fact that the Human Rights Committee never aspired to participate in social and economic issues, the communist–nationalist majority routinely deplored the Committee's "negligence" in this field in the hope of weakening its influence and discrediting its agenda in the public eye. Kovalyov attempted to explain the nature of the Committee's work and emphasized that other parliamentary committees existed that were devoted to social and economic issues. But the parliament had no patience for complexities and refinements.[48]

Why wasn't the Committee doing anything to assist the Russian population in their economic turmoil? Why did they work exclusively with former dissidents, victims of political repression and prisoners? These were frequent reproaches.[49] By 1993 the attacks became more vitriolic, culminating in a Supreme Soviet vote on the question: "Has the work of the Human Rights Committee in the defence of social and economic rights been unsatisfactory?"[50] The result: 74 in favour, 38 against and 17 abstained.[51] And if deputies lacked information on the work of the Committee, then the attacks invariably shifted to offensives against Kovalyov personally.[52] He was commonly denounced as a man who could not overcome his "hatred towards the regime", who did not care for the majority of Russians living on the poverty line, and who was engaged in "commercial activity" in violation of parliamentary protocol. Deputy D. Bubyakin proposed that he be dismissed from his position.[53]

The hostility which Kovalyov faced was clear from the very first session. As it turned out, this struggle with the parliament not only became an exceedingly familiar motif in the life of the Committee, but seriously drained Kovalyov and other committee members of enormous amounts of energy.[54] Frustrated by the jostling for power in the parliament, its attempts to simply engage in the task at hand grew increasingly difficult. As Siomina recalled: "There was also the struggle within the parliament, which took away a lot of energy. The first parliament was 85 per cent Communists ... It was understood that the tasks of the parliament were secondary to the struggle over who would dominate, who would dictate the life of the parliament."[55] Part of the reason for this particularly harsh attack in June 1993 can be explained by Kovalyov's support for Yeltsin in the presidential and parliamentary stand-off over Gaidar's reform package. The Sixth Session of the Supreme Soviet in June marked one of the heights of a crisis that had been brewing since December 1992. As a sign of support for Yeltsin and the reform package, Kovalyov joined a reform coalition and Russia's Choice, an all-Russian voters' association that anticipated elections for a new parliament. As the arguments from both sides became dangerously polarized, the reaction of the conservative majority to what were clearly moves to undermine the parliament after the April referendum was not so surprising.

But Kovalyov showed a remarkable ability to push forward in an undemocratic parliament. His political confidence grew as a result, strengthening his ability to reckon with his opponents and win supporters by reasoned and well-informed arguments. Unfortunately his manner of speech – often paternal and irritating – also had the knack of making him enemies, and the most obvious of these was Ruslan Khasbulatov. When the bipolar division emerged in the parliament, relations between the Chairman and the Committee rapidly deteriorated.[56] Khasbulatov clearly did not appreciate Kovalyov's outspoken criticism regarding his chairmanship of the Soviet. Kovalyov clashed with Khasbulatov as early as April 1991. The chairman candidly encouraged deputies to vote in favour of the "Law on the Militia". Contravening the inviolability of the person, the law permitted unsanctioned searches of homes and businesses. Moreover, it sanctioned the use of firearms if a person *suspected* of a crime attempted to flee. In the case that a militia officer killed or wounded a citizen, the incident would not be treated as a criminal case but as an administrative investigation conducted by the militia themselves. Khasbulatov prevented Kovalyov from speaking in the session when he sought to express his objections to the law. A mere 13 deputies voted against it.[57]

The Human Rights Committee appealed to the Committee on Constitutional Supervision of the USSR to examine the law in view of the international treaties and obligations signed by the Soviet Union.[58] When Khasbulatov took the decision to expel Chechen refugees and migrants from hotels around Moscow early in 1992, Kovalyov issued a public protest and supported the call from several deputies for an inquiry.[59] In September 1992 he called for Khasbulatov's dismissal. By the end of the summer of 1993, Khasbulatov had made several attempts to merge the Human Rights Committee with the Committee on Legality and Order. An appendage of the Interior Ministry and the Procurator's Office, the Committee on Legality and Order was responsible for the "Law on the Militia". According to Sirotkin, "the attempt to unite us with a committee chaired by a militia general, with half of the staff composed of agents of the KGB, Ministry of the Interior and the army was clearly a covert way of liquidating the Committee."[60]

Kovalyov and his colleagues were undoubtedly marginalized by the larger power struggle between Khasbulatov and the executive. Moreover, Kovalyov's personal support for Gaidar and the economic policy of "shock therapy" that Khasbulatov openly and aggressively rejected complicated the picture further. Although Kovalyov had complete control over the direction of the Committee's work, the only executive authority he could muster was with Yeltsin personally and certain members of his circle, notably Foreign Minister Andrei Kozyrev, and the success of many of his initiatives was dependent on that fragile balance. As the Russian republic began to move against the remaining USSR power centres, as first witnessed by Yeltsin's takeover of the oil, natural gas, coal, hydroelectric and nuclear industries, his seizure of the USSR Finance Ministry, the Soviet mint and the USSR procuracy, Kovalyov clearly wanted to show his allegiance to Yeltsin in the uncertain period between the August coup and the signing of the Belovezh Agreement of December 8.[61] His relationship with the President was strengthened when Yeltsin showed him the GKChP (State Committee for States of Emergency) arrest list of August 19, devised largely by KGB officers who started their careers in the Fifth Directorate for suppressing dissent. The list contained the names of seventy people, including Kovalyov and former political prisoners Lev Timofeyev, Gleb Yakunin and Sergei Grigoryants.[62] Without a clear separation of powers, however, a resolution of the constitutional vacuum or a decisive party vision, he could not achieve a fraction of the structural reform he aspired to.

While Kovalyov may have had difficulty convincing the Supreme Soviet of his views, he was acutely conscious of the powers of the press to reach the broader public and promote his plan for the education of society on the rights of the individual. His daily life became hectic in the coming years as he became a favourite with the liberal press. It was not unusual for him to do two or three interviews a week in 1990 and 1991 with reporters from papers as diverse as the conservative *Trud* and *Selskaya Zhizn'* to the pro-reform paper *Nezavisimaya Gazeta*.[63] The importance of Kovalyov's role as a public spokesman for human rights cannot be underestimated. He raised the same issues tirelessly to different papers, explaining carefully and simply the extent and breadth of Russia's human rights problems and their origins. His early interviews lack some of the frustration and rhetoric that characterizes his publications in later years. But in trying to build a human rights culture he

Figure 3.1   Sergei Kovalyov with President Yeltsin and President Bush, The
White House, Washington, June 1992

Source: Memorial Archive, Moscow.

understood and always appreciated the power of the press to spread his
message and he undoubtedly favoured a competitively organized, market-
based press rooted within civil society. He played a large role in ensuring
that the press in the Soviet Union was transformed into a robust forum of
public debate. Its liberal minority not only supported his political stance, but
respected his commitment to their profession.

The problems of the Human Rights Committee were not confined to its
relationship with the Supreme Soviet. The final composition of the
Committee was divided into two parts – a full-time staff of seven people and
twelve deputies, the majority of whom were members of Democratic Russia.[64]
Certain members of the staff complained that the work of the Committee was
hampered by the ambition of the deputies who spent too much time on the
tribune and not enough time thinking about either a vision for the Committee
or the colossal task that lay ahead.[65] "This was the first convocation of
deputies," recalled Siomina, "and there was already a lot of ambition. They
had won the elections and this feeling of victory was the main thing, there was
no consciousness of how much work lay ahead, its volume, its contents and
how it might be achieved. No one was thinking about this, except Kovalyov
who knew what he wanted."[66] This created a certain tension between the staff
and the deputies, and the clear lack of resources, time and experience
prevented the Committee from establishing a proficient infrastructure or
formulating a long-term working plan.[67] Most of its work was left to the staff

and to five of the deputies, characterized by Committee member Oleg Orlov as the "workhorses" of the Committee: they comprised Kovalyov, Sergei Sirotkin, Mikhail Arutuynov, Anatoly Kononov and Alexander Kopylev.[68]

To understand the shortcomings of the Committee also requires an appreciation of the way in which the Supreme Soviet had worked under the Soviet Union. Deputies attended twice a year for three days to raise their hands to laws which they had neither drafted nor, in all probability, read. So long as the inner circle of the CPSU determined all state and party policy, the Supreme Soviet remained neither acquainted with genuine parliamentary traditions nor equipped with the appropriate technology necessary to function as a parliament. It was not until 1991 that the Committee received its first computer, which was donated by the Human Rights Project Group. One year later they received a fax machine.[69]

Kovalyov himself did not prove to be an outstanding organizer. There would be so many changes to react to over the course of the next three years that he was constantly divided between the need for long-term planning and a fear that circumstances might swiftly change.[70] Not a capable manager, and unaccustomed to giving orders, he preferred to work with close friends like Boris Zolotukhin and Arseni Roginsky. But Kovalyov also knew what he wanted and, despite the many problems the Committee encountered and his own shortcomings, he realized that they had been given the opportunity to influence the democratic process in the Soviet Union. He rarely raised his head for the next three years.[71]

States of Emergency

The most urgent task for Kovalyov was to facilitate the drafting of a law on States of Emergency. Since a state of emergency permits governments to temporarily withdraw certain individual rights and freedoms in the interests of state security, Kovalyov was anxious to secure a new law. He was keenly aware that individuals were largely defenceless for the duration of a state of emergency and were often threatened by governments who abuse special powers given in good faith, to swiftly enforce a state of emergency with restrictions on civil and political rights out of proportion to the threat.

Kovalyov could easily observe what was going on around him and suspected that the vulnerable balance of power near the end of Gorbachev's rule might precipitate such an action. The frequency in which states of emergency were called into being across the Soviet Union was testimony to that concern. In 1990 emergency situations were in force in a number of areas – three in Azerbaidzhan, two in Armenia and Georgia and one each in Tadzhikistan, Uzbekistan, Kirgizia and Moldavia.[72] Kovalyov also recognized that once they had been effected they were often difficult to bring to an end.[73] Azerbaidzhan and Tadzhikistan had been under a state of emergency for over a year.

With his increased understanding of Western and international human rights law, Kovalyov realized that human rights violations occurring during states of emergency had become a problem of international concern. Three of the major treaties, the International Covenant on Civil and Political Rights (ICCPR), the European Convention on Human Rights and the Four Geneva Conventions of 1949 in their Common Article 3 sought to set reasonable standards of government behaviour by stipulating those rights which remained fundamental during a state of emergency.[74] Divided into derogable and non-derogable rights, there is a general consensus in these treaties on at least two rights that are non-derogable during a state of emergency. These are the right to protection against the arbitrary deprivation of life and against the subjection of individuals to torture or to cruel, inhumane or degrading treatment.[75] The ICCPR which Kovalyov used as inspiration for the drafting of the law adds "that the right to freedom of thought, conscience and religion ... is also non-derogable."[76] Frequent rights subject to derogation during a state of emergency include the liberty and security of person, liberty of movement, protection of privacy, freedom of expression and opinion and the right of peaceful assembly.[77] Surveying the specific problems, the international community also recognized that a state of emergency often threatened the independence of the judiciary, often leading to the purging of judges or the establishment of separate courts of justice.[78] The threat of administrative detention without charge and without intention to place the detainee on trial was also a major concern.[79]

Kovalyov began work on the draft law some time in 1989 under the auspices of the Human Rights Project Group (HRPG). He recognized that the absence of a model law on states of emergency and the divergences in international treaties were testimony to the problems legislators encountered when formulating a list of non-derogable rights, procedural and limitation clauses while trying to take account of the historical experience of individual countries. His first concern was the implementation of international standards into the domestic laws of the Soviet Union. This was not only because of the weakness of treaty-based and other international monitoring systems, but also because he appreciated how important it was for the Soviet Union to actively support the standards set by the international community as a step to resolving its own domestic problems and building trust abroad. He worked together with Lavut, Zolotukhin, Professor Ernest Ametistov, Ernest Orlovsky and Vladimir Golytsin. For guidance they relied upon the International Covenant on Civil and Political Rights and the Law on States of Emergency of the Federal Republic of Germany, the drafting of which had taken twelve years to satisfy the German parliament.[80] While drafting their law, Kovalyov also prepared and distributed a 48-page report entitled *With Regard to Legislation Governing States of Emergency* to Supreme Soviet deputies. This document included a copy of the Committee's own draft law, excerpts from Nicole Questiaux's 1982 United Nations study on states of siege or emergency, earlier Soviet decrees on the subject and the relevant provisions of French, West German, US, Spanish and Greek laws.[81]

On April 3, 1990, a month after Kovalyov's election to the Congress, a law was passed at Gorbachev's initiative by the Supreme Soviet "On Governing States of Emergency".[82] There were two distinct features of the Soviet law. One overriding characteristic was the standard vagueness that accompanied many Soviet laws. On fundamental questions such as the basis on which a state of emergency could be introduced, the law stated rather obliquely in Article 1 that "large-scale disturbances" and "national disasters, epidemics, industrial accidents or epizootics" could serve as the basis to introduce a state of emergency.[83] No time frame was stipulated for the duration of the state of emergency, which was defined simply as a "temporary measure".[84] According to Article 11 troops could be introduced in "exceptional cases", with no other criteria given to regulate the action of troops in accordance with the severity of the situation.[85] The second dangerous aspect was the prerogatives conferred on the President, providing for direct Presidential rule with powers to suspend local government and replace it with his own executive organ or appointed representative.[86] House arrest was possible without stated reason.[87]

The vagueness of the Soviet law probably increased Kovalyov's resolve to pass his version, which was both comprehensive and detailed. His first genuine opportunity to promote his draft came with his appointment to the Human Rights Committee. On February 1, 1991, a decree was passed "On the Political Situation in the RSFSR", point 7 of which authorized the drafting of a law on States of Emergency. Kovalyov understood the importance of defining the grounds on which a state of emergency could be introduced. He divided the grounds into two categories. In the first instance, according to Article 4 of his draft, a state of emergency could only be introduced if there was "a real, extreme and unavoidable threat to the safety of the citizen or the constitutional system of the republic, the elimination of which is impossible without the introduction of a state of emergency". The preconditions for introducing a state of emergency were "attempts to forcibly change the constitutional order", "massive disorder", "inter-ethnic conflict", the "blockade of separate regions", or a "threat to the life and security of the citizen or to the normal functioning of state institutions".[88] The second grouping, as outlined in Article 4, was linked to "natural disasters", "epidemics, epizootics" and "large-scale industrial accidents which threaten the health and life of the population and which necessitate rescue and restoration operations".[89]

The most important difference between Kovalyov's and the Soviet draft was the issue of parliamentary control.[90] According to the Committee's draft, a state of emergency could only be introduced by a decree of the President of the Russian Federation, or a decree of the Presidium of the Supreme Soviet RSFSR, and would have to be passed over to the Supreme Soviet for approval. The Supreme Soviet had the right to amend the decree, but had to approve or reject the introduction of a state of emergency within twenty-four hours.[91] A state of emergency introduced on the entire territory of the RSFSR could not last for longer than thirty days and a new decree had to be approved if the President or Presidium sought to prolong the state of emergency.[92] The law emphasized that such a decree had to explain the circumstances serving as the basis for introducing a state of emergency in accordance with Articles 3 and 4. It had to include a list detailing the terms of the emergency measures and an "exhaustive" list of the temporary limitations on the rights and freedoms of the citizen. The planned duration of the state of emergency, the state organs responsible for the implementation of the measures to resolve the emergency situation and the exact terms under which they operate, also had to be outlined.[93] In one of several references to the rights of the public, the law also stipulated in Article 12 that the decree had to reach the population through the press no less than six hours before the decree went into force.[94] According to Article 41, the General Secretary of the United Nations had to be notified within three days, with an accompanying list of the rights withheld under the state of emergency as stipulated by the ICCPR.[95]

Kovalyov and the other authors of the draft recognized the importance of ensuring that the legislature continued to function during an emergency situation. The draft stipulated that the legislature maintain all controlling functions and oversee the implementation of the state of emergency. By dividing the preconditions of a state of emergency into two groupings, they were able to avoid a degree of arbitrariness by detailing the measures that were acceptable to resolve the situation under either Part A or Part B of Article 4.[96] They expressed concern that, under the Soviet law, the measures to resolve a state of emergency could be implemented in one of only two ways: either by direct Presidential rule or by the establishment of a commanding officer.

Kovalyov and the Human Rights Committee found this option unacceptable. In the new draft, it stipulated three degrees of government control, dependent on the intensity of the threat.[97] The first and milder form, as outlined in Article 16, was that all local branches of executive power would be maintained, but would be directly answerable either to the President, to his appointed representative, or to the Presidium of the Supreme Soviet.[98] The second measure, in Article 17, provided for the establishment of a coordinating committee which was to assume part of the powers of the local executive organs.[99] The third form was that the Supreme Soviet of the Russian Federation could give permission for the Ministry of Internal Affairs of the RSFSR, the Chairman of the State Committee on Defence and Security and the Committee on State Security of the RSFSR to organize an operations staff and a commanding officer on the territory of the state of emergency.[100] The third variant was only applicable in the case of attendant violence, massive disorder or a threat to the constitutional order.[101] An interesting addition to Article 21 was that the names of military commanders and staff taking immediate part in the implementation of a state of emergency were to be kept in the archives of the Committee of the Council of Ministers RSFSR on emergency situations.[102]

The two groupings also allowed the authors of the draft to stipulate which rights could be subject to derogation. Under a threat to the "constitutional order" (Part A), Article 23 outlined the derogable rights – which included: a curfew; restrictions on the freedom of the press, on publishing, and on photocopying machines; the suspension of political parties, public organizations, mass movements "standing in the way of the normalization of the situation"; document-checks; and the limitation or prohibition of the sale of weapons. Article 24 outlined the conditions of Part B under a "natural disaster": the temporary evacuation of citizens where rescue operations were taking place, a system to distribute food products and items of the first necessity, the establishment of a quarantine, the mobilization of government bodies, institutes and organizations to assist in rescue operations.

The authors of the draft stressed that there were to be no changes to the court system. According to Article 34, the establishment of separate courts of justice was prohibited and there were to be no expedient measures taken that violated the criminal code.[103] In the case of administrative detention, a person could be held for up to thirty days. Persons without documents could be detained for up to three days. Changes to the constitution were forbidden, as were the holding of elections and referendums.[104] This included the provision made under the ICCPR that no person or group was to be discriminated against on the "basis of race, nationality, sex, language, religion, political convictions or social origin".[105] They sought also to observe the sovereign rights of the republics by stipulating that each republic had the right to declare a state of emergency under the condition that it be approved by that republic's Presidium of the Supreme Soviet. The exception to this was when a republic was threatened with massive violence and disorder endangering individual lives: at such times a state of emergency may be introduced quickly and without forewarning.[106]

Kovalyov cannot be credited with the work on the final stages of the law. The final draft was completed by the Committee's lawyer, Sergei Sirotkin, with advice and comments from the Committee on Legislation, the Committee on Security and the Committee on Freedom of Conscience. The law was finally presented to parliament on May 7, 1991, and passed in the first reading on the condition that minor amendments proposed by the Committee on Legislation be included by the second reading. The minor amendments were introduced and it passed on May 17, 1991, and was directly made law.[107]

Kovalyov was no doubt satisfied that the Committee's first law was passed in accordance with international human rights legislation and international treaties. It set a good example. Despite the fact that his draft was more exhaustive than its Soviet predecessor, the May 1991 law would be

Figure 3.2   Sergei Kovalyov with Bogdan Kl'emchak. Camp Zone 35, Perm
Oblast, 1990

forced to experience all the vicissitudes of Russia's fledging democracy.
Indeed controversy around the law would arise at the two most contentious
moments of Kovalyov's career: October 1993, and December 1994. Abused
and even ignored in the process, it would be violated by the Mayor of
Moscow when he expelled individuals of Caucasian origin from the capital,
and by President Yeltsin when he ordered the storming of the breakaway
republic of Chechnya.

The penal system

Hardly less important to Kovalyov was the reform of Russia's penal system.
During his tenure as Chairman of the Human Rights Committee, he took
every opportunity to visit prisons and camps across Russia and the United
States to interview prisoners and investigate living conditions.[108] Conscious
of the physical and psychological ordeal of imprisonment, part of his motivation can be traced to his personal experience as a political prisoner. His
concern, however, had deeper roots in the history of Russia's notorious
treatment of its prisoners and the marginalization of penal reform in
government budget and policy.

Gorbachev's government acknowledged the need to improve penal conditions with the 1986 amendments to the *Corrective Labour Code*, by markedly extending prisoner privileges.[109] The amnesties of prisoners of conscience and political prisoners in 1987 and 1988 also demonstrated its commitment to reform. Yet while the amnesties marked an important political decision in the new regime, they did little to improve the penal conditions in the more than one thousand facilities across the Soviet Union. Senior Procurator Tabakova admitted in June of 1990: "I am familiar with the penal systems in many countries. And I have come to the conclusion that ours is the hardest. Up to this day GULAG traditions are still alive and well in prison camps in certain regions of the country, where prisoners are totally dependent on the administration."[110] In 1990 there were between 680,000 and 760,000 prisoners in the Soviet penal system, with an additional 200,000 in pre-trial detention, 10,000 sentenced prisoners awaiting disposition of appeals, and 160,000 people involuntarily confined in alcohol and drug treatment colonies.[111] The rapid deterioration of the USSR's economy from 1985 had a serious effect on the food supply to camps and colonies and witnessed the closure of many factories, removing what limited opportunities prisoners had to earn a small wage.

Kovalyov decided to launch his reform initiative with an investigation of several camps and prisons.[112] Although familiar with camp life in the past, he needed to assess the changes since *perestroika* to determine the crucial problems that could be addressed on a minimal budget and in a predominantly hostile parliament. His first trip to Russia's Corrective Labor Institutions (*upravlenie ispravitelno-trudovie uchrezhdenii*)[113] in his capacity as Chairman of the Human Rights Committee took place between August 6–12, 1990. He was accompanied by deputies A. Kononov and Y. Khrulev and two consultants, V. Parfenov and A. Roginsky. They headed some 1,000 kilometers east of Moscow to Kazan, the capital of the former Tatar Autonomous Soviet Socialist Republic. There they visited Kazan prison, the juvenile colony and detention cells. Further east along the Volga river to Chistopol prison, the last address of Kovalyov's seven-year sentence. He met with former Camp 36 inmate, Mikhail Kazachkov still serving a fifteen-year sentence for "treason," "contraband" and "currency speculation."[114] From there they went north east to the notorious Camp Perm Complex in the Ural Mountains where they visited Perm Zone 35 and the Perm juvenile colony.[115] In late 1990, twenty political prisons still languished in Zone 35[116] (Figure 3.2).

It must have seemed a strange turn of fate for Kovalyov to return to Camp 36. In a literary Memoir, entitled *Art and the Gulag*, he recalled:

> At a distance of fifteen years it was hard to recognize anything. Some things I had forgotten (although at the time I thought one couldn't even obliterate them with acid) and others had changed terribly. Abandoned in 1987, the Zone had fallen apart and gone to seed: some barracks had disappeared, others were quite dilapidated, their window panes broken,

a strip of no mans land overgrown with weeds, the guard towers falling down. In some places, barbed wire hung loose, in others it had disappeared altogether.[117]

At each destination, the sub-committee arranged meetings with the camp administration and representatives of the Department of Internal Affairs. At both the Perm Camp Complex and Chistopol prison Kovalyov met with some of his former captors whose attitude to him now appeared to be one of "fear and servility". "They all met us standing to attention," he remembered. "Someone asked me … Don't you want revenge?"[118]

It seems likely that Kovalyov chose Chistopol prison because he could easily assess the changes. While permitted to visit cells at random, he noted that prisoners had more freedom to personalize their cells with pictures torn from journals and magazines, with jars of flowers, and in some cases with small electric stoves. They were allowed tools to carve wooden boxes. Plywood screens had been installed in front of the toilets for privacy. But the improvements were superficial. The cells remained overcrowded. Solitary confinement at Kazan and Perm were congested, with "dull lighting, shocking food and filth".[119] Prisoners with tuberculosis were confined to *shizo* and their injections intravenously administered to them through a hole in the door. The arbitrariness with which prisoners were sent to solitary confinement remained a prominent feature of prison life.[120]

It was the complete absence of any mechanism to regulate the behaviour of camp staff towards prisoners that exasperated Kovalyov. The enthusiasm he later expressed for the American penal system was perhaps slightly naive, but he was drawn to the seemingly uninhibited relationship between staff and prisoners. "There was no servility, insincerity or mutual animosity," he claimed, "and on the whole the prisoners understand that the wardens are simply trying to make a living."[121] He could not help but be astounded that American prisoners concerned about cholesterol levels had the right to insist on margarine over butter. His enthusiasm is understandable when he depicts his own experiences in the camps:

You may violate the dress code everyday and nobody will ever notice it, until they want to put you in *shizo*. In the sleeping quarters in winter it is cold … The old guys used to get into bed with their *valenki* on (felt boots). Of course, anyone who was a little younger undressed according to the regulations. But we put everything that was warm over the top of us. A duty officer would enter with a deputy. He would say to a prisoner:

"Why are you violating internal regulations?"

"Because it is cold, Citizen Major."

"Quick, take your jacket to the cloakroom."

Turning to the deputy, the Duty Officer would say "Write a report, refusal to fulfill orders." And all around you there are thirty other people still lying there with their jackets covering them. He doesn't even look at the rest ... The poor fellow is carted off to *shizo*. Formally this is all within the limits of the law ... if you request the law, they will show you the regulations on beds. But in essence, it is arbitrariness and mockery. I am sure this is done specifically in order that a prisoner feels a humiliating dependence, not on the law or the state, but on the mood of a specific person.[122]

The *zek* culture emerged as a result of the appalling conditions in the camps.[123] The term materialized to define the customs fostered by prisoners to survive in their environment. Camp staff were also driven by the need to supplement their wages and better their own miserable existence in the isolated camps, and they keenly participated. But the prisoners were often driven by motives of survival or the prospect of luxuries such as tea and cigarettes. Kovalyov wondered if, after decades of mutual suspicion and hostility, prisoners and staff could ever establish humane working relations.[124] The first step to achieve this was to eliminate the conditions which forced prisoners to rely on these activities.

Kovalyov appointed Oleg Orlov to head a sub-committee on penal reform. On his return from Washington in early September 1991, where he served as Yeltsin's envoy to the American congress on the outcome of the August coup, he formed a small sub-committee to draft amendments to the *Corrective Labour Code*. This group consisted of Kovalyov, Oleg Orlov, current director of Memorial's Human Rights Centre, and Arseni Roginsky, historian with Memorial. Over the course of the next six months, they met regularly in the evenings at Memorial's Human Rights Research Centre to work on the draft.[125]

Kovalyov took his second trip to the camps in December 1991 with representatives of the Ministry of Internal Affairs. Although it was a working trip, it was also organized in response to a massive strike conducted by prisoners in November. As early as July 1989, the Peschanka District Colony in the Ukraine conducted a strike over living and working conditions. This was followed by further strikes at the Rzhevskoi colony in the Kalinin *oblast*, the Tselinograd Special Regime Colony and, in October 1991, an uprising in the Krasnoiarsk Strict Regime Colony over staff abuse and inhumane conditions in the punishment cells.[126]

The controversy around the November 1991 strike, however, was fuelled by Valery Abramkin. A chemical engineer by education, Abramkin (1947–) was editor of the underground *samizdat* publication *Poiski*. He was in labour camp from 1979 to 1985, and later headed the Public Centre to Aid the Humanisation of the Penitentiary System and is one of the most committed and energetic advocates of penal reform in Russia. On October 29, Abramkin called on prisoners across Russia to strike for two hours on November 13 to protest against the inhumane conditions of their detention. He succeeded in convincing members of the Moscow Helsinki Group to appeal to prisoners to outline their demands and issue a public statement to the Ministry of Internal Affairs and the Supreme Soviet RSFSR.[127] Their key demand was to bring Russian legislation and penal conditions into line with the Convention Against Torture and Other Cruel, Inhumane or Degrading Treatment or Punishment which came into force in the Soviet Union on June 26, 1987. The Kargopolskii Corrective Labour Institution, located 300 kilometres south of the sea port Arkhangelsk, included among its demands: (i) to remove all camp medical services from under the direct control of the Ministry of Internal Affairs; (ii) to abolish all restrictions on correspondence, printed matter and parcels; (iii) to conduct an investigation into the dietary norms of prisoners and staff. At the same time the staff at Kargopolskii demanded improved working conditions and an increase in their pay. Both prisoners and staff demanded that the 50 per cent tax taken by the Ministry of Internal Affairs from the prisoners, ostensibly to pay for their upkeep, be abolished.[128] Over 80 per cent of the prison and camp populations across Russia was estimated to have taken part in the strike.

Kovalyov denounced Abramkin's action as a "provocation".[129] This position seems to have been driven more by principle than by concern for the impression he might convey as Chairman of the Human Rights Committee. In contrast to his colleagues at the Moscow Helsinki Group, of which he was still an active member, Kovalyov could not support Abramkin's decision. He expressed concern for several reasons. Such a protest could have provoked the camp administration and resulted in a violent conflict between staff and prisoners, a point which was later cruelly validated. He was worried that the Human Rights Committee had only just established the sub-committee to begin drafting the amendments to the *Corrective Labour Code* on penal reform. He was anxious for the fate of the amendments. "This was the perfect 'trump card' for deputies of communist persuasion," argued Orlov. "Why give them more rights when you can't even discipline them now? And Abramkin had broken one of the unspoken rules between former prisoners and prisoners still inside. A free person never has the right to suggest, advise or provoke a protest. These rights are reserved for those on the inside."[130]

Regardless of Kovalyov's criticisms, Abramkin's decision actually drew massive media attention to the problem of human rights violations in Russia's penal system. It may also have motivated the Duma to act more urgently on the legislation which was passed almost eight months to the day after the strike. Indeed Zolotukhin and Kovalyov stressed that the amendments were essential if they wanted to calm the situation in the camps.[131] Abramkin sent the sub-committee a proposal outlining his suggestions for changes to the penal system. The proposal provided a good starting point for the group.

Abramkin advocated the fundamental restructuring of the prison system, calling for the construction of new prisons, training centres for personnel and the replacement of old staff. While Kovalyov and his colleagues entirely supported Abramkin's proposals, they did not know how they could possibly realize them. The difficulty was that they could not utterly transform the penal system without massive financial support from the government budget or the support of the Supreme Soviet. They decided instead to amend the existing legislation, and by doing so they attempted to solve two major problems. Their first aim was to improve the fundamental conditions for prisoners and establish incentives. Their second aim was to eliminate, as far as possible, the arbitrary exercise of power by the camp administration by removing certain powers from their jurisdiction.[132] The Ministry of Internal Affairs, however, would remember the strikes of 1991 and the attempts to remove its powers. It would retaliate in its own way.

Family and social ties

The sub-committee recognized that one of the most important amendments was to broaden the guidelines for contact between prisoners and their family and friends. To alleviate the feeling of complete isolation that accompanies imprisonment, Kovalyov and the authors insisted in Article 26 that prisoners in general regime colonies could receive visits six times a year of up to four hours without the presence of a prison warden. They could also receive six long visits per year of up to three days in which prisoners could live with their family in separate quarters, either inside or outside the colony. In order to secure a meeting outside the colony, prisoners would have to appeal to the camp administration and procurator for permission.[133] Articles 63 to 70 stated that, for prisoners in strengthened regime colonies, visits were to be four short and three long stays. In the strict regime colonies for recidivists and the special regime colonies for dangerous recidivists, they were to receive three short visits and two long visits. Those confined to prisons were to be allowed three short and one long visit and those in strengthened prison regimes, one short visit. Prisoners were given the right to change the dates of either their short or their long visits.[134] The camp administration could not reduce the number of meetings with family as a form of punishment.

The sub-committee introduced in Article 26 the right of every prisoner to four telephone conversations a year of up to fifteen minutes when the technical means were available (except for those prisoners confined to *shizo*).[135] The sub-committee insisted that every prisoner be given twelve days of annual leave, and particularly well-behaved prisoners could appeal to take their holidays with their family, outside the colony. To apply for this leave they had to have served over half their term.[136]

Correspondence

In keeping with their aim of minimizing the isolation experienced by prisoners, the sub-committee abolished the limitations on correspondence. According to Article 30, prisoners could receive and send as many letters and telegrams as they wished with no restrictions on the number of pages. The delivery of letters to prisoners and the sending of them by the administration had to be completed no more than three days from the day of receiving the letter. Telegrams had to be delivered immediately.[137] Conscious of the importance of food parcels as supplements to an insufficient diet, the sub-committee significantly increased in Article 28 the number of parcels allowed by each prisoner, with the incentive of further packages dependent on behaviour. The number per year for prisoners in general and strengthened regime colonies doubled from three to six packages (*peredach, banderol*). For good behaviour the sub-committee increased this number to twelve packages. In the special regime colonies for recidivists and dangerous recidivists they were to have the right to four packages, and for good behaviour, twelve. They removed the camp administration's right to impose restrictions on the weight of packages. This responsibility was regulated by the postal office and could not exceed the maximum weight stipulated by postal rules.[138] Prisoners were no longer required to have served one-third of their term before receiving a parcel. The sub-committee introduced the right to have any literature, and to subscribe to magazines and newspapers, although a prisoner would not be allowed more than ten books or journals at a time. Literature acquired by post was not included as part of the package allowance. The administration retained the right to read correspondence and inspect parcels. Correspondence between prisoners, unless family, was allowed only with the permission of the administration.[139] Again, the number of parcels allocated to each prisoner could not be restricted as a form of punishment. Those confined to *shizo* or *pkt* could receive their parcels at the end of their confinement.

Employment

The penal reform sub-committee maintained the tradition that all prisoners were obliged to work. Given the general conditions in the penal camps, its decision to preserve this tradition suggests that it understood the importance of a wage for the health and well-being of prisoners. Yet it insisted in Article 39 that the monthly wage could not be lower than the minimum wage established by law.[140] Incentives were given in Article 51 for workers who exceeded their quota, such as permission to receive an additional package, an extra visit, permission to spend extra money, early release, transfer to a more lenient institution, extended walks of up to two hours in the general regime colonies and one hour in the strengthened regimes.[141] Prisoners could do voluntary construction work on their own buildings, but they were not allowed to work on buildings which accommodated the camp administration. With the money earned in the colonies, prisoners were free to purchase food products from the colony store, pay for health care and medicines, negotiate with insurance agencies and conduct monetary transfers.[142] The administration could not deprive prisoners of the right to buy food, products, clothes or cigarettes, even if they had violated a regulation.

In early 1992, Kovalyov pointed out to Yeltsin that they urgently needed to amend the legislation on prisoner wages. His letter resulted in the presidential decree: "On changes to the RSFSR system of payment of work conducted by prisoners and by persons detained in medical and rehabilitation clinics" which abolished the 50 per cent reduction in wages, as the prisoners at Kargopolskii had demanded during their strike. Taken from the prisoners under the pretext that it was used for their upkeep, 50 per cent clearly exceeded what the Ministry of Internal Affairs was spending on each prisoner.[143] The corresponding amendments were later introduced into the code.[144]

The penal reform sub-committee insisted that the time prisoners spent working in the camps be accrued as part of their work experience. Since the number of working years determines salary in Russia and is essential when computing pensions, the sub-committee contended that prisoners were entitled to the same benefits as other free persons.[145]

Special privilege prisoners

It was important to Kovalyov and his colleagues that pregnant women, women with children under three living in penal colonies, invalids of Categories I and II, men over sixty, women over fifty-five, sick prisoners and prisoners confined to quarantine enjoy certain privileges. The first as stipulated in Article 47 was that the above categories were not obliged to work.[146] Under the 1986 code, invalids of Categories I and II worked a forty-two hour week. Tuberculosis patients worked at least four hours per day. Women returned to work directly after feeding their child.[147] With the 1992 amendments, the above categories were entitled to free food, boots, clothes and bed linen, and could receive money by transfer from family or friends. They could work if they chose. Seriously ill prisoners, pregnant women, women with children and invalids of Categories I and II, irrespective of their place of confinement, were allowed twelve packages a year.[148]

According to Article 57, on appeal to court, pregnant women or women with children under three convicted for a term of less than five years could postpone their sentence until they had given birth or their child has reached three years of age. A child could stay with its mother on the colony up until the age of three and then leave with the mother's permission to live with relatives, an appointed guardian or at a children's home. If the mother's sentence was due to end before the child turned four, she could appeal to the administration to keep her child on the colony until the end of her sentence.[149] During their annual twelve-day holiday, women prisoners could take their children for short visits to their family.

The camp administration in penal camps was prohibited from punishing pregnant women, women with children and invalids of Category I with terms in *shizo* or *pkt*. In general or strong regime prisons, the above categories could not be confined to *kartser*.[150]

Prisoner redress

While stressing the significance of improving general living and working conditions for prisoners, it was essential to the sub-committee that prisoners be able to defend their own rights. According to Article 10, they stressed that all prisoners had to be informed of their rights and obligations, the conditions of work and rest stipulated by the law. They were guaranteed access to legislative acts that pertained to criminal justice and the internal regulations of the Corrective Labour Institutions.[151]

Moreover, any suggestions, statements or complaints written by prisoners and addressed to a procurator, court or government organ could not be examined by the administration and had to be forwarded within twenty-four hours.[152] In case of a threat to the prisoner's life, his health or a criminal action against him/her, the prisoner had the right to request a transfer to another location. The administration was obliged to respond to this request or to eliminate the threat within the camp or prison. In the event that the request was denied, the administration had to state the reasons for the refusal.[153] The sub-committee felt that, even if the request was denied, the administration could then be held accountable for any subsequent events. "We were concerned," said Orlov, "that there had been numerous cases of placing prisoners in cells where they were subject to beatings and rape, either by prisoners or camp staff, in order to extract testimony."[154] The amendment was seen as one step in curbing the ability of the administration to pressure prisoners.[155]

Punishment

The changes relating to modes of punishment made by the sub-committee were directed at the articles they considered especially cruel and which sought to undermine a prisoner's human dignity and health. Its first move was to prohibit the use of the straitjacket, an instrument it believed was rarely used for its original purpose of controlling violence, but rather as an instrument of torture.[156]

The sub-committee outlined a series of punishments in the event that a prisoner violated internal regulations, from the mildest to the most severe, not unlike those established in the 1986 law. Several examples of the milder forms included an informal warning or the summoning of a prisoner by the camp administration for a formal reprimand which may entail outside cleaning duties except of the staff residence or offices of the administration. Prisoners could also be deprived of visits to the camp cinema, concerts or participation in sporting activities. Privileges previously conferred to prisoners for exceeding work norms or good behaviour, as stipulated in articles 62–5, 69, 75 and 76, could be revoked. The most severe punishment was placement of prisoners in punishment cells, transfer to a closed prison, or to a more severe regime facility.[157]

The system of confining individuals to punishment cells was well known in Soviet history. There were three basic types of cells used for punishment.

- *Shizo*[158] (a punishment cell) was the hardest: the size of the cell could vary between 6ft x 7ft and 10ft x 11ft and the maximum confinement was for a period of fifteen days. Most had small windows that let in very little light and air, and some had no windows at all. Beds were wooden or metal pallets without any kind of mattress or bedding. Prisoners could not wear coats or warm outer clothing, even in winter. Before the amendments, prisoners confined to *shizo* could not use their exercise time. If a visit was scheduled during that time they would lose it.[159]
- *Pkt*[160] (internal camp prison) was for longer-term punishment up to a maximum period of six months. In a special regime colony, it could be up to one year. Prisoners usually worked in an isolated room. They were allowed to smoke, read and take exercise. Usually the cells had better lighting and conditions than *shizo*. Mattresses were provided.[161]
- *Dizo*[162] (a disciplinary cell) combined aspects of *pkt* and *shizo* for short-term punishment of up to fifteen days. Prisoners could work, exercise and keep personal items in the cells. Mattresses were provided.[163] Punishment in cells was often accompanied by food rations.[164]

All three forms of punishment continued to exist under the Russian penal system. The sub-committee stipulated that, in all three forms, each prisoner was entitled to an individual sleeping place with a mattress and sleeping linen. In *shizo*, a prisoner could request from the warden that extra clothing be brought to the cell when needed. Every prisoner was entitled to a walk of up to thirty minutes.[165] To avoid the use of consecutive sentences and the abuse of cell punishment, the sub-committee specified the maximum period allowed to detain prisoners during the course of one year. The maximum term in *dizo* could not exceed forty days, in *shizo*, sixty days and in *pkt*, six months.[166] Prisoners in general, strengthened or strict regime colonies could be transferred to *pkt*; prisoners in special regime camps for dangerous recidivists could be confined to a cell for up to a year; individuals in prisons could be transferred to a strict regime colony for recidivists for a period of two to six months. Prisoners living in normal living quarters in special regime colonies for dangerous recidivists could be transferred to *pkt* in that camp.[167]

The new amendments stipulated that prisoners confined to *pkt*, *shizo* or *dizo* were prohibited meetings (although the meeting could be rescheduled), the right to acquire food products and items of the first necessity, to receive packages (which would be retained and given to them on completion of the term) or to use board games.

Freedom of conscience

Kovalyov and his colleagues understood the importance of guaranteeing freedom of conscience and religion. In Article 53, the legislation provided for believers to worship and to practise any religion while in the colony or prison. Prisoners could conduct religious ceremonies, receive literature and invite others to participate, except persons confined to *shizo, pkt* or *dizo*. Men were no longer forced to shave their heads and could wear a beard or a moustache. The sub-committee felt it was important for the psychological well-being of women to be allowed to dress as they wished.

The consequences

The sub-committee knew well enough that its amendments were not the final solution to the problem. More than a third of the complaints received by the Supreme Soviet Human Rights Committee between June 1990 and October 1993 concerned conditions or incidents in the colonies and prisons. In the Committee's report on the Observance of the Rights of Man and the Citizen in the Russian Federation for 1993, they noted that they were troubled by a number of ongoing problems related to employment and medical facilities. The decline in Russia's general economy witnessed a breakdown in the strong association between the colonies and the industrial ministries. The conditions for a growing number of prisoners deteriorated as the total figure of unemployed reached 124,900 in 1994. Left without the wages to purchase food and basic necessities, to provide assistance to their families, or the opportunity to pay for medical services and vacations, prisoners had little opportunity to improve their general living conditions or to take advantage of the amendments proposed by the sub-committee. A worsening of living conditions invariably led to a deterioration in the health of prisoners and the medical facilities on the colonies remained short of supplies, equipment and competent staff. The unsanitary conditions facilitated the spread of diseases like tuberculosis. In 1994 there were 22,224 tubercular prisoners, and the failure to implement the Anti-Tuberculosis programme in 1992–95 meant that thousands of people infected with the disease were kept in *shizo* or isolation zones in ordinary colonies and not in special TB colonies. Many sick people were released each year still infected with the disease.[168]

The amendments of the sub-committee removed some of the powers of the camp administration to punish and pressurize prisoners. Even if they failed to secure regulation on the use of force, the right of the prisoner to complain or to request a transfer might at least force camp staff to contemplate the consequences of their actions. On the basis of prisoner complaints and petitions, the procurator's office found 2,537 employees of investigation jails and corrective labour facilities in 1994 guilty of violating the law and committing various abuses.[169] The majority were disciplined, and 146 were dismissed from the Interior Ministry and 92 were handed over to the courts. Any headway in this area, however, was interrupted when all the criminal cases opened to investigate prisoner complaints concerning the unlawful use of force were halted by the procuracies in late 1994.[170]

The sub-committee had not anticipated that the passing of its amendments would be accompanied by the deployment of *Spetsnaz* forces (special troops) to "discipline" prisoners.[171] The use of *Spetsnaz* troops in the colonies was an alarming development. Orlov attributed the deployment of the troops to their amendments. He argued that, since the sub-committee significantly curtailed the powers of the administration to punish prisoners, they sought other external means of intimidation. "Complete with black masks, the troops were sent in under such pretences as a 'narcotics inspection'," said Orlov, "and have hit and beaten prisoners half to death."[172] This was particularly acute in 1994 in Novokuznets investigation prison, when approximately 100 prisoners slashed their wrists in a mass suicide attempt. An investigation conducted by the Presidential Human Rights Commission under Kovalyov linked the vicious incident to the fierce beating of detainees by a *Spetsnaz* division.[173] By the time of their second report, for 1994–95, the Committee warned that the situation had seriously deteriorated. The recommendations outlined in the 1993 report had not been considered by the relevant departments and ministries and their calls for an independent, civilian review board to monitor human rights in the penal system were ignored. It was the same *Spetsnaz* troops sent into the prisons that were later deployed against the seperatist movement in Chechnya.[174]

The banning of the Communist Party[175]

On July 28, 1992, one month after the successful passage of the legislation on penal reform, Kovalyov appeared as a witness during the Constitutional Court proceedings on the Soviet and RSFSR Communist Parties. President Yeltsin accused the Communist Party of acting as an accomplice in the August 1991 Putsch. He banned the Communist Party with three successive decrees dated August 23, August 25 and November 6, 1991. These decrees suspended the activity of the RSFSR Communist Party, froze the assets of the Russian and USSR Communist Parties, banned these parties from operating on RSFSR territory and seized their assets.[176] In mid-November 1991, thirty-six deputies, the majority of whom were members of the Communists of Russia fraction, petitioned the Constitutional Court to overrule the decrees which, they argued, contradicted the right to political pluralism and the right to property.[177]

In response to the appeal, several liberal deputies, including Kovalyov, Boris Zolotukhin, Viktor Sheinis and Oleg Rumyantsev issued a counterclaim. The liberals argued that, since Article 6 on the leading role of the Communist Party had been revoked in March 1990, Yeltsin's decrees were in accordance with the Constitution. The President, they asserted, had the right to outlaw a party that ruled by force.[178] They also appealed to the court to rule on the very constitutionality of the Soviet and RSFSR Communist Parties since they seized power during the October 1917 Revolution.[179] The Constitutional Court decided to combine the two petitions into one case.[180]

The liberals founded their case on the argument that the "CPSU acted as a substitute for the legislative, executive and judicial branches". It argued that the CP was not a political party, but a structure that absorbed the state within itself.[181] The CPSU ruled for decades through institutions that gave the outward appearance of being based on law – constitutions, parliaments and elections.[182] The liberals sought to prove that the Communist Party *was* the government of the USSR, if not in name then in fact, from 1917. And it had, therefore, violated all four Soviet Constitutions, beginning with the first in 1918.

The Court ruled that it could only examine the activity of the RSFSR Communist Party after March 14, 1990, the date when Article 6 was revoked, and not from October 1917 when the Bolsheviks first seized power. It ruled that Yeltsin did have the right to revoke the property and assets of the Communist Party and that the Party used its control over the KGB and the military to manipulate the entire government. The court ruled that the Soviet government was the Politburo, the Central Committee and its local structures. The court upheld Yeltsin's decree on the requisition of property and ruled that practically all the ruling structures of the Communist Party, apart from the primary party organizations, from the central apparat to the federal, republican, *oblast*, *krai* and *raion* levels violated the Constitution after the passing of Article 6.[183]

One cannot underestimate the symbolic significance of Kovalyov's short but well-crafted 4,000-word testimony. His address was carefully planned to illustrate the direct relationship between the violation of human rights in the former USSR and the political course of the CPSU. He systematically substantiated his argument with primary documents retrieved during his work on the transfer of KGB files to the state archives in 1991.[184] Presented close to twenty years after his arrest, Kovalyov's testimony to Russia's highest court was also a tribute to members of the Soviet Union's human rights movement, a public acknowledgment of the years of persecution suffered under the deliberate and conscious policies of the CPSU.

Kovalyov's position was that the CPSU bore "not criminal, but moral responsibility" for the Soviet era.[185] He divided his testimony into three parts. He began his speech by arguing that the CPSU consciously and deliberately pursued a foreign policy that resulted in the isolation of the Soviet Union from the world community. He argued that the Soviet Union's position on human rights was formed in the Central Committee of the CPSU during the debates on the Universal Declaration of Human Rights in the wake of World War Two. He pointed to the hypocrisy of the Soviet delegation who readily signed international treaties and documents, but remained "categorically against the creation of some kind of international controlling mechanism".[186] He cited three references from Interior Ministry files in which the struggle of the Soviet delegation to the United Nations Human Rights Commission against the controlling mechanisms proposed by other countries was discussed. "Sheltering behind the thesis of sovereignty," Kovalyov declared, "instructions were given to vote against the examination of complaints by the United Nations Human Rights Commission, against the right of the international court to settle such complaints and the establishment of posts such as the High Commissioner on Refugees".[187]

Twenty-four years after the Initiative Group sent their first letter to the United Nations, Kovalyov declared in his speech to the Constitutional Court that the silence of the United Nations in response to their letter was a consequence of the international politics of the CPSU. It is doubtful that Kovalyov agreed with the UN's decision not to investigate the complaints sent by the group in compliance with the Soviet Union's veto on international control. But before all else he blamed the politics of his own country.[188] Unlike the Initiative Group's third letter to the United Nations on September 26, 1968, which openly criticised the United Nations and declared that "the silence of an organization of international law unties the hands of those who will be inspired to further persecutions," Kovalyov declared in his testimony that the "CPSU's decisions in international politics untied their hands in internal politics."[189]

In the second part of his testimony, Kovalyov linked the international politics of the CPSU with the suppression of dissidents. "The entire Soviet conception of human rights was built on the priority of collective over individual rights," he stated. "It is this ideology which lay the basis of all the methods of struggle with human rights activists."[190] Having largely secured the isolation of the Soviet Union from international interference, the struggle against the movement, Kovalyov argued, was conducted by the KGB with the full consent of the Central Committee. "I support the following logic," he declared, "that what the KGB did, it did to implement the politics of the CPSU and only the CPSU".[191] To prove that the repression of dissidents was a carefully contrived action, Kovalyov highlighted a document sent to Central Committee members in the autumn of 1966 by Nikolai Savinkin, Deputy Head of the administrative department. The document recommended that Article 70 of the Criminal Code be amended in response to the growing number of protests, appeals and flyers in circulation. The problem with Article 70, according to Savinkin, was that individuals could only be charged once their intention to weaken and undermine the Soviet regime had been proved. Savinkin proposed that a new article be drafted which did not require such evidence. The result was the well-known article 190–1: "From 1968 to 1986 with the exception of 1976," Kovalyov informed the Court, "under two basic political articles of the criminal code 2468 people were convicted" [Article 70 and Article 190–1]. "The only aim of these repressions, from my point of view, was the desire of the CPSU to preserve, in any way, its ideological monopoly".[192]

Kovalyov then sought to prove that, even during *perestroika*, the link between the KGB and the CPSU remained strong and unchanged. He opened the third part of his testimony by questioning the motives that compelled the CPSU to release political prisoners in 1987. Convinced that the decision was driven by nothing more than political expediency, he quoted from a document signed by KGB head Viktor Chebrikov which stated that the motivation to release political prisoners convicted under Articles 70 and 190 was "to strengthen the unity of the party and the nation ... the release of [prisoners] is to our political advantage and underlines the humanity of the Soviet regime".[193] For Kovalyov, the demeaning conditions surrounding the release of political prisoners only substantiated his claim. In an effort to illustrate that the KGB continued to suppress the movement with the approval of the CPSU, he highlighted the problems with the December 1987 seminar, the instruction of September 6, 1989, which called for the burning of 583 volumes of Sakharov's dossier and Gorbachev's order to "crush" the 1989 "KGB and *Perestroika*" seminar.[194]

The court, however, dismissed the liberals' counterclaim. It argued that the CPSU ceased to exist in August, 1991, and the Russian Communist Party remained unregistered.[195] The liberals hoped that the Constitutional Court would act as a public venue to expose the crimes of the party and legally implicate the CPSU for the crimes committed since 1917. Indeed they hoped the case would symbolize the first step in a long line of national gestures compelling Russian society to confront its own past. It was an ambitious undertaking. Kovalyov was frustrated that judge Valery Zorkin refused to examine the question of the constitutionality of the Party, dismissing what he characterized as "historical questions" from the proceedings. "The monstrous documents taken from the Party archives ... testified that the Party was the main organizer of widespread, terrorist activity against the population of the country," declared Kovalyov. "Zorkin stubbornly refused to examine them and called them the 'Dead Sea Scrolls'."[196]

Many commentators argued that the proceedings bore all the signs of a political spectacle.[197] Although the court was never vested with criminal jurisdiction, *Izvestiya* declared in its pages that "Russian society seemed to expect ... a Russian Nuremberg process, with the resulting de-communisation (similar to de-nazification) ..."[198]

The denazification programme in Germany did expose for the first time the problems of defining guilt, responsibility and liability into judicial categories. Kovalyov systematically rejected the idea of assembling individuals whose actions could be deployed to implicate the CPSU as a whole. Constitutional Court Judge Anatoly Kononov warned: "It is not so simple to create a clean mechanism that divides the sheep from the goats."[199] Kovalyov feared that criminal punishment would launch an interminable number of bitter struggles and false accusations that would seriously protract the democratization process. For that reason he rejected a repeat of the lustration laws passed in the Czech Republic in 1992 against the former state security service, the StB. As Havel himself maintained, there was always the problem of finding sufficient evidence to implicate people.

An attempt to isolate the guilty would also exonerate the rest of the population. Kovalyov was convinced that every Soviet citizen shared some responsibility for the actions of the Soviet regime. He saw the acknowledgment of this as an overriding national issue.[200] He argued during his testimony:

> I believe that if a result emerges from this trial, then so too will an understanding of our national guilt, of the fact that we were its best pupils, that we so easily accepted the ideology of the older brother and the first among equals and we willingly supported the persecution of exceptional people never having read a line of their work but who we reprimanded with so many. There would emerge an understanding of the responsibility the Party bears and how this responsibility is greater than for the rest of us. For whoever holds the wealth of power must also bear the weight of responsibility that power entails. But we too allowed this government to be chosen, we allowed this ongoing lawlessness. If we ourselves had been better, along with them – this would not have been possible. And we will remain its dependents, opening our mouths like jackdaws and crying – "Give me work, Give me pay. Give me shops that are full" – until we realize that we ourselves are responsible for everything that has happened.[201]

For Kovalyov, there was no moral equivalence between the actions of the Communist Party and the Soviet population at large. What he actually had in mind for his project of "moral cleansing" was never entirely clear. It appeared that he believed in some kind of re-education and national repentance project that would expose the population at large to the crimes of the regime as a way for Russian society to look openly and honestly at itself. The banning of the Communist Party and the exposure of its crimes was one way to force the facts on society.

More radical liberals believed that democratization in Russia could never really take place without lustration. By the time of the Chechen war, Kovalyov's own views on the purging of the state security services and administration appeared to grow a little ambiguous. While driving through Grozny, a Moscow journalist said to him: "Look, Sergei Adamovitch – this is all your work! Can't you see that you are guilty of all this. You and your sissiness, your rejection of lustration, your unwillingness to hunt out the witches."[202]

Despite the Constitutional Court's refusal to engage in a historical debate over the constitutionality of the Soviet and RSFSR Communist Parties, Kovalyov had at least succeeded in one of his ambitions as Chairman of the Human Rights Committee. However modest his achievement, his half-hour testimony, presented in a slow, methodical manner, was televised almost in full.[203] This kind of publicity only helped Kovalyov to realize one of his long-term objectives: to persuade Russian society, however irritating it may have become, that it shared the burden of its own history.

Declaration of the Rights and Liberties of Man and the Citizen

The major practical task for Kovalyov once he became Chairman of the Human Rights Committee was to draft Section Two, *On the Rights and Liberties of Man and the Citizen*, of the 1993 Constitution of the Russian Federation. On June 16, 1990, during the RSFSR Congress of People's Deputies, a Constitutional Commission was established comprising some 120 people. Under the direction of Oleg Rumyantsev, an independent sub-committee comprised of Kovalyov, Sergei Sirotkin and Boris Zolotukhin was entrusted with Section Two of the draft constitution relating to human rights. Travelling back and forth from Moscow to the state dacha at Archangelsk for ten weeks in the autumn of 1990, the sub-committee finished its draft in November.[204]

Kovalyov and the authors were convinced that human rights had to serve as the basis of any viable constitutional order. They sought to replace the 1977 Constitution with a draft that celebrated the inalienable rights of the individual as the supreme value.[205] Openly rejecting the socialist doctrine of collective rights, the authors sought to completely reverse the traditions of their predecessors and move Russia closer to Western Europe in spirit and practice. The institutionalization of the inalienable rights of the individual into the country's supreme legal document would give Russian society a fundamental set of laws to which it could aspire.

The first problem the sub-committee encountered was to access the constitutions of democratic countries. Not readily available in Moscow's libraries, they only managed to find scattered excerpts in books.[206] For this they were helped by Alexander Sobyanin. Well known as Sakharov's election campaigner and one of the founders of Democratic Russia, Sobyanin was appointed Secretary to the Constitutional Commission in 1990. He obtained copies of the US and Mexican constitutions, and Sakharov's draft constitution of 1989, all of which served as guides for the sub-committee's draft.[207]

By November 1990 Kovalyov and the draft's authors were satisfied that their text embodied the fundamental democratic ideals. The difficulties began once the first draft was introduced into the plenary session of the Constitutional Commission. The Constitutional Commission was comprised of former party and state representatives and established by the Presidium of the Supreme Soviet when it was still under the chairmanship of Politburo member Vitaly Vorotnikov.[208] As a result of the huge number of amendments proposed by the conservative majority, the draft was so transformed that Rumyantsev was forced to retreat. A revised version of the constitution was rejected by the Russian parliament in 1991. After the failure of the August coup, a second draft was prepared and presented by Rumyantsev to the RSFSR Supreme Soviet on October 10, 1991. The draft was again rejected.[209]

Despite the arguments between the liberals and the conservative majority over the constitution, the sub-committee managed to hold onto its elaborate section *On the Rights and Liberties of Man and the Citizen*. Its approach was attacked by the majority, who remained "completely orientated toward the old Soviet conception of human rights," recalled Sirotkin. "The so-called priority of economic and social rights".[210] In the interim, the uncertainty surrounding the constitutional crisis urged the sub-committee to frame its draft as a separate document. Inspired by the Universal Declaration of Human Rights and the International Covenant on Civil and Political Rights, they titled the document *The Declaration of the Rights and Liberties of Man and the Citizen*. Although ostensibly the same as its original draft of Section Two of the draft constitution, the declaration was an inspirational, non-binding document. It was passed by the RF Supreme Soviet Deputies after two readings on November 22, 1991.[211]

Yeltsin's political tactics were opening the way for the Human Rights Committee to shape the Russian Federation's new position on human rights. The declaration was also a response to the Soviet Declaration of Human Rights and Liberties passed by the USSR Congress of People's Deputies some two months previously, on September 5, 1991 – the last decree before its collapse.

The passing of the *Declaration of the Rights and Liberties of Man and the Citizen* did not arouse much press attention, but it was officially enshrined that:

> ... basic rights and liberties in conformity with the commonly recognized principles and norms of international law shall be recognized and guaranteed in the Russian Federation ... The basic rights and liberties of the human being shall be inalienable and shall belong to everyone from birth.[212]

Civil rights granted in the declaration included: physical integrity rights, such as the right to life (Art. 7) and protection against torture (Art. 8(4)), due process rights such as the right to a fair trial (Art. 32), the presumption of innocence (Art. 34) and the right to legal representation (Art. 37). Everyone had the right to the inviolability of person and private life (Art. 8(1) and Art. 9(1)). Forced labour was prohibited (Art. 23(4)). Under political rights, everyone was to enjoy the right to freedom of association (Art. 20) and to assemble peacefully (Art. 19). Everyone had the right to freedom of thought, conscience and religion (Art. 14 (1)). Everyone was to have the right to freedom of expression and the unimpeded expression of opinion and belief (Art. 13(1)). Every citizen had the right to participate in affairs of the state, to elect and to be elected (Art. 17).[213]

The prolonged struggle to reach a consensus over the draft constitution continued into 1992. By the time of the Sixth Congress in April 1992, the majority still refused to include *The Declaration of the Rights and Liberties of Man and the Citizen* into the Constitution as Section Two. It remained an unbinding declaration. Following his victory at the April 25 referendum, Yeltsin began a push for a new constitution with the help of Sergei Alekseev, former

Chairman of the Committee on Constitutional Supervision, and Vice-Premier Sergei Shakhrai. By the time of the Constitutional Convention in Moscow in June 1993, *The Declaration of the Rights and Liberties of Man and the Citizen* was introduced in full into Yeltsin's new draft constitution. It was another six months before the draft constitution was put to a national referendum.

Human Rights Commissioner

The final article of the *Declaration of the Rights and Liberties of Man and the Citizen* declared that "Parliamentary control over the observance of human rights and civic freedoms in the RSFSR shall be exercised by a Parliamentary Commissioner for Human Rights (Art. 40)."[214] The struggle to establish an independent office for Russia's first parliamentary Human Rights Commissioner to receive citizens' complaints outside the judicial system took Kovalyov and his colleagues close to three years to realize.[215] During its first month, the Committee received over one thousand letters from across the Soviet Union. The complaints ranged in concern from verdicts passed in criminal and civil trials to unsubstantiated arrests. There were complaints concerning conditions in detention centres, unlawful dismissals and problems related to housing. Each complainant sought legal advice and redress against the administration.[216]

Kovalyov was unable to dismiss the letters or entrust them to the office of the General Procurator. Despite the fact that it was not part of the Committee's mandate to secure redress for individual complaints or supervise the executive branch, Kovalyov insisted that they should attempt to reply formally to every letter and to offer advice where possible.[217] Ilya Burmistrovitch, a mathematician and former political prisoner, was employed to work full-time with two volunteers to deal with the correspondence and establish a systematic mechanism to manage the complaints. It was decided that each letter was to be answered within a two-week period. For more complicated cases, a response was expected within a month. By 1993, the Committee had more than 10,000 complaints in its offices and had resolved less than 10 per cent of them.[218] As Siomina, Kovalyov's chief aid, recalled, the Committee repeatedly failed to meet its own deadlines and often relied on other methods.

> We also used telephone justice. It was inevitable … One major example of our use of telephone justice was with the penal system. Because there is no regional prison system, it is possible for a resident of one end of Russia to be consigned to a prison at the opposite end. This effectively violates the rights of a prisoner to meetings, since under the present economic conditions, relatives cannot afford to travel to him, or even to send him parcels. Relatives appeal to us to arrange a prisoner's transfer to another region.[219]

The failure of the Committee to manage the complaints proved to be one of its greatest disappointments. Its efforts were well-intentioned, but without the administrative expertise or the money to employ adequate staff, the rising number of letters only served to remind Kovalyov of the urgency of establishing a post for a Human Rights Commissioner and an accompanying office staffed by trained lawyers and administrators. Kovalyov believed that, psychologically, this was one of the most crucial institutions for the building of a human rights culture in Russia, and he never failed to stress its importance. Founded on the idea of protecting citizens from state organs in individual cases of injustice, the post of Human Rights Commissioner also encourages the administration to act in a more sensitive way to the needs of citizens. For Kovalyov, proving to the Russian public that the government was taking steps to treat them with proper consideration by accepting responsibility for administrative negligence or arbitrariness had two distinct advantages. It would build public confidence in state institutions and, by educating citizens on individual rights, it might gradually reverse the dominant Soviet theory of the primacy of the state over the individual.

In the 1970s, the Soviet regime dismissed the office of Ombudsman as it existed in Western countries as a "bourgeois" institution. In an article for *Sovetskoe Gosudarstvo i Pravo*, Y. Shemshuchenko and G. Murashin argued that the very nature of the office forces workers into a compromise when they appeal to a Human Rights Commissioner. "Subject to political pressure from his peers in the parliament," argued the authors, "the Ombudsman is also a representative of the ruling class whose interests he is obliged to protect."[220] The office's effectiveness was also called into question: "Unlike the Procurator in the Soviet Union ... the recommendations of the Ombudsman are not based on the law ... but on the persuasiveness of the Ombudsmen's arguments and his ability to gain the trust of the parliament, the administrative organs, courts and press."[221] For the critics of the office, this "was testimony to the lack of interest of the ruling class in some form of serious control over state organs."[222]

The authors maintained that the Soviet Union's own General Procurator was better equipped to play the role of protector of individual rights. Viewed as the fourth branch of government under Soviet law, Art. 164 of the USSR Constitution entrusted the General Procurator and his subordinate procurators with "supreme supervision".[223] Empowered to receive complaints concerning officials and the administration, the procurator had two roles. He conducted general supervision over state agencies to ensure that all acts of the agencies and officials were in accordance with the law. He also supervised the administration of criminal justice.[224] The office of the General Procurator was an instrument of the system, and its dual roles as guardian of the state and protector of individual rights were clearly irreconcilable. Any individual complaints addressed to the Procurator seeking redress were always secondary to the Procurator's role as defender of state interests.

Kovalyov denounced the General Procurator as an "unnatural chimera". He hoped that the office of the Human Rights Commissioner would eventually replace this highly centralized and rigidly controlled institution. The draft law for the office modelled by the Committee and a team of consultants was based on the classic model of a parliamentary Ombudsman, as in Sweden and Great Britain, with its opportunities to influence the administration and strengthen parliamentary traditions.[225] The authors of the draft favoured a centralized system spanning the entire Russian Federation.[226] Once established, the Russian office would be one of the largest in the world with an anticipated 160,000 complaints in the first year and a staff of 270.[227] As soon as the Committee felt confidant that they could find suitably qualified individuals to represent the office, they hoped to establish a system of local Ombudsmen.

The draft law outlined three primary tasks for the Russian Human Rights Commissioner. One was to receive complaints and assist in "remedying violated rights".[228] The Commissioner was to "examine complaints about actions, failures to act or decisions ... of state agencies, agencies of local government and government officials which in the opinion of the petitioner, violate his rights or restrict his liberties ..."[229] The Russian Human Rights Commissioner was not to examine complaints concerning decisions of the Federal Assembly or of the legislative organs, nor complaints about decisions of judges and courts, unless it related to the violation of procedure during court proceedings.[230] A complaint had to be submitted to the Commissioner in writing within one year from the time of the violation.[231] All complaints submitted to the Commissioner were exempt from government fees.[232]

The most characteristic feature of the office of the Human Rights Commissioner was that it did not have the power to resolve complaints. It did have the power to submit recommendations to any government establishment and to assist in the resolution of conflict. On receiving a complaint the office of the Human Rights Commissioner had several options. It could initiate an investigation of the complaint, inform the complainant of other measures taken to defend his rights, pass on the complaint to an appropriate official or agency competent to resolve the complaint, or decline to initiate an investigation. The Commissioner was obliged to inform the complainant of the decision and, on initiating an investigation, he informed the agency or official against whom the complaint was lodged.[233] The Commissioner could open an investigation on his own initiative in cases of wide-scale or gross human rights violations.[234]

When carrying out his investigation the office of the Human Rights Commissioner could freely visit state and local government agencies. It could request from state organs, local government and its officials, information, documents and materials necessary to conduct an investigation. If court proceedings had been violated during a criminal, civil or administrative case, it could request information.[235] The agency against whom the complaint was lodged was given the opportunity to explain any matters relevant to the case. The complainant was to be informed of those explanations.[236]

Some of the options for the office of the Commissioner, once the investigation had finished, included the following. It could inform the complainant that no violation of his rights or liberties had been established. In the case of a violation it could send its findings to the official or agency in question, recommending possible and necessary measures to remedy the violation. The office could file a petition with a court in defence of the citizen's rights and liberties, petition the agency to initiate disciplinary or administrative proceedings against officials responsible for violating actions, or petition a court or procurator to review a court decision.[237] The office could publish its findings and was obliged to inform the agency or official of its decision to publish. Within one month after receiving the recommendation, an agency or official was obliged to consider it and send a written reply to the Commissioner. If the recommendations had not been put into effect, the department had to explain the reasons why.[238]

The second task of the office of the Human Rights Commisioner was constantly to apply pressure to state organs to improve legislation affecting human rights.[239] Kovalyov hoped that the office would function as a research base capable of determining weak points in domestic policy. According to the draft law, if the office recognized a recurring problem it had the right to conduct an examination of the relevant government agency and forward its proposals to amend or add to existing legislation, to draft new legislation or suggest improvements in administrative procedure. It could also recommend that legislation be amended to ensure compliance with international norms and standards.[240]

The third task of the office was to "educate people about human rights and liberties and the methods for their defence."[241] Complainants would learn more about their own powers as citizens as a result of their consultations with the office and through the process of defending their case. By publishing the results from investigations, the authors hoped they could reach the public and educate them using the case method. It was thirty years since Valery Chalidze had argued that the most effective way individuals could learn about their rights was by defending their individual grievances. The authors of the draft also hoped that public accountability within agencies for their administrative actions would educate the individuals working in those organs. This was perhaps their most difficult challenge. Moreover, the draft law stipulated that the office of the Human Rights Commissioner had to publish an annual report on human rights in Russia drawing attention to priority issues, making recommendations for improvement, and, hopefully in the interim, educating and changing attitudes.

The personality of the Human Rights Commissioner was foremost in the minds of the authors of the draft. For the Committee's lawyer, Sergei Sirotkin, the success of the office in Russia depended largely on the personality of the Human Rights Commissioner.[242] For Siomina, the Human

Rights Commissioner "in a post-totalitarian society must be a teacher. I think that's the best way of describing his role."[243] The power of the office rested in the moral authority of the Commissioner to practise diplomacy and tact to influence administrations. Acting as the conscience of the government, the Commissioner had to try to build a culture of discussion, compromise and good faith. In the public sphere, he had to be capable of obtaining the trust of a sceptical Russian public, of drawing its attention to human rights problems and of educating them in the importance of solving those problems for the success of Russia's democracy. The Committee, of course, was hopeful that Kovalyov would assume that role. Given his unpopularity, though, they were concerned that he would never secure the two-thirds majority in the Duma required for his appointment.

The aspect of the office which most appealed to Kovalyov was its independence.[244] Unconstrained by political concerns, he would be free to pursue the protection of human rights and develop the office. Particularly significant for Kovalyov was the Commissioner's power to demand official documents, materials and information which satisfied his long-term struggle for *glasnost* in government structures. What Shemshuchenko and Murashin had seen as the Ombudsman's weakness was for Kovalyov the role's strength. He believed that the protection of human rights did not always fit into the precise "judicial formulas" prescribed by the courts, and that conflict could be resolved outside the court system. "There has to emerge in Russia," he argued, "an institute whose strength and influence are not based on the right to give orders, but on the ability to convince."[245]

It was over this final point that the struggle for the office began. The Committee's first problem was to ensure that Article 40 of the *Declaration on the Rights and Liberties of Man and the Citizen*, that provided for the creation of the appointment of a Human Rights Commissioner, be included in the draft constitution. The Declaration had been introduced as Part Two of the Constitution in April 1992, but only on condition that Article 40 be discarded. The Committee failed to secure the two-thirds majority to secure Article 40. Its main opponents were the office of the General Procurator, headed by Valentin Stepankov, and the Interior Ministry. The General Procurator easily protected his position with a substantial number of his own representatives in the Supreme Soviet and corpus of deputies. The Military Procurator's office, also with a substantial number of representatives in the Soviet, was especially concerned that the new office would open an investigation into all the violations taking place in the army.[246]

The Procurator's office and the Interior Ministry were supported by the Communist Party. The Committee had to convince the Communist bloc that the office was not an institute of power that the democrats were attempting to control for their own political ends. The Committee's opponents questioned why it did not want to give the Human Rights Commissioner full powers (*vlastnie polnomichie*) to initiate legislation and criminal proceedings. According to Siomina:

The communists even drafted their own law. They insisted that the Ombudsman have complete powers so that he be a type of Prosecutor. Understand, it was not with malicious intent, it was a sincere lack of understanding of what the office of Ombudsman meant. I say this quite responsibly, because there was an open conversation with Oleg Mironov, one of the authors of the alternative draft, and he occupies a serious place in the Communist bloc. He recounted to us what the basic fears of the communists were. They decided that this new institution is being created, headed by Kovalyov ... and that the democrats were not that stupid not to want complete powers for this institution.[247]

There were discussions in the Duma, private meetings and meetings in the parliamentary Committee on Legislation.[248] The irony was that the Communists hoped to secure full powers for the Ombudsman so they could appoint one of their own representatives. At that time, given the make-up of the Congress, it was more probable that they could ensure a two-thirds majority vote for their own candidate.

The provision for the Human Rights Commissioner did finally go into the presidential draft at the Constitutional Convention in July 1993. Again, Yeltsin was supportive of the Committee's initiatives. The 1993 Russian Constitution passed by referendum in December included in Article 31(e) a provision for the appointment of a Commissioner on Human Rights. Sirotkin, however, was not satisfied with the article: "I think that the article on the Commissioner should have been placed in the section on human rights and contained more detailed provisions," he argued. "Unfortunately now there is only mention that the State Duma appoints the Commissioner, who acts on the basis of a federal constitutional law. And moreover, even this was not easy to achieve."[249] The Committee's next task would be to secure a federal constitutional law and Kovalyov's appointment.

Freedom of movement

Kovalyov was not involved in every aspect of the Committee's work, but he was an energetic facilitator. To this degree he facilitated the establishment of the sub-committee on Refugees. It was headed by Mikhail Arutuynov, an engineer who worked for the Agricultural Science Institute in Moscow for twenty years. He was put forward as a candidate by his fellow employees in the March 1990 elections and became an energetic and committed advocate of the rights of refugees and forced migrants. One of the most important laws passed by the sub-committee was the "Law on Freedom of Movement and Freedom of Choice of Residence" on June 25, 1993, effective from October 1, 1993.[250] This law officially abolished Russia's notorious *propiska* system. Article 1 of the law stated:

In accordance with the Constitution of the RF and international acts about human rights, every citizen of the Russian Federation has the right to freedom of movement and freedom to choose one's place of residence within the Russian Federation. Persons who are lawfully situated in the Russian Federation but are not citizens have the right to freedom of movement, to choose their place of temporary or permanent residence within the Russian Federation in accordance with the Constitution and laws of the Russian Federation and international treaties of the Russian Federation.[251]

The law stipulated that all citizens had the right to appeal to the courts if there were grounds to suppose that discrimination had taken place.

Despite the passing of the law, the *propiska* system remained a strong tradition. The new system established under the June 1993 law stipulated that all citizens had to follow a simple registration procedure and notify the authorities in the case of a change of address. No official authorization to live in a certain place was necessary. This new law was quickly contradicted by the establishment of special *propiska* commissions.[252] The new commissions were assisted by the executive organs in direct violation of the 1993 law and the December 1993 Constitution, and the Russian militia continued to demand from citizens that they fulfill the regulations of the *propiska*.[253] It was noted that the situation appeared particularly acute in cities like Moscow, the Moscow region, St Petersburg, Krasnodar and Stavropol territories, Vladimir, Voronezh, Nizhegorod and Rostov.

The Committee was fighting a difficult battle in its efforts to abolish this ancient and primitive method of social control. The internal passport system had existed in Russia in one form or another since the Time of Troubles.[254] The June law was meant to take effect in Russia on October 1, 1993, but the state of emergency introduced on October 7 forced a suspension of the law. In November, the Moscow authorities flagrantly contradicted the law when an order on "The temporary conditions on stays in Moscow" was introduced.[255] One of the conditions was that, if a citizen from the near abroad stayed in the capital for more than twenty-four hours, he was obliged to register with the militia and pay a fee of 10 per cent of the minimum Russian wage. Failing to register incurred a fine of 3–5 times the minimum wage. A repeat offender was fined fifty times the minimum wage and evicted from Moscow.[256]

After the order of the Moscow authorities in November, the Committee witnessed a rise in the number of sub-statutory acts and orders, either placing restrictions on the law or ignoring it altogether. The Moscow and St Petersburg authorities claimed that the *prospiska* system was necessary to aid the struggle against crime, which served increasingly as an excuse for the issue of such orders. The Committee called on the Federal Migration Bureau to abolish all discriminatory acts, to abolish all fines and taxes, and to establish a system that guaranteed citizens the right to freedom of movement and registration without fear of discrimination. The Committee also drafted a law on basic identification documents, such as passports and identity documents. It stipulated that a passport is a document to be used only for departing the country, and a plastic identity card would be used within Russia. They succeeded in submitting the draft law, but it was not adopted.[257]

The virtual preservation of the *propiska* system violated more than the right of the citizen to choose his place of residence. Failure to register one's place of permanent residence inevitably entailed restrictions on other rights, including basic social and economic rights such as the right to work, and to receive free medical care and municipal benefits.

October 1993

President Yeltsin's decision to dissolve the Congress of People's Deputies and the Supreme Soviet on September 21, 1993 also marked the end of the Human Rights Committee. The most controversial event in Kovalyov's public career – his support of Yeltsin's order to fire on the White House on October 4 – overshadowed his three-year commitment to democratic reform and tireless campaigning for human rights issues. His decision contravened a personal philosophy grounded in the theory of evolutionary change. For the first time, he openly sanctioned political expediency and violence to open the way for the long awaited constitution.

In the lead-up to the October events, Kovalyov was ambiguous about the mounting crisis between the President and the parliament. In the middle of 1992, he admitted that the 1977 Brezhnev Constitution did not provide for a way out of the crisis and expressed concern that, if a referendum was used as the basis to dissolve the parliament, a "dangerous precedent" would be established. "And what if, suddenly, the new one doesn't turn out to be so good? What then? Another referendum?"[258] he asked. Admitting that it was a difficult and complicated choice, he contemplated an idea proposed by Alexander Sobyanin that the deputies stand for election again, but seemed only partially and reluctantly committed to the idea.[259] By the time of the secret ballot to impeach Yeltsin in March 1993, however, his position had changed. In the weeks leading up to the April referendum, he argued that: "The only way is for the people to have the highest sovereignty and primary rights. Appealing to them as the President is doing will decide the fate of the opposition."[260]

Kovalyov was concerned with the results of the ballot to impeach Yeltsin, which fell short by only seventy-two votes. On March 29, members of the parliamentary reform coalition refused to vote in the Ninth Congress, except on the issue of confidence in the Congress. In the interval between the sittings, Kovalyov read a statement he had failed to present to parliament when blocked from the floor by Khasbulatov. "We attend the Congress only as witnesses," he declared. "The Ninth Congress was convened by the Supreme Soviet leadership for the single purpose of toppling the President, legally elected by the nation ... The spirit and letter of the law are being violated and we will not participate in the trampling of democratic principles."[261] For Kovalyov, the ballot to impeach Yeltsin was the symptom of a much deeper concern. He grew convinced that the stand-off between the President and the "irreconcilable opposition" would eventually force Russia to "make a choice between democracy and totalitarianism". Although sharply criticised for this simple dichotomy, he had legitimate reasons to be concerned. The constitution was "full to the brim of irreconcilable contradictions",[262] the parliament was blocking democratic reform, rewriting the constitutional rules and gradually depriving Yeltsin of power with the intent to transform him into a ceremonial head of state. "There is no doubt", he later argued, "that the victory of Khasbulatov and his supporters ... would have meant the end of democracy, the end of parliamentarianism and the final result, the end of freedom in Russia."[263]

Sensing that he would get nowhere with an unsympathetic Congress, Kovalyov nevertheless remained unsure how they could resolve the crisis. When asked in an interview in April, "Are you inclined toward revolution?", he responded:

> I have already said that I am not a revolutionary, but let's be honest: it is not logically possible to keep living under this suspended constitution and there is no strictly legal way out of the existing crisis ... In any case the way out will be a long one. This may even be our forty years in the desert.

One day earlier, on April 10, he had declared "that the idea of compromise [with the parliament] is not possible; either it is re-elected or it is dissolved."[264]

When Kovalyov stood up in parliament on April 27 and appealed to the deputies to resign, he used Yeltsin's victory in the referendum as his basic argument.[265] He hoped that the referendum would persuade the corpus of deputies to step down. While the parliamentary majority was still demoralized by its defeat and the victory of the democrats, Kovalyov believed that Yeltsin still held a strong bargaining position. Perhaps naively, he believed that the President and the parliament could have reached an agreement under these conditions and avoided the bloodshed that accompanied the October events. He was disappointed on both accounts.

Kovalyov later admitted that he was prepared to support an order to dissolve the parliament directly after the referendum.[266] But the moment was soon lost. He argued that the interim period between April and September gave Khasbulatov time to gather forces. Kovalyov visited Yeltsin, unannounced, in Valdai in the summer of 1993 to express his concern about the Speaker's frequent closed meetings with military commanders.[267]

Kovalyov remained concerned about Khasbulatov's growing influence. On the morning of September 21, in a session of the Supreme Soviet, he reproached the speaker for inflaming the crisis with public speeches about Yeltsin's weakness for alcohol. Khasbulatov replied: "What are you talking about, Sergei Adamovich? Don't you know that troops are on their way to Moscow?"[268] He then heard from N. Ryabov that Yeltsin would be appearing on the eight o'clock news to announce the dissolution of both the Supreme Soviet and the Congress of People's Deputies and would be calling for new parliamentary elections for December 12 under Decree 1400, "On the Step-by-Step Constitutional Reform of the Russian Federation". Kovalyov went directly to the Kremlin to contact his friend and colleague, Foreign Minister Andrei Kozyrev. He hoped to organize a meeting with Yeltsin, but the President had left for the state dacha. Kovalyov asked Kozyrev to warn Yeltsin that he thought Decree 1400 "was a serious and dangerous mistake" and that they should postpone the televised speech. After Kovalyov watched Yeltsin announce the dissolution of the legislature on the eight o'clock news, he went to the White House to collect his belongings. "I decided straight away that I would submit to Decree 1400," he said.[269] Five days later, on September 26, Yeltsin issued decree No. 1450 on the creation of a Presidential Human Rights Commission of the Russian Federation and appointed Kovalyov chairman of the new Commission directly under the President.

The events of October 3 and 4 marked the climax of the political crisis. In the early afternoon of October 3, mass rallies were organized by two hard-line demagogues: Viktor Anpilov of the neo-communist workers' Moscow movement, and Vitaly Urazhtsev, leader of one faction of the "shield" (Shchit) organization. They broke through a heavy police cordon to meet Rutskoi and Khasbulatov standing on the balcony of the White House. Rutskoi told them "to form up detachments and take the mayor's office, then on to Ostankino",[270] and Khasbulatov incited them to "seize the Kremlin by storm with tanks".[271] At 4.30 p.m. they stormed the mayor's office. They attacked the Moscow Telephone Centre and a building of the Moscow Military District to seize weapons. There were orders to blockade all airports and train stations. They stormed the military counter-intelligence headquarters in Moscow, demanding that they send telegrams to units throughout the country requesting them to carry out the orders of Rutskoi and Khasbulatov.[272]

On the early morning of October 4, special military forces launched an artillery attack against the White House. Within hours the rebellion was crushed. The eighteenth floor of the parliament building was completely destroyed by the fire, taking with it the offices and archive of the Human Rights Committee. The number of people who died in the October events is estimated at 147.[273]

On October 3, Kovalyov stood amid the crowd outside the White House as pro-parliamentary forces gathered. On the same day he issued a public appeal to the "citizens of Russia" in the name of the Chairman of the Human Rights Committee:

Today I was in the crowd. It moved with red and black-yellow flags toward the White House, breaking through a cordon of police, assaulting and killing members of the militia. The crowd cried out – "All power to the Soviets", "Down with Yeltsin". And they even cried, "Shoot – shoot the democrats, the militia, the Jews and blacks ..." For my entire life I have tried to fight against the arbitrariness of power. But I am firmly prepared to defend these rights from a crowd of *pogromshiki*, from a possessed crowd whose leaders have passed guns over to them ... One thing I know with conviction: We – the political prisoners of Stalin, Khrushchev and Brezhnev's camps, our children and grandchildren – we do not want to return to the yoke of Soviet power. The shadows of the dead millions are with us.[274]

Kovalyov sought his theoretical foundations for the dissolution of the parliament in the supremacy of constitutionalism. In his much-criticised article in *Moskovskii Novosti* on October 3, he argued that Yeltsin had acted on the will of the people when he dissolved the parliament on September 21. He declared: "The President by definition must be the guarantor of constitutionalism. But what is constitutionalism – following the bad letter of a bad law or the fundamental principles of constitutionalism?" Although he avoided a discussion of the fact that he had sanctioned the dissolution of a democratically elected parliament, he never characterized the whole process as legal. He asked rhetorically:

Haven't we resorted to the principle of revolutionary expediency? Today democratically minded public opinion does not like this parliament – and orders it to resign. And tomorrow it does not like the new one, and the next president issues a decree on the dissolution of the corpus of deputies. What will then happen with Russia's nascent parliamentarianism? I hope that the present precedent will not become its tombstone. Of course one cannot exclude the probability of early dissolutions of the parliament. It is important that the new Russian constitution includes an article regulating the conditions of procedure for holding early elections for parliament and president.[275]

Kovalyov was aware that a dangerous precedent was being set. The young human rights activist, Yan Rachinsky of Memorial's Human Rights Centre, and the famous dissident and writer, Andrei Sinyavsky, criticised Kovalyov in the pages of *Nezavisimaya Gazeta*. Sinyavsky lamented that "his own tribe of intellectuals, instead of forming some kind of opposition to Yeltsin ... are welcoming all his undertakings and appealing again for wide measures ... This is how Soviet power began."[276] Another exile, the well-known legalist Valery Chalidze, also expressed his personal unease with Kovalyov's decision.[277]

While Kovalyov failed to answer his own question on "revolutionary expediency", his critics were more resolute. Rachinsky attacked Kovalyov for his "creative approach to constitutionalism"[278] and argued that the Chairman's support for Yeltsin's politically expedient decree symbolized the "disappearance of the moral authorities". "When a choice had to be made between power and the law, between the president and the constitution," he argued, "practically all the respected deputies turned to the side of power."[279]

Rachinsky expressed his deep concern for Kovalyov's oversimplification of a complex crisis. "It is completely incomprehensible to me how ... the deeply respected Kovalyov could draw the conclusion that the fundamental majority of voters have become used to following the logic of black and white: there are democrats and there are communists."[280] This simple dichotomy of reformers vs. revanchists, democrats vs. communists deployed by Kovalyov, puzzled even his admirers. For many of his peers this crude oversimplification of events only served to exacerbate the situation. His one-sidedness prevented him from seriously addressing the fact that he supported the dissolution of a congress to which he himself had been demo-cratically elected in March 1990. Of equal consequence, he failed to acknowledge that some of the concerns expressed by the Congress over Gaidar's shock therapy were legitimate ones. His self-proclaimed ignorance of economics blinded him to a fundamental aspect of the political struggle.

Kovalyov argued that the struggle to preserve democracy in post-Soviet Russia meant the end of the parliament. He insisted some years later that, although he did not agree with Yeltsin's decree, he decided to support it. He felt compelled to support Yeltsin's decision as a sign of allegiance to the democrats.[281] This was perhaps the essence of the tragedy for his admirers. Moreover, he equated the success of democratic reform in Russia too closely with Yeltsin's career. He became infatuated with the idea of the President as the leader of democracy, and two years later he admitted that this was his "personal sin".[282]

Kovalyov nevertheless believed that his role had shifted from the imme-diate concerns of the individual to the wider demands of institutionalizing human rights. He had always argued against the use of radical measures that violated individual rights, but this criticism was lodged from the sidelines. Now he espoused wide measures when he thought that the struggle to insti-tutionalize human rights was threatened. His commitment to practical politics over solitary dissidence was no more evident than in October 1993:

> Today I have come to realize that in many respects it is easier to sacrifice one's career, welfare and freedom in order to defend human rights from totalitarian violence than it is to secure the implementation of human rights through working at practical politics. At this time we are not just defending the rights of separate individuals – we are called upon to ensure that human rights become firmly rooted in our society. We must entrench them in the fundamental principles of our future Constitution. We must use them as the cornerstone for building a new Russian state.[283]

In Kovalyov's defence, we cannot underestimate how convinced he was that the crisis not only meant the end of democracy, but that Russia was on the brink of civil war on October 3. This partly explains his continued support of Yeltsin in the wake of October. When he stood outside the White House he was confronted for the first time by thousands of people, openly violent and aggressive. And his public appeal to the citizens of Russia is testimony to his fear of an imminent civil war. Conceding himself that he believed in Yeltsin, he nevertheless remained adamant that Russia was threatened with the end of democracy in October 1993, and he never moved from this position.

Notes

1 See R. Sakwa, *Russian Politics and Society*, London and New York: Routledge, 1993. See also J. Ostrow, *Comparing Post-Soviet Legislatures: A Theory of Institutional Design and Political Conflict*, Columbus: Ohio State University Press, 2000.
2 S. Kovalyov, "Pochemy v SSSR net pravozashchitnogo dvizheniya", *Vek XX i Mir*, No. 6 (1991): 9–11. See also "Pravozashchita: shag vpered ili dva shaga nazad?" *Rysskaya Mysl'*, No. 3842, August 24, 1990: 9. "Chelovecheskoe izmerenie nashei bedy", *Rysskaya Mysl'*, No. 3831, June 8, 1990: 1, 2. *Literaturnaya Gazeta*, No. 23, June 6, 1990: 2.
3 In interviews with Alexander Daniel, Ludmilla Alekseeva, Alexander Lavut and Oleg Orlov, none of them were able to recall the article. See A. Daniel, personal interview with E. Gilligan, Moscow, June 1998; L. Alekseeva, personal interview with E. Gilligan, Moscow, June 1998; A. Lavut, personal interview with E. Gilligan, Moscow, June 1998; O. Orlov, personal interview with E. Gilligan, Moscow, June 1998.
4 S. Kovalyov, "Pochemy v SSSR net pravozashchitnogo dvizheniya", *Vek XX i Mir*, No. 6 (1991): 9.
5 A. Podrabinek, "Kto skazal, chto v SSSR net pravozashchitnogo dvizheniya?", *Ekspress Khronika*, No. 33 (210), August 13, 1991: 8.
6 *Ibid.*
7 S. Kovalyov, "Pochemy v SSSR net pravozashchitnogo dvizheniya", *Vek XX i Mir*, No. 6 (1991): 10–11.
8 S. Kovalyov, "Speech to the International Helsinki Federation Meeting: Moscow, May 29–June 5, 1990", New York: Kline Archive, pp. 1–3.
9 S. Kovalyov, *Novoe Vremya*, No. 25, June 19–25, 1990: 25.
10 See L. Alekseeva, personal interview with E. Gilligan, Moscow, July 1999; A. Lavut, personal interview with E. Gilligan, Moscow, July 1999. A. Daniel, personal interview with E. Gilligan, Moscow, July 1999.
11 Podrabinek, *op.cit.*, 8. See also M. Landa, "Eto nasha zhivaya istoriya i my – tak ili inache – ee uchastniki", *Rysskaya Mysl'*, December 7–8, 1991: 3. Despite the differences between Podrabinek and Kovalyov, Kovalyov would always support *Ekspress Khronika*. See "Pochemy neobkhodimo poddershat Ekspress-Khroniku?", *Ekspress Khronika*, February 9–16, 1995: 4.
12 S. Kovalyov, "The Lessons of street-rally democracy – No grounds for mistrust", *New Times*, No. 10, March 6–12, 1990: 6. See also "Speech at the International Helsinki Federation Meeting: Moscow, May 29–June 5, 1990", New York: Kline Archive, pp. 1–3.
13 S. Kovalyov, "Second speech at the Moscow Conference on the Human Dimension (CSCE)", New York: Kline Archive. See also S. Kovalyov, "The wise state opens its borders", *New Times*, No. 39, 1991: 25–7.
14 S. Kovalyov, cited in "Civic Action", *New Times*, No. 8, 1990: 10.

15 *Ibid.*
16 S. Kovalyov, "Pochemu v SSSR net pravozashchitnogo dvizheniya", *Vek XX i Mir*, No. 6 (1991): 10.
17 S. Kovalyov, "Chelovecheskoe izmerenie nashei bedy", *Rysskaya Mysl'*, No. 3831, June 8, 1990: 2.
18 S. Kovalyov, "Dissident s parlamentskim mandatom", *Referendum: Zhurnal Nezavisimikh Mnenii 1987–1990 No. 1–37*, Paris: *Rysskaya Mysl'*, 1992: 175.
19 "Izbiratelnii blok Demokraticheskaya Rossiya", *Rysskaya Mysl'*, No. 3813, February 2, 1990: 1.
20 O. Orlov, personal interview with E. Gilligan, Moscow, June 1998. Henceforth, Orlov (1998). Other members included Sergei Stankevich, Ilya Zaslavski and Arkady Murashev.
21 M. Landa, "Sergei Kovalyov: fakty biografii", *Pravozashchitnik 2*, April–June 1997: 79.
22 "Nostalgiya po 99,9%", *Rysskaya Mysl'*, No. 3818, March 9, 1990: 1, 2.
23 Orlov (1998).
24 *Directory of Russian MPs*, United Kingdom: Longman Group, 1992, p. vii.
25 Orlov (1998).
26 Orlov (1998).
27 See "Inoi chuoi", *Izvestiya*, No.159, August 25, 1995: 7. See also Orlov (1998).
28 M. Landa, "Cooperation between Rights Defenders and the Authorities", *Express Chronicle: Human Rights Information Agency – English Weekly News Digest*, March 21, 1997: 15. See also A. Sinyavsky, *The Russian Intelligentsia*, New York: Columbia University Press, 1997, p. 67.
29 Orlov (1998). Kovalyov also heard from some members of his electorate that people had been visiting flats, spreading the rumour that he had not been in camp under Article 70 but for rape. See "Nostalgiya po 99,9%", *Rysskaya Mysl'*, No. 3818, March 9, 1990: 2.
30 S. Kovalyov, "In Moscow, The Dissident Politician: Sergei Kovalyov, Keeping His Promise to Sakharov", *Washington Post*, March 7, 1990: B1.
31 Orlov (1998).
32 *Directory of MPs*, pp. 138–9.
33 Cited in "Sergei Kovalyov: ne vizhu smysla mstit", No. 2, 1992, New York: Kline Archive, p. 2.
34 Kovalyov won in the first round. This was surprising since under the new laws the successful candidate, irrespective of the number of candidates, had to receive 50 per cent of the votes cast.
35 L. Siomina, personal interview with E. Gilligan, Moscow, December 1995. Henceforth, Siomina (1995). See also *Pervaya Sessiya Verkhovnogo Soveta RSFSR Biulleten"*, No. 7, July 3, 1990, Moskva: Verkhovnii Sovet RSFSR, 1990, p. 3.
36 The final vote was 705 for and 229 against.
37 Siomina (1995).
38 Siomina (1995).
39 *Pervaya Sessiya Verkhovnogo Soveta RSFSR, Biulleten' No. 6*, July 3, 1990, Moskva: Verkhovnii Sovet RSFSR, 1990, p. 54. Henceforth, *Biulleten' No .6.*
40 *Pervaya Sessiya Verkhovnogo Soveta RSFSR, Biulleten' No. 7*, July 3, 1990, Moskva: Verkhovnii Sovet RSFSR, 1990, p. 4. Henceforth, *Biulleten' No. 7.*
41 A. Kononov, *Biulleten' No. 7*: 4–5.
42 S. Kovalyov, *Biulleten' No. 6*: 53.
43 S. Kovalyov, *Biulleten' No. 6*: 53–4.
44 S. Sirotkin, "Sotsialnie i ekonomicheskie prava v proekte constitutsii RF", *Sotsialnie Problemi i Prava Cheloveka*, Moskva: Moscow Helsinki Group, 1993, pp. 35–6.

45 S. Kovalyov, *Shestaya Sessiya Verkhovnogo Soveta Rossiiskoi Federatsii, Biulleten' No. 47*: June 7, 1993, Moskva: Verkhovnii Sovet RSFSR, 1993, pp. 34, 38.

46 "Moscow – Third Conference on the Human Dimension of the CSCE September 10–October 15, 1991". Available online at: http://www.osce.org/docs/english/1990–1999/hd/mosc91e.htm (accessed March 2003).

47 S. Kovalyov, "Conference with State Duma Deputy, Sergei Kovalyov", *Federation News Service*, 26/2, April 18, 2000.

48 *Biulleten' No. 47*: 37, 40, 41, 43.

49 *Biulleten' No. 47*: 37, 40, 41.

50 *Biulleten' No. 47*: 47.

51 This question was raised by Sergei Mikhailov from the South Sakhalin Territorial District. See *Biulleten' No. 47*: 47. Note, 108 deputies did not vote.

52 *Biulleten' No. 47*: 40.

53 *Biulleten' No. 47*: 44, 39, 46. Note, the Committee clearly felt some pressure to respond to social and economic issues. The 1994–95 report of the Presidential Human Rights Commission introduced a new section on social rights. See *On the Observance of the Rights of Man and the Citizen in the RF (1994–95)*, p. 71.

54 Siomina 2 (1995).

55 Siomina 2 (1995).

56 S. Sirotkin, personal interview with E. Gilligan, Moscow, November 1995. Henceforth, Sirotkin (1995).

57 S. Kovalyov, *Chelovek i Pravo*, No. 16 (1992): 4. See also "VS RSFSR prinyal zakon o militsii", *Nezavisimaya Gazeta*, No. 48, April 20, 1991: 1. "Novgorodskoe veche v Moskve", *Novoe Vremya*, No. 32, 1991: 10–11. Part of the reason for the support of the bill was that it included the long-awaited and important dissolution of CPSU organizations within the law-enforcement bodies.

58 Nothing resulted from this appeal because the Committee on Constitutional Supervision was dissolved in December 1991.

59 See "Sergei Kovalyov: fakty biografii", *Pravozashchitnik 2*, April–June 1997: 80. See Sirotkin (1995).

60 Sirotkin (1995).

61 J. Dunlop, *The Rise of Russia and the Fall of the Soviet Empire*, Princeton, NJ: Princeton University Press, 1995, p. 267.

62 Dunlop, *ibid.*, 208.

63 L. Siomina, personal interview with E. Gilligan, Moscow, July 1998. Henceforth, Siomina (1998).

64 Siomina (1995).

65 Orlov (1995) and Siomina (1995).

66 Siomina (1995).

67 Siomina (1995) and Orlov (1995).

68 Orlov (1995).

69 Siomina (1995).

70 L. Siomina, "Letter to Edward Kline", undated. From the contents of the letter it was probably written some time in early 1992.

71 S. Kovalyov, *Moskovskii Novosti*, April 11, 1993, No. 15: 11.

72 *Amnesty International Annual Report 1990*, London: Amnesty International, 1990, p. 86.

73 S. Kovalyov, "Osleplenie polifema ili o polze raznikh tochek zreniya", *Narodni Deputat*, No. 11, 1992 (574): 107. See also S. Kovalyov, "Voina v Zakavkaze – Vashe Mnenie?", *Rysskaya Mysl'*, No. 3812, January 26, 1990: iv.

74 J. Fitzpatrick, *Human Rights in Crisis: The International System for Protecting Rights During States of Emergency*, Pennsylvania: University of Pennsylvania Press, 1994, p. 50.
75 Fitzpatrick, *op.cit.*, 35. Note that each treaty stipulates separate provisions with the non-derogable rights.
76 See "International Covenant on Civil and Political Rights", A/RES/2200 A (XXI), 16 December, 1966. Arts. 4, 6 , 7 (paragraphs 1 and 2), 11, 15, 16, 18. See also "Zakon Rossiiskoi Sovetskoi Federativnoi Sotsialisticheskoi Respubliki o Chresvychainom Polozhenii", St. 27.
77 Fitzpatrick, *op.cit.*, 36.
78 Fitzpatrick, *op.cit.*, 33.
79 Fitzpatrick, *op.cit.*, 38.
80 S. Kovalyov, "Osleplenie polifema ili o polze raznikh tochek zreniya", *Narodni Deputat*, No. 11, 1992 (574): 107.
81 See "Planning and General Support Proposal", submitted to the Ford Foundation by the Human Rights Project Group, December 5, 1989, New York: Kline Archive, pp. 4–5.
82 "Law Governing States of Emergency", April 3, 1990, *Current Digest of the Soviet Press*, Vol. XLII, No. 19, 1990, p. 54. Henceforth, *Law*. Please note this is an abridged version.
83 *Law, Art. 1.*
84 *Law, Art. 1.*
85 *Law, Art. 11.*
86 *Law, Art. 16.*
87 *Law, Art. 1.*
88 "Zakon Rossiiskoi Sovetskoi Federativnoi Sotsialisticheskoi Respubliki O Chresvychainom Polozhenii", St. 4, Pt. A. Henceforth, *St.*
89 *St. 4. Pt. B.*
90 S. Sirotkin, "Tretya Sessiya Verkhovnogo Soveta RSFSR", *Biulleten' No. 27*, May 7, 1991, Moskva: Verkhovnii Sovet RSFSR, 1991, p. 60.
91 *St. 11.*
92 *St. 13.*
93 *St. 10.*
94 *St. 12.*
95 *St. 41.*
96 *St. 10, 22, 23, 24.*
97 Sirotkin, *op.cit.*, 59.
98 *St. 16.* See also Sirotkin, *op.cit.*, 61.
99 *St. 17.* See also Sirotkin, *op.cit.*, 61.
100 *St. 18.* See also Sirotkin, *op.cit.*, 61.
101 Sirotkin, *op.cit.*, 61.
102 *St. 21.*
103 *St. 34.*
104 *St. 38.*
105 *St. 26.*
106 *St. 6.* See also Sirotkin, *op.cit.,* 63.
107 *Biulleten' No. 27*: 63, 64, 73. See also *Biulleten' No. 30*: 61–86.
108 Siomina (1998).
109 *Prison Conditions in the Soviet Union*, New York: Human Rights Watch, 1991, p. 41.
110 N. Tabakova, "V zone osobogo ravnodushiia", *Moskovskaya Pravda*, June 8, 1990: 4. See also "The Zone, 1989: The Soviet Penal System under Perestroika", *Radio Liberty Report*, September 15, 1989, p. 4.
111 *Amnesty International Report 1990*, Amnesty: London, 1991, p. 10.

112 S.Kovalyov, 'Odnazhdy propal prezidentskii ukaz', *Literaturnaya Gazeta*, No. 33 (5513) August 17, 1994, p.11.

113 See, *The Stalinist Penal System: A Statistical History of Soviet Repressions & Terror 1930-53*. J. Pohl, London: McFarland & Company Ince., Publishers, 1997, p. 10. See also, *Commission on Human Rights: Fifty-first session. Item 10 (a) of the provisional agenda - Report of the Special Rapporteur, Mr Nigel S. Rodley, submitted pursuant to Commission on Human Rights resolution 1994/37 Addendum Visit by the Special Rapporteur to the Russian Federation.*

114 M. Kazachkov, 'Dolomat menya do kontsa im ne udalos', *Ekspress Khronika*, No. 51 (176) December 18, 1990, p. 4. Kazachkov was arrested on November 21, 1975 under articles 64, 78, 88 & 154, p.3.

115 S. Kovalyov, 'C.A. Kovalyov: Vse eti dela nado nepesmatrivat', *Ekspress Khronika*, No. 34 (159) August 21, 1990, p.8. See also, *Rysskaya Mysl'*, No. 3842 August 24, 1990, pp. 1, 8.

116 In the spring of 1991, Kovalyov appealed to Yeltsin for an amnesty of the prisoners. The decree drafted by Kovalyov disappeared and it was not until after the August coup that a new decree was drafted and the Amnesty took place. The last ten political prisoners received amnesties and were released at the end of 1991 and beginning of 1992.

117 S. Kovalyov, *Tvorchestvo i byt gulaga*, Moskva: Zvenya, 1998, p. 6.

118 S. Kovalyov, "Sergei Kovalyov: ne vizhu smysla mstit", No. 2, 1992, New York: Kline Archive, p. 2.

119 *Ibid.*

120 S. Kovalyov, *Tvorchestvo i byt gulaga*, Moskva: Zvenya, 1998, p. 62. See also "C. A Kovalyov: vse eti dela nado nepesmatrivat", *Ekspress-Khronika*, No. 34 (159), August 21, 1990: 8.

121 Kovalyov, *op.cit.*: 8.

122 S. Kovalyov, "Sergei Kovalyov: ne vizhu smysla mstit", No. 2, 1992, New York: Kline Archive, p. 2.

123 Abbreviated from the Russian word for prisoner, *zaklychennyi.*

124 Kovalyov, *ibid.*, 2.

125 Orlov (1998).

126 *Prison Conditions in the Soviet Union*, New York: Human Rights Watch, 1991, p. 45.

127 *Nezavisimaya Gazeta*, No. 134, October 29, 1991: 1. See also *Demokraticheskaya Rossiya*, No. 35 December 6, 1991: 8.

128 "Zakliuchennye osnovatelno podoshli k aktsii protesta", *Nezavisimaya Gazeta*, No. 145, November 16, 1991: 1.

129 *Ibid.*

130 Orlov (1998).

131 See *Biulleten' No, 27*: 5, 70.

132 Orlov (1998).

133 "O vnesenii izmenenii i dopolnenii v ispravitel'no-trudovoi kodeks RSFSR, ugolovnii kodeks RSFSR i ugolovno-protsessualnii kodeks RSFSR", *Vedomosti* 29 (1992): 2086–101, St. 26. See also "O soblydenii prav cheloveka v zavedeniyakh penitentsiarnoi sistemi", *Doklad o soblydenii prav cheloveka i grazhdanina v Rossiiskoi Federatsii za 1993 god.*

134 *St. 63, 64, 65, 69, 70.*

135 *St. 26.*

136 *St. 51.*

137 *St. 30.*

138 *St. 28.*

139 *St. 30.*

140 *St. 39.*

141 *St. 51.*
142 *St. 22.*
143 Orlov (1998).
144 Orlov (1998).
145 Orlov (1998).
146 *St. 37.*
147 *Prison Conditions in the Soviet Union*, New York: Human Rights Watch, 1991, p. 36.
148 *St. 28.*
149 *St. 57.*
150 *St. 53.* For an explaination of the terminology *shizo*, *pkt* and *kartser.*

151 *St. 10.*
152 *St. 35.*
153 *St. 82.*
154 Orlov (1998).
155 Orlov (1998).
156 Orlov (1998).
157 *St. 53.*
158 *"Shtrafnoi izoliator "*
159 *Prison Conditions in the Soviet Union*, New York: Human Rights Watch, 1991, p. 41.
160 *"Pomeshchenie kamernogo tipa"*
161 *Prison Conditions in the Soviet Union*, New York: Human Rights Watch, 1991, p. 41.
162 *"Ditsiplinarnyi izoliator"*
163 *Prison Conditions in the Soviet Union*, New York: Human Rights Watch, 1991, p. 41.
164 *Ibid.*
165 *St. 53.*
166 *St. 54.*
167 *St. 53.*
168 See *On the Observance of the Rights of Man and the Citizen in the Russian Federation (1994–1995).* Report of the President"s Commission on Human Rights, translated by Catherine A. Fitzpatrick for the Human Rights Project Group, March 1996. Henceforth, *Report.* See also "Doklad o sobludenii prav cheloveka i grazhdanina v Rossiiskoi Federatsii za 1993 god", *Prava Cheloveka v Rossii, Vypusk 1*, Moskva: Prava Cheloveka, 1995, p. 211. Henceforth, *Doklad.*
169 *Report*: 67, 68.
170 *Report*: 67, 68.
171 *Doklad*: 211.
172 Orlov (1998).
173 *Report*: 68.
174 "Stenogramme of interview with Sergei Kovalyov by David Remnick", New York: Kline Archive, unpublished, undated, p. 5.
175 This is better known as the trial of the CPSU. But according to Judge Anatoly Kononov, it was not a trial of the CPSU but rather a hearing on the constitutionality of the three decrees issued by Yeltsin regarding the banning of the Communist Party.
176 D. Barry, "The Trial of the CPSU and the Principles of Nuremberg", *Review of Central and East European Law*, No. 3, (1996): 255.
177 Barry, *op.cit.*, 255.

178 A. Kononov, personal interview with E. Gilligan, Moscow, September 1999. Henceforth Kononov (1999).

179 Kononov (1999).

180 *Materiali dela o proverke konstitustionnosti Ukazov Presidenta RF, kasayshikhsya deyatel"nosti KPSS i KP RSFSR, a takshe o proverke konstitustionnosti KPSS i KP RSFSR*, Moskva: Spark, 1996, p. 3.

181 "It is easy to defend the strong: Andrei Makarov on the prospects of the trial of the CPSU", *Moscow News*, No. 28, 1992: 6.

182 Barry, *op.cit.*, 260.

183 Kononov (1999).

184 S. Kovalyov, "Vystuplenie Kovalyova v Konstitustionnom sude", June, 1992 Melbourne: Personal collection, E. Gilligan. Henceforth, *Vystuplenie.*

185 Kovalyov, *Vystuplenie.*

186 Kovalyov, *Vystuplenie.*

187 Kovalyov, *Vystuplenie.*

188 Kovalyov, *Vystuplenie.*

189 Kovalyov, *Vystuplenie.*

190 Kovalyov, *Vystuplenie.*

191 Kovalyov, *Vystuplenie.*

192 Kovalyov, *Vystuplenie.*

193 Cited by Kovalyov, *Vystuplenie.* See also Ts.Kh.C.D – Centre for Contemporaray Documentation. F.89, P.18 D.111 N.2521-Ch December 26, 1986. Memorandum from the KGB to CPSU Central Committee, p. 4.

194 Kovalyov, *Vystuplenie.*

195 For the ruling of the court regarding Yeltsin's three decrees, see Barry, *op.cit.*, 258.

196 Kovalyov, *Vosp.*, 81.

197 See Barry, *op.cit.*, 256. See also Yuri Feofanov, "The Establishment of the Constitutional Court in Russia and the Communist Party Case", *Review of Central and East European Law*, No. 6, (1993): 629.

198 Cited in Feofanov, *ibid.*, 623.

199 Kononov (1999).

200 S. Kovalyov, "Obshaya vina, obshaya otvetstvennost", *Moskovskii Novosti*, No. 5 January 31, 1991: 3. See also S. Kovalyov, "Tak zhit v takom gosudarstve", *Karta*, New York: Kline Archive, date unknown, pp. 7–10.

201 Kovalyov, *Vystuplenie.*

202 Kovalyov, *Vosp.*, 92

203 Siomina (1998).

204 Siomina, (1985 and 1998).

205 Siomina (1998).

206 Siomina (1998).

207 Siomina (1998).

208 B. Zolotukhin, "Mozhet li Rossii vyiti iz konstitutsionnogo kriziza?", *Rysskaya Mysl'*, No. 3981, May 28–June 3, 1993: 7.

209 "Constitution Watch: Russia", *East European Constitutional Review*, Vol. 1, No. 1 (Spring), (1992): 6.

210 S. Sirotkin, personal interview with E. Gilligan, Moscow, November 1995. Henceforth, Sirotkin (1995).

211 Sirotkin (1995). See also "Deklaratsiya Prav i Svobod Cheloveka i Grazhdanina", *Vedomosti – Sezd Narodnogo Deputata i Vekhovnogo Soveta RSFSR 52*, (1991), st. 1864–5: 2101–7.

212 Section One, Chapter Two. Constitution of the Russian Federation. Articles 17 and 18. Available online at:

http://www.departments.bucknell.edu/russian/const/ch2.html   (accessed   June 2000).

213 "Deklaratsiya Prav i Svobod Cheloveka i Grazhdanina", *Vedomosti-Sezd Narodnogo Deputata i Vekhovnogo Soveta RSFSR 52*, (1991), st. 1864–5: 2101–7.

214 "Deklaratsiya Prav i Svobod Cheloveka i Grazhdanina", St. 40. See also L. Boitsova, V. Boitsova and V. Rudnev, "Upolnomochennii po delam nesover-shennoletnikh", *Sovetskaya Ustitsiya*, No. 19–20, October (1992): 10.

215 Better known in Western countries as the office of the Federal Ombudsman.

216 "Otchet Komiteta Verkhovnogo Soveta Rossiiskoi Federatsii po pravam cheloveka", Melbourne: Personal collection, E. Gilligan, p. 11.

217 S. Kovalyov, "Ombudsmeny i sudebnye garantii zashchiti prav cheloveka", *Yuridicheskaya Zashita Prav Cheloveka*, Moskva: Moskovskaya Khel'sinskaya Gruppa, February, 1993, p. 152. See also I. Burmostrovitch, personal interview with E. Gilligan, Moscow, December 1995; V. Petrovich, personal interview with E. Gilligan, Moscow, December 1995.

218 S. Kovalyov, "Ombudsmeni i sudebnie garantii zashchiti prav cheloveka", *Yuridicheskaya Zashchita Prav Cheloveka*, Moskva: Moskovskaya Khel'sinskaya Gruppa, February, 1993, p. 152. See also "Ombudsmen upol-nomochen zashchitit", *Obshaya Gazeta*, January 17, 1994: 4.

219 Siomina (1995).

220 Y. Shenshuchenko and G. Murashin, "Institut ombudsmena v sovremennom burzhyaznom gosudarstve", *Sovetskoe Gosudarstvo i Pravo*, No. 1, (1971): 139–44.

221 Shenshushenko and Murashin, *ibid.*, p.143 .

222 Shenshushenko and Murashin, *ibid.*, 143.

223 Cited in J.M.F. Feldbrugee, *Russian Law: the end of the Soviet system and the role of law*, Dordrecht and Boston: M. Nijhoff, 1993, p. 205.

224 Feldbrugge, *op.cit.*, 206.

225 V. Boitsova, *Slyshba zashchiti prav cheloveka i grazhdanina: mirovoi opit*, Moskva: Vek, 1996, p. 6. See also "The Price of Independence: The Office of Ombudsman and Human Rights in the Russian Federation: A Report of the Lawyers Committee for Human Rights, March 1995".

226 For a copy of the draft law, see "Poyasnitelnaya zapiska k proektu federalnogo konstitutsionnogo zakona ob ynolnomochennom Rossiiskoi Federatsii po pravam cheloveka", *Rossiiskii Biulleten Po Pravam Cheloveka*, Vypusk 4, 1994: 179–80. Henceforth. *Proekt. St.* See also "Zakonodatelnaya reglamentatsiya deyatel'nosti upolnomochennogo po pravam cheloveka v Rossiiskoi Federatsii", *Pravozashchitnik 2*, 1997: 63.

227 "The Price of Independence: The Office of Ombudsman and Human Rights in the Russian Federation: A report for the Lawyers Committee for Human Rights, March, 1995", p. 14.

228 *Proekt. St. 1.*

229 *Proekt. St. 16.*

230 *Proekt. St. 16.*

231 *Proekt. St. 17.*

232 *Proekt. St. 18.*

233 *Proekt. St. 20.*

234 *Proekt. St. 21.*

235 *Proekt. St. 23.*

236 *Proekt. St. 25.*

237 *Proekt. St. 28.*

238 *Proekt. St. 29, 34.*

239 *Proekt. St. 1.*

240 *Proekt. St. 30.*
241 *Proekt. St. 1.*
242 Sirotkin (1995).
243 Siomina (1995).
244 S. Kovalyov, "Ombudusmen upolmomochen zashitit", *Obshaya Gazeta*, No. 20/45, New York: Kline Archive, year unknown, p. 4.
245 S. Kovalyov, "Ombudsmeni i sudebnie garantii zashchiti prav cheloveka", *Yuridicheskaya Zashchita Prav Cheloveka*, Moskva, February, 1993. p. 153. See also "Ombudsmen znachit zastupnik: interviu s Sergeem Kovalevym", *Rysskaya Mysl'*, No. 4057, December 15–21, 1994: 9.
246 Sirotkin (1995). See also Kovalyov, "Ombudsmeni i sudebnie garantii zashiti prav cheloveka", *Yuridicheskaya Zashchita Prav Cheloveka*, Moskva, February 1993, p. 156.
247 Siomina 2 (1995).
248 Siomina (1995).
249 Sirotkin (1995).
250 M. Aruntynov, personal interview with E. Gilligan, Moscow, December 1995. Henceforth, Aruntynov (1995).
251 Cited in "Pasportnaya sistema i sistema propiski v Rossii", *Biulleten' Po Pravam Cheloveka*, (1994), p. 14.
252 See "On the Observance of the Rights of Man and the Citizen in the Russian Federation (1994–1995): Report of the President's Commission on Human Rights", Melbourne: Personal collection, E. Gilligan. Henceforth, *Report (1994–1995)*.
253 *Report (1994–1995)*.
254 "Pasportnaya sistema i sistema propiski v Rossii", *Biulleten' Po Pravam Cheloveka*, (1994): 15. Note that the other two important laws passed by the sub-committee comprise the "Law on Refugees of the Russian Federation" on February 19, 1993, and "On Forced Migrants" on February 19, 1993.
255 *Belaya Kniga Rossii.*, p. 71. See also "Doklad o sobludenii prav cheloveka i grazhdanina v Rossiiskoi Federatsii za 1993 god", *Prava Cheloveka v Rossii – Mezhdunarodnoe Izmerenie, Vipusk 1*, Moskva: Prava Cheloveka, 1995: 206–9.
256 *Belaya Kniga Rossii.*, p. 71.
257 Aruntynov (1995).
258 S. Kovalyov, *Moskovskii Novosti*, April 11, 1993: 11.
259 S. Kovalyov, "Khvatit li zdravogo smysla", *Vek*, No. 15, 1992: 2.
260 S. Kovalyov, *Moskovskii Novosti*, April 11, 1993: 11.
261 S. Kovalyov, "Deputatu trusyat pered referendumom", *Nezavisimaya Gazeta*, April 10, 1993, No. 68 (583): 4.
262 *Ibid.*
263 Kovalyov, *Vosp.*, 85–8.
264 "Deputaty trusyat pered referendumom", *Nezavisimaya Gazeta*, April 10, 1993, No. 68 (583): 4.
265 "Russian Parliament must be decent enough to resign, says reformer MP", *RIA-Novosti*, April 26, 1993: 2.
266 Kovalyov, *Vosp.*, 78.
267 Kovalyov, *Vosp.*, 84.
268 Kovalyov, *Vosp.*, 90.
269 Kovalyov, *Vosp.*, 84.
270 A. Rutskoi, cited in J. Dunlop, *The Rise and Fall of the Soviet Empire*, Princeton University Press, Princeton 1993, p. 320.
271 R. Khasbulatov, cited in Dunlop: 320.
272 Dunlop, *ibid.*, 320.
273 Kovalyov, *Vosp.*, 80.

274 S. Kovalyov, "Obrashchenie predsedatelu komiteta no pravam cheloveka C.A Kovalyova k grazhdanam Rossii, Okt, 1993", *Moskva Osen – 93: Khronika Protivostoyaniya*, Moskva: Respublika, 1995, p. 424.
275 S. Kovalyov, "Parlament umer, da zdravstvuet parlament!", *Moskovskii Novosti*, October 3, 1992: 2.
276 A. Sinyavsky, "Vse eto uzhe bylo: Pochemy ya segodnya protiv Eltsina", *Nezavisimaya Gazeta*, No. 295, October 13, 1993: 5.
277 V. Chalidze, Letter to E. Gilligan, April 1997, Melbourne: Personal collection E. Gilligan.
278 Y. Rachinskii, "Posmertnaya pravota kommunisticheskoi propagandi, ili kratkie zametki o tom, kak vazhno ne putat formu i soderzhanie", *Nezavisimaya Gazeta*, October 19, 1993, No. 199: 5.
279 Rachinskii, *ibid.*, 5.
280 Rachinskii, *op.cit.*, 5.
281 Kovalyov, *Vosp.*, 89.
282 Kovalyov, *Vosp.*, 86.
283 S. Kovalyov, "Kovalyov"s speech to the Founding Congress of the Political Movement – Russia's Choice", October 16–17, 1993. Translated by E. Kline, New York: Kline Archive, p. 2.

4 The Presidential Human Rights Commission

This study has shown that the Russian Federation is taking serious steps in the region of human rights as one of the foundations of the Constitutional system ...

1993 Presidential Human Rights Report

The aftermath of October

The shelling of the White House in Moscow in October 1993 cast a long shadow over Sergei Kovalyov's career. The new Russian Constitution was founded on the blood of the 147 Russian citizens who were killed in the conflict that took place on October 3 and 4. For all his explanations, Kovalyov was criticised by many of his contemporaries for supporting political expediency. The result was to undermine his reputation as Russia's leading human rights activist, at least within certain intellectual circles, and to provide ongoing material for his harshest critics. A seed of doubt was also planted in the minds of the democratic public, tarnishing his once unblemished reputation as Russia's custodian of the principles of non-violence and evolutionary politics. Talk of his unfaithfulness to those principles raised the question of whether he would resort to a similar position again. He was not to fully recover his reputation until the beginning of the Chechen war in November 1994.

Many of Kovalyov's major areas of reform came under direct threat as a result of the shelling of the White House. He reacted quickly to the human rights violations that occurred in October by taking part in a committee with instructions to look into the activities of the law enforcement organs during the crisis.[1] The measures taken by the Russian government to suppress the rebellion seriously breached the provisions of the Committee's law "On States of Emergency". Alexander Kulikov, Deputy Minister of Internal Affairs, was Commandant during the state of emergency effective in the capital from October 3 to October 18.[2] He acknowledged that, between October 3 and October 5, 95,000 people had been detained in detention centres; 35,000 for violating the curfew, 54,000 for administrative infractions and 6,000 for unspecified acts. Moscow's mayor, Yuri Luzhkov, exploited the state of emergency to purge Moscow of people of Caucasian and Central Asian nationalities. The Moscow Major's Office appealed to the public to use "special telephones" to inform on persons living in the capital without residence permits – 9,779 people were evicted from Moscow for being without a *propiska*.[3] The Committee's landmark law "On Freedom of Movement and Freedom of Choice of Residence" abolishing the *propiska* was flagrantly ignored by Luzhkov. After October 18, he ordered a clean-up of Moscow and implemented a mandatory registration system for all people coming from the former Soviet republics. For a first violation, the accused was fined five times the monthly wage. Repeat offenders were placed under administrative arrest for fifteen days or deported from the capital.[4]

Kovalyov sought to ensure that the government was made accountable for its misdeeds in October. His concern over the crackdown was evident in his decision to appeal to the President publicly in the pages of *Izvestiya*. He expressed concern not merely for the violation of the federal law "On States of Emergency", but for Yeltsin's decree "On Additional Measures to Guarantee the State of Emergency in the City of Moscow", which had ostensibly over-ruled the Federal law. He sought permission from Yeltsin in his public appeal to instruct Procurator-General Kazannik, to examine cases of human rights violations by the MVD, the Militia and the Ministry of Security, and to allow the International Red Cross access to those arrested on October 3–4. He appealed for an examination of all acts and orders published between October 3 and October 18 to establish that they were in accordance with international obligations.[5] He also asked for an investigation of the work of public organizations which had been suspended during the state of emergency, most notably the right-wing newspapers *Pravda* and *Sovetskaya Rossiya*.[6] Despite Kovalyov's efforts, the Procurator-General took action on only 115 cases of human rights violations in October, a fraction of those who registered complaints. Not one criminal case reached the courts when both the organizers of the 1991 August coup and October 1993 were privately amnestied.[7] The violations that occurred in October served to remind Kovalyov of the sheer frustration of seeking accountability for the actions of government agencies in Russia. This failure to secure adequate redress for the victims was one of the first signs of his marginalization in Yeltsin's entourage during 1994.

In the aftermath of the October events, Kovalyov grew increasingly busy with political affairs. On October 16, he addressed the founding congress of the new political bloc, Russia's Choice, in anticipation of the forthcoming December elections. In the opening speech to the Congress, he was optimistic for the democrats:

> The democratic forces can win – not just the elections but substantive political and economic reforms – only if their collaboration survives the elections … If Russia's democrats can work together, then I am confident we can win the elections and – more important – secure for Russia the stability, reforms, democracy and safeguards for human rights and civil liberties which it so desperately needs.[8]

Split over whether to form a party or an electoral bloc, Kovalyov was finally elected Chairman of the Russia's Choice movement, the option favoured by Gaidar and Foreign Minister Andrei Kozyrev. The new party was coined the "party of power".

Kovalyov's optimism regarding the elections was shattered when the results were released on December 12. The outcome illustrated that the democratic reformers were woefully uninformed about the mood of the Russian public. Russia's Choice won more seats than any other bloc, but the extremist parties and candidates won the largest share of the seats in the 450-member chamber. After being elected a people's deputy for the Varshavskii electoral district, Kovalyov declared:

> At this time my country is passing through one of the most complex and dramatic moments in its history. On the one hand, the new Constitution has been adopted and we have held the first democratic election since 1917. On the other hand, representatives of extremist political tendencies have ridden the wave of democracy to gain a strong position in the new parliament. Among them is the Liberal Democratic Party which is led by Vladimir Zhirinovsky, a man whose views are in complete opposition to both liberalism and democracy.[9]

Alarmed by Zhirinovsky's success, Kovalyov joined the council for the newly formed Russian Anti-Fascist Movement (RAM) on December 21. He explained Zhirinovsky's success in a number of ways. He argued that the electorate did not vote so much for Zhirinovsky and the communists as "against" the costs and burdens of economic reform. He insisted that "Russian voters [had not] yet learnt that elections are the mechanism through which ordinary citizens exercise control over their country's policies. They more often think of elections as a means to simply express their discontent."[10] He also believed that the popularity of fascist ideas in Russia was directly linked to the omnipotence of the state bureaucracy. He argued that the tendency to favour fascist ideas "... was not only a result of Zhirinovsky's promises of social and economic reform, but directly linked to a general feeling of social defencelessness amongst the population."[11] He admitted that he could no longer ignore the social tensions that accompanied Russia's economic instability. He had underestimated the extent to which years of economic suffering had affected the electorate and called for an easing of the "negative effects of economic reforms on society, toward providing shock-absorbers that people could feel and understand ..."[12]

While the democrats were shocked by the results of the elections, they still awaited the passing of the Russian constitution. The constitutional plebiscite for Yeltsin's 1993 draft Constitution coincided with the December elections. The plebiscite witnessed an official turnout of just over 55 per cent of voters. Roughly 60 per cent were in favour of the amendments to the

Constitution and 40 per cent against. Yet suspicions were aroused over the handling of the process by the Central Electoral Commission and Yeltsin's decision to call a plebiscite to sidestep the referendum laws which would have drastically altered the results.[13]

Yet what paradoxically united Russia's Choice and Zhirinovsky's Liberal Democratic Party was their support for the new constitution. The aspect favoured by the two political parties was the strong presidential power granted to Yeltsin. In the hope of avoiding a repeat of the conflict that took place between the President and the legislature in October 1993, the authors of the draft had been sure to give Yeltsin control over government appointments, policy formation, the power to issue decrees and edicts and to dissolve the legislature. Commentators later argued that the constitution was tailor-made for Yeltsin, and its success depended largely on its interpretation. Concern was expressed that these powers might one day fall into the "wrong hands".[14] And indeed, Yeltsin would misuse his powers, much to the detriment of Russia's struggle for democracy.

Kovalyov did not strongly criticise the disproportionate powers given to the President. For him, stability was the primary objective of the new constitution.[15] He acknowledged the gaps and deficiencies in the basic law and he knew that it would not necessarily solve the ongoing political crisis between the executive and the legislature. But he hoped that they had set in motion a constitution that would one day reflect the true spirit of Russia. In a speech on May 21, 1994 to celebrate the birthday of Sakharov, he declared:

> Today we live in a country where a new constitution has been passed that proclaims human rights to be the basis of the legal system, where the legislative foundations for political freedom and the supremacy of rights have been laid. We live in a country where the democratic achievements of the people succeeded in suppressing an attempt at armed *revanche*, where freedom of speech has become the norm and where finally a tendency toward public agreement and reconciliation is taking shape.[16]

Kovalyov's satisfaction with the new constitution did not solve his growing problems with the President. Yeltsin anticipated a new political advantage in Zhirinovsky's unexpected victory in the elections. He began to placate the Zhirinovsky voters by noticeably shifting Russia's foreign and domestic policy. Kovalyov, his leading "Westernizer" was sidelined in the process. The attempts by Russia's leading human rights activist to force the authorities to submit to some form of public control grew increasingly difficult. Kovalyov acknowledged the marked change in Yeltsin's policies, but unlike many of his former dissident colleagues he continued his support for the President over the following year.

The new Commission

The extent to which Kovalyov was determined to promote human rights issues was no more evident than in his decision to accept the post of Chairman of the Presidential Human Rights Commission. While preoccupied with securing a democratic majority in the new Duma in the months leading up to the December elections, he was also anxious to replace the public platform he lost when the Human Rights Committee had been dissolved along with the old parliament. On September 26, five days after his decision to dissolve the Congress of People's Deputies, Yeltsin signed decree No. 1458 establishing a Presidential Human Rights Commission.

The President informed Kovalyov of his appointment as Chairman of the new Presidential Human Rights Commission through the newspapers.[17] Unlike March 1990, when Yeltsin persuaded Kovalyov in a personal conversation to head the Human Rights Committee, Kovalyov was given little option. He accepted the post for the same reasons that compelled him to finally accept the chair of the Supreme Soviet Committee. He saw the appointment as an opportunity to influence the government administration and to voice his human rights concerns. The difference was that, by the end of 1993, he had significantly more to lose. He and his colleagues were still anxious to pass the law on the Human Rights Commissioner in the parliament. They were in the middle of compiling Russia's first government human rights report for 1993. They hoped one day to witness the implementation of the laws they had passed under the Supreme Soviet. Moreover, Kovalyov was concerned that he and his colleagues might lose their power to influence the drafting of laws. He was concerned about his crucial role as international spokesman for Russia's new policy on human rights, epitomized in his April 1992 address to the UN Human Rights Commission. In short, he risked losing his public profile in domestic politics and the modicum of influence he had painstakingly built up.

Kovalyov was aware that his new position had been given to him by way of a political trade-off for his loyalty in October. The mood under which the new Commission was established did not match that which accompanied the beginning of the old Committee. The Commission was established under what was tantamount to presidential rule in the lead-up to the elections, and it was not until November that a further decree, No. 1798, was issued outlining the terms and conditions under which the Commission would operate. Kovalyov and his team took what was left of their files from the burnt offices at the White House and moved to *Dom* 3/8 at *Staraya Ploshad*, the former offices of the Central Committee. The first session of the Commission was not convened until December 15.

The Presidential Human Rights Commission was divided into two sections – a public commission and an administrative body. Its public profile was raised by the honorary membership of prominent individuals in the public commission, such as human rights activist Elena Bonner,[18] lawyer and former

Chairman of the Legislative Committee Boris Zolotukhin, Foreign Minister Andrei Kozyrev, Sergei Averintsev, Alexander Mikhailovitch, Sergei Alekseev, Igor Golembiovskii, Duma Deputy Mikhail Molostvov, former dissident and Head of the Department of International Humanitarian and Cultural Collaboration under the Foreign Ministry Vyachaslev Bakhmin and writer Fasil Izkander. The key staff comprised former members of the Human Rights Committee: Mikhail Arutyunov (vice-chairman), Alexander Kopylev (vice-chairman), Sergei Sirotkin (vice-chairman) and Kovalyov's chief aid, Lydia Siomina. With the exception of the chairman, the vice-chairmen and a total staff of thirty-five, the remaining members worked as volunteers.[19] With vastly improved technical support, the prospects for the future looked promising.

Particularly significant were Kovalyov's negotiations with Yeltsin in the interim period between September 26 and the signing of the second decree, No. 1798, on November 1. It was agreed that the Commission would serve as the nucleus of the office of the Human Rights Commissioner once the federal constitutional law establishing the office was passed by the Duma.[20] Kovalyov and his colleagues attached a separate document to Decree 1798 detailing the status of the Presidential Human Rights Commission. The mandate, tasks and rights of the Commission were practically identical to those outlined in the draft law on the Human Rights Commissioner. The mandate of the Commission was:

1   To aid the President of the Russian Federation to guarantee fundamental human rights and freedoms.
2   To respect and monitor human rights and freedoms in the Russian Federation.
3   To amend legislation in order to guarantee human rights and freedoms.
4   To defend the rights and protect the citizens of the Russian Federation, situated outside its borders.
5   To strengthen international collaboration to guarantee rights and freedoms, recognized by international law and the legislation of the Russian Federation.[21]

The document stated that one of the primary tasks of the Commission was educational. Each year it was required to issue an annual report outlining the human rights situation in Russia and suggesting ideas for improvement. The report would be distributed to all government departments and to the public. The Commission was to keep the legislative and executive organs up to date on human rights violations. It would examine normative acts and orders to establish that they were in accordance with international law. Moreover, the Commission was to receive citizens' complaints, including those addressed to the President.[22] In order to investigate individual or mass cases of human rights violations the Commission was able to request information, documents or materials from state departments or individuals necessary to adequately understand the case. The Commission was to pass recommendations to government departments, who were to respond within fifteen days. Experts could be recruited to investigate cases.[23] It was agreed that, once the office of the Human Rights Commissioner was established, the Presidential Human Rights Commission would continue to exist as a small consultative body to the President.[24]

The problem of developing a system for analysing complaints that plagued the Human Rights Committee continued.[25] Ilya Burmistrovich and Yuri Shikhanovich remained with the Commission, but the complaints continued to pile up. Because it was anticipated that the office of the Human Rights Commissioner would be established in the near future with a large budget and staff qualified to manage the complaints, the problem remained unsolved. The work of the Commission was seriously affected by the impermanence of its position. "The temporary status of the Presidential Commission", recalled Siomina, "had a psychological effect on its employees. A person working temporarily puts down few roots. So from November, we worked for two years without systematizing our work."[26] The failure of Kovalyov to systematize the Commission's work particularly irritated his successor, Vladimir Kartashkin. The new Chairman later bitterly assailed Kovalyov for failing to establish a working structure.[27]

The fundamental weakness of the Commission was its status. The decree stated that the Commission was an "independent subdivision of the Presidential Administration ..." (*samostoyatelnoe strukturnoe podrazdelenie Administratsii Presidenta RF*).[28] The difficulty rested in the precarious position that the Commission occupied as an "independent" structure preparing the staff for the office of the Human Rights Commissioner, and as a subdivision *pri prezidente* (under the President). Each side interpreted the status of the commission differently. Kovalyov saw his role under the President as an overseer, ensuring that Yeltsin abided by his constitutional duty as the guarantor of the rights and freedoms of the citizens of Russia. He insisted on the Commission's independence in precise accordance with the letter of Yeltsin's decree.[29] This detachment from the presidential structures and his tendency to utter independent judgements made Kovalyov's position difficult. Attempting to be both consultant and critic of the President proved too disrupting. For all his democratic proclamations, Yeltsin became increasingly frustrated with the vocal criticisms emanating from the presidential structures. Kovalyov's hardest battle was to convince his colleagues that criticism could be constructive.

This conflict of interest was complicated by Kovalyov's appointment on January 21 as Russia's first Human Rights Commissioner.[30] In what became known as the "gentlemen's agreement", the deputies in the first session of the Duma negotiated to distribute key parliamentary posts among the blocs in proportion to their size. At first glance, Kovalyov's appointment was a major victory for the democratic forces. It continued to arouse the suspicion of its opponents that the office of the Human

Rights Commissioner might eventually be used by the democratic parties to wield significant influence in the towns and provinces of Russia.[31] Yet no law had been passed to accompany the appointment. Kovalyov accepted the post in defiance of Article 103.e of the constitution, which stipulated that a Human Rights Commissioner was to be appointed on the basis of a Federal constitutional law. His successor, the communist Oleg Mironov, criticised Kovalyov on the popular television programme *Geroi Dnya* for accepting the post in violation of the constitution.[32]

For Kovalyov, the difficulties of operating in a lawless state became more apparent. While he struggled to secure the office of the Human Rights Commissioner for Russia, he defied the constitution in the process. Undoubtedly, he became more impatient and anxious to push forward. He believed that the office of the Human Rights Commissioner was one of the most important democratic institutions for Russia. Contrary to those who criticised Kovalyov as a radical Westernizer, he never believed that a simple solution was feasible, nor was he naive enough to believe that Western democratic institutions could be transplanted in their entirety to Russian soil. He believed in the importance of creating institutions that protect the citizen from a despotic state, and he was driven by his personal philosophy that the task of the intellectual was to create ideals. But he was constantly caught in the contradiction between slow, evolutionary change, the belief that progress should adjust itself to the actual pace of historical change, and the role of the intellectual to push forward, to create visions for Russia's future. It is in his struggle for Section Two of the Constitution and the post of Human Rights Commissioner that we see this contradiction played out most acutely. Whatever may be thought about the means Kovalyov supported to implement these two institutions, his decision was no doubt weighed against what they had already achieved and how far they had come from March 1990 or, for that matter, from 1964.

As essential as visions are for any country, especially those undergoing a period of dramatic change, on their own they are not enough. By 1994, Kovalyov's ability to push forward could not conceal the fact that his many talents were undermined by his poor organizational skills. He and the majority of his colleagues were inexperienced in the day-to-day demands of administrative and managerial chores. As Siomina later confessed, "all we had was common sense".[33] Kovalyov had shown his commitment to practical work in the Human Rights Committee, but he had been relatively free to pursue his own goals. The presidential administration demanded something new of him. He was expected to fulfill the Commission's mandate, and the expectations that accompanied it were higher. One of its functions was to handle complaints, and the Commission was now accountable to individuals. It was also responsible for the reputation of what would one day be the office of the Human Rights Commissioner. Kovalyov's struggle to meet these demands is no more evident than in the Commission's first case.

Human Rights Commissioner: Case No. 1

The first case of the Presidential Human Rights Commission was an extremely challenging one. In early December of 1993 it received a letter from Svetlana Romanuk, a member of the Moscow Committee for the Survival of Youth. Romanuk expressed her concern about the recent establishment of Viktor Stolbun's boarding school for adolescents in the town of Stupino in the Moscow *oblast*.[34] Stolbun was known in narrow circles in the 1970s for his cure for alcoholism, the so-called Stolbun method. The self-proclaimed medical practitioner reappeared again at the beginning of the 1990s.[35] His boarding school known as *Phoenix* and the accompanying rehabilitation centre, *Spasitel* (Saviour), was based in a pioneer camp which belonged to the Ministry of Atomic Energy. Stolbun was alleged to be conducting experiments on children, administering electrical charges in the coccyx, anal and perineal regions with the aim of reducing psychological tension.[36] These alleged practices were causing a strong public reaction, especially in the summer of 1994. Romanuk appealed to Kovalyov to investigate the school.

Stolbun had begun to arouse suspicion in 1992. In the summer of that year, he moved his school, together with the 150 adolescent students, to Torzhok in the Tver region, after growing pressure from the local Stupino press and the media in the capital. It was rumored that the Stupino administration had decided to withdraw its financial backing for the school once the newspaper campaign began. In Torzhok, Stolbun organized accommodation in an old sanatorium. He continued to advertise on the television and in the newspapers, claiming that for two-hundred dollars teenagers from the ages of fourteen to sixteen could undergo the selection process. Reports later confirmed that the director and his wife, Valentina Streltsova, intentionally selected children who were having trouble at school, suffering from either self esteem problems or psychiatric disorders. According to Siomina, Stolbun "gathered damaged children.... Children with colossal personality complexes in communication and in self-esteem."[37] For some specialists, the boarding school proved a convenient way for parents to escape the responsibilities of raising a difficult child.[38] Moreover, part of the attraction, actively promoted by Stolbun, was that the students finished school at sixteen and were assured entry into an institution of higher learning. According to the advertisements, any child, even those not making satisfactory progress or lacking direction, could complete the entire school programme in one year, excel, and go directly into any institute of higher learning.[39] The electrical charges inflicted on the children were said to accelerate the learning curve by removing the signs of hyperactivity that distracted the children from their studies.[40] The controversy around the school was heightened by the open and public support of Stolbun by the Minister of Education A.G. Asmolov, the popular children's writer Eduard Uspensky, and the director of children's films Rolan Bikov. Stolbun was also alleged to have treated Brezhnev, Andropov and Ligachev.[41]

The Commission decided to undertake an investigation of the school under pressure from the press and Romanuk's appeal. After a preliminary study of the question, they organized specialists in child psychiatry and psychology, pedagogues, and members of the Commission to visit Torzhok. On April 28, the Commission had its first open session on the case. Svetlana Romanuk, the most tireless campaigner for the closure of the school, presented her findings. She argued that the children were deliberately isolated from their surroundings and information sources: television, radio and newspapers. She expressed concern that the majority of students did not return to their parents, but stayed on at the school as teachers or aides, and that the students were only guaranteed entry into those higher education institutes which were private and did not require entry examinations. "As Russia heads towards building a lawful, democratic society," declared Romanuk, "it's difficult to believe that we could allow medical experiments on children and present them to the wider community as if they were outstanding pedagogical experiments with phenomenal results."[42] She concluded that the electrical charges administered in the anal regions had distinctly sexual overtones. For Romanuk, the idolization of Stolbun by the students was reminiscent of a sect.[43]

The Commission employed consultants to help with the investigation. One of the specialists who investigated the school as part of the Commission's team of experts was Vice President of the Independent Psychiatrists' Association, Emanual Gushansky. As Kovalyov's chief aide confirmed two years later, Gushansky believed that the school was a dangerous social phenomenon. He laid particular stress on the fact that there was no medical evidence for the treatment being administered to the children. Gushansky described the feelings they experienced immediately after the procedure: "At first there is complete lethargy, followed by a short sleep and then a gradual resurgence in energy." He expressed concern that the children were becoming dependent on the practice. Moreover, he believed that the electrical charges were being performed without the permission of the children or the children's parents.[44] Gushanskii's colleague, Elena Brono, and members of the Independent Association of Child Psychiatrists and Psychologists noted little independence among the students. According to Brono the children were "in complete isolation, there were no newspapers, radio or television … The children were never on their own and kept busy from morning until evening." The experts were concerned that the children would experience serious difficulties when trying to adapt to life outside the school.[45]

Of equal concern was that Stolbun was not a doctor. He had no licence to treat children with tests that had no scientific foundation. The Deputy Procurator of the Moscow *oblast*, General Sugrobov, pointed out at the open session on April 28 that "Stolbun was violating Article 4 and 18 of the law of the Russian Federation pertaining to the right of the individual to informed agreement to render psychiatric help and the right to receive psychiatric help from professionals."[46] By February 1995, the General

Procurator of Russia instituted proceedings against Stolbun on the basis of Article 221 of the Criminal Code for assuming the role of a doctor.[47]

Kovalyov's chief aide, Lydia Siomina, visited *Phoenix* for one day. A philologist by profession and the former principal of a secondary school, Siomina had sought permission from Kovalyov to live with the children for a week in order to conduct a thorough investigation. He had refused her request.[48] Siomina invited Tatyana Velikanova, Kovalyov's old friend and co-editor of the *The Chronicle of Current Events*, with her to the school. Since returning from internal exile in the mid-1980s, Velikanova had worked as a mathematics teacher. The third member of the team was a specialist in paediatric psychology from the Institute of Child Psychiatry and Psychology.[49] The women spent the day with different groups, speaking with the children and teachers, monitoring classroom activity and watching choral performances. "When all three of us met afterwards," Siomina claimed, "it turned out that we had the same impression: we expressed it in different words, but we had a completely unanimous viewpoint, that this school was hiding something, something serious."[50]

On the eve of the first session of the Commission regarding the Stolbun case on April 27, Kovalyov decided to visit the school personally. According to Siomina's account, he had fully supported the conclusions of the experts before his visit.[51] As it turned out, he had significant differences with other members of the Commission, notably Elena Bonner and Sergei Averintsev, during the six-hour session the following day.[52] He argued that the children had appeared content to him. As a whole the Commission and the recruited experts were united in their opposition to the school and were irritated by Kovalyov's repeating of the words: "I've never seen so many happy children. They are all damaged, all ugly ... But they are all happy."[53] His unyielding position dragged out debates on the question for several months.

Kovalyov's position was severely weakened by the fact that he had no justification for his argument, except that the children appeared happy. It was around this premise that the rumour emerged shortly after that he was under pressure from the authorities to discourage further investigation into the boarding school.[54] But according to Siomina his reaction was shaped by inexperience:

> I think that Sergei Adamovich took the children's happiness so seriously because he is not a professional in this field. He has his children, but his life's priority was rights defence, and with ten years of prison and exile, he didn't bring up his children in the full sense of the word. To use a Russian expression, he took the children's happiness for "pure money" ... His standard line was that Soviet schools were schools that repressed children, that was his stereotype, which isn't completely true.[55]

Kovalyov's position on the Stolbun school was surprising. One would have expected him to reject Stolbun's dominant theory of the importance of the collective over the individual that the experts had noted. If that did not influence his decision, his knowledge of the abuse of psychiatric medicine under the Soviet regime would surely have compelled him to investigate the case further. Siomina and Velikanovna urged him to change his mind, without success.

The Commission never succeeded in issuing a final resolution. Romanuk wrote to Yeltsin on August 22, 1994 that, because of:

> ... Sergei Kovalyov's lack of objectivity and his lack of desire to fulfill his obligations Boris Nikolaevitch, I appeal to you with the question: Whose rights is the Human Rights Commissioner defending? How can you trust the defence of human rights by Kovalyov when he knows about the EXPERIMENTS ON CHILDREN ...[56]

The members of the Commission drafted a resolution. It stated that the status of the school and the licensing of its activities did not enter the competence of the Commission. The draft claimed that there was evidence to suggest that the parents and the children were not always informed about the regulations and provisions of the school. It explained that the method of administering electric currents practised on the children had no scientific foundation and had not been sufficiently tested. For this reason it could not be used. The findings concluded that the relevant educational and health ministries should conduct a careful examination of the school over several weeks.[57] The conclusions were never released.[58]

In effect, the Commission completely absolved itself of any responsibility and prevented the investigation from moving forward. It did not pass on recommendations to the suitable departments suggesting appropriate action, as was stipulated in its mandate. After interest in the case waned, Commission members went to Washington to observe American investigatory procedures. From this experience they understood how poorly they had handled the Stolbun matter.[59] "I must say," said Siomina, "we investigated this affair very unprofessionally. Where could our experience have come from for this? It was our first serious investigation. When a year later we went to the United States ... to see how they approached their investigations ... We immediately understood all our mistakes in this case."[60]

But inexperience could not be the only excuse for the poor handling of this case. By dismissing the expert findings, Kovalyov failed to take into account the arguments and specialized knowledge of the Commission's consultants. Nor did he try to reconcile his own opinion with that of the experts by investigating the school further. Ruling out valid evidence in favour of opinion and intuition was neither a diplomatic nor a professional handling of events and showed his lack of managerial and administrative talents at their worst. It is hard to determine what the main impetus was behind his decision, but it is worth noting that he did not mention the school in his *Memoirs*. As Human Rights Commissioner, Kovalyov could no longer pick and choose his causes. If the Commission was to be respected for its objectivity, it had to undertake cases, regardless of their appeal or lack thereof. The Commission's first case was a memorable failure.

Decree on banditry and organized crime

Within six weeks of the opening session on the Stolbun case, Kovalyov was drawn into yet another public debate. On June 14, Yeltsin issued Decree No. 1226 "On Urgent Measures to Protect Citizens Against Banditry and Organized Crime." On June 17, Kovalyov reacted to the decree by calling a session of the Commission for June 20. The decree was issued in response to a report by the Chairman of the Parliamentary Committee on Security, Viktor Ilyukhin, who was previously responsible for the draft laws "On the Struggle Against Corruption" and "On Introducing Changes and Additions to the Criminal Procedural Code RSFSR", all of which were rejected by the Committee on Legislation under the Supreme Soviet. The worst features of these draft laws were revived in the June 14 decree.[61] Illyukhin declared to the State Duma that the members of his committee were unanimous that "today, crime is really Russia's national tragedy. There must be a decisive struggle with crime. Very extreme measures are needed now ..."[62]

The concern about mounting crime statistics was well-grounded. The crime figures in Russia had doubled since 1988, from 1,220,362 registered crimes to 2,632,708 in 1994.[63] For Kovalyov, however, the absence of a judicial process for search warrants and the likelihood of illegal detention were among the provisions of Decree No. 1226 that he found alarming. The law enforcement organs could initiate a preliminary investigation of any person or enterprise suspected of being involved in organized crime before a search warrant was secured. Individual, cooperative or enterprise property could be searched or phone-tapped as well as any relatives or persons living with the suspect up to five years prior to the charge. The decree stipulated that the authorized representatives of internal affairs and counterintelligence agencies had the right to inspect the buildings and premises of enterprises, institutions and organizations irrespective of the forms of ownership, to familiarize themselves with documentation, and also to examine transport facilities, their drivers and passengers.[64] Banking and commercial confidentiality would not be an obstacle to obtaining information and documents on the financial activities of any person. If the law enforcement organs believed that there were grounds to convict an individual, he could be held in detention for up to thirty days without being charged.[65]

The Decree on Banditry violated the constitution and the criminal code on several counts. Most notably, it was the absence of any judicial procedure for intiating an investigation or search warrants that violated the following articles: Art. 25: the home is inviolable; Art. 23.2: each person has the right to privacy of correspondence, telephone conversations and postal, telegraph and other communications; and Art. 22.2: detainment cannot exceed 48 hours without court sanction.[66]

The Commission took action on June 20. Kovalyov issued a public appeal to the President, using the opportunity to highlight the President's role as stipulated by the 1993 constitution: "According to the Constitution," he declared, "you as President are the guarantor of the rights and liberties of man and the citizen ... The Human Rights Commission appeals to you to suspend the existing Decree No. 1226 dated June 14, 1994."[67] While the members openly sympathized with Yeltsin's concern about rising crime figures, they were not convinced that it was necessary to use extreme measures.[68] They argued that the struggle would be better waged respecting the limits of the existing laws and through reform of the law enforcement organs. The Commission was convinced that, if implemented, the decree would be accompanied by arbitrariness, unwarranted detention, intrusion into the private activity of citizens, the criminilization of the militia and the corruption of the bureaucracy.[69] As Sirotkin recalled, "Yes, the facts that we gathered testify that, as we predicted, the decree precipitated wide-scale violations ... it made no contribution to the struggle against crime."[70]

Kovalyov was convinced that Yeltsin had come under the influence of similiar decrees adopted in the republics of Bashkortostan and Tatarstan. Situated north of Mongolia, the republic of Tuva had issued a decree on June 29, 1993 "On the Strengthening of the Legal Base of the Struggle with Premeditated Murders on the Territory of the Republic of Tuva". It stipu-lated that, in a case in which a juvenile commited a murder, one of the parents was to be punished in the criminal trial. In the case of a murder during a party at which alcohol was consumed, the party organizers could be jailed for up to two years. Although the decree was abolished within a month, the mere fact that such measures had been considered alarmed Kovalyov.

In the Republic of Bashkortostan in the Southern Urals and the Republic of Tartastan on the Volga, extreme measures to fight crime had already been in use for over a year. In Bashkortostan, 500 people had been detained in connection with the murder of one official. Not one of the detainees was charged. Three attempted suicide and two admitted their own guilt indepen-dent of each other.[71] "Our fear", wrote Kovalyov to Yeltsin, "is that the decree will be accompanied by the arbitrary acts of the law enforcement organs which have already been confirmed by reports from Bashkortostan and Tartastan where similiar judicial acts are in force."[72] Boris Yeltsin had indeed taken a short trip to Tatartstan on May 30. Fourteen days later the decree on Banditry had appeared. After the signing of the decree, the Minister of Internal Affairs of Tatarstan, Iskander Galinov, praised Yeltsin's anti-crime decree. He argued that the President had borrowed much from Tatarstan's experience.[73]

At a meeting of the Collegium of the General Procurator's office on June 21, the Acting Procurator, General Aleksei Ilyushenko, supported Illyukhin's report. Kovalyov was present at the collegium along with procurators from the most important regions throughout Russia, as well as Sergei Filatov,

Head of the Presidential Administration, and Sergei Stepashin, First Deputy Director of the Federal Counterintelligence Service (FSK). Illyushenko announced that the state programme for combating crime for 1994–95 would cost up to 5 billion rubles and the agencies of the Procurator's office would be assigned a coordinating role in the implementation of the programme. The procedures for implementing the decree were to be distributed to local and provincial areas.[74] The following day in the Duma Kovalyov declared: "The picture we are now observing consists of the following: the departments who are responsible for fighting crime are establishing for themselves convenient, comfortable roles in their struggle with crime. Yes, for the departments work is becoming far more convenient. And what about the citizens?"[75]

Kovalyov found it extremely difficult to reconcile himself to the decree, and considered resigning. He was persuaded by his colleagues to remain with the Commission, but his growing apprehension urged him to appeal to the President again.[76] This time Yeltsin responded by giving Kovalyov permission to form a working group to monitor the implementation of the decree – a token gesture at best. The Commission did not have the resources to track the outcome of the decree. Kovalyov argued that it gave him and his colleagues the power to investigate cases to try to facilitate a lawful outcome. They did manage to gather some statistics, but little else was achieved.

The Duma also voted against the decree, 246 to 6. But the legislature was patently ineffective and Yeltsin refused to withdraw the decree. It was implemented on June 27 and the President warned that the Russian Armed Forces would be deployed to aid the fight against crime.[77] By the end of June, a huge operation was launched by the Regional Administration for Combating Organized Crime with the Moscow Criminal Investigation Department, the Administration on Economic Crimes and 20,000 soldiers. They checked on 689 facilities in Moscow and the police detained 2,251 people, with 759 administrative charges brought against them.[78]

For Kovalyov, the Decree on Banditry and Organised Crime was symptomatic of Yeltsin's overall reaction to Zhirinovsky's electoral success in December. Yet he could not get across to his opponents that a coercive government is in fact a weak government. Nor could he convince them that any extreme measures instigated by the government would in fact reach far beyond the perpetrators of organized crime into the everyday lives of individual citizens. Kovalyov had shown his commitment to institutionalized democracy in the shape of formal structures like the constitution, parliament, the courts and electoral systems since 1990. This was only one aspect of his struggle. Local traditions anchored in Russia's political culture presented an even greater challenge for him. Although the disparity between these two forces had largely shaped his struggle, culture's power to constantly generate and encourage old prejudices and habits of thinking was no more evident than in the debates evoked by Yeltsin's June 14 decree.

Kovalyov had hoped that Russia's transition would be shaped by a government that encouraged respect for the law. He also hoped that the new government would encourage civil society to build on its own forces. The decree of June 14 dampened these hopes considerably. Finding it increasingly difficult to promote respect for the rule of law, he found himself in a quandary: to stay meant that he had to work with Yeltsin, who was doing less to encourage democratic reform; to go meant that he would lose any power he still had to influence the authorities. His influence was declining since neither his letters, his fifteen-minute interview on NTV, nor the press campaign against the decree had the slightest influence on Yeltsin. And Yeltsin's concession to Kovalyov to form a monitoring group worked as both a token gesture and a way to keep the Chairman quiet. At stake was not just Kovalyov's personal integrity, but the more fundamental question of the government's real commitment to democratic reform.

Despite the fact that Kovalyov's influence was clearly declining in the government camp, he continued to demonstrate his ability to live with uncertainty. He remained vocal and committed to an open and honest politics. By December of 1994, his commitment to these principles would do much to keep Russia's political integrity intact. For the time being, members of the presidential administration were more intent on preserving the administrative methods of a bureaucratic elite than they were on adjusting to the requirements of a struggling democratic transition.

Russia's first human rights report

One positive event ten days after the June 14 decree was the ratification of the European Convention on Human Rights by the Russian parliament. This coincided with the publication shortly after of the Presidential Commission's first annual human rights report, entitled *The Observance of the Rights of Man and the Citizen in the Russian Federation for 1993*. The Commission experienced few problems with publishing the report, but after it was forwarded to Yeltsin and the Public Chamber on July 5, the Chamber quickly revoked its decision to conduct a broad discussion on human rights problems on July 16 to coincide with its public release and sought to classify it for official use only.[79]

Instead the Public Chamber agreed to discuss *The Federal Programme of Action in the Field of Human Rights*.[80] This document grew out of Kovalyov's participation in the World Conference on Human Rights in Vienna in June 1993. Kovalyov was encouraged by the discussions at the conference and Russia's support for the promotion and protection of human rights as a matter of priority for the international community.[81] Part of the conference's mandate was to invoke "the spirit of our age and the realities of our time which call upon the peoples of the world and all Member States of the United Nations to rededicate themselves to the global task of promoting and protecting all human rights and fundamental freedoms so as to secure full and universal enjoyment of these rights."[82]

Kovalyov continued to lament the great gap between Eastern and Western conceptions of individual rights, particularly among the Islamic countries.[83]

He joined the world conference in its condemnation of the ongoing aggression against the Republic of Bosnia and Herzegovina, the ethnic cleansing, war crimes and crimes against humanity, particularly the targetting of its Muslim population. The Russian Federation was the only country to vote against the declaration introduced by Pakistan's representative on behalf of the Organization of the Islamic Conference on account of point 6, which called for "Lifting the arms embargo against the Republic of Bosnia and Herzegovina in order to enable it to exercise its right to self-defence in accordance with Article 51 of the Charter and implementing all necessary measures under the Charter in order to reverse the aggression perpetrated by Serbian forces." In a letter to Yeltsin, Kovalyov pointed out that, despite the verbal agreements he received to his objection, many of those countries later abstained from voting. Among them were Australia, France, Great Britain and the United States.[84] It was a controversial decision.

One of the outcomes of the Vienna Conference was the "Vienna Declaration and Programme of Action". This aspirational document inspired Kovalyov to return to Moscow to draw up a *Federal Programme of Action in the Field of Human Rights for Russia*. Devised in consultation with the Ministry of Foreign Affairs under Andrei Kozyrev, the programme comprised eight sections covering legislation in the field of human rights; the judicial defence of human rights and legal aid; non-judicial defence of human rights; NGOs; human rights education and distribution of information; human rights and Russia's foreign policy; the defence of socially vulnerable persons; national minorities; persons deprived of freedom; military personnel; refugees and forced migrants. In the programme they detailed the general problems in each of these areas and proposed solutions.[85]

The Federal Programme was an idealistic document in the manner of any number of international treaties and declarations. Unfortunately, it remained in draft form. Yet it was the 1993 report issued by the Commission which was equally, if not more, important in the depth of its commitment to self-criticism and fact-finding research. Compiled with the assistance of Memorial's Human Rights Centre, The Soldiers' Mothers Committee, The Mothers' Rights Foundation, the International Red Cross, International Amnesty, the Moscow Investigation Centre on Human Rights, the law enforcement organs, federal ministries, departments and trade union associations, both the 1993 and 1994/1995 reports are essential historical documents which reflect, for the first time, a serious attempt by the Russian government to face the objective reality of human rights violations in Russia.[86]

The Commission experienced problems in acquiring accurate information and statistics. Its report is fundamentally devoted to trends in the capital and on this level it is fairly narrow in its scope. The Commission did not pay adequate attention to the problem of labour rights and conditions in the military, and its statistics on the number of non-combatant deaths in the army failed to take into consideration normal mortality figures.

The first conclusion of the Commission's report was that Russia was taking serious steps at human rights reform. Yet worrying traditions and practices continued to weaken its progress. Much of the report was devoted to the violations that occurred as a result of October 1993 and the Decree on Banditry and Organized Crime.[87] Among other ongoing concerns was the increased flow of refugees from Southern Ossetia, the Prigorodny district zone of the Ossetian–Ingush conflict, Abkhazia, Tajikistan and other conflict-torn locations. The Commission singled out Moscow's local government as the most consistent violator of human rights, especially against refugees and forced migrants.[88] Thousands of refugees had been placed in hotels and dormitories around Moscow pending the resolution of their residential status. These places became and continued to be permanent places of residence. Many refugees had been waiting up to three years for a decision. In the meantime, they suffered from discrimination over work and housing. In its October 1993 directive, the local government sought to deport refugees to military installations and, in violation of the Committee's laws "On Refugees and Forced Migrants", the Moscow government stopped the city's Migration Service from registering applications for legal status as refugees or forced migrants on November 5, 1993.[89]

The Commission recognized "Freedom of Movement and Freedom to Choose One's Place of Residence" as one of Russia's most acute problems. According to the figures of the Federal Migration Service there were more than 500,000 foreign citizens and persons without citizenship in the Russian Federation who were residing in violation of the visa-passport regime in 1993 in Moscow and the Moscow region. On July 1, 1994 the Moscow government introduced a special charge for a residence permit for people from other cities.[90] Russian citizens coming to Moscow to become residents would pay 500 times the minimum monthly wage. For CIS citizens the fee was 1,000 times the wage, and for those from the far abroad it was 1,500 times.[91]

Others areas of concern included the situation in the penal system. The general conditions and facilities were in serious violation of fundamental rights. Inadequate medical services, no public monitoring of the penal administration, the horrible conditions of preliminary detention and investigation, its overcrowding, limited correspondence and complaints about beatings and intimidation remained ongoing concerns. The situation for persons sentenced to death was considered especially inhumane, since no time periods for considering appeals had been established.[92]

The largest concern regarding labour rights was the general failure to pay salaries and wages. At the beginning of 1994 the total amount owing to individuals across Russia was, according to the report, 800 billion rubles. Violations also extended to forced vacations, violation of the right to hiring and firing, and serious occupational health and safety concerns.[93]

The army continued to work according to old laws and traditions. Insufficiently open to society and with cruel and degrading initiation rituals, in 1993 2,572 serviceman died, 9,292 sustained injuries of varying severity and 462 committed suicide. This all took place during combat training and work being performed to help the economy. Non-combat losses in the armed forces were still labeled as classified information. The military courts maintained their independence from the general judicial system making it even more difficult to access information and initiate investigations. The Commission also considered the use of soldiers as forced labour to be a violation of their individual rights.[94]

The office of the Human Rights Commissioner established

Soon after the report was publicly released, the State Duma passed the first reading of the draft law on the Office of the Commissioner of Human Rights on July 21, 1994. Kovalyov said in his speech to the Duma: "There has not been one case in the last ten years in Austria when a recommendation passed down by the Austrian Ombudsman to a ministry was not fulfilled." Someone shouted from the hall of the Duma: "But that is Austria; in Russia no-one will listen to you."[95]After the draft was approved at the first reading, it was then sent for comments to the Supreme Court, Constitutional Court, Supreme Court of Arbitration, committees and commissions of the Duma, parliamentary factions and the President.

In August, Yeltsin decided to jump-start the Ombudsman's office by decree. In Decree 1587 "On providing the means for the Office of the Human Rights Commissioner to fulfill its function", financial allocations were made for staff and premises in anticipation of the federal law. Alexander Chebotarev was appointed manager of the start-up committee, along with the Russian–American Project Group. An organizational blueprint for the Human Rights Commissioner's office was devised and specifications drawn up for an information system and communications network to service it.[96] In November 1994, the United Nations Development Program (UNDP) and the Russian Federation's Commissioner for Human Rights held a successful three-day international seminar in Moscow on the prospective Russian office.

Kovalyov accepted the general trend prevalent in Yeltsin's administration of the primacy of Presidential decrees. The Duma still had the power to prevent laws from being passed and, in October, when the law on the Human Rights Commissioner was being heard for the second time, the Commission lost out by three votes.[97] The year 1994 was an ambigious one for Kovalyov. While Yeltsin was taking wider measures to appease the Zhirinovsky voters, he was also taking steps to keep Kovalyov inside the Presidential administration. Kovalyov remained resilient and open to change. But he would continue to vocalize his concerns, and his commitment to an open and transparent politics was never more apparent than in his final year in the Presidential Administration.

Notes

1 "S predlozheniyami soglasen. Deistvyite", *Izvestiya*, No. 203, October 23, 1993: 2.
2 "The Curfew in Moscow – It's over and done with", *The Current Digest of the Post Soviet Press*, Vol XLV, No. 42 (1993): 11.
3 See "Doklad o sobludenii prav cheloveka i grazhdanina v Rossiiskoi federatsii za 1993 god", *Prava Cheloveka v Rossii – mezhdunarodnoe izmerenie*, Moskva: Prava Cheloveka, 1995, pp. 231, 232. Henceforth, *Doklad*.
4 See *Doklad*, p. 231. See also "Human Rights Organizations Talk About Cleansing in Accordance with the Ethnic Principle", *The Current Digest of the Post Soviet Press*, Vol XLV, No. 42 (1993):10.
5 "S predlozheniyami soglasen. Deistvyite", *Izvestiya*, No. 203, October 23, 1993: 2.
6 "Yeltsin's Difficult Road Toward Elections", *RFE/RL*, Vol. 2, No. 41, October 15, 1993: 2.
7 See *Doklad*, p. 233. See also S. Kovalyov, "Nasledie Sakharova. Idei i praktika", *Memorial Aspekt*, June 9, 1994: 2. "Press Conference with State Duma Deputy Sergei Kovalyov", *Federal News Service*, 26/2, April 18, 2000.
8 S. Kovalyov, "Sergei Kovalyov's Speech to the Founding Congress of the Political Movement Russia's Choice", October 16, 1993, p. 1. Translated by E. Kline, New York: Kline Archive.
9 Kovalyov, *op.cit.*, p. 2.
10 Kovalyov, *op.cit.*, p. 2.
11 S. Kovalyov, "Draft Speech by Sergei Kovalyov", New York: Kline Archive, undated, untitled.
12 S. Kovalyov, "Sergei Kovalyov's speech to the Council on Foreign Relations", December 20, 1993, pp. 1–5. Translated by E. Kline, New York: Kline Archive.
13 "Russia's Plebiscite On a New Constitution", *RFE/RL Research Report*, Vol. 3, No. 3, January 21, 1994, pp. 1, 3. See also "Falsification of Results of December Vote Announced", *RFE/RL News Briefs*, May 2–6, 1994, Vol. 3, No. 19, 1994: 5.
14 "Russia's Draft Constitution", *RFE/RL*, Vol. 2, No. 48, December 3, 1993, pp. 9–15.
15 "Konstitutsiya Za i Protiv", *Moskovskie Novosti*, No. 49, December 5, 1993: 10.
16 S. Kovalyov, *Nauchno – prakticheskaya konferentsiya, posvyashchennaya 73-i godovshchine so dnya rozhdeniya A. D Sakharova*: May 21, 1994, Moscow: Yuridicheskaya Literatura, p. 11.
17 S. Kovalyov, "On the New Russia", *The New York Review of Books*, April 18, 1996: 12.
18 Note that Elena Bonner also supported Yeltsin during the October events. See "My podderzhivaem prezidenta", *Izvestiya*, September 25, 1993: 3.
19 "Ukaz Prezidenta Rossiiskoi Federatsii ob Obespechenii Deyatel'nosti Komissii Po Pravam Cheloveka Pri Prezidente Rossiiskoi Federatsii, No.1798", New York: Kline Archive, November 1, 1993.
20 S. Kovalyov, "The Ruling Element and Society: Who Will Prevail?", *Moscow News*, No. 31, August 11–17, 1995: 1–2.
21 *Polozhenie o komissii po pravam cheloveka pri Prezidente Rossiiskoi Federatsii*, Melbourne: Personal collection, E. Gilligan: 1. Henceforth, *Polozhenie*.
22 *Polozhenie*, p. 2.
23 *Polozhenie*, p. 3.
24 S. Kovalyov, "Ombudsmen znachit 'zastupnik'", *Rysskaya Mysl'*, No. 4057, December 15–21, 1994: 9.
25 L. Siomina, personal interview no. 2 with E. Gilligan, Moscow, December 1995. Henceforth, Siomina 2 (1995).
26 Siomina 2 (1995).

27 Siomina argued that they failed to systematize their work. See Siomina 2 (1995). For V. Kartashkin on the work of the Presidential Human Rights Committee, see "Blesk i nisheta dvizheniya pravo zashchitnikov", *Rossiiskaya Gazeta*, No. 35 (1645), February 20, 1997: 5.

28 Siomina 2 (1995).

29 Kovalyov, *Vosp.*, p. 90.

30 "Sergei Kovalyov Pervyi Ombudsman Rossii", *Izvestiya*, January 22, 1994: 1.

31 Siomina 2 (1995).

32 "Geroi Dnya", *NTV*, Channel 4, Moscow, May 22, 1998: 7.30 p.m.

33 Siomina 2 (1995).

34 S. Romanuk, "Prezidentu RF Eltsinu B. N.", August 19, 1994. Melbourne: Personal collection, E. Gilligan. Romanuk cites in her letter the two occasions she appealed to the commission, December 8, 1993 and July 4, 1994.

35 In the mid-1980s, Stolbun had a small commune where he treated people with schizophrenia, asthma and ulcers. For accounts by former members of the commune, see "Rai bez Pamyati", *Moskovskii Komsomolets*, December 30, 1993: 2.

36 "Prokurator zanyalas Stolbunom", *Rossiiskaya Gazeta*, February 1, 1995: 2. See also "Rai bez Pamyati", *Moskovskii Komsomolets*, December 30, 1993: 2.

37 Siomina 2 (1995).

38 "Kto plachet no Stolbunu? Eksperimentu nad podrostkami kalechat ikh psikhiky", *Rossiiskaya Gazeta*, June 7, 1994: 2. See also "Pedagoga budet sudit", *Trud*, September 3, 1995: 2.

39 *Moskovskii Komsomolets*, December 30, 1993: 2.

40 *Ibid.*

41 *Ibid.*

42 S. Romanuk, "Tekst vystypleniya zayavitelya – S.V. Romanuk na otkritikh slyshaniyakh v kommissii po pravam cheloveka 28/04/94 po povodu raboti shkoli internat-eksternat Feniks". Available online at: http://info.sandy.ru/socio/public/youth/stolbun/romanuk_about_stolbun.htm (accessed June 2000).

43 *Ibid.*

44 E. Gushanskii, "Bednaya Liza mogla byt schastlivoi, esli by sbrosila trusiki i doverilas doktoru Stolbunu", *Kuranti*, No.100 (867), May 28, 1994: 4.

45 See "Begstvo ot svobody", *Sevodnya*, June 4, 1994: 14. See also "Elektrod na nyatoi tochke", *Trud*, June 3, 1994: 2; "Kto plachet no Stolbunu? Eksperimentu nad podrostkami kalechat ikh psikhiky", *Rossiiskaya Gazeta*, June 7, 1994: 2.

46 "Procurator zanyalas Stolbunom", *Rossiiskaya Gazeta*, No. 24, February 1, 1995: 4. See also "Pedagoga budet sudit", *Trud*, September 3, 1995: 2.

47 *Ibid.*, 4.

48 Siomina 2 (1995).

49 Siomina could not recall her name.

50 Siomina 2 (1995).

51 Siomina 2 (1995).

52 "Kovalyov – v Portugaliu, a Stolbun – v beshentsi", *Kuranti*, No. 115 (882), June 18, 1994: 4.

53 This was quoted from Siomina 2 (1995) and in "Kto plachet po Stolbunu? Eksperimentu nad podrostkami kalechat ikh psikhiky", *Rossiiskaya Gazeta*, June 7, 1994: 2.

54 S. Romanuk, "Prezidentu RF Eltsinu B.N.," August 19, 1994, Melbourne: Personal collection, E. Gilligan, pp. 1–2.

55 Siomina 2 (1995).

56 Romanuk, *op.cit.*,

57 "Zaklychenie Komissii po pravam cheloveka pri prezidente RF po resultatam spetsialnogo rassledovaniya faktov narysheniya prav detei v eksternoi shkole – internate Feniks Stypinskogo raiona Moskovskoi oblasti", undated, Melbourne: Personal collection, E. Gilligan.
58 Siomina (1998).
59 Siomina 2 (1995).
60 Siomina 2 (1995).
61 Zolotukhin, B. "Conservativnaya chast Dumi orientirovana na stroitelstvo polit-seiskogo gosudarstvo", *Rysskaya Mysl'*, No. 4035, June 23–29, 1994: 3.
62 V. Ilyukhin, *Gosudarstvennaya Duma: Stenogramma zasedanii*, Tom. 6, June 22, 1994, Moskva: Respublika, 1994, p. 515.
63 *Prestupnost'i pravonarusheniya, 1998*, Moskva, 1999: Sheet 1.
64 Cited in "Punitive bodies given the green light", *Moscow News*, No. 26, July 1–7, 1994: 2.
65 "Punitive bodies given the green light", *Moscow News*, No. 26, July 1–7, 1994: 2.
66 See The Constitution of the Russian Federation. Available online at: http://www.departments.bucknell.edu/russian/const/ch4.html (accessed June 2000).
67 S. Kovalyov, "Komissiya po pravam cheloveka pri prezidente Rossii obsuzhdaet zakon o bor'be s prestupnost'iu: Obrashchenie B. N. Yeltsinu", *Rysskaya Mysl'*, No. 4036, June 30–July 6, 1994: 2.
68 Sirotkin (1995).
69 Kovalyov, *ibid.*, p. 2. See also Sirotkin (1995).
70 Sirotkin (1995).
71 S. Kovalyov, cited in *Gosudarstvennaya Duma: Stenogramma zasedanii*, Tom. 6, June 22, 1994, Moskva: Respublika, 1994, pp. 529–30. See also "Nashe Budushee – svobodnie grazhdane svobodnoi strani", *Rossiiskaya Gazeta*, No. 150 (1007), August 9, 1994: 4.
72 S. Kovalyov, "Komissiya po pravam cheloveka pri prezidente Rossii obsuzhdaet zakon o bor'be s prestupnost'iu: Obrashchenie B. N. Yeltsinu", *Rysskaya Mysl'*, No. 4036, June 30–July 6, 1994: 2.
73 "Tatarstan Minister Defends Yeltsin's Anti-Crime Decree", *RFE/RL News Briefs*, Vol. 3, No. 25, June 13–17, 1994: 16.
74 "Crime Leaves No Time for Reform of the Prosecutors Office", *The Current Digest of Post-Soviet Press*, Vol. XLVI, No. 25 (1994): 11.
75 S. Kovalyov, cited in *Gosudarstvennaya Duma: Stenogramma zasedanii*, Tom. 6, June 22, 1994, Respublika, Moskva, 1994, p. 529.
76 Kovalyov, *Vosp.*, p. 92.
77 "Army to Aid in Fighting Crime," *RFE/RL News Briefs*, Vol. 3, No. 25, June 13–17, 1994: 6.
78 "Operation Hurricane Sweeps through Moscow", *Current Digest of Soviet Press*, Vol. XLVI, No. 25 (1994): 13.
79 "For Official Use Only: Scandal over Kovalev's Report", *New Times*, August 1994: 24. See also Kovalyov in "Odnazhdi propal prezidentskii ukaz", *Rossiiskaya Gazeta*, August 17, 1994, No. 33 (5513): 11.
80 Arutyunov (1995).
81 "Prezidentu Rossiiskoi Federatsii B. N. Eltsinu ob itogakh vsemirnoi konferentsii po pravam cheloveka, No. 16711", New York: Kline Archive, July 20, 1993.
82 "The World Conference on Human Rights, Vienna Declaration and Program of Action", Available online at: http://www.unhchr.ch/html/menu5/wchr.htm (accessed July 1999).
83 Siomina (1995).
84 "Prezidentu Rossiiskoi Federatsii B. N. Eltsinu ob itogakh vsemirnoi konferentsii po pravam cheloveka, No. 16711", New York: Kline Archive, July 20, 1993.

85 "Federal'naya programma deistvii v oblasti prav cheloveka (proekt)", *Prava Cheloveka v Rossii*, Moskva: Prava Cheloveka, 1995, pp. 250–80.
86 *Doklad*, p. 189.
87 *Doklad*, pp. 230–5.
88 *Doklad*, p. 198.
89 *Doklad*, p. 199.
90 *Doklad*, p. 208.
91 *Doklad*, p. 208
92 *Doklad*, pp. 210–18.
93 *Doklad*, pp. 223–9.
94 *Doklad*, pp. 218–23.
95 "Ombudsmen 'znachit' zastupnik", *Rysskaya Mysl'*, No. 4057, December 15–21, 1994: 9.
96 "Proekt postroeniya edinoi sistemu informatsionno-kommunikatsionnogo obespecheniya rabochego apparata upolnomochennogo po pravam cheloveka v RF", New York: Kline Archive, 1995.
97 Siomina 2 (1995).

5　The Chechen war 1994–96

Life has always been cheap in Russia, especially under the Bolsheviks. But you introduced a new "democratic" and "humanitarian" strain into this shameful national tradition. For a whole year in Chechnya you have been restoring "constitutional order" and "civil rights" with bombs and missiles.

Sergei Kovalyov to Boris Yeltsin[1]

I call upon all the political forces in Russia, upon the world community, to stop the destruction of non-combatants, of civilians.

Sergei Kovalyov[2]

The origins of the Chechen war

The war in the breakaway republic of Chechnya was the most dramatic period of Kovalyov's turbulent career. Like so many of his colleagues, he was shocked by the Russian attack on Grozny in November 1994. His first year as Chairman of the Presidential Human Rights Commission had seen him struggle to adapt to the customs and demands of the Presidential Administration, and kept his attention firmly fixed on events in the capital. Events in Chechnya forced new and unexpected challenges upon him, forcing him to bear witness to a cruel campaign against the breakaway republic and take a public stand against the inordinate violence of the Russian troops and forces of the MVD.

Kovalyov's contribution to Russian society's knowledge of human rights violations in the Northern Caucasus was unparalleled. His relentless public criticism of the military campaign made a vital contribution to the military ceasefire signed on August 30, 1995 and the Khasavyurt Peace Treaty signed in neighbouring Dagestan on August 6, 1996. But the price of Kovalyov's anti-war activism was the defeat of his reform agenda. As he raised his voice louder in protest against President Yeltsin's directives in the Caucasus, he was so marginalized in the process that his managerial and administrative aspirations for the Presidential Human Rights Commission fell to an all-time low.

After Kovalyov emerged as the leading opponent of the Chechen war, he was denounced by nationalists for ignoring ethnic tensions in the Northern

Caucasus. Yet in fact he had long been concerned about the region. Of the many factors that converged to produce this crisis, Kovalyov argued that it was the failure of the law "On the Rehabilitation of Repressed Peoples", passed by the Supreme Soviet on April 26, 1991 that constituted a critical moment in the lead-up to a succession of bloody events in the region. He struggled to persuade the Supreme Soviet in 1991 to address the law's limitations. He was outspokenly critical of the legislation, its inadequate legal provisions, the want of implementation procedures and potential for disturbing consequences.[3] In particular, he was concerned about Article 6 that allowed for the restoration of the original borders before the ethnic populations were forcibly deported to Siberia, the Far East and Central Asia in 1945.

The law was astonishingly vague. It provided that "the realization of territorial rehabilitation of repressed peoples will be provided for on the basis of legal and organized measures to restore the national-territorial borders that existed before the unconstitutional forcible changes."[4] The law was drafted by Nikolai Medvedev, Chairman of the Commission on National-State Structures and Inter-Ethnic Relations. It was presented for examination at the third session of the Supreme Soviet on March 22, 1991.[5] Khasbulatov openly attempted to force the law through on the first reading, but failed. The Supreme Soviet largely supported his urgings to pass the law without reworking the draft. Many deputies argued that compensation for the repressed peoples was a matter of urgency. Kovalyov insisted that more attention should be paid to reworking Article 6 and that it was not enough, as Khasbulatov suggested, to redraft the law over the lunch break.[6] Kovalyov wanted the deputies to define how, and on what basis, territorial boundaries were to be rehabilitated. Who would hold the power to conduct negotiations and to what degree would the republics participate in the process?[7] In Kovalyov's view, the restoration of justice required detailed negotiations and the meticulous drafting of legislation. Khasbulatov responded with derision: "Look at him – he defends the rights of every prisoner, but he does not want to defend the rights of entire peoples! That's the Committee on Human Rights for you."[8]

During the second reading, Kovalyov proposed his own amendments. Yet, after failing to secure the two-thirds majority for the changes, the following dialogue took place between Kovalyov and the Speaker:

> "Excuse me, but I intend to make a statement. I'm very pleased to see that the issue of deportation is being discussed. But as to the law in its entirety, I intend to vote against it and I would like to briefly explain the reasons why. I have this right."
>
> "No. Why? That's fine. You go ahead and vote against it. The fourth microphone please."
>
> "Ruslan Impanovich, you are violating ..."
>
> "Sergei Adamovich, I'm not violating anything. I patiently allowed everyone to vote for your amendments."

"The amendments aren't the point ..."
"I'm not satisfied either. But that doesn't mean that I have to lay it on everyone else. That's enough."
"The point is about the violation of ..."
"Turn off the third microphone. Fourth microphone ..."[9]

Kovalyov was attacked by the parliament for being bureaucratic in his approach.[10] His aim was to ensure that future relations between the Soviet Union and its repressed minorities would be defined by the law rather than through the arbitrary exercise of government power or the discretionary application of goodwill. The Human Rights Committee failed to ensure adequate legal provisions for the Law on Repressed Peoples or to coordinate responsibility for its implementation between the federal ministries, departments, and the republican, *krai* and *oblast* levels of government. It did manage to postpone the passing of the law until the third reading on April 26, and insisted on one minor but marginally important amendment. The amendment to article 6 stated that:

> ... the implementation of territorial rehabilitation when necessary must be determined by a transition period. The decisions about the establishment of a transition period and the restoration of borders are to be taken by the Supreme Soviet of the RSFSR.[11]

It was not long before the anticipated tension over border claims arose in the Northern Caucasus. The law's failure to stipulate a process was the reason given by Memorial's Human Rights Centre for the bloody conflict that arose between North Ossetia, Ingushetia and Chechnya in the autumn of 1992.[12] The conflict emerged over border claims by both North Ossetia and Ingushetia to the Prigorodny region and Chechnya's claim to the Sunzhenskogo region.[13] In the spring of 1991, Chechnya had declared its independence from Ingushetia and threatened to attack Russian troops situated on parts of Ingushetian territory which had belonged to Chechnya before the two republics were merged in 1934. After successful negotiations, no attack took place.[14] The Security Council met in December 1992 and decided to strengthen its forces in the entire Northern Caucasus region.[15]

While the failure of the law to adequately stipulate the terms of rehabilitation was a significant factor in the situation in the Northern Caucasus, the deteriorating political situation inside Chechnya, the Moscow government's reluctance to negotiate and its prejudice toward the Chechen peoples were no less significant. A crisis had been escalating since November 27, 1990, after the National Congress of Chechen Peoples (NCCP) under the influence of Doku Zavgaev, First Secretary of the Chechen Ingushetian Oblast Committee, passed a declaration "On the State Sovereignty of the Chechen–Ingush Republic". Since Bashkortostan and Tartarstan had made similar claims to a negotiated degree of independence in response to

Yeltsin's urging to "take as much sovereignty as you can handle", the Supreme Soviet anticipated an analogous agreement could be reached with the Chechen–Ingush Republic.[16]

But while the Soviet Government was distracted by the August coup in Moscow in 1991, the National Guard under the auspices of the National Congress of Chechen Peoples seized power. With the arrival of Soviet Airforce General Dzhokar Dudayev in Grozny in the spring of 1991, and the domination of a more radical faction within the NCCP, a declaration was passed that unilaterally declared Chechnya's separation from Ingushetia and independence from the Soviet Union. Dudayev announced the creation of the Chechen Republic of Ichkeriya.[17] By the end of August, the NCCP had taken control of the government and called for a "campaign of civil disobedience".[18] The Russian federal authorities grew anxious about the escalating situation. They sent Khasbulatov to Grozny, where he recommended that Chechnya's Supreme Soviet disband. He called for a Provisional Council to be installed and arranged for elections to be held on November 17, 1991. But the NCCP ignored the orders from Moscow and held elections on October 27, electing Dudayev as President. On November 2, the Fifth Congress of People's Deputies in Moscow declared the elections unlawful.[19]

From 1992, Dudayev was recognized *de facto* by the Russian government as the President of the breakaway republic. He insisted that all negotiations be conducted at the executive level with Yeltsin.[20] But the President refused to meet the Chechen President. The Russian government's decision to leave the Deputy Prime Minister, Sergei Shakhrai, as head of the negotiation process exemplified its insensitivity and political ineptitude. Dudayev had refused to conduct negotiations with Shakhrai, who was a Cossack by birth, traditionally considered an enemy of the Chechens and supposedly sympathetic to the Cossacks living in the northern regions of the republic.[21] By spring 1994 Shakhrai declared that "the possibility of a political dialogue with Dudayev has been exhausted".[22] The Head of the Presidential Administration, Sergei Filatov, declared that negotiation with those in power in Chechnya was only possible once Chechnya recognized that it remained part of the Russian Federation.[23]

On December 16, 1993 Shakhrai had created a puppet government in Chechnya under the leadership of Umar Avturkhanov in the northern territory of Nadterechni.[24] Avturkhanov's Provisional Council was recognized as the only legitimate power in Chechnya and the Russian government started to pay pensions and wages to the people of Upper Terek. Under the direction of Deputy Nationalities Minister General Alexander Kotenkov, the Russian government began to supply weapons and ammunition to the Provisional Council.[25] According to Kogan-Yasni: "Neither from the side of the Federal Authorities of Russia nor from Dudayev's side in Grozny did they work out a systematic approach for a realistic resolution to ... this political crisis."[26] According to Sergei Sirotkin, co-chairman of the Presidential Human Rights Commission, "the possibility of settling the Chechen crisis on a civilized basis had not been exploited."[27]

The growing tension in the breakaway republic was neglected by the human rights community, which continued to give precedence to the conflict between Ossetia and Ingushetia. Kovalyov himself had been satisfied with the assurances of Sergei Filatov throughout the summer and autumn of 1994. Filatov had told him that the Russian authorities were sympathetic to the "opposition" under Avturkhanov and would keep supplying pensions to the people of Northern Chechnya in the hope that it would form a stronghold against Dudayev (who had rejected funds from Moscow), but they would not participate in a forceful resolution to the problem.[28] Yeltsin himself confirmed this in a public announcement on August 12, 1994, when he declared that:

> Forcible intervention in Chechnya is not permissible ... we in Russia have succeeded in avoiding inter-ethnic clashes only because we have refrained from forcible pressure. If we violate this principle with regard to Chechnya, the Caucasus will rise up. There will be so much turmoil and blood that, afterwards, no one will forgive us.[29]

Kovalyov had come close to becoming involved in the mounting crisis. He had joined his colleagues at Memorial in examining possible solutions to the conflicts over border claims between Ingushetia and Ossetia on President Yeltsin's request.[30] In September 1994, he was on a monitoring trip in Assinovskaya, a small Cossack village situated on the border between the Chechen and Ingushetian Republics. It was at that time that he received a telephone call from the President's advisor on National Security, Yuri Baturin, asking if he would be willing to go to Chechnya to mediate with Dzhokar Dudayev. He agreed to the proposal. Yet Baturin called back later to say that the meeting would not be going ahead.[31]

This abortive attempt to employ Kovalyov as a mediator with Dudayev was one of the great missed opportunities in the history of the Yeltsin administration. As preparations advanced for the military campaign, Kovalyov was kept in the dark, despite his role as personal advisor to Yeltsin as Chairman of the Human Rights Commission. The plans for the military campaign were formulated under the guidance of Yeltsin's new circle of ministers and advisors: General Alexander Korzhakov, Head of the Presidential Security Service; Nikolai Yegorov, Minister for Nationalities and Regional Affairs; Oleg Lobov, Secretary of the Russian Security Council; Sergei Stepashin, Minister of Security; Viktor Yerin, Minister of Internal Affairs; and Pavel Grachev, Minister of Defence.

The reasons for Baturin's return call to Kovalyov were directly connected to the impending campaign. The decision to use force had already been agreed upon. Soon after Baturin called Kovalyov in Assinovskaya, Nikolai Yegorov and General Alexander Kotenkov moved to the border of Chechnya to prepare for the overthrow of Dudayev.[32] On November 24, the Kremlin relaunched its puppet government under a new name – The Government of National Rebirth in Chechnya.[33]

The capture of Grozny

The Chechen war began with a debacle. On November 26, unmarked Russian tanks advanced to the centre of the Chechen capital in the direction of the Presidential Palace opposite Freedom Square. The Russian tank crews were attacked by forces loyal to Dudayev. Some soldiers were taken prisoner, while others were forced to retreat. Three days later, Yeltsin warned Dudayev that all factions had to surrender their weapons within twenty-four hours. In response, Dudayev threatened that all prisoners taken in the attempted storm would be shot if Moscow did not acknowledge them as members of its own army.[34] On the same day, Yeltsin declared that the Russian government had been unable to prevent the "internal conflict in Chechnya" and were concerned that "the opposing sides [were] recruiting mercenaries from abroad."[35] Within a week, it was disclosed that the entire November 26 operation had indeed been organized by the Russian government under the direction of Sergei Stepashin, Head of the Federal Counter Intelligence Service (FSB) using Russian soldiers privately contracted through the FSB.[36]

The Russian Security Council tried hard to conceal its role in the failed invasion. It continued to insist that it was an internal conflict between the Provisional Council and Dudayev's forces. The Minister of Defence, Pavel Grachev, had known about the plans one month before and the FSB had recruited their tank crews from within the ranks of the Russian Armed Forces.[37] In the pages of *Rossiiskie Vesti* and in a declaration to the State Duma on November 30, Grachev insisted that the Russian Army had taken no direct part in the November 26 operation.[38] This is probably correct. According to Kovalyov, Grachev remained sceptical about the war, well aware of the deteriorating conditions within the army and its limited capability for strategic and coordinated action. Allegedly he was accused of cowardice during a session of the Security Council.[39] Responsibility for the operation was handed over to private forces organized by the FSB.

On November 28, two days after the failed storming, the Kremlin called an emergency meeting of the Security Council. Yeltsin's strategy for resolving the "Chechen crisis" and Pavel Grachev's role in implementing it were by this time unambiguous. It was during this meeting that the decision to send the Russian Army into Chechnya was taken. Yeltsin agreed to and signed the secret Decree No. 2137 that introduced a State of Emergency in the Republic of Chechnya "to secure the cessation of the armed conflict, disarm and liquidate the armed formations on the territory of the Chechen Republic".[40] The President did not seek the approval of the State Duma to introduce a State of Emergency, in direct violation of the Human Rights Committee's law "On States of Emergency". The ruling was taken behind the closed doors of the Security Council where it was agreed that the army would be sent in on December 11 with a task force of 23,700 men.[41] In preparation, the airports in Grozny were bombed the following day.

Grachev declared in the papers one week later that "if a peaceful resolution to the Chechen crisis cannot be found, then a lawful government will be restored by forceful means." He added that the "troops would not destroy the city of Grozny".[42]

Kovalyov was disturbed by what was happening. Once he heard about the failed storming, he approached Yeltsin's public spokesman, Georgy Satarov, to be told that the November 26 attack had been a measure to hasten the negotiation process and that there would be no further military action. His anxieties were reinforced when Satarov told him that the President was unavailable since he had been hospitalized for a small operation on his nose. Evoking memories of Yeltsin's similar disappearance in October 1993, Kovalyov informed the press of the President's absence.[43]

The tension over the impending campaign coincided with the second reading of the law on the Human Rights Commissioner. On December 9, the State Duma met in one of its final sessions for 1994. The arguments concerning the law circled around two fundamental points. Should the Human Rights Commissioner have the power to initiate criminal proceedings? Should the office be an appendage of, or independent of the State Duma? As Sirotkin recalled, "there were proposals that would have removed the restrictions on political activity thereby making the Commissioner an institution for the struggle against the President. This was a very dangerous tendency."[44] Kovalyov's position was nevertheless compromised by the fact that he had failed to leave Russia's Choice once appointed Human Rights Commissioner. He insisted that, until the law was passed, he would remain Chairman of Russia's Choice, without conceding that Yeltsin's August decree was, in fact, a law in and of itself. The Communist and Liberal Democratic factions managed to block the law.[45] In mid-December, Kovalyov nevertheless departed for Chechnya to see what was taking place. Under the auspices of the office of the Human Rights Commissioner, he established a working group to travel to the breakaway republic to monitor events.

Kovalyov was already on a collision course with Yeltsin. The President signed a second – this time public – decree. Decree No. 2166 stated: "I charge the Russian government in accord with points (e) and (f) of Article 114 of the Constitution of the Russian Federation to *use all available means* [my italics] to guarantee state security, the rule of law, civil rights and liberties, the defence of public order, the fight against crime and the disarming of illegally armed formations" situated in the Republic of Chechnya.[46]

The immediate result was a breakdown in communication between Kovalyov and the President. Kovalyov struggled to secure permission for his investigation from Yeltsin. He was unable to secure seats on a flight to Chechnya for his working group. At the end of his speech that evening in Moscow at *Dom Medikov* on December 14, the anniversary of Sakharov's death, he concluded: "Today Andrei Sakharov would be there where blood is flowing in Grozny, in Chechnya. I am certain of this."[47] The Minister of Foreign Affairs Andrei Kozyrev approached him after his address to tell him that First Vice-Premier Oleg Soskovets was waiting for him on the telephone. Soskovets promised that he would organize a flight for Kovalyov and his working group for the following morning. The group consisted of Duma deputies Leonid Petrovsky (the Russian Communist Party), Valery Borshchov (Yabloko), Mikhail Molostvov (Russia's Choice) and Kovalyov's close friend and colleague, Oleg Orlov, Director of Memorial's Human Rights Centre. He was told that only five people could go because of a shortage of seats on the plane.[48]

The next morning, Kovalyov and his working group departed from Moscow's Chkalovskaya Military Airport in an empty plane. As they were flying over Voronezh, they were informed that they would be returning to Chkalovskaya due to ice on the airstrip in Mozdok. On arriving back, they noticed a mail plane was due to leave for the Military Headquarters in Mozdok, but were refused permission to join the flight. They returned the following morning to be refused again, whereupon they drove to the civilian airport, Vnukovo and took a domestic flight to Mineralnyie Vodi. From there, they drove via Nazran, the capital of Ingushetia, to Grozny by car.[49] By this time, the Ministry of Defence was restricting access to and from the Northern Caucasus. This was the first of repeated attempts to hinder Kovalyov's monitoring activity in Chechnya.

On December 13, the Russian State Duma gathered in Moscow to discuss the situation. The leader of Russia's Choice, Yegor Gaidar, tried to convince the deputies to overturn their 1993 decision that the holding of elections in Chechnya had to be a precondition for negotiations. Gaidar insisted that the question of Chechnya's independence could not be the first issue in the negotiation process. The December 13 session of the Duma marked the beginning of the vehement attack by the Liberal Democratic Party of Russia on Russia's Choice, and on Kovalyov in particular. V. Marichev blamed Russia's Choice for the events in Chechnya since Russia's Choice was ostensibly the "government party". M. Burlakov raised a question of confidence in Kovalyov. "What!" he declared. "Didn't he know they were violating human rights there? He has been in this job for an entire year and not an inch of progress has been made in the republic."[50] He requested that a vote of confidence be taken regarding Kovalyov's position.[51] No decisions on the question of utilizing force in Chechnya were taken.

Meanwhile, in Nazran, Kovalyov and his working group were met by Duma deputy Viktor Kurochkin. Kurochkin had met with Dudayev on December 10 and been told by the Chechen President that he was prepared to negotiate. Kurochkin contacted the Chairman of the Federation Council in Moscow, Vladimir Shumeiko, who said he would try to pass the information on to the President, but when Kurochkin called again on the following day he was told not to call again.[52] Kovalyov wanted to head directly to Mozdok where the command centre for the Russian campaign in Chechnya was stationed, but was convinced to go to Grozny on finding out about the planned blockade of the capital.[53] President Ruslan Aushev of Ingushetia organized a car and escorts for the group to travel along the north road to Chechnya. As they drove towards Chechnya they met Russian troops headed for the capital. On December 11, three columns of tanks had entered the breakaway republic, one from Mozdok in the north, another from Vladikavkaz in the west and a third from Kizlyar in the east. On the evening of December 15, Kovalyov's group reached the Presidential Palace in Grozny without incident. They found no sign of fighting and the Presidential Palace in Grozny was under the guard of armed Chechens.[54]

On the same day, the Russian government secured its media support. A Temporary Press Agency was set up in Mozdok and declared its support for President Yeltsin's decision to send in troops.[55] The Agency was set up under *Roskompechat'*, (Order No. 1886-p.) under the direction of S. Grizunov with representatives from the Ministry of Nationalities, the Ministry of Emergency Situations, the MVD, FSB and Ministry of Defence.[56] The two papers that became apologists for the state's position were *Rossiiskaya Gazeta* and *Rossiiskie Vesti*.[57] Order No. 1360 of December 9 stated that all journalists would need permission to work in the Northern Caucasus, and to work in Grozny they needed special accreditation from the Military Headquarters in Mozdok. They could be deprived of their accreditation if deemed to be spreading disinformation or inciting racial or religious hatred.[58] Over the course of the next few months, Kovalyov and his group would spend much of their time responding to misinformation issued by the government's propaganda agencies. Kovalyov's group went directly to the Presidential Palace to try to arrange a meeting with Dudayev. They first met Shamsuddin Yousef, Minister of Foreign Affairs of the Chechen Republic of Ichkeriya. Orlov recalled that, after the group explained that they were in Chechnya to investigate human rights violations, the Foreign Minister arranged for the provision of a flat on Prospekt Avtarkhanov for the group, with Chechen escorts.[59]

The most tragic aspect of the war in Chechnya was the failure of the Russian government to secure all precautions to prevent civilian casualties. As the Russian troops headed for Grozny on December 11, no corridors were established to evacuate the civilian population from the capital or the surrounding villages, despite Yeltsin's assurance to the contrary to the Chechen people on December 17: "We will strive to reduce to a minimum the use of force which, unfortunately, might lead to possible victims among the civilian population."[60] Thousands of people had abandoned the city after the bombings of November 29 and December 1, but thousands, especially elderly Russians and Chechens, were stranded in Grozny.[61] They either had no relatives to help them move or were too impoverished to move themselves. Many refugees had left for the mountains of Southern Chechnya, a Chechen stronghold, or for the neighbouring republics of Ingushetia and Dagestan.[62]

Grozny was relatively quiet in the days between December 16 and 19. Kovalyov and his group drove around the surrounding villages of Pervomaiskaya, Dolinskii and Assinovskaya situated to the north-west and west of Grozny. Russian troops were then firing on the village of Pervomaiskaya, while Chechen detachments were trying to hold the village from the outskirts. Kovalyov and the group drove further west to Dolinskii where they witnessed intense howitzer shelling of civilian buildings. South of Dolinskii in Assinovskaya they discovered that Russian troops were prevented from entering the village by crowds of people. Armed volunteers stood behind a line of women and children, but no shots were fired. They drove into the village and spoke with soldiers and commanders.[63] They discovered that the Russian soldiers under the guidance of the Ministry of Defence were concerned about the MVD troops, after complaints from the locals of looting and violence. Many soldiers petitioned their commanders to remove the MVD divisions in order to avoid tension between civilians and servicemen.[64] As Kovalyov recalled: "We didn't hear any talk about constitutional order, about Russian state interests, about the unity of the Federation. All those with whom we talked were saying completely different things. 'Why have they sent us here? Who is this war for? How can we fight against our own people? When will they take us out of here?'"[65] As Orlov later argued: "Who bore the fundamental responsibility for the death of peaceful civilians at this early stage [was] still questionable ... but later, when it approached the stage of bombing Grozny, it became clear that what was happening was a massive violation of human rights."[66]

By the time of Kovalyov's return to Grozny on the evening of December 19, the situation had changed considerably. For the first time, he and his colleagues witnessed the bombing of the capital by Russian military aircraft. The following morning they went out to observe the damage, agreeing to stay together to formulate a common position. For that reason Kovalyov had attempted to facilitate the formation of a group that represented a cross-section of the State Duma; Leonid Petrovsky of the Communist Party, Valerii Borshchev from Russia's Choice and Mikhail Molostvov from Yabloko.[67] The group could only investigate an insignificant part of the bomb damage.[68] They travelled to the intersections of Moskovskaya and Noya Bauchidze Streets, a district of one-story buildings where two bombs had left enormous craters. Four buildings had been completely destroyed, three houses were irreparably damaged and eleven more were seriously damaged. There were no military targets in the area.[69]

On the night of December 21–22 the city was again bombed. During the night, the working group heard up to fifteen explosions, and by midday the following day there was a series of large explosions. One rocket had struck the intersection of Prospekt Kirov and Sadovaya Street. When they visited the site, Kovalyov's group discovered that a nine-storey building and the "Kosmos" cinema had been hit by a rocket strike the night before. The bomb that fell around midday had killed approximately twelve people in their cars, twenty-two homes were seriously damaged and three one-storey buildings were completely destroyed. The next day, after a night of intensive strikes, the group observed that the children's department store, *Detskii Mir*, and the bank alongside had been struck. Both were on fire. By the night of December 23–24 the bombs were falling only five hundred metres from the flat: they later observed that one of the bombs had dropped on Avturkhanov Street and the second on Rosa Luxembourg street.[70]

The two top floors of House 5-a on Luxembourg Street were completely destroyed and most of the occupants had spent the night in the basement. One family, Anna Volkova and her son and daughter-in-law, had remained in their apartment. It was the fate of this family that Kovalyov often narrated to recapture the tragedy of the war for civilians. Later, at a press conference, he said:

> A very old woman is sitting on the sidewalk with the few possessions she saved from her fourth-floor apartment which was destroyed by a bomb. Next to her lie the bodies of her son and daughter-in-law covered with a blanket. Volkova is sitting on a stool behind a small cart with a flannel blanket – passer-bys are leaving money for the funeral services on it.[71]

What horrified Kovalyov was not merely the devastation, but the fact that the bombs and rocket strikes were falling on civilian buildings, not military targets. In an interview on the television programme *Itogi* on December 20, he declared: "The firing, perhaps, is directed at military targets, but the strikes are falling on people's homes. I have seen the destruction of people's homes with my own eyes. I have seen the corpses of peaceful citizens, clearly not combatants."[72] His successive appeals from Grozny focused world attention on the indiscriminate use of force:

> What is happening is clearly an enormous human tragedy. We have seen the disarmament of bandit groups turn before our eyes into chaos, into an all-out civil war … The Chechen nation, like any other nation, can make mistakes in its choice of leaders and ideals. But this does not give anyone the right to conduct a debate with them in the language of bombing and bombardment …[73]

In fact, while the Russian Air Force was bombing Grozny, the Ministry of Defence was facing serious divisions among its military elite. On December 15, Defence Minister Grachev dismissed a group of senior officers who had refused to send their troops into Chechnya once they recognized the potential for large civilian losses.[74] Grachev visited the military headquarters in Mozdok on December 21 and ordered Colonel General Eduard Vorobyov, First Deputy Commander of the Russian Ground Forces, to assume command. With equal insistence, Colonel Vorobyov refused to send troops in, convinced that they were not battleworthy and that poor weather conditions would only lead to further random strikes. Vorobyov was quickly replaced by Lieutenant General Anatoly Kvashin, and Pavel Grachev took a more personal role in the planning of the storm of Grozny for December 31.

Vorobyov later ran for parliament in the autumn of 1995, on the same ticket as Gaidar and Kovalyov.

Kovalyov continued to insist on negotiations. On December 23, Russian Foreign Minister Andrei Kozyrev contacted Kovalyov in Grozny to determine the possibility of negotiations with Dudayev. At their own initiative, Kovalyov and Orlov met with the Chechen President, but found it difficult to engage in a constructive conversation. Orlov noted that Dudayev was fixed on the idea of Chechen sovereignty and persisted in steering the conversation back to the topic of Russian imperialism. According to Orlov, "[i]t was a wild and endless monologue," that kept them at the Presidential Palace for several hours.[75] While Dudayev was hostile to Russia's treatment of Chechnya, he did not rule out negotiations. He agreed that the first priority was to organize a ceasefire. He agreed to the preliminary condition that Russian and Chechen troops could only be moved with the consent of both parties and that they needed to establish a joint commission to monitor the ceasefire. The question of Chechnya's status and disarmament would be discussed once the ceasefire was implemented. Orlov believed that Dudayev was prepared to come to some compromise regarding the Republic's status.[76] Kovalyov and Orlov went directly to Gudermes to send a telegram to Kozyrev in Moscow, explaining Dudayev's position, since the phone lines were down in Grozny. There was no response from the capital. Kovalyov never found out whether the telegram reached Kozyrev, although the Foreign Minister later declared that he had passed on the telegram to the Security Council, which ignored it.[77]

On December 24, the Russian Air Force bombed the Chechen Council of Ministers building and a mass of dwellings on Griboedov Street. According to General Petr Deinekin, the Chief Commander of the Russian Air Force, the last bomb dropped on Grozny was at 18.55 on the same day.[78] Several weeks later, the Commander revealed that due to heavy cloud and fog over the capital, the Russian Air Force had been unable to use laser-directed bomb and rocket strikes until December 29. It had intended to strike the television tower, the television station and several factories.[79] Kovalyov's frustration intensified when he heard a report from the Temporary Press Agency claiming that Dudayev's forces were bombing their own capital.[80] "You are able to stop this vicious circus of lies and murder," he wrote to Yeltsin on December 24:

> Only you are in a position to stop this senseless war … Every day, with our own eyes, we see planes bombing residential buildings. Every day we see the corpses of peaceful civilians, fragments of people, some without heads and others without legs. Boris Nikolaevitch, I'm ashamed to answer the questions concerning this war. When will this stop?[81]

The urgency Kovalyov felt to organize a ceasefire is best conveyed in his appeals to President Yeltsin, the Soldiers' Mothers Committee and the

International Community. Often dictated by telephone to Lydia Siomina at the Presidential Human Rights Commission and then passed on to Memorial in Moscow, these appeals are records of Kovalyov's amazement and outrage:

> It's time for a cardinal decision while we still have a choice. This opportunity will not be repeated. This is obvious while standing here under these bombs; we either have to stop what is happening or protect a return to a repressive government. That is, of terror, and not only in Chechnya. Boris Nikolaevitch, I understand that I'm coming to you from a position of resistance. But it's necessary. You have to understand that you are catastrophically wasting time. You do not need these people who are heading this war ...
>
> I know that my appeals do not always reach you and therefore, as Commissioner of Human Rights of the Russian Federation, while I still hold this post, I appeal to all the political forces of Russia, all the peaceful communities to stop the annihilation of a peaceful population. There must be a quick renewal of negotiations. I know for sure that the Chechen side is prepared for them.[82]

Two themes preoccupied Kovalyov in his appeals. The first was that Chechnya was "a nation in arms". He argued that the village locals would continue to join Dudayev's special forces to defend their homes and families regardless of their allegiance to Dudayev if strikes continued. The second was his concern for the growing number of victims, Russian and Chechen civilians, Russian and Chechen soldiers. This fear for combatants and non-combatants alike permeates all his appeals.

In the days between December 26 and December 31, Kovalyov was preoccupied with trying to organize humanitarian corridors for the evacuation of civilians. It was estimated that three convoys had left the Chechen Republic since the outbreak of fighting. Civilians had gathered at a bus stop near the railway station after hearing about the convoy through word of mouth. On December 26 and 27, Ingushetia's State of Emergency Ministry organized the evacuation of more civilians in eight buses. As the convoy approached the Ingushetian and Chechen border, it was stopped by Chechen forces and ordered to return to the capital. On hearing this, Kovalyov and Orlov went to the Presidential Palace and spoke with Dudayev's aide, Mavlen Salamov. He suggested that the decision to stop the convoys had been taken within Dudayev's closest circle that suspected the Ingushetians might be aiding the Russian troops. Salamov told them to gather lists of people who wanted to leave and a convoy would be organized under the aegis of the Human Rights Commissioner.[83] For two days, Kovalyov and his group visited apartments and bunkers gathering names, and on December 31 returned to the palace with the lists for a meeting with the Vice-president, Zelimkhan Yandarbiev, to decide on the question of the first convoy. At the same time,

Kovalyov appealed to the world community for urgently-needed medical supplies to be sent to hospitals in the capital.[84]

In Moscow, Nikolai Yegorov, Minister of National and Regional Affairs, announced plans for a full-scale storming of Grozny. Commander Deinekin's announcement on December 24 that the bombing of Grozny had ceased was directly refuted by Kovalyov, who continued to report bomb and rocket strikes after Christmas Eve.[85] Yeltsin himself declared that the bombing had ceased on December 27,[86] and Foreign Minister Andrei Kozyrev asked Kovalyov to return to Moscow since his mission had finished.[87] The same day, Kovalyov reported from Grozny that six rocket or bomb strikes had fallen on the city during the night and nine rockets and a bomb had been dropped on Urus-Martan, a region south of Grozny and a gathering point for refugees.[88] On December 28, Kovalyov and his group witnessed the first artillery fire on the capital in preparation for a storm with ground troops. On both December 29 and 30 Dudayev appealed again to Yeltsin for negotiations. Disappointed and frustrated, Kovalyov complained that the Russian side only wanted "unconditional capitulation" and criticised Moscow for insisting on unconditional disarmament.[89] He argued that this demand was completely unrealistic.[90]

Kovalyov's central concern was to get the civilians out of Grozny. As it turned out, just as he arrived at the Presidential Palace for the meeting with Yandarbiev on December 31, the storming of Grozny had begun. He and other deputies were persuaded by Isa Idigov, Chairman of Economic Affairs, to stay in the presidential bunker. Among those confined to the metre bunker were Oleg Orlov, Mikhail Molostvov, Valery Borshchev, Lev Ponomarev, Gleb Yakunin, Viktor Sheinis and Chechen Vice President Yandarbiev. Kovalyov managed to reach a Russian commander of one of the divisions heading for Grozny through a radio set up in the basement. The name of the commander is unknown. Kovalyov explained to him that Russian deputies had been unexpectedly caught in the Presidential Palace and were anxious to leave before the beginning of the planned storm. In consultation with Vice-President Yandarbiev, Kovalyov worked out a plan to evacuate them and passed their plans onto the commander. He promised to call them back, but never did.[91]

By midnight of December 31 they were joined by Russian soldiers taken prisoner from Maikopskaya Brigade No. 131 and Rifle Battalion No. 81. Both Kovalyov and the Soldiers' Mothers Committee were startled by how young the soldiers were. From conversations with the recruits that evening he discovered that, in order to capture the city on December 31, a fresh unit which had never served together had been hastily gathered, half of whom were badly trained eighteen- and nineteen-year-old boys in their first year in the army.[92] Defence Minister Grachev claimed several weeks later that they were the only soldiers available at the time and proudly added that these "eighteen-year-old boys died for Russia and they died with a smile on their faces. A memorial must be built for them."[93] Kovalyov also ascertained that the order to storm Grozny had been given orally and there was neither a written order nor documentation outlining a plan for the attack.[94] Grachev had anticipated that all four columns that had entered Chechnya on December 11 would converge on the capital, yet the eastern and western groups had hardly moved.[95] New Year's Eve passed by as Chechen and Russian deputies congratulated each other on the forthcoming year.

It appeared that Yeltsin and his supporters were not prepared to change the direction of their policy. But while they were ignoring Kovalyov's pleas for a political settlement and humanitarian assistance, they did their utmost to discredit his appeals that were appearing in *Izvestiya* and on the liberal television channel *NTV*. It was not only the forces of Russian nationalism that took advantage of the opportunity created by Yeltsin's decision to send troops into Chechnya, but *Rossiiskaya Gazeta* and *Rossiiskie Vesti*, the government newspapers which only a few months earlier were praising the benefits of an independent Human Rights Commissioner, quickly moved to criticise Kovalyov for his alleged attack on Russian statehood. They wished to fix in the public mind the image of Kovalyov as the inveterate dissident and an equally inveterate Westernizer. On the centre spread of *Rossiisskie Vesti* were two photographs, one of Kovalyov on the left and one of Pavel Grachev on the opposite page. In between the two images were war scenes of Russian soldiers firing on Chechen forces, Russian tanks and civilians in flight. The headline, "Let him have his say", was placed under Kovalyov's photograph, where he was accused of acting in "a dissident fashion", "of gathering a mosaic of facts", and of using the war to muster "political capital".[96] For the Head of the Presidential Administration, Sergei Filatov, Kovalyov "had done very little" to help the situation in Chechnya. For others like Sergei Shakhrai, his behaviour was reminiscent of a "religious fanatic". For one journalist he was "a torturer of Frogs" (in reference to his student dissertation topic of many years earlier).[97] And finally, for the leader of Russian National Unity, Alexei Vedenkin, he deserved to have a bullet put through his head.[98]

The hypocrisy behind the public smear campaign against Kovalyov was that the military and government press were seeking a means to blanket the internal chaos within the Russian army. As they struggled to present a united front in the media, Kovalyov's reports of chaos and discord were coming out in a constant stream in the liberal press. The disorder was clearly evident up until January 1995. Morale in the army was dangerously low, with soldiers hurriedly recruited from a mixture of combined forces, from districts as far apart as Vladivostok and Kaliningrad, and from forces as diverse as naval officers and Interior Ministry riot police. They had never served together, nor through lack of defence funding had they all undertaken training in large military manoeuvres.[99] Politically, Yeltsin and his circle were caught up in contradictions they could not resolve, beginning with Yeltsin's power struggle in the RSFSR and his infamous slogan: "Take as much sovereignty as you can handle", and Article 6 of the law "On

Repressed Peoples". As Foreign Minister Kozyrev said to Kovalyov later in January: "We can't take the path back; we can't recognize our mistakes; for the simple reason that if we retreat in the Chechen conflict, inevitably the question will arise as to what to do with those who are guilty."[100]

Meanwhile, the Russian forces had failed to capture Grozny on New Year's Eve. The following day the firing had quietened down enough for deputies Viktor Sheinis, Lev Ponomarev and Gleb Yakunin, and *Izvestiya* journalist Irina Dement'eva, to leave the bunker and return to Moscow with the news of the failed storming.[101] Kovalyov remained. The news reports from Moscow declared that the December 31 storming had been a success. On January 4, Vice-Premier Nikolai Yegorov stated that the government of the National Rebirth of Chechnya under Salambek Khadzhiyev "will arrive in Grozny tomorrow and get down to work."[102] He added that the remaining armed formations located in the surrounding mountains would be destroyed by spring.[103] In contrast, Kovalyov and Orlov were reporting in the pages of *Izvestiya* that Dudayev's forces continued to maintain a strong hold on the centre of the capital.[104] On January 4, Kovalyov decided to leave the Presidential bunker to return to Moscow to try to arrange a meeting with President Yeltsin. He heard over the radio that Yeltsin had on December 28 decreed (No. 2224) the formation of a Temporary Commission for Monitoring Human Rights and Civil Liberties in Chechnya and appointed the new Justice Minister, Valentin Kovalyov of the Russian Communist Party, as the Commission's Chairman. In the same way that he had learnt of his appointment to the Presidential Human Rights Commission, Kovalyov learned that he had been appointed Vice-Chairman of the Temporary Commission without any consultation. On January 2, he also learnt of his nomination for the Nobel Peace Prize by fellow biologist and deputy Nikolai Vorontsov. Kovalyov arrived back in Moscow on January 5 and found himself the focus of media attention. At his first press conference, he made no secret of his feelings of frustration, anger and shock about the events still taking place. He later expressed some regret for his strident language. On leaving Grozny he had witnessed the corpses of Russian soldiers killed in the failed December 31 storming and left lying on the streets. "The bodies of Russian soldiers have been lying in the streets for days," he declared; "some have been gnawed by dogs."[105] All his objections were founded on the failure of the authorities to protect individual liberties in Chechnya, from those of the Russian soldiers to those of the Russian, Chechen and Ingushetian citizens: "I have come to Moscow to look the officials in the eye, to try to find out who is lying," he declared:

> It is impossible to live in a country where the first persons lie ... Our team is convinced that the possibilities for negotiation are far from exhausted, and that all possibilities should be investigated. We know for a fact that it's the Russians, and not the Chechens, who are stalling peace talks. Of course, negotiations will be exceptionally difficult and lengthy, but to begin them is simple.[106]

The question of the right of the Chechen nation to independence came up during the press conference. He argued that the Moscow government had probably ruined its chances of keeping Chechnya within the Russian Federation. He believed that the decision to use force in the republic and then to prolong the attack in an uncompromising and brutal manner only served to isolate the republic further.

The question of adequate provisions to decide on the question of self-determination soon became a dominant theme in his public life. As the conflict in the Northern Caucasus escalated, and he began to seek support from foreign governments to place more pressure on Russia, Kovalyov severely criticised the vagueness of Article 1 of the International Covenant on Civil and Political Rights on self-determination, posing the questions "How does a community exercise its right to self-determination?" and "What is the procedure for secession?"[107] He argued that the division of powers required a basic level of goodwill from both sides, as well as appropriate laws and procedures.[108] If this basic requirement was absent, then without prescribed laws the chances for success were limited.

Kovalyov never publicly shared his personal views on Chechen sovereignty in the early days of the war. Given the political tension surrounding this issue, it was prudent of him to remain silent on the question. At the press conference, he expressed his anxiety about Dudayev's political motives and raised the question of the degree to which the Chechen President was driven by legitimate claims for independence or by his own personal power. Although he hinted that he would be disappointed to see the break-up of the Russian Federation, he never denied Chechnya's right to self determination. "I have no sympathy for Dudayev's unilateral declaration of Chechen independence," he stated. "There was much to criticise in Chechnya's human rights record during the three years it was governed by Dudayev ..."[109] But he argued that the unity of the Russian Federation could not take precedence over the lives of its citizens. And the war had made the task of negotiations far more difficult than they had been in 1991. He argued, most strongly, that it was Russia's failure to take into account its historical relations with the Chechens, the arrogance and political opportunism of Yeltsin's circle, that had prevented them from reaching a peaceful agreement with the republic, both prior to November 1994 and after.[110]

Indeed, Kovalyov's colleague, former member of the Human Rights Committee of the Supreme Soviet and aide to Kovalyov during his trips to Chechnya Oleg Orlov, agreed that the period between 1991 and 1994 was marked by serious human rights violations against Russian-speaking peoples in Chechnya. Orlov acknowledged that after two trips to Chechnya he had not succeeded in writing a report and conceded that not enough attention had been paid to violations during the period of Dudayev's regime.[111] Similarly, Mikhail Arutyunov, a Deputy Chair of the Presidential Human Rights Commission and refugee specialist admitted that the "Commission did not examine the situation and events in Chechnya."[112] They could never have guessed, however, that the human rights community would eventually be used by the apologists of the war as a scapegoat for the deteriorating situation in Chechnya prior to 1994.[113]

While the primary reason for Kovalyov's return to Moscow was to meet with Yeltsin, he was uncertain of what he would gain from the meeting. His appeals from Grozny had been ignored, his attempts to organize negotiations between the opposing sides had fallen on deaf ears, and the prospect of convincing the President to remove Russian troops from Chechnya was remote. In the forthcoming months, he was to become a constant irritant to the security apparatus in its efforts to pacify Chechnya. The President's reluctance to meet him was unmistakable. When his request for a meeting was denied on January 5, he replied angrily: "If the President doesn't think that the death of thousands of his own citizens isn't important, then he doesn't need to see me."[114] He concluded the phone conversation with the warning that he would not hide the President's response from the press.[115] This threat served its purpose. Several hours later Yeltsin's aide called back to say that the meeting would take place the following day.[116]

In many ways this meeting signified the final breakdown of the collaboration between Russia's Human Rights Commissioner and President Yeltsin. On January 6 at one o'clock, Kovalyov met with the President in the Kremlin. According to Kovalyov, this hour-long meeting was essentially a monologue. When he informed the President that his declaration on December 27 regarding the cessation of bombing in Grozny was mistaken and that the bombing of Grozny continued, Yeltsin retorted: "You have one-sided information, Sergei Adamovitch. I know for sure that the bombing has stopped." When Kovalyov asked the President for humanitarian assistance and evacuation corridors to remove the civilians, the wounded and the dead, Yeltsin told him it was still "too early".[117] It was clearly difficult for Kovalyov to accept that his years of trust in Yeltsin had been mistaken. He found it difficult to accept that the President was aware of what was happening and, unlike the aftermath of October 1993 or the controversy that surrounded the June 1994 Decree on Banditry, the President was now ignoring him and making no attempt to take his concerns into account. It was abundantly clear that Yeltsin had no intention of forming an alliance with Kovalyov on a tragic debacle that he and his circle had initiated. Given his inability to influence the President, Kovalyov turned to Prime Minister Viktor Chernomyrdin, Gaidar's replacement in 1992 who had expressed wavering interest in a peaceful settlement.

Kovalyov grew increasingly involved in peacemaking efforts in the region. Two days after his meeting with Yeltsin, he returned to Nazran with Alexander Daniel and Oleg Orlov. Throughout the conflict, Kovalyov had remained in frequent contact with Yegor Gaidar and, through the offices of the Ingushetian Vice-President Boris Agapov, Gaidar arranged for Kovalyov to speak with Chernomyrdin on the possibility of organizing a truce. On January 9, Chernomyrdin approved the idea of a 48-hour truce to remove the dead soldiers and evacuate the wounded and non-combatants, to start the following day. He told Kovalyov that he had passed on the necessary orders to the military. Kovalyov was asked by Chernomyrdin to make contact with both sides and explain the conditions of the ceasefire. He met with Aslan Maskhadov, then Head of the Armed Forces of the Chechen Republic of Ichkeriya and later elected President of Chechnya in 1997, and with Vice-President Zelimkhan Yandarbiev. The Chechen side agreed to the ceasefire. But negotiating with the Russian security apparatus was not so easy. When he tried to contact Russian Generals A.V. Kvashnin and L.V. Shevtsov at the Military Headquarters in Mozdok, he was unable to get through to them.[118]

Kovalyov's attempt at peace was quickly cut short. Later that evening it was announced on the radio that the truce on humanitarian grounds was to be replaced with an ultimatum, on the order of President Yeltsin.[119] The conditions were that if the Chechens gave up their weapons and released the prisoners of war, they would be guaranteed safe passage to their homes. Kovalyov quickly disassociated himself from the new terms and informed Chernomyrdin's office, the press and the Soldiers' Mothers Committee that Russia's Generals "were delaying the burial of their dead sons and the evacuation of the wounded."[120] His group returned to Grozny on January 10 and found it relatively calm. By midday, shooting had begun again and "it was obvious", recalled Orlov, "that neither side took the truce seriously."[121] Aslan Maskhadov met with General Ivan Babichev, Commander of the Western Division of the Russian Armed Forces, and the General informed the Chechen leader that they were not prepared to negotiate on the terms of the ceasefire. There was no evacuation of the wounded or the dead.[122] The storming of Grozny continued until January 19.

It is a credit to Kovalyov's perseverance and his skill for devising new strategies that he continued to insist on a ceasefire. The following day he sent his "Proposal for a Truce in Grozny and a Broader Peacemaking Effort in Chechnya and the Caucasus" to Andrei Kozyrev and Viktor Chernomyrdin. The crucial points of the proposal were: the establishment of a Joint Military Control Commission; the physical separation of the opposing sides by a distance sufficient to preclude the exchange of rifle fire; the removal of the dead and the evacuation of civilians and wounded soldiers; the exchange of prisoners; the staged withdrawal of troops of the Russian Armed Forces; gradual disarmament and the redeployment of regular military units of the Russian Armed Forces and the Ministry of Internal Affairs to permanent stations, with the police assigned responsibility for maintaining law and order. In conclusion, the proposal called for a national round table conference on Chechnya and negotiations without preliminary conditions.[123]

When Viktor Chernomyrdin appeared on Russian television four days later, the terms of his agreement were exactly the same as those in Kovalyov's proposal.[124] His address of January 16 marked the first government attempt to conduct negotiations on the basis of Kovalyov's truce conditions since the outbreak of war. Chernomyrdin announced that a meeting was to be held in Moscow on January 17 between Taimas Abubakarov (Chechen Finance Minister), Usman Imaev (Chechen Minister of Justice and General Procurator), Sergei Shakhrai (Russian Vice-Premier) and Vyacheslav Mikhailov (Chairman of the State Committee on Federal and National Affairs).[125] On January 17, Chernomyrdin met the Chechen representatives and agreed on a phased ceasefire. The Chechen side planned for the ceasefire to begin on the following day at 5 p.m. The next day, Yeltsin declared that he was unwilling to begin negotiations with Dudayev "who conducted genocide against his own people".[126] On January 19 the Presidential Palace in Grozny was captured by General Rokhlin's 8th Corps from Volgograd.[127] Yeltsin declared on the same day that the "military operation [was] practically wrapped up".[128] Russian air and artillery bombardment of targets in Chechnya, however, continued, as did the ground fighting in and around Grozny. On January 18, Abubakarov and Usman waited in Nazran for a meeting with the Russian representatives of the military, who failed to show up.[129] The Russian flag was raised on the Presidential Palace on January 20.

Kovalyov returned to Moscow on January 24 to announce that the truce was broken. He handed out leaflets dropped by the Russian Armed Forces on local villages, threatening retaliation:

> If there is open firing from your village, we will retaliate without hesitation with powerful missile strikes!
>
> Residents of Bamut! You have been betrayed. People in Dudayev's entourage are saying that he has fled abroad with his family. Dudayev's closest aides are hauling truckloads of property stolen from the Chechen people out of Grozny. They are calling upon you to resist so that they can get away with as much as possible.[130]

Pavel Grachev announced that "no kind of truce is possible. Only an ultimatum." "That peacemaker Kovalyov," he pronounced, "is an enemy and traitor of Russia. He is meeting up with everyone down there."[131]

At the same, Valentin Kovalyov's Temporary Commission to monitor Civil Rights and Liberties in Chechnya had started working, as had Nationalist film-maker Stanislav Govorukhin's Parliamentary Commission to Investigate the Causes of the Chechen war.[132] On January 4, Valentin Kovalyov returned from Chechnya to announce in a Press Conference that there were no human rights violations taking place in Chechnya.[133] The following day he was appointed Russia's new Minister of Justice by Yeltsin and at the same time he was expelled from the Russian Communist Party for defying its official protocol not to enter any government post in protest against the direction of economic reform.[134] He later argued that "there is no armed conflict between the Republic of Chechnya and the Russian Federation … What we have is something on an entirely different plane: there are armed formations seeking independence and threatening national integrity."[135]

On January 27, Kovalyov resigned from his appointment as Vice-Chairman of the Temporary Commission. Its members refused publicly to condemn the use of warfare, or to demand an immediate ceasefire, humanitarian aid, exchange of POWs, evacuation of the wounded and burial of the dead.[136] Kovalyov's claim about the urgent need for humanitarian assistance was confirmed by Istvan Gyarmati, Personal Representative of the OSCE Chairman-in-Office who led the OSCE delegation to Grozny. He concluded that the "humanitarian situation is a catastrophe of serious proportions" and that "the need for humanitarian aid is very large in all parts of Chechnya and the neighbouring regions. Detained Chechens in the prison wagons in Mozdok that we met had been badly beaten and were in urgent need of medical care."[137] This was confirmed by Lorenzo Amberg's mission from the Department of Foreign Affairs in Switzerland. The emergency management consultant Frederick Cuny also concluded in his report that "there were approximately 30,000 civilians still in Grozny with little food or water". The Russian authorities refused to acknowledge the existence of the civilians, claiming that the only people left were "supporters of the bandits."[138] In the end it was not until February 18, 1995 that permission was given for the first delivery of humanitarian aid to Grozny by the International Red Cross.[139]

The parliamentary hearings of January 26 dramatized the polarization of the Russian Duma on Chechnya. Kovalyov was summoned by the Duma to explain the results of his investigations. He was given two hours' notice to prepare his report. In his speech, he again stressed the ongoing human rights violations: "Both sides are guilty of human rights violations," he declared, "but the scale of their violations cannot be compared."[140] He stressed the need for a ceasefire and humanitarian aid for the civilians and soldiers. He proposed that the Duma appeal to the Presidential Administration for humanitarian corridors to be organized to provide a safe haven for civilians. He concluded his report with the words:

> The need for humanitarian aid is very great in all parts of Chechnya and the neighbouring regions. Right now, today, the main thing is to stop the war. We ought to immediately adopt a resolution about a ceasefire, about the creation of a humanitarian corridor, about the evacuation of the civilian population. The population must be supplied at least with items of prime necessity: medical supplies, food, even drinking water, because there's none in the town. Grozny isn't a city any more – it's a pile of bricks, with the burnt-out skeletons of buildings sticking up all over the place. People are living in the cellars underneath.[141]

During the January 26 hearings, Kovalyov proposed that the State Duma:

1   condemn the military operation in Chechnya as a way of resolving a political non-international dispute by military means;

2 condemn the use of weapons of mass destruction and their indiscriminate effect;

3 agree without delay on a ceasefire;

4 appeal to the government for humanitarian corridors to be organized and other means of rescuing the civilian population.[142]

Not since the "aggressively obedient majority" vilified Sakharov in 1989 had a Russian parliamentarian been subject to the denunciations that were showered on Kovalyov. Yuri Kuznetsov of the Liberal Democratic Faction led the criticism against Kovalyov by accusing him of hiding in a cellar for forty days in Grozny, and appealed to the Duma to remove him from office. Burlakov, also of the Liberal Democratic Faction, accused Kovalyov of neglecting his duty: "Where was he when the mass violation of human rights was taking place? Why didn't you evacuate a single civilian? My relatives died there and its your fault. Pharisee!"[143] Boiko accused Kovalyov of an "anti-state approach",[144] and his unavoidable confinement to the bunker of the Presidential Palace during the storming of Grozny between December 30 and January 4 became the source of a stream of condemnations. "Who is he defending?" asked Zhirinovsky:

The bandits, rapists and troublemakers … people who are fighting against our Constitution, our State, with weapons in their hands! And millions of citizens have suffered. Suffered from the disintegration of the USSR as a result of the activity of his political movement … Why wasn't he monitoring human rights violations in our city? Why was he sitting in a basement in a city where a war is going on?[145]

Kovalyov did not go without support among other deputies. Deputy Minzhurenko from Russia's Choice asked, in response, to Zhirinovsky's question:

And where in general should the Russian Human Rights Commissioner have been? Of course he should have been [in Grozny] where [there was] a massive violation of human rights. We don't understand how to fight for human rights in our country. This is a completely new thing. Sergei Adamovich himself doesn't know what to do. He tries to appeal to public opinion, he tries to appeal to our conscience, but unfortunately, he does not always succeed.[146]

Members of the parliament resorted to the Soviet lexicon of denunciation and accused Kovalyov of being a Western agent. Deputy A. Gerber of Russia's Choice asked what was the reason for the accusation, especially since the West was keeping a low profile regarding the war. "I think he is most of all an agent for himself, of his own conscience."[147] The intensity of the proceedings was best illustrated by the speech by Valery Borshchov

(Yabloko), a liberal deputy who had accompanied Kovalyov to Grozny on his first trip:

> I was with Sergei Adamovitch in the delegation. The left wing present here very often use the word "Russian", invoke the name of Russia, and evidently consider themselves Russian patriots. From this podium, the great Russian patriot Alexander Isaevich Solzhenitsyn spoke, and as you recall, he said: there's no more important task than safeguarding our people. I don't remember anyone objecting to his words. This is in fact our main task. And so it astonished me that no one – I'm talking about this part of the hall, the majority – is disturbed that a nation is being destroyed. Naturally, bombs and bullets don't discriminate according to ethnicity. That's clear. Naturally, when a city is destroyed, Russians and Ingush and Jews die too. And if you take into account that many Chechens sent their women and children to their native villages, then it is also evident that the majority of those dying are Russian. Why doesn't this bother you at all, you who like to think you're Russian patriots?
>
> The authorities have done nothing to evacuate civilians! Nothing at all has been done! People camped out in the bus terminal, waiting for a bus to come along. I recall when the Ingush Ministry for Emergencies organized four convoys, and they stormed the buses trying to leave. Our Russian authorities ignored the problem. It was Sergei Adamovitch who raised the issue with the Chechen authorities, telling them that organization was needed. And they said, for God's sake, make lists. It was actually necessary to settle this with them. Four convoys left without difficulty. But understandably, tensions increased as the fighting came closer. Thanks to Sergei Adamovitch, people went around to the cellars and compiled lists. He's the one who raised the issue – no one else cared. Why didn't you care? Why doesn't anyone care that in that cold, hungry city children are dying?
>
> We moved into the cellar only after they bombed our apartment. We lived on the fourth and second floors. On January 5, we were forced to move into the cellar of the house where we were living. It was a cold, damp cellar. But it wasn't us that mattered – there were children there! Three, five, six years old, six months. Why did you refuse to adopt a resolution calling for a ceasefire? That upsets me. You're juggling with words, you're playing political games, and you spit on your Russian people, honourable Russian patriots![148]

Kovalyov's precarious position grew worse. The Chechen leadership awarded Kovalyov a medal for his contribution to the "Cause of Defending Human Rights at a Time of Open Aggression and Genocide directed by the Government of the Russian Federation at the Chechen Nation", In an interview, Alla Dudayev, the wife of the Chechen President, described Kovalyov as her favourite Russian politician.[149] The question of Kovalyov's patriotism became the central preoccupation of the government and military press. He fell victim to the ridiculous charge that his "inadequate patriotism" was distorting the public perception of events in Chechnya and undermining the battle to preserve the unity of the Russian Federation.

Kovalyov contributed to the controversy with inflammatory public statements. He enraged nationalist opponents by announcing on the television programme *Itogi* that "Patriotism is the last refuge of the scoundrel" and that Tolstoy and Pushkin were his intellectual allies against xenophobic nationalism. Journalists Vadim Kozhinov and Marina Yureva of *Rossiiskaya Gazeta* quickly responded. Kozhinov argued that one only had to look at Tolstoy's novels to understand what kind of patriot he was, with his "strong criticisms of the West" and his antipathy towards the "supremacy of individual ownership". Kochinov recalled Pushkin's support of the suppression of the Polish Uprising in 1831 as a direct symbolic refutation to Kovalyov's position regarding the Chechen war. According to Kozhinov, Pushkin was baptized Russia's "National Poet" and "Patriot" for enthusiastically championing Russian unity and denouncing the West for interfering in Slavic problems. Kozhinov quoted from the poem "To the Slanderers of Russia", where Pushkin argued that the suppression of Poland was Russia's internal affair, "an argument between the Slavs". Kozhinov then set out to demonstrate that the West had always resented Russia for liberating her from Napoleon in 1812 and, thereafter, constantly sought fault in Russia's internal affairs. He concluded by dividing Pushkin's contemporaries into two groups. The first group consisted of "Pushkin, Chadeev, Chukovsky, Baratinsky, Gogol and Tutchev – all supporters of the suppression of the Polish uprising, who would not only be remembered for their great talents, but for their loyalty to the Russian state." The second group were, "a group of like-minded people in the mould of Kovalyov, talentless heretics who would almost certainly be cast onto the trash heap of history." To protect themselves against the charge that they were threatening the Poles, the editor of *Rossiiskaya Gazeta* added as a footnote: "We are not calling for the restoration of the borders of the Russian Empire in Pushkin's time, or to infringe upon the sovereign republic of Poland. We are simply using historical examples to refute Kovalyov's claim."[150]

To reinforce Kozhinov's article, *Rossiiskaya Gazeta* ran another article two days later by Marina Yureva, in which she praised Kozhinov for his "deeply argumentative" article. The same could not be said of Yureva's polemic, which chose invective over argument. It argued that "Patriotism [was] one of the inherent traits of our national character … Russia was always special … with its traditions … its humanism." She concluded with the accusations that Kovalyov suffered from "megalomania" and a "persecution complex".[151]

Kovalyov became the focus of a wider campaign to discredit the human rights movement. The attacks escalated, with accusations of negligence and irresponsibility for events in Chechnya prior to the December attack. The broadsheet *Rossiiskaya Gazeta* devoted an entire section to the rights defence movement under the general heading "For the Attention of Human Rights Defenders", over a period of approximately two months. Its front page listed cases where Russians had fallen victim to crime in Chechnya. Typical examples included:

> Veteran of the Great Patriotic War V. N. Kovalenko lives in Mayakovskaya Staropromislovskaya region. In April 1993 robbers burst into his flat, threw a bag over his head, bound him and severely beat him. His flat was pillaged.

Another example:

> On May 11, 1993 around one o'clock in the morning, two armed Chechens opened garage No. 31 'Olympic' which belonged to a Mr Smirnov. They wheeled out a Zhiguli and drove it away.[152]

More disturbing for Kovalyov was the fact that one of his most famous dissident colleagues was making the same argument. On June 7, 1995 Solzhenitsyn wrote:

> The painful destruction of the situation in Chechnya lasted three years. There was violence, robbery, the eviction of non-Chechens from their apartments etc. *Ekspress-Khronika* wrote in June 1992, every third Chechen citizen had experienced violence (half a year later, the correspondent who wrote that article killed himself). Where were all you Moscow human rights activists, from Sergei Kovalyov down to you personally? Why was it that not one of you was moved by these sufferings? Why did none of you go to Chechnya *then, when it was still not too late* in order to witness crimes and help the victims?[153]

On January 27 the Duma deferred its decision to dismiss Kovalyov as Human Rights Commissioner. On the same day he attempted to fly to Grozny with an OSCE delegation but the Defence Ministry intervened to prevent him joining the group. He was told that the passenger list could only be altered with Grachev's personal approval. He had already received permission to fly from Valentin Kovalyov the previous day. But he suspected that Grachev was aware that he was going to investigate the filtration point in Mozdok organized with the authorization of Grachev and Nikolai Yegorov, which had been the subject of reports of beatings, torture and summary executions.[154]

Instead he flew to Strasbourg, where he presented one of his most outspoken speeches against the war to the Council of Europe. He then travelled to Geneva where he headed the Russian delegation to the annual meeting of the 52nd UN Human Rights Commission. He openly supported the Council of Europe's decision to defer Russia's admission

WANTED

SERGEY KOVALYOV

SERGEY KOVALYOV

Figure 5.1   Sergei Kovalyov, Moscow Times, October 27, 1995: p. 8
Source: Moscow News, Moscow.

Figure 5.2   Sergei Kovalyov in Geneva as head of the Russian Delegation of the UN Commission on Human Rights (undated)
Source: Memorial Archive, Moscow.

and maintained Sakharov's principle that Russia needed both pressure and support. "If the problem is to be approached in an honest and responsible way," declared Kovalyov, "I will have to state with regret that the situation with human rights in Russia does not meet high European standards, nor will it meet them for some years to come." He recommended that a timetable be established by which Russia could fulfil a given objective.[155] While the Communists and Nationalists would interpret this as a candid betrayal of their country, Kovalyov would see the switch from the domestic to the international arena as a legitimate way of mustering support and leverage. He said in his speech that he did not want to defer Russia's admittance indefinitely, but did not feel that Russia was in a position to honour its own constitutional principle of the priority of international commitments over the country's internal legislation.[156] His speech was regularly interrupted by heckling from one of his most outspoken critics, the ultra-nationalist leader Vladimir Zhirinovsky, who also attended the Strasbourg conference, both to publicly attack Kovalyov and to argue against the proposed integration of the Baltic States into the European Union.[157] Zhirinovsky's behaviour led to his microphone being turned off and his expulsion from the parliament.[158]

The parliamentary assembly concluded that it "unreservedly condemns the indiscriminate and disproportionate use of force by the Russian military, in particular against the civilian population ... The Assembly resolves to freeze its examination, for the time being, of Russia's request for membership of the Council of Europe."[159] The UN Commission on Human Rights expressed its "deep concern over the disproportionate use of force by the Russian Armed Forces in Chechnya" on February 27, 1995. The Russian government refused to allow the UN Human Rights Commissioner to conduct a monitoring mission to Chechnya.[160] After months of negotiation, however, the OSCE was able to organize an assistance group to visit Chechnya in April.

Throughout 1995, the Russian Duma did little to end the Chechen war other than to produce a series of declarations and appeals. Every constructive attempt to stop the bloodshed was blocked by the nationalist factions. There was little support for the initiative to amend the constitution to give the Duma more control of the actions of the Defence Ministry. The liberal factions wanted to ban the use of money from the budget for military activities in Russia, but only 100 deputies voted for this. Zhirinovsky's faction always supported the power ministries. From January 1, the Russian Democratic Party under Glaz'ev, Govorukhin and Travkin, practically all the members of the Agrarian Party and three-quarters of the Shakhrai–Shokhin faction, also supported the war. In a letter to Yeltsin on January 27, Kovalyov wrote of being hindered in his work:

> Boris Nikolaevich! With your decree you commanded me to fulfill my constitutional function without waiting for the Duma to pass the appro-

priate federal law. I see only two ways out of this situation. Either you disavow your decree of August 4, 1994 "On measures to guarantee the constitutional function of the Human Rights Commissioner". Or you and Viktor Chernomyrdin establish constitutional order in the state and governmental apparatus. Only you are in the position to achieve this.[161]

He acknowledged that he would prefer to conduct quiet diplomacy, but as the heads of state continued to ignore him, he had "no other choice than to shout".[162]

Kovalyov's long struggle to become Russia's first Human Rights Commissioner ended on March 10, 1995. The Duma voted to dismiss him from his post in defiance of the factional agreement of January 1994.[163] His allies attempted to block the passing of the law on the Human Rights Commissioner until new elections were called, but all their protests were ignored. The final vote, instigated by nationalist Sergei Baburin, was 240 deputies for, 75 against, 3 abstentions and 128 absent or not voting.[164] It was another eighteen months before the law on the Human Rights Commissioner was passed and Oleg Mironov of the Russian Communist Party was appointed.[165] For the time being, Kovalyov maintained his position as Chairman of the Presidential Human Rights Commission and continued to monitor events in Chechnya.

Рисунок Вадима Мисюка.

Figure 5.3   "You have the right to remain silent. You have the right
to a meeting with Sergei Kovalyov ...", *Nezavisimaya
Gazeta*, January 31, 1995: p. 1

Samashki and Budyonnovsk

Over the next three months, Kovalyov was at the centre of one of the fiercest controversies of the first Chechen war. Between April 7 and 8, 1995, the village of Samashki, located 25 kilometres west of Grozny, was attacked by MVD forces. The attack provoked a retaliation campaign by Chechen guerillas in the small industrial town, Budyonnovsk, two months later. Both events drew Kovalyov back into a controversy that involved Stanislav Govorukhin, nationalist film-maker and Head of the Duma Commission to Investigate the Causes of the Chechen War.

Once the Russian flag was flying over the Presidential Palace in Grozny, Dudayev's supporters were forced into the surrounding villages and mountain regions. The MVD established Checkpoint No. 13 some 8 kilometres from Samashki on December 17. The Russian forces blocked off part of the route from Rostov to Baku to the south west, putting Samashki on the remaining major route from Ingushetia to Grozny.[166] Sporadic fighting had begun in the region as early as December 11, despite requests by the village elders that those who wanted to fight move to Grozny. By February 21, negotiations between Lema Abdulkhajiev, head of Samashki's village administration, along with the village elders, and General Lieutenant Yuri Kasalapov had begun. The elders were given three days to organize the removal of any rebel forces from the village. On March 7, the residents of Samashki agreed to the conditions and the rebel fighter unit moved into a forest south of Samashki. The signed agreement was delivered to Kasalapov,[167] but the uncertainty as to whether the rebels had actually left the village eventually served as the pretext for an MVD attack with OMON troops on the village.[168]

The railway line between Sernovodsk and Samashki was the reason for the failure of the agreement. A military train arrived in Samashki to clear and repair the rail track to carry supplies and Russian troops. Pro-Dudayev fighters came out of the mountains to try and convince the village elders not to allow the train to come into Samaskhi, and two Russian soldiers were wounded. On March 26, Russian helicopters shelled the village and the elders agreed to allow the military train to pass through while they stood along the rail track to prevent any clashes between Dudayev's men and Russian troops. The train, however, failed to pass and returned to Sernovodsk.[169]

On April 6, General A.S. Antonov offered the elders another ultimatum, the requirements of which included handing over 264 automatic weapons, 2 machine guns, 1 armed personal carrier, and agreeing to allow the MVD units into the village. If the demands were not met, a full-scale weapons check would be conducted by the MVD forces. The elders declared that they could not answer for Dudayev's forces, but their local militia did not have that many guns and they could only hand over 50 at the most. The General refused to negotiate.[170] On April 7, General-Colonel A.C. Kulikov of the MVD declared that Dudayev's main commander, Shamil Basaev, Head of the Abkhazian battalion, was in Samashki. According to witness testimonies only about 40 local militia remained in the village; neverthless 350 Russian soldiers of the MVD and the OMON troops took part in an operation to cleanse the village of Dudayev's fighters. Divided into ten separate storming groups, the term "cleansing" was used to mean the checking of every street and individual home.[171] Aerial bombardments hit the village on the morning of April 7. Between seven and nine o'clock, armed personal carriers opened fire on the village, with shelling beginning approximately twenty-five minutes before the 4 p.m. deadline.[172] There were several attacks that the local militia testified to,[173] but the presence of any members of the Abkhazian battalion in Samashki at that time is highly doubtful. This was confirmed by the village militia, members of the Abkhazian battalion and witness testimonies.[174]

General Antonov proudly boasted that "this was the first completely independent military operation conducted by the Interior Ministry troops in history."[175]

From April 8, a new observer mission organized by Memorial began to interview witnesses. Memorial's Human Rights Centre established a new monitoring group in the wake of Kovalyov's dismissal on March 10. The group was headed by Kovalyov and included Duma deputies and representatives from the Russian–American Human Rights Project Group. Since his dismissal Kovalyov had begun to work more closely with his old friends and colleagues at Memorial, Arseni Roginsky and Oleg Orlov. The observer mission took accounts of premeditated arson, theft and beatings,[176] they were shown syringes on the street suggesting the use of narcotics by Russian soldiers. The mission concluded that 103 civilians had died – 90 men and 13 women.[177] The most chilling testimonies came from civilian men who had been rounded up and taken to the screening point in Mozdok and a temporary detention centre in Assinovskaya. According to Razyev Khasan, the men were forced to run with dogs chasing them to a helicopter that then transported them to Mozdok.[178] Those detained in Mozdok were confined to pits in the ground, masked and beaten during interrogation until they confessed that they were armed rebels. They were not given any water until 36 hours after their arrival. On April 11, Razyev Khasan was released on the condition that he sign a statement declaring that he had no grievances against the Russian authorities.[179]

When Kovalyov returned from Samashki, he declared that the attack had been a "punitive operation" against the village.[180] He gave accounts of witness testimonies and the general findings of Memorial's Observer Mission. "The military activities against the village of Samashki," he threatened, "will be subject to careful investigation."[181] The report released by Kovalyov and Memorial in November under the title "All Available Means" was contested in a public debate by Stanislav Govorukhin and his Parliamentary Commission to Investigate the Causes of the Chechen War. Seven months after the events in Samashki, on November 20, 1995, Govorukhin released his own report entitled "Govorukhin's Commission" at a press conference in Moscow. His report rejected the figures, testimonies and evidence of Memorial's documentation of events, but only managed to secure signatures from six of the ten members that made up his commission. After returning from Samashki, Govorukhin declared: "for me Samashki is still a mystery. I find all this bloody arithmetic distasteful ..."[182] He concluded in his report that "The Parliamentary Commission ... did not find one confirmation that Russian soldiers had brutally treated peaceful civilians in the village of Samashki", and that no punitive operation had ever taken place.[183] Oleg Orlov responded with the article"The New Patriotism of Stanislav Govorukhin", in which he convincingly contested Govorukhin's version of events.[184]

Govorukhin's report blamed the Russian press and human rights activists for a one-sided account of events in the village. He argued that 90 per cent of the information distributed to the West was a conscious lie used to inspire Dudayev's separatist activity, which he called "a conspiracy of the mass media against the President, the government, the parliament, against Russian statehood and the Russian people."[185] According to Govorukhin, Kovalyov and his colleagues were responsible for Dudayev's retaliatory the attack on Budyonnovsk. For Govorukhin, the attack on Budyonnovsk was the result of what the separatist leader and his followers had read in the Russian press.[186]

> Imagine a young Chechen reading an account of Kovalyov's press conference where he details the mistreatment of prisoners-of-war by soldiers ... [or] a young Chechen Highlander, who has decided to lay down his arms, then learns about Russian atrocities from the tales of human rights activists. Of course, after such an unpleasant discovery, he will go off to fight with new intensity. Who should we blame for this?[187]

In the wake of the Samashki events, Dudayev's rebel forces under the leadership of Shamil Basaev took hostages in the small industrial town of Budyonnovsk, 140 kilometres from Grozny, on June 13. Aslambek Izmailov, a Chechen fighter, declared that they "were forced to take such a step to stop the destruction of our people."[188] Having lost their headquarters in the mountain village of Shatoi, approximately 150 fighters arrived in the small town with a population of 54,000, took hostages from the streets and seized the local hospital.

Kovalyov arrived with Orlov three days later and phoned Gaidar for help in the negotiation process.[189] Minister of Defence Grachev did not believe that the crisis could be settled through negotiations and advocated the use of force as soon as possible.[190] The following day, Kovalyov woke to the sound of artillery fire. The hospital was on fire and the Russian forces were storming it. During the fighting, which lasted for five hours, it was estimated that eighty people died.[191] Five hostages were killed by Basaev's forces after the rebel leader's demand for a Press Conference did not take place on time.[192]

Figure 5.4   Sergei Kovalyov in Budyonnovsk, Stavropol, June 1995
Source: Memorial Archive, Moscow.

Kovalyov appealed to Prime Minister Viktor Chernomyrdin to begin negotiations. He believed that Chernomyrdin, who had earlier supported the ceasefire on January 10 that had been overruled by Yeltsin, genuinely sought peace in the Caucasus.[193] Chernomyrdin asked Kovalyov to form a negotiation team.[194] But it was not until Sunday morning that Kovalyov was allowed access to the hospital.[195] The negotiations between him and Shamil Basaev lasted for less than an hour. They agreed that in return for the release of the hostages, Basaev and his forces would be guaranteed safe passage to Chechnya and they would take with them around 100 volunteers until they arrived at their point of safety. The agreement stated that urgent negotiations would resume immediately on the withdrawal of Russian troops from

Chechnya and the disarmament of Chechen forces. Once the ceasefire was under way, all political questions would be settled by peaceful means.[196] But the Kremlin completely ignored the point that all political questions were to be solved exclusively on the basis of negotiations, instead stating that the negotiation process would be conducted by a new commission.[197]

Basaev refused to accept the new conditions. This rejection resulted in the well-known televised drama between Chernomyrdin and Basaev. The rebel leader requested that Chernomyrdin publicly endorse the conditions of Kovalyov's draft. Chernomyrdin responded that all military activity would cease on the condition that the hostages be released before Basaev and his men left the city.

Kovalyov was called to the main headquarters, where the Head of the Stavropol Administration, Yevgeny Kuznetsov, demanded that he leave Budyonnovsk. He was prevented from re-entering the hospital,[198] and it was not until the following morning, after Basaev declared that he would not go anywhere without Kovalyov, that he was called back to the Headquarters.[199] Believing that Kovalyov's group was the only guarantee of his safety, Basaev forced the authorities to get Kovalyov back to the hospital.[200] Kovalyov volunteered to go with Basaev, along with the hundred other volunteers, to ensure the release of the remaining hostages.[201]

The Russian authorities insisted that Kovalyov, Orlov and the remaining hostages all sign the following document: "I, the undersigned, am voluntarily joining Shamil Basaev's bandit group and leaving with them for the Chechen Republic and I am aware of all possible consequences of my decision."[202] They were taken in six buses towards Chechnya. On Wednesday June 21, Kovalyov and the others were released. He was subsequently hospitalized, having suffered a minor heart attack during the crisis.[203]

It took this violent event to convince the Russians to begin genuine negotiations.[204] Within two months, the Russian government agreed to a military ceasefire, signed on August 30, and the Khasavyurt Peace Treaty signed in neighbouring Dagestan on August 6, 1996 finalized the withdrawal of the federal forces from Chechnya.[205] A decision about Chechen sovereignty was put aside for five years. Kovalyov estimated that some 27,000 persons had died in Chechnya in the months between December and February 1994–95.[206] He openly acknowledged that the figure could be out by up to 20 per cent, and estimated that 400,000 people had been displaced by the war.[207]

This, however, would not be the end of the Chechen campaign.

The Constitutional Court

Kovalyov sought redress for events in Chechnya in the most traditional means for a rights defender. He appealed to the Russian Constitutional Court. In late June he and a group of parliamentary deputies appealed to the Constitutional Court to examine the constitutionality of the decrees and resolutions which initiated the Chechen war. Their argument was that the

Presidential Decrees of November 30 and December 9, 1994, and the corresponding resolution had

> ... formed a single system of normative legal acts that resulted in the unlawful use of the Armed Forces of the Russian Federation since their use on the territory of the Russian Federation is only legally possible within the framework of a regime of a state of emergency or a state of martial law. It is stressed that these measures resulted in the unlawful restriction and massive violation of the constitutional rights and freedoms of Russian citizens.[208]

The decrees under examination included No. 2137 of November 30, 1994, "On Measures to Restore Constitutional Legality and Law and Order on the Territory of the Chechen Republic", Decree No. 2166 of December 9, "On Measures to Stop the Activities of Illegal Formations on the Territory of the Chechen Republic and in the Zone of the Ossetian-Ingush Conflict", Resolution No. 1360 of December 9, 1994, "On Ensuring State Security and Territorial Integrity of the Russian Federation, Legality, the Rights and Freedoms of Citizens and Disarmament of Illegal Armed Formations on the Territory of the Chechen Republic and Adjacent Areas of the Northern Caucasus", and Decree No. 1883 of November 2, 1993, "On the Main Provisions of the Military Doctrine of the Russian Federation".[209]

The most contentious point was the secret decree of November 30, 1994. This decree commissioned the Defence Ministry to establish a leadership group to lead the action to "disarm and liquidate the armed formations, to introduce and support the regime's State of Emergency". It did so in secret, without seeking the approval of the State Duma, in defiance of the Law on States of Emergency (May 17, 1991). All the bureaucratic mechanisms of the Chechen campaign were established under the auspices of this decree.[210] Matters were complicated even further when Yeltsin secretly rescinded it after attending an OSCE conference in Budapest on December 5. In Budapest he signed a Code of Behaviour concerning Military-Political Aspects of Security. In the code (point 36) it was stipulated that "Every participating state shall guarantee that any decision about the direction of its armed forces for the execution of internal security will be taken in accordance with Constitutional Proceedings".[211]

In what appeared to be a clumsy attempt to bring the decree into line with the Budapest Code, the President abolished the November 30 decree and replaced it with a new one on December 9. All mention of a state of emergency, or reference to the law on states of emergency, was removed, and all knowledge of the decree's existence was concealed until the eve of the Constitutional Court hearings, when a letter from the President's Administration (A19–2), dated July 3, removed its confidential status. Thirty-one copies of the abolished decree were distributed on December 12.[212]

Kovalyov left hospital in Moscow on July 10 to present his testimony to the Constitutional Court. He argued that, according to Part 2 of Article 74 of the "Law on the Constitutional Court", the constitutionality of the decrees could be examined with all their attendant consequences. For Kovalyov, the hypocrisy of the documents was reflected in the fact that, amid the optimistic phrases of constitutional law and order, nowhere was there a description of the character and method of action that would eventually lead to the killing of thousands of innocent victims. This was not "simply hypocrisy", he argued "but direct mockery".[213] His testimony was short and succinct. He outlined the violations he had witnessed personally and his attempts to negotiate a ceasefire with both the Russian government and the *de facto* Chechen leader. He accused Yeltsin of "criminal negligence".[214]

Yeltsin's legal team, led by Sergei Shakhrai and Yuri Baturin, argued that the President had in fact been forced to defend Article 80 of the Constitution stating that:

> The President shall be the guarantor of the Constitution of the Russian Federation, and of human and civil rights and freedoms. In accordance with the procedure established by the Constitution of the Russian Federation, he shall take measures to protect the sovereignty of the Russian Federation, its independence and state integrity, and ensure concerted functioning and interaction of all bodies of state power.[215]

According to the Presidential lawyers, Yeltsin had been forced to act since the human rights community had ignored the deteriorating situation in Chechnya prior to 1994.[216] These arguments echoed the speeches of Zhirinovsky and Kuznetsov in the parliamentary hearings of January 26 and 27.

The Constitutional Court ruled that it would not examine the first decree, since it had been abolished and no human rights violations had occurred between November 30 and December 9. Nor would it examine the decrees according to the "appropriateness of the actions carried out on their basis".[217] It rejected the submission that a state of emergency had to be introduced "to ensure state integrity and constitutional order" and the Russian government's violation of the 1949 Geneva Convention on the protection of citizens during non-international conflicts, on the basis that domestic legislation was not in accordance with the convention. It ruled that the President of the Russian Federation, being the Commander in Chief of the Armed Forces, "had the right to ensure state security". The court ruled that the Presidential decree of December 9, 1994, was not in breach of the Constitution, but simultaneously recommended to the parliament that it pass a clearer set of laws governing the use of troops within the Russian Federation.[218] Federation Council Deputy Issa Kostoyev lamented that the verdict represented the victory of the "law of force, not the force of law".[219]

Justice Minister Valentin Kovalyov declared: "I am fully satisfied with today's decision ... The court was able to stay away from political passions and base its judgements strictly on the law. It is a great achievement."[220] All eighteen judges signed the ruling, but at a press conference the following day seven of the judges admitted that they did not fully agree with the court's decision.[221]

Kovalyov's argument that the consequences of the decrees had to be included when the court was assessing the constitutionality of the decrees was supported by Constitutional Court Judge Anatoly Kononov. In an article written after the ruling, Kononov argued that it was within the limits of the Law on the Constitutional Court (Part II, Article 74) to consider the extent of the consequences. He did not believe that each decree was to be examined individually and that, since the government had continued to work under the auspices of the dissolved decree of November 30, there were grounds to include it. He maintained that:

> Judging and evaluating the acts of the President and the Government of the Russian Federation regarding the well-known events in Chechnya, the Constitutional Court retreated from the demands of Part II of Article 74 of the Federal constitutional law "On the Constitutional Court of the RF" on the necessity to take into consideration, not only the literal meaning of the examined acts, but the attached meaning to their interpretation in light of human rights practice and its place in the system of rights treaties.[222]

Kovalyov was bitterly disappointed with the court's ruling. He declared that:

> ... the real cause of the war in Chechnya is neither in Grozny nor in the entire Caucasus region; it is in Moscow. The war pushed aside that corner of the curtain that obscured the real power struggle for control of Russia. Unfortunately, it is not liberal, but the most hard-line forces – those from the military–industrial complex and the former KGB – who are celebrating that victory in the power struggle now.... the true goal of the war in Chechnya was to send a clear-cut message to the entire Russian population: "The time for talking about democracy in Russia is up. It's time to introduce some order into this country and we'll do it whatever the cost."[223]

Resignation

Within a week of the Constitutional Court decision, the Head of the Presidential Administration Sergei Filatov publicly condemned Kovalyov. He criticised the Human Rights Commissioner for his declaration that Yeltsin was a "constitutional criminal". "It is unacceptable," argued Filatov, "to direct that sort of remark at the President, if you are at the same time in the employ of the President."[224] That same week, Yeltsin prepared a decree to liquidate the Presidential Human Rights Commission.[225] But the decree remained unsigned.

For his work in Chechnya, Kovalyov was awarded numerous Human Rights Awards across the world. The Council of Europe honoured him with its 1995 European Human Rights Prize in Strasbourg. He received the Raoul Wallenburg Prize, named after the famous Swedish diplomat known for his efforts to save thousands of Jews during World War Two. The International League for Human Rights in New York awarded him its 1995 Human Rights Prize. The Czech Republic honoured him with its *Chelovek Cheloveky* human rights award. He also received an award from Freedom House in Washington, and the Theodore Khekker Prize in Germany. He was the founding laureate of the Nuremberg International Human Rights Prize.

Kovalyov resigned from the Presidential Human Rights Commission on January 23, 1995. In his resignation letter to Yeltsin, he wrote:

> You began your democratic career as a forceful and energetic crusader against official deceit and Party despotism, but you are ending it as the obedient executor of the will of the power-seekers in your entourage ... I considered myself obliged to remain in your administration as long as my status enabled me on occasion, even if only in isolated instances, to counteract government policies that had violated human rights and humanitarian values. Perhaps even now such opportunities have not been totally exhausted. But I can't go on working with a president whom I believe to be neither a supporter of democracy nor a guarantee of the rights and liberties of my fellow citizens. I hereby inform you that, as of today, I resign as Chairman of the President's Human Rights Commission, as a member of the Presidential Council, and as a member of all other presidential bodies.[226]

Kovalyov was deeply alarmed by the Chechen war and the indiscriminate violence that accompanied the campaign. Yeltsin's move away from the liberal forces, his arrogance and sanctioning of a bombing campaign on a city full of innocent victims, was an unforgivable turn in government policy. "Presidential decisions are made almost in the same back-room fashion as in the era of the Politburo," wrote Kovalyov to Yeltsin. "You and the heads of government feed us such transparent lies that we're simply left dumbfounded."[227]

While others, like former dissident Father Gleb Yakunin, left Russia's Choice, Kovalyov remained with the liberal party to secure a seat in the Duma in the December 1995 elections. Sensing that Russia's Choice was no longer the "party of power", Yeltsin's advisors organized two new pro-Yeltsin factions, *Stabilnost* and *Rossiya*.[228] The alliance between Yeltsin and the liberal reformers had finished. The divide over the war had taken on greater significance than the divide in political factions.

What the tragedy of the war signified for Kovalyov was that his attempts to marry a political and a human rights sensibility in Russian politics had fallen to a low-water mark, and that Yeltsin's human rights aspirations were mere rhetoric. Beyond the personal tragedy was the larger tragedy of a war that led to the unnecessary killing of thousands of civilians and combatants, a war that was pursued and whitewashed under the banner of human rights discourse. Above all, Kovalyov believed in his loyalty to Russia, to an open and honest politics, not in his personal loyalty to the Presidential Administration. He believed in compromise, and he understood the complexities of working in a country with a crumbling infrastructure and weak institutions. He tried hard to avoid the moral absolutes that led to black-and-white solutions, but he could not stomach the lies. "The fragile bridge of trust between society and the state," he said with disappointment, "created with such difficulty in the face of century-old suspicion, has once again been destroyed."[229]

Notes

1 S. Kovalyov, *The New York Review of Books*, February 29, 1996: 29.
2 S. Kovalyov, "Ne znat, ne slyshat, ne ponimat: khronika – pozitsiya – mneniya", Vol. 2, Moskva: Memorial Arkhive, p. 12. A chronicle of the appeals and declarations written during the first month of the Chechen war.
3 S. Kovalyov, "Osleplenie polifema, ili i polze raznikh tochek zreniya", *Narodnii Deputat*, 11 (1992): 104–10. Henceforth, *Narodni*.
4 See Zakon, "O reabilitatsii repressirovannikh naradov RSFSR", *Vedomosti S'ezda Narodnikh Deputatov RSFSR i Verkhovnogo Soveta RSFSR 18* (1991) pp. 537–8. See also Memorial, *Cherez Dva Goda Posle Voiny*, Moskva: Memorial, 1994, p. 17.
5 See "Tret'ya Sessiya Verkhovnogo Soveta RSFSR", *Biulleten' No. 19 Sovmestnogogo Soveta Respubliki i Soveta Natsional'nostei*, March 22 (1991): 34–85. Henceforth, *Biulleten' 19.*
6 Kovalyov, *Biulleten' 19*, pp. 48, 57.
7 Kovalyov, *Biulleten' 19*, pp. 48, 57.
8 Kovalyov, *Vosp.*, p. 98. See Kovalyov, *Narodni*, pp.104–10.
9 R. Khabulatov and S. Kovalyov, "Sovmestnoe zasedanie 3-i sessii V/S RSFSR", *Biulleten' 21*, April 21, 1991: 106.
10 Kovalyov, *Narodni*, pp. 104–110.
11 See "Tret'ya Sessiya Verkhovnogo Soveta RSFSR", *Biulleten' No. 25 Sovmestnogogo Soveta Respubliki i Soveta Natsional'nostei*, April 26, 1991, p. 62.
12 Memorial, *Cherez Dva Goda Posle Voiny*, Moskva: Memorial, 1994, p. 18.
13 *Ibid.*
14 J. Dunlop, *Russia Confronts Chechnya: Roots of a Separatist Conflict*, Cambridge: Cambridge University Press, 1998, p. 173.
15 Dunlop, *ibid.*, pp. 178–9.
16 Cited in J. Dunlop, "Gathering the Russian Lands: Background to the Chechen Crisis", Working Papers in International Studies 1–95–2, The Hoover Institution, Stanford University, 1995, p. 1.
17 Dudayev added the name Ichkeriya to Chechnya soon after his declaration of independence. Ichkeriya is a region in Chechnya where the toughest resistance against Russian and other foreign invaders has taken place historically. It is the region of the "Noxh-Mak-Kual" tribe. See "Current Chechen Profile: Chechnya at a Glance". Available online at http://www.anima.com/article/glance.html (accessed March 2000).

18 See E. Kline, "The Conflict in Chechnya, Briefing Paper", March 3, 1996, New York: Kline Archive, 1996, p. 6.
19 V. Kogan-Yasni, *Perekresta Chechenskie*, Moskva: Yrebus, 1995, p. 8.
20 Kogan-Yasni, *ibid.*, pp. 19–20.
21 Kogan-Yasni, *op.cit.*, p. 25.
22 S. Shakhrai, cited in Dunlop, *op.cit.*, p. 197.
23 S. Filatov, cited in Kogan-Yasni, *op.cit.*, p. 15.
24 Kogan-Yasni, *op.cit.*, pp. 21–2.
25 Dunlop, *op.cit.*, pp. 122, 126. See Kogan-Yasni, *op.cit.*, p. 26.
26 Kogan-Yasni, *op.cit.*, p. 20.
27 Sirotkin (1995).
28 S. Kovalyov, "Opros svidetelya Sergeya Kovalyova", *Voina v Chechne – Mezhdunarodnii Tribunal III*, Moskva: Glasnost, 1995, p. 269. Henceforth, Kovalyov, *Opros.*
29 B. Yeltsin, "Yeltsin Opposes Intervention by Force", *The Current Digest of the Post-Soviet Press*, Vol XLVI, No. 32, 1994: 12.
30 See *Two Years After the War: Problem of Displaced Persons in the Zone of the Ossetian-Ingush Conflict*, Moscow: Memorial Human Rights Centre, 1994.
31 S. Kovalyov, "Konstitutsionnoe prestuplenie", *Novoe Vremya*, No. 29, July 1995: 11. See *Vosp.*, p. 104.
32 Yeltsin did not respond to Dudayev's letter of October 3, 1994 in which the Chechen leader requested a meeting with the President. See "Pis'mo Prezidentu RF B. N. Yeltsinu", in Kurochkin's *Missiya v Chechnye*, Moskva: Pomatur, 1997, pp. 142–3. Note that Avturkhanov's forces reached Grozny on October 15, but for unknown reasons retreated. See Dunlop, *op.cit.*, p. 193.
33 Kogan-Yasni, *op.cit.*, p. 27.
34 See *Rossiya – Chechnya: tsep' oshibok prestyplenii*, Moskva: Zven'ya, 1998, p. 33. Henceforth, *Rossiya.*
35 B. Yeltsin, "Offitsial'nii Groznii ugrozhaet Moskve vtoroi Kavkazskoi voinoi", *Rossiiskie Vesti*, No. 2226 (650), November 29, 1994: 1.
36 Kovalyov, *Opros*, p. 245.
37 P. Felgenhauer, *The Chechen Campaign*. Available online at: http://www.anima.com/article/chapter3.html (accessed March 2001).
38 See *Rossiya*, 32.
39 S. Kovalyov, "Stenogram of an interview with Sergei Kovalyov by David Remnick", New York: Kline Archive, unpublished, undated, p. 2. See Kovalyov, *Opros*, p. 263. P. Grachev, "Offitsial'nii Groznii ugrozhaet Moskve vtoroi Kavkazskoi voinoi", *Rossiiskie Vesti*, No. 2226 (650), November 29, 1994: 1.
40 Ukaz No. 2317c "O Meropriyatiyakh po vosstanovlenie konstitutsionnoi zakonnosti i pravoporyadka na territorii Chechenskoi Respubliki". For a copy of the decree, see Kurochkin's *Missiya v Chechne*, Moskva: Pomatur, 1997, pp. 144–6.
41 Felgenhauer, *op.cit.* See Dunlop, *ibid.*, p. 205.
42 P. Grachev, "U voennikh na yazike miroliubivaya leksika, a v ume – silovoi shchenarii", *Rossiiskie Vesti*, No. 232 (656), December 7, 1994: 1.
43 Kovalyov., *Vosp,* p. 91.
44 Sirotkin (1995). See also "Ombudsman znachit 'Zastupnik', " *Rysskaya Mysl'* (No. 4057), December 15–21, 1994: 9.
45 Sirotkin (1995).
46 Ukaz No. 2166 "O Merakh po presecheniu deyatel'nosti nezakonnikh voorushennikh formirovanii na territorii Chechenskoi Respubliki i v zone Osetino-Ingushskogo konflikta", New York: Kline Archive.
47 S. Kovalyov, "Ne znat, ne slyshat, ne ponimate: khronika – pozitsiya – mnenie", Moskva: Memorial Archiv, p. 9.
48 Kovalyov, *Opros*, pp. 247–8.

49 O. Orlov, "Missiya Kovalyova na fronte", *Memorial Aspekt*, No. 13, June 1995: 3.
50 M. Burlakov, *Biulleten' No. 71, Stennogramma zasedanii Gosudarstvennoi Dumi*, December 13, 1994, pp. 7–9.
51 See *Biulleten' No. 71.*, pp. 7–9.
52 Kurochkin, *op.cit.*, p. 21.
53 Kurochkin, *op.cit.*, p. 30.
54 Orlov, *op.cit.*, p. 3.
55 *Rossiiskie Vesti*, No. 237 (661), December 15, 1994: 1.
56 *Ibid.* See *Chechenskaya Tragediya: Kto Vinovat.* Y. Nikolaev (ed.), Moskva: Novosti, 1995.
57 See "Pasporyazhenie pravitel'stva RF ot 1 Dekabrya, 1994, No. 1886-p", *Informatsionnaya Voina v Chechne; fakti, dokymenti, svidetel'stva*, Moskva: Prava Cheloveka, 1997, p. 329.
58 *Rossiya*, 269–70. See Article 6, "Postanovlenie ot 9 Dekabrya, 1994 No. 1360", New York: Kline Archive.
59 Orlov, *op.cit.*, pp. 3–4.
60 "Obrazhenie Prezidenta RF k zhitelyam CR", *Rossiiskie Vesti*, No. 237 (661), December 17, 1994: 1.
61 Frederick Cuny concluded that approximately 30,000 civilians were still left in Grozny. See Cuny, F., "An Assessment of the Humanitarian Situation in Chechnya, Ingushetia and Ossetia", February 28, 1995, New York: Kline Archive, p. 7.
62 See *Russia's War in Chechnya: Victims Speak Out*, Vol. 7, No.1, January 1995, Human Rights Watch: Helsinki, p. 3.
63 Orlov, *op.cit.*, pp. 3–4.
64 "The Situation in Samashki", Memorial Report 12/1994–04/1994. Available online at http:www.anima.com/war/sem_hor.html (accessed March 2001).
65 Kovalyov, *Vosp.*, p. 109.
66 Orlov, *op.cit.*, p. 4.
67 O. Orlov, Personal interview no. 3 with E. Gilligan, Moscow, August, 1999. Henceforth, Orlov 3 (1999).
68 O. Orlov, "Opros svidetelya Olega Orlova", *Voina v Chechne – Mezhdunarodnii Tribunal III*, Moskva: Obshestvenni fond "Glasnost", 1995, p. 122. Henceforth, Orlov, *Opros*.
69 Orlov, *Opros*, p. 121.
70 Orlov, *Opros*, pp. 121–37.
71 S. Kovalyov, "Press Conference, Moscow, January 5, 1996", New York: Kline Archive. Henceforth, *Press Conference*. See S. Kovalyov, "Nel'zya vesti gryaznuiu voinu i odnovremenno provodit' demokraticheskie preobrazovaniya", *Pravozashchitnik 2*, 1996, p. 17. Henceforth, *Pravozashchitnik.*
72 S. Kovalyov, "Ne znat, ne slyshat, ne ponimat: khronika – pozitsiya – mneniya", Vol. 2, Moskva: Memorial Archiv, p. 12.
73 Kovalyov, *op.cit.*, p. 14.
74 See *Rossiya*, 189.
75 O. Orlov, "Missiya Kovalyova na fronte", *Memorial Aspekt*, No. 13, June 1995: 3.
76 Orlov, *op.cit.*, p. 3.
77 Kovalyov, *Vosp.*, p. 60.
78 According to V. Shumeiko, at the Security Council meeting of January 6, 1995 the same claim was repeated. See *Rossiya*, 152.
79 See *Rossiya*, 189. See "Report of the President's Commission on Human Rights (1994–1995)", New York: Kline Archive, p. 21.
80 See *Informatsionnaya Voina v Chechne; fakti, dokymenti, svidetel'stva*, Moskva: Prava Cheloveka, 1997, p. 407.

81 S. Kovalyov, "Ne znat, ne slyshat, ne ponimate: khronika – pozitsiya – mnenie", Moskva: Memorial Archiv, p. 23.
82 Kovalyov, *op.cit.*, p. 23.
83 *Rossiya*, 307.
84 Orlov, *Opros*, p. 132. See M. Borshchev, ""Proceedings of the Russian State Duma, January 26, 1995. Translated by E. Kline, New York: Kline Archive.
85 Kovalyov, *Opros*, p. 256.
86 See *Rossiya*, 38
87 Kovalyov, *Opros*, p. 262.
88 S. Kovalyov, *Izvestiya*, No. 251, December 30, 1994: 1.
89 S. Kovalyov, *Moskovskie Novosti*, No. 66, December 25, 1994–January 1, 1995: 1.
90 *Ibid.*
91 Kurochkin, *op.cit.*, p. 48.
92 Kovalyov, *Pravozashchitnik*, p. 17. See Kurochkin, *op.cit.*, p. 42. The prisoners were released in the spring.
93 P. Grachev, "Ostanovit'sya? My ne ostanovimsya!", *Moskovskie Novosti*, January 22–29, 1995: 1. See *Nezavisimaya Gazeta: Spetsvypusk 2: Chechnya kak eto bylo*, Moskva: Chernomor'ya, 1992, p. 62.
94 Kovalyov, *Press Conference.*
95 Felgenhauer, *op.cit.*
96 "Pyst' zvuchit ego golos", *RossisskieVesti*, No. 246 (670), December 28, 1994: 19.
97 S. Filatov, *Rossiiskie Vesti*, December 22, 1992: 1. For others like Sergei Shakhrai, his behaviour was reminiscent of that of a "religious fanatic". See S. Shakhrai, *Rossiiskaya Gazeta*, July 14, 1995: 2. He was also labelled a "Frog Torturer", *Moskovskaya Pravda*, September 23, 1995: 5.
98 Kovalyov, *Vosp.*, p. 130.
99 Felgenhauer, *op.cit.*
100 A. Kozyrev, cited by Sergei Kovalyov in *Argumenti i Fakti*, No. 29, July, 1995, p. 3.
101 Kurochkin, *op.cit.*, p. 51.
102 N. Yegorov, "Yeltsin orders a halt to bombing of Grozny", *Ria-Novosti*, January 5, 1995. RB00176: 1
103 Yegorov, *op.cit.*, p. 1.
104 *Izvestiya*, January 6, 1995: 44. Republished in *Nezavisimaya Gazeta: Spetsvypusk 2: Chechnya kak eto bylo*, Moskva: Chernomor'ya, 1996, p. 62.
105 Kovalyov, *Pravozashchitnik*, p. 17.
106 Kovalyov, *Press Conference.*
107 S. Kovalyov, "Nel'zya zhit v takom gosudarstve", *Karta*, No. 9, 1995: 7–8.
108 *Ibid.*
109 S. Kovalyov, "Statement by Sergei Kovalyov, Member of the Russian State Duma: Commission on Security and Cooperation in Europe, May 1, 1995", New York: Kline Archive. See S. Kovalyov, "How the West shouldn't react to Events in Chechnya", *Demokratizatsiya: The Journal of Post-Soviet Democratization*, Vol. III, No. 4, (1995): 396–8.
110 S. Kovalyov, "Statement by Sergei Kovalyov, Member of the Russian State Duma: Commission on Security and Cooperation in Europe, May 1, 1995", New York: Kline Archive.
111 O. Orlov. "Missiya Kovalyova na fronte", *Memorial Aspekt*, No. 13. June, 1995: 3.
112 Arutyunov (1995).
113 K. Lubarsky, *Ogonyok*, July 30, 1995: 57.
114 Kovalyov, *Vosp.*, pp.110–11.
115 Kovalyov, *Vosp.*, pp. 110–11.
116 See K. Lubarsky, "Kovalyov and Yeltsin", *New Times*, February 1995: 9–12.
117 Kovalyov, *Vosp.*, pp. 110–11.
118 Kovalyov, *Vosp.*, p. 67.

119 "Press release, Office of the Commissioner for Human Rights, January 10, 1995", Translated by E. Kline, New York: Kline Archive.
120 *Ibid.* See *OMRI Daily Digest*, Vol. 1, No. 9, January 12, 1995: 1.
121 Orlov (1998).
122 Orlov (1998).
123 S. Kovalyov, "Proposal for a Truce in Grozny and a Broader Peacemaking Effort in Chechnya and the Caucasus", New York: Kline Archive.
124 "Itogi", Channel 4, *NTV*, January 16, 1995.
125 *Rossiya*, 43.
126 B. Yeltsin, cited in *Centre of Political-Geographical Investigations Bulletin*, January 9, 1995, Memorial Arkhiv, p. 33.
127 Felgenhauer, *op.cit.*
128 B. Yeltsin, cited in "Peregovorov vozmoshno, no ne s Dudaevym", *Rossiiskaya Gazeta*, January 19, 1995: 1. See V. Yelisenko, *Rysskaya Mysl'*, No. 4062, January 26–February 1, 1995: 4.
129 "Peregovorov vozmoshno, no ne s Dudaevym", *Rossiiskaya Gazeta*, January 19, 1995: 1.
130 "Report of the President"s Commission on Human Rights (1994–1995)'', New York: Kline Archive, p. 29.
131 P. Grachev, *Rysskaya Mysl'*, No. 4062, January 26–February 1, 1995: 1–2.
132 The commission was established on January 13, 1995. See *Komissiya Govorukhina*, Moskva: Laventa, 1995.
133 "Constitution Watch: Russia", *East European Constitutional Review*, Vol. 4, No.1 (1995): 25.
134 *Ibid.* See "Communists Denounce Valentin Kovalev's Nomination", *OMRI Daily Digest*, Vol. 1, No. 9, January 12, 1995: 2.
135 V. Kovalyov, "Liubaya popytka diskreditirovat' armiiu – antigosudarstvenna", *Krasnaya Zvesda*, January 24, 1995: 1.
136 S. Kovalyov, "Resignation Letter to the Temporary Commission to Monitor Civil Rights and Liberties in Chechnya, January 27, 1995", Translated by E. Kline, New York: Kline Archive.
137 I. Gyarmati, cited in E. Kline's "The Conflict in Chechnya: Briefing Paper", March 3, 1996, New York: Kline Archive, p. 14.
138 F. Cuny, "An Assessment of the Humanitarian Situation in Chechnya, Ingushetia and Ossetia, February 28, 1995", New York: Kline Archive, p. 7.
139 *Ibid.*
140 S. Kovalyov, "Proceedings of the Russian State Duma, January 26, 1995", translated by E. Kline, New York: Kline Archive. Henceforth, *Proceedings*. See "Sergei Kovalyov's report to the Deputies of the State Duma, January 10, 1995", translated by E. Kline, New York: Kline Archive.
141 S. Kovalyov, "Sergei Kovalyov's report to the Deputies of the State Duma, January 10, 1995", translated by E. Kline, New York: Kline Archive.
142 Kovalyov, *Proceedings*, p. 150.
143 M. Burlakov, *Proceedings*, p. 158.
144 M. Boiko, *Proceedings*, p. 160.
145 V. Zhirinovsky, *Proceedings*, p. 158.
146 A. Minzhurenko, *Zasedenie*, p. 176.
147 A. Gerber, *Zasedenie*, p. 178.
148 M. Borshchev, *Proceedings*, p. 243.
149 *Khace*, No. 38, September 23, 1995: 2.
150 This article was in response to an interview with Kovalyov on the television program, *Itogi*, where he allegedly said that Pushkin was not a patriot. See V. Kozhinov, *Rossiiskaya Gazeta*, January 31, 1995. No. 23: 1.
151 M. Yureva, "Poltari Izvilini", *Rossiiskaya Gazeta*, February 2, 1995: 2.

152 "K svedeniiu bortsov za prava cheloveka", *Rossiiskaya Gazeta*, February 4, 1995: 1, 2.
153 A. Solzhenitsyn, *Literaturnaya Gazeta*, June 7, 1995: 1.
154 S. Kovalyov, "Open Letter to President Boris Yeltsin, January 27, 1995", Translated by E. Kline, New York: Kline Archive. See *Usloviya soderzhaniya zaderzhannykh v zone vooruzhennogo konflikta v chechenskoi respublike obrashchenie s zaderzhannymi*, Moskva: Memorial, 1995.
155 S. Kovalyov, "Russia Needs both Pressure and Support", *New Times*, March 1995: 52.
156 Kovalyov, *op.cit.*, p. 52. See "Report on Russia's request for membership in the light of the situation in Chechnya", Council of Europe, Parliamentary Assembly, Doc. 7230, January 31, 1995.
157 R. Tiwari, "Russia – human rights: Zhirinovsky's Strasbourg Heckling Censured", Moscow, January 31. An Inter Press Service, 1995. Worldwide distribution via the APC networks.
158 D. Yakushkin, "Caucasian War Leaves Russia on the Roadside", *Moscow News*, No. 5, February 3–9, 1995. See S. Kovalyov, "Belaya vorona Rossiiskoi politiki", *Obshaya Gazeta*, February 3, 1995: 3.
159 "Report on Russia's request for membership in the light of the situation in Chechnya", Council of Europe, Parliamentary Assembly, Doc. 7230, January 31, 1995.
160 Human Rights Watch Report, "Russia: Partisan War in Chechnya on the Eve of the WWII Commemoration", Vol. 7, No. 8: May, 1995.
161 S. Kovalyov, "Sergei Kovalyov's open letter to President Boris Yeltsin", January 27, 1995. Translated by E. Kline, New York: Kline Archive, p. 2.
162 *Ibid.*
163 "Pravozashchitniki schitayt uvolnenie Sergeya Kovalyova nezakonnym: Borba za mesto upolnomochennogo po pravam cheloveka nachalas", *Moskovskie Novosti*, No. 50, March 18, 1995: 3. See "Dismissal by Deputies: Communists and Nationalists joined forces to fire Russia's highly esteemed Human Rights Commissioner", *Moscow Times*, March 12, 1995: 18.
164 E. Kline, "Letter to Associates and Friends of Sergei Kovalyov, March 12, 1995", New York: Kline Archive, p. 1.
165 See G. Chistyakov, "Upolnomochennym po pravam cheloveka v Rossii stal predstavitel' kommunisticheskoi partii", *Rysskaya Mysl'*, No 4224, May 28, 1998: 1, 24. See I. Velikanova, "Ombudsmen ishchet sebe kryshu", *Obshaya Gazeta*, No. 21, May 28, 1998: 2; see also V. Komarova, "Zakonodatel'naya reglamentatsiya deyatel'nosti upolnomochennogo po pravam cheloveka v Rossiiskoi Federatsii", *Pravozashchitnik 2* (1997): 63–73.
166 *Vsemi Imayishi Stredstvami*, Moskva: Memorial, 1995, p. 87. Henceforth, *Vsemi*. See "The Situation in Samashki", Moscow: Memorial Report 12/1994 – 04/1994. Available online at http:www.anima.com/war/sem_hor.html (accessed June 1999).
167 *Vsemi*, pp. 90, 93.
168 "Statement by Sergei Kovalyov, member of the Russian State Duma: Commission on Security and Cooperation in Europe. May 1, 1995", New York: Kline Archive.
169 *Vsemi*, p. 93.
170 *Vsemi*, p. 94 .
171 *Vsemi*,p. 97.
172 "The Situation in Samashki", Moscow: Memorial Report 12/1994 – 04/1994. Available online at httP://www.anima.com/war/sem_hor.html (accessed March 1999).
173 *Vsemi*, p. 99.

174 *Vsemi*, p. 99.
175 *Vsemi*, p. 5.
176 *Vsemi*, p. 101.
177 *Vsemi*, p. 107. On the main street Sharipova, 45 of the 95 houses were burnt down or made uninhabitable.
178 R. Khasan, cited in *Vsemi*, p. 102. See "The Situation in Samashki", Moscow: Memorial Report 12/1994 – 04/1994.
179 *Vsemi*, p. 106.
180 S. Kovalyov, *Rysskaya Mysl'*, No. 4075, April 27–May 3, 1995: 4.
181 *Ibid.*
182 The Open Hearings, May 29, 1995, "Chechnya – Human Rights 1991–1995", organized by Stanislav Govorukhin, cited in *Kommisiya Govorukhina*, Moskva: Laventa, 1995, p. 121.
183 *Ibid.* See Govorukhin, cited by Kronid Lubyarsky in "Let the Duma Pay Me in Rubles", *New Times*, No. 37, 1995: 19.
184 O. Orlov, *Memorial Aspekt*, June 1995: 2.
185 S. Govorukhin, *Kommiciya Govorukhina*, Moskva: Laventa, 1995, p. 113.
186 Govorukhin, *ibid.*, pp. 114, 115. See Kronid Lubyarsky, *ibid.*, p. 19.
187 S. Govorukhin, *Moskovskaya Pravda*, June 7, 1995: 1.
188 S. Izmailov, *Izvestiya*, June 23, 1995: 4.
189 S. Kovalyov, "Missiya v Budyonnovsk: Kak eto bylo", *Novoe Vremya*, July, 1995, No. 26: 12. See *New York Times*, June 17, 1995: 6.
190 P. Grachev, *The Times*, June 17, 1995, No. 26: 12.
191 S. Kovalyov, "Speech by Sergei Kovalyov at Human Rights Watch Meeting, New York, March 9, 1996", Melbourne: Personal collection, E. Gilligan.
192 S. Kovalyov, "Stenogram of interview with Sergei Kovalyov: New York, October 22, 1995", New York: Kline Archive, unpublished. No author's name given, p. 6. See S. Kovalyov, "Speech at Human Rights Watch, New York: March 6, 1996", Melbourne: Personal collection, E. Gilligan.
193 Kovalyov, *Vosp.*, p. 111.
194 Y. Albats, *Izvestiya*, August 25, 1995: 4.
195 See account of Kovalyov's arrival at the hospital written by Yakov, a journalist with *Izvestiya* who was also a hostage. *Izvestiya*, June 23, 1995: 4.
196 S. Kovalyov, *Novoe Vremya*, July, 1995 No. 26: 13.
197 Kovalyov, *ibid.*, p. 13.
198 Kovalyov, *ibid.*, p. 13.
199 Kovalyov, *op.cit.*, p. 13.
200 S. Kovalyov, "Besprintsipnyi Kovalyov: Pravozashchitniku za derzhavu ne obidno, a stidno", *Nezavisimaya Gazeta*, December 1, 1995: 5.
201 Kovalyov, *ibid.*, p. 5.
202 Yakov, *op.cit.*, p. 4.
203 Kovalyov, *ibid.*, p. 5.
204 Kovalyov, *Vosp.*, pp. 116–17.
205 V. Yemelyanenko, "Preliminary Peace reached in Chechnya", *Moscow News*, August 4–10, 1995: 1. See S. Kovalyov, "Russia takes a detour on the road to the rule of law", *International Practioner's Notebook*, Issue 60, August 1995: 4–8.
206 On the Observance of the Rights of Man and the Citizen in the Russian Federation (1994–1995). Report of the President's Commission on Human Rights. Translated by Catherine A. Fitzpatrick for the Human Rights Project Group, March 1996, New York: Kline Archive.
207 V. Gomez, *OMRI Daily Digest*, No. 38, Part 1, February 22, 1995.
208 *Judgement of the Constitutional Court of the Russian Federation, July 31, 1995*, European Commission for Democracy through Law. Document available from Lenin Library, Moscow 96–46 71–4, p. 1. Henceforth, *Judgement*.

209 *Judgement*, p. 1.
210 A. Kononov, "Osoboe Mnenie", Melbourne: Personal collection, E.Gilligan. See personal interview with E. Gilligan, Moscow, September 1999.
211 K. Lubarsky, "Vstat! Sud Idet", *Novoe Vremya*, No. 29, July, 1995: 8–11. See K. Lubarsky, "V ozhidanii verdikta", *Novoe Vremya*, No. 30, July, 1995: 8–11; see also K. Lubarsky, "Shemyakin Sud", *Novoe Vremya*, No. 32, August, 1995: 8–10.
212 K. Lubarsky, "Vstat! Sud Idet", *Novoe Vremya*, No. 29, July, 1995: 8–11.
213 S. Kovalyov, *Vystuplenie Sergeya Adamovicha Kovalyova na zasedanii Konstitutsionnovo Suda*, Moskva: Evraziya, 1995, p. 12.
214 Kovalyov, *op.cit.*, p. 12.
215 Article 80, Section One, Chapter Two. Constitution of the Russian Federation. Available online at: http://www.departments.bucknell.edu/russian/const/ch2.html   (accessed   June 2000).
216 See questions directed at Sergei Kovalyov during the proceedings of the Constitutional Court in *Vystuplenie Sergeya Adamovicha Kovaleva na zasedanii Konstitutsionnovo Suda*, Moskva: Evraziya, 1995, pp. 11–30. See V. Maslennikov, "Sergei Kovalyov zashchishaet kogo?", *Rossiiskaya Gazeta*, July 14, 1995: 2. "Yuri Baturin: Prezident imel pravo", *Rossiiskaya Gazeta*, July 14, 1995: 2.
217 V. Rudnev, "Vstat' konstitutsionnyi sud idet: Slushaetcya 'Delo v Chechnye'", *Izvestiya*, July 8, 1995. p. 1. See V. Rudnev, "Konstitutsionnyi sud obrashchaetsya za pomoshch'iu k ekspertam", *Izvestiya*, July 14: 2.
218 *Judgement.*, pp. 3–11. See A. Kirpichnikov, "Resheniya o vvode voisk v Chechniu priznany konstitutsionnymi", *Sevodnya*, August 1, 1995: 1.
219 I. Kostoyev, cited in *Moscow Tribune*, No. 143, August 1, 1995: 1, 2.
220 V. Kovalyov, cited in *Moscow Tribune*, No. 143, August 1, 1995: 1, 2.
221 *Moscow Tribune*, No. 143, August 1, 1995: 1, 2.
222 Kononov, A. "Osoboe Mnenie", Melbourne: Personal collection, E. Gilligan. See A. Kononov, personal interview with E. Gilligan, Moscow, September 1999.
223 Kovalyov, *Vystuplenie*, p. 10.
224 S. Filatov, "Kovalyov insult may kill group", *Moscow Tribune*, No. 144. August 2, 1995: 1.
225 E. Tregubova, "Prezident zamenil Komissiiu po pravam cheloveka 'Otdelom po zhalobam'", *Sevodnya*, August 1, 1995: 3. See A. Podrabinek, "Prezidentu nadayela igra v 'prava cheloveka'", *Ekspress Khronika*, No. 28, August 4, 1995: 1; see also M. Pavlova-Sil'vanskaya, "'Kremlevskaya Kadril' vokrug Sergeya Kovalyova", *Novoe Vremya*, No. 32, August 1995: 12–13. "Konets prezidentskoi Komissii po pravam cheloveka", *Pravozashchitnik*, No. 3, July–September, 1995: 4–6.
226 S. Kovalyov, *New York Review of Books*, February 29, 1996: 29. S. Kovalyov, *Izvestiya*, January 24, 1996: 2. See K. Lubarsky, "Kovalyov & Yeltsin", *New Times*, February 1995: 6–7.
227 S. Kovalyov, *Izvestiya*, January 24, 1996: 2.
228 M. McFaul, "Eurasia Letter: Russian Politics after Chechnya," *Foreign Policy*, Summer 1995: 158.
229 S. Kovalyov, *Izvestiya*, January 24, 1996: 2.

6   Troubling times

Will the authorities domesticate the rights defenders who join such commissions, making them "court" defenders of human rights? It is a complicated
question and impossible to work out any universal means for resolving it ...
But to me it is senseless to refuse any interaction with the authorities.
                    Oleg Orlov, Director, Memorial Human Rights Centre

The Kiva Syndrome

By July of 1996, the only remaining members of the Presidential Human
Rights Commission were Deputy Chairman Aleksandr Kopylev, ex-foreign
minister Andrei Kozyrev and writer Fazil Izlander.[1] The rest of Kovalyov's
colleagues, notably his chief aide Lydia Siomina and the Commission lawyer
Sergei Sirotkin, had resigned. Within six months, the Presidential Human
Rights Commission was reorganized. Kovalyov's replacement was Professor
Vladimir Kartashkin, the well-published apologist of the Soviet regime
whom Kovalyov had first met in 1988 during the preparatory meetings for
the Human Rights Project Group. Fyodor Burlatsky was proposed as a
candidate for the post of Human Rights Commissioner.[2] It was finally
decided that Oleg Mironov of the Russian Communist Party would assume
that appointment.[3]

The revival of the Presidential Human Rights Commission was inaugu-
rated in the winter of 1997 with a series of defamatory articles in
Rossiiskaya Gazeta and *Nezavismaya Gazeta*.[4] Written by new Commission
member Aleksei Kiva, there were three fundamental themes to the articles.
Kiva's leading motif was that the human rights movement had harmed the
process of democratization in post-Soviet Russia. "It is not the role of a
human rights activist to attack the state," Kiva claimed. "A human rights
activist ... is a tactful teacher."[5] He criticised Kovalyov for being a victim of
"the anti-state syndrome" with "the consciousness of an underground
man".[6] Second, he argued that the human rights community was never
interested in the "common man". "Our human rights activists," he wrote,
"have been preoccupied with God knows what, except the defence of the
elemental rights of the common man." And third, he argued that the most

important component in the building of a human rights culture in Russia was patriotism. "It's impossible to ignore the fact that, for many dissidents, the West has become their second home."[7]

Kiva's articles provoked a strong reaction among the human rights community, especially the Moscow Helsinki Group (MHG). In June 1996, Yeltsin issued a decree that stated that the Presidential Human Rights Commission was to cooperate with the Moscow Helsinki Group and other human rights organizations to form an Expert Council on human rights.[8] Although the Chair of the Moscow Helsinki Group, Ludmilla Alekseeva, and the Director of Memorial's Human Rights Centre, Oleg Orlov, were prepared to participate in the Expert Council, they both issued public declarations in March 1997 shortly after the publication of Kiva's articles. "The articles' arrogant and even scornful tone towards rights defenders," wrote Alekseeva, Orlov and Lev Ponomarev, "aroused hostility towards the Presidential Human Rights Commission amongst rights defenders who were previously prepared to cooperate for the sake of improving the human rights situation in the Russian Federation."[9] The MHG called on President Yeltsin to dissolve the Commission in its current form:

> The Kartashkin Commission recognizes only an educational role for rights defenders. The role is truly great, and rights defenders are actively engaged in legal education. But the members of the Presidential Commission regard any criticism of state organs and of individual officials that violate human rights as impermissible, classifying it as destructive and illegitimate for the human rights movement as such.[10]

The question of cooperation between human rights movement and government in Russia in 1997 remained unresolved. The public declaration by the Moscow Helsinki Group sparked the cooperation debate yet again. Shortly after Sergei Kovalyov's resignation, the writer Andrei Sinyavsky heaved a sigh of relief: "I am glad that Sergei Kovalyov has returned to the dissident movement," wrote Sinyavsky, "and I hope he will feel more comfortable in this role than in Yeltsin's service. Every cloud has a silver lining. Otherwise our Sergei Adamovich would be serving as a human rights adviser to Mr Cannibal."[11] Malva Landa accused Kovalyov of creating a "democratic veil" around Yeltsin. A shallow accusation that neglected the complexity of his position, Landa's simplification of events is more damaging than constructive. Sinyavsky's claim is equally unconstructive. For the young human rights activists of Memorial, Kovalyov's decision to resign was a welcome one.[12]

More importantly, Kovalyov's colleagues in the Presidential Human Rights Commission lamented his decision to resign. His chief aid Lydia Siomina wondered about who would educate the authorities on human rights questions: "[F]or me, the question is unambiguous," she acknowledged. "To cooperate with the representatives of the authorities, yes, it means to engage in difficult, unnoticed daily work to educate them. And rights defenders must not abandon this task ..."[13]For Commission member and specialist on refugees Mikhail Arutyunov: "Kovalyov's resignation was a great loss to the Commission."[14]

Five months after his resignation, Kovalyov wrote to the board members of the Russian–American Human Rights Project Group: "For now, human rights activity is being entirely pushed back into the civic sphere. We human rights advocates have once again become dissidents in some sense ... The change in the overall situation perhaps affects me most of all. For me, it is obvious that priorities must be changed ..."[15]

Derzhavnost' and Vladimir Putin

With his career no longer strained by the administrative demands of the Presidential Human Rights Commission, Kovalyov had more time to pursue other activities. He worked on his *Memoirs* and a collection of essays entitled *Sergei Kovalyov: The Pragmatics of Political Idealism* (*Sergei Kovalyov: Pragmatika Politcheskogo Idealizma*) over the following years. He remained in the public eye by maintaining a rigorous schedule of press appearances as well as travelling frequently in Europe to speak on Russia, the rise of Vladimir Putin and the second Chechen war. For him, the most disappointing development at the end of Yeltsin's presidency was the cynical collapse of the Khasavyurt Peace Treaty and the ongoing brutality in Chechnya. His public activism on this issue reached unprecedented levels.

In the wake of the first Chechen campaign and his subsequent resignation, Kovalyov started to speak about the changes in the Russian government. As early as 1996, he began to formulate his ideas on the decisive turn in Russian domestic and international policy that began in late 1993 and culminated with the beginning of the second Chechen campaign in September 1999. At a meeting at Human Rights Watch in New York in March 1996, he argued:

> This is not the ideology of classical communism as it was formulated in the late twentieth century in Europe nor as it existed in Russia for a very brief period after the 1917 revolution. This is a new form of an ideology that has been gaining more and more influence, which could be described by the untranslatable Russian word *derzhavnost'* (statism). This is the oriental deification of the state, the placing of the state above society.... Naturally there is not a single Russian politician who has stated it in the words I have just used. It's just that it is very familiar to us because of our recent past and is recognizable to us in terms of other words and in the actions of the present Russian leadership.[16]

For Kovalyov, the concept of *derzhavnost'* was accompanied by a distinct revival of Eurasianism. The geopolitician Alexander Dugin began to gain prominence in political circles as a political advisor with his main work, *The Foundations of Geopolitics: The Geopolitical Future of Russia* (*Osnovi Geopolitiki: Geopolitichiskoye Budushiye Rossiyi*), a treatise on the new Eurasianism.[17] The new President, Vladimir Putin, confirmed this himself in November 2000 when he said: "Russia has always seen itself as a Euro-Asiatic nation."[18] This doctrine soon grew evident in Putin's strategy of the new Eurasian Economic Community, the Russian–Iranian Strategic Partnership and the Russia–China summit.[19] Kovalyov's aspirations for a Russia that would one day be a part of Western Europe appeared to be seriously threatened.

In the *New York Review of Books* in 2001 he declared that an "unknown KGB lieutenant-colonel named Vladimir Putin shot out of the shadows like an imp out of a snuffbox and landed in the center of Russian politics."[20] Indeed, in 1998 Yeltsin positioned Putin as head of the domestic intelligence agency, the FSB and the Security Council. On New Year's Eve 1999, he announced during his resignation speech that Putin would be appointed acting President. Within three months, in a remarkable turn of events, "the unknown KGB lieutenant-colonel" was elected President of the Russian Federation. As Yeltsin's decline grew increasingly imminent, Kovalyov argued that the Presidential Administration had found in Putin a competent actor capable of playing the role of strong man to secure its own position in the future government. "A large part of the electorate," he argued ,

> ... holds conservative or even reactionary views and was intended to see in Putin a man with the potential to restore old Soviet values, a bearer of the imperial idea, a proponent of the "strong state" in the traditional Russian understanding of this concept ... In order to win the affection of these conservative voters, Vladimir Vladimirovich unleashed the second Chechen war, gave speeches about the necessity of reviving the military–industrial complex, dedicated a memorial plaque to the late Yury Andropov, toasted Stalin's birthday with Zuganov, declared he was proud of his service in the KGB, and swore allegiance to his Chekist past.[21]

For Kovalyov, of course, the rise of the new President of Russia, a former KGB apparatchik, was a paradox too shattering to ponder. Beyond Chechnya, his concern rested with the fate of the mass media which were being called on not to take an anti-state position.[22] "Putin ... like a true Chekist," he argued, "is more concerned with controlling public life, particularly information, than with dictating tastes."[23] Moreover, Kovalyov split decisively with Yegor Gaidar when the economist took what he characterized as an exceedingly rational approach, not only to the election of Yeltsin in the 1996 Presidential elections, but to Putin's support of the economy.[24] Surprisingly, Aleksander Solzhenitsyn also came out in support of the death penalty for Chechen "terrorists".[25]

It was not only Kovalyov, but the human rights community in general who expressed concern about the direction of Putin's leadership. This resonated in the All-Russia Emergency Congress in Defence of Human Rights, held in Moscow in January 2001, the largest conference in the history of the Russian human rights community with over 1,000 human rights activists present from across the country. Although debate lingered around the word "emergency" in the title of the conference, all agreed that there were grounds for concern. Kovalyov argued that "we must calmly and without hysterics keenly analyse the scale of the dangers that may be awaiting us in the future. What is the exact nature of these dangers?"[26] A General Resolution was issued by the participants concluding that "the foundations of the Constitution have been eroded, leading to what can be described as a constitutional crisis.... the restrictions and violations of human and civil rights and freedoms in various areas of life bear unmistakable signs of a slide towards authoritarianism."[27] For Kovalyov, it was the establishment of a Constitutional Assembly under Putin with 400 members – 100 of those personally selected by the new President – to amend the Constitution and the ongoing war in Chechnya that most alarmed him.

A separate resolution was issued that condemned the growing pressure on the press and the resurgence of state propaganda. Working groups were established to coordinate action between organizations. Among the working groups established under the " 'Common Action' Group of Activists" were groups on anti-war lobbying, judicial reform, prison reform, military reform, media freedom and independence, protection against ethnic and racial discrimination.[28] As had happened many times before, the tasks that the community had set themselves were voluminous and their physical, financial and human resources were stretched.

"The most influential forces in Russia today are attempting to establish an authoritarian regime," wrote Kovalyov some time later in The *New York Review of Books*. "How can one describe for the Western reader the repulsive sensation of returning to a past only slightly refurbished? It's something like being forced into filthy old clothes several sizes too small that you thought had been thrown out long ago."[29]

The second Chechen war: September 1999–

The rise of Vladimir Putin as Prime Minister in August 1999 coincided with the beginning of the second Chechen campaign one month later. This campaign continues to be shaped by excessive force and insidious methods of warfare that involve terrorizing the civilian population of Chechnya and targeting men of fighting age with arbitrary detention and summary execution. For Kovalyov, the position of the West after its intervention in Kosovo and East Timor was "cowardly, lazy and lacking in foresight ... The West will wait for events to unfold and pay a high price when events do not turn out well," he said. "This is the time for people to do their duty.... When people do their duty, they find that their actions have an effect."[30]

Figure 6.1   Sergei Kovalyov speaking at the Parliamentary Assembly of the Council of Europe, Strasbourg, September 2000

Source: Memorial Archive, Moscow.

He argued convincingly that the success of Putin's presidential bid grew out of the war. "The powers that they acquired in the course of the elections", he declared, "were supported by the majority of the population, thanks to the unbridled hysteria around the so-called war on terror."[31] After Aslan Maskhadov won the 1997 presidential election in Chechnya with an overwhelming majority, the new Chechen government sought to re-establish stability in the wake of a two-year war that had completely destroyed not only its capital, but the surrounding villages. Putin took the first opportunity to re-enter Chechnya in September 1999 after extreme Chechen fighters took their battle into neighbouring Dagestan. For Kovalyov, "the executors of this criminal intrusion were Islamic extremists and fanatical nationalists who had not been given official posts from the new Chechen government. I want to say that Commander Putin cynically played this situation as a trump card for victory in the parliamentary and presidential elections."[32]

The attack on neighbouring Dagestan was followed shortly after by the controversial apartment bombings in Moscow and the southern Russian city of Volgodonsk that killed 300 people. Rumours circulated that the FSB, not Chechen extremists, were responsible for the wave of bombings to provide justification for the return of Russian troops to Chechnya. After a failed attempt by Kovalyov and Duma deputies to establish a parliamentary committee to investigate these claims, Kovalyov formed a public committee made up of interested deputies to investigate the detonator found in an apartment block in Ryazan on September 22, 1999. The local FSB claimed that it was a fake detonator that had been part of an unspecified training operation.[33] To date, Kovalyov's commission has found no further evidence implicating either the Chechens or the FSB.[34]

The Russian government termed the operation launched in Chechnya in September 1999 as an "anti-terrorist" operation. It was based on the "1998 Law on the Suppression of Terrorism" and the "1996 Law on Defence", and gained momentum after the September 11 attacks in New York in 2001.

In January of that year, Putin transferred all official authority for overseeing the military operation in Chechnya from the Ministry of Defence to the FSB. Kovalyov described Putin as "the Russian Pinochet".[35] The disappearances that typify the second Chechen war are accompanied by frequent terror campaigns against the Chechen population through "sweep" operations that include the closure of streets or entire villages, with frequent looting and the arbitrary detention of men. These sweep operations have also taken place in refugee camps in neighbouring Ingushetia. Documentation from those detained at the Chernokozovo Detention Centre, the temporary filtration points spread across Chechnya, the mass grave with 51 bodies found in Dachny in February 2001, the discovery of four makeshift graves in Alkhan-Kala and the summary executions, are a fraction of the evidence that testifies to a shameful and disgraceful period in twentieth-century Russian history.[36]

In February 2002, Kovayov arrived in Washington to deliver a speech before the American Foreign Policy Council. The ongoing sweep campaigns (*zachistki*) continued to haunt his speeches. He labelled the perpetrators of these acts "death squads" that he suspected operated with the approval of the highest level of government. "If [top military and government officials] know of these death squads, then why are they keeping silent?" he asked.

> And if they don't know of these death squads, the question is: Why don't they? We are always finding, all across Chechnya, mass graves of civilians. Sometimes it's not even a grave but a heap of dumped bodies. Whenever we can identify the bodies, it turns out each grave or heap contains people not from that local area, but instead from all across Chechnya. The bodies belong to people who had been detained at different checkpoints in different parts of Chechnya, yet somehow they are turning up in a grave together, often quite far from where they were detained.[37]

For Kovalyov, economic reasons were one of the driving motives in the war. He did believe that the army sought revenge for its defeat in the last campaign. But more disquieting, he declared, was that the "Generals, officers and soldiers are making a fortune from this war by trading oil.

Detained Chechens are released for money. They sell corpses back to their relatives. They are constantly looting. Here in Moscow the soldiers are begging on the streets because they are so poor. But in Chechnya the money they get isn't bad and they can 'get a bit extra'. This war is feeding our Generals, it is shaping and advancing their careers. This is their world and their philosophy."[38]

Kovalyov often drew comparisons between Europe's – and particularly NATO's – response to events in Chechnya and Kosovo and East Timor's vote for independence in August 1999. "The world after Kosovo", he believed, "knows that it is standing at a crossroads." Would the Western world intervene to stop the violence in Chechnya, as they had done in Kosovo and East Timor, with bomb strikes and ground troops? Would the violence against innocent civilians compel them to respond in equal measure and with equal persistence for a peaceful resolution? It would not. As Kovalyov noted paradoxically, "Russia is using NATO's methods to achieve Milosevic's ends."[39]

As part of a broader public initiative, he supported a proposed Temporary UN Administration in Chechnya. Ilyas Akhmadov, the exiled Foreign Minister of the Chechen Republic of Ichkeria, devised a plan that was publicly issued in July 2003 calling for the implementation of the United Nations Trusteeship System. Akhmadov argued that Maskhadov would accept the prospect of conditional independence, assistance with economic reconstruction and the replacement of Russian forces with an international force. The model proposed was very similar to that proposed for Kosovo in 1999.[40] Kovalyov signed the petition prepared by the European Transnational Radical Party in support of the plan on July 11, 2003.

The Conscience Committee of the United States Holocaust Memorial Museum put Chechnya on its Genocide Watch list in May 2000. In a disheartening speech, Kovalyov shamefully concluded: "Actually, we are on the border of genocide. The question is: will we allow ourselves to cross the line."[41] By 2003, many believed that Russia had already crossed that line.[42] For Sergei Kovalyov, at the age of 73, a challenge of a different order had only just begun.

Notes

1 S. Mulin, "Pravozashchitniki predchuvstvuyut plokhie vremena", *Nezavisimaya Gazeta*, February 7, 1996: 2.
2 Siomina (1995).
3 "Kommunist Oleg Mironov – upolnomochennii po pravam cheloveka", *Izvestiya*, May 23, 1998: 1.
4 A. Kiva, "Blesk i nishcheta dvizheniya pravozashchitnikov", *Rossiiskaya Gazeta*, No. 35 (1645), February 20, 1997: 5. "Blesk i nishcheta dvizheniya pravozash-chitnikov", *Rossiiskaya Gazeta*, No. 36 (1646), February 21, 1997: 5. "Ot dissidentstva k samozvanstvu", *Nezavisimaya Gazeta*, April 29, 1997: 8.
5 A. Kiva, "Blesk i nishcheta dvizheniya pravozashchitnikov", *Rossiiskaya Gazeta*, No. 35 (1645): February 20, 1997: 5.

6 A. Kiva, "Ot dissidentstva k samozvanstvu", *Nezavisimaya Gazeta*, April 29, 1997: 8.
7 A. Kiva, "Blesk i nishcheta dvizheniya pravozashchitnikov", *Rossiiskaya Gazeta*, No. 36 (1646), February 21, 1997: 5.
8 "O nekotorikh merakh gosudarstvennoi podderzhki pravozashchitnogo dvizheniya v Rossiiskoi Federatsii". See *Pravozashchitnik 2*, April–June, 1996, pp. 59–60.
9 "Moscow Helsinki Group calls for dissolution of Presidential Human Rights Commission", signed by Ludmilla Alekseeva, Lev Ponomaryov and Yuri Orlov. *Express Chronicle Weekly Digest*, March, 7 1997: 1.
10 *Ibid.*
11 A. Sinyavsky, *The Russian Intelligentsia*, New York: Columbia University Press, 1997, p. 56. See also M. Landa, "Cooperation between rights defenders and the authorities", *Express Chronicle, English Weekly News Digest*, March 21, 1997.
12 Kline (1996).
13 Siomina (1995).
14 Arutyunov (1995).
15 S. Kovalyov, "Letter to Human Rights Project Group Board Members", July 12, 1995, New York: Kline Archive.
16 S. Kovalyov, "Speech to Human Rights Watch", March, 1996, Melbourne: Personal collection, E. Gilligan.
17 I. Berman, "Slouching Toward Eurasia?", *Perspective*. Vol. XII, No. 1, September–October 2001. Available online at: http://www.bu.edu/iscip/vol12/berman.html (accessed June 2003).
18 V. Putin, cited in Berman, *ibid.*
19 Berman, *ibid.*
20 S. Kovalyov, "The Putin Put-On", *The New York Review of Books*, August 9, 2001: 29.
21 Kovalyov, *op.cit.*, p. 29.
22 Kovalyov, *op.cit.*, p. 29.
23 Kovalyov, *op.cit.*, p. 31.
24 S. Kovalyov, "Litsom k litsu: Sergei Kovalyov", March 5, 2000. *Radio Svoboda.* Available online at http://www.svoboda.org/programs/FTF/2000/FTF.030500.asp (accessed March 2003).
25 "Russia's Solzhenitsyn Wants Death Penalty Restored", *Reuters*, April 29, 2001. Available online at http://groups.yahoo.com/group/solzhenitsyn-l/message/173 (accessed March 2003).
26 S. Kovalyov, "Ugroza pravovomu gosudarstvu i konstititsionnyim osnovam demokratii v strane". Available online at http://www.hro.org/ngo/congress (accessed March 2003).
27 "General Resolution of All-Russia Extraordinary Congress in Defense of Human Rights". Available online at http://www.gdf.ru/arh/file009e.shtml (accessed September 2003).
28 *Ibid.*
29 Kovalyov, *op.cit.*, p. 31.
30 "Human Rights Campaigner Warns Chechen War Signals Dangerous Turn in Russia Away From Civil Society Values", February 25, 2000. Available online at http://www.eurasianet.org/departments/recaps/articles/cep022500.shtml (accessed March 2003).
31 S. Kovalyov, "Ugroza pravovomu gosudarstvu i konstititsionnyim osnovam demokratii v strane". Available online at http://www.hro.org/ngo/congress (accessed March 2003).
32 *Ibid.*
33 "Putin's Shadow", *The Wall Street Journal Europe*, August 3, 2002. Available online at http://www.tjetjenien.dk/baggrund/bombs.html#wsj (accessed March 2003).

34 "Kniga 'FSB vsryvaet Rossiiu' fakti ili versii?", *Radio Svoboda*, June 11, 2002. Available online at http://www.somnenie.narod.ru/bl/roitman.html
35 S. Kovalyov, "Litsom k litsu: Sergei Kovalyov", *Radio Svoboda*, March 5, 2000. Availableonline at : http://www.svoboda.org/programs/FTF/2000/FTF.030500.asp (accessed September 2003).
36 See, "Last Seen ...: Continued 'Disappearances' in Chechnya", *HRW Report*, April 2002, Vol. 14, No. 3 (D). See also "Into Harm's Way: Forced Return of Displaced People to Chechnya", *HRW Report*, January 2003, Vol. 15, No. 1(D). "Swept Under: Torture, Forced Disappearances, and Extrajudicial Killings During Sweep Operations in Chechnya", *HRW Report*, February 2002, Vol. 14, No. 2 (D). "Burying the Evidence: The Botched Investigation into a Mass Grave in Chechnya", *HRW Report*, May 2001, Vol. 13, No. 3 (D). All available online at http://www.hrw.org/reports/world/russia-pubs.php (accessed August 2003).
37 S. Kovalyov, cited in "Kovalyov Takes Grim Message to US", *Moscow Times*, February 18, 2003: 1.
38 S. Kovalyov, "Nikto ne rasstrelival zalozhnikov", *Rabochaya Demokratiya*. Available online at http://www.1917.com/index.html (accessed June 2003).
39 "Russia justified Chechnya raids", *Boston Globe*, October 29, 1999: 3.
40 I. Akhmadov, "The Russian-Chechen Tragedy: The Way to Peace and Democracy – Conditional Independence Under an International Administration 2003", Kline Archive, New York.
41 S. Kovalyov, cited in "Human Rights Campaigner Warns Chechen War Signals Dangerous Turn in Russia Away From Civil Society Values", February 25, 2000. Available online at: http://www.eurasianet.org/departments/recaps/articles/cep022500.shtml (accessed August 2003).
42 Elena Bonner and Vladimir Bukovsky both signed an appeal to President Bush in which they cited their ongoing concern about crimes against humanity and genocide against the Chechen nation. The *New York Times*, September 23, 2003: 6. See also Akhmadov, I. "The Russian–Chechen Tragedy: The Way to Peace and Democracy – Conditional Independence Under an International Administration 2003", Kline Archive, New York.

Conclusion

> There needs to be a critical mass of people who understand that democracy
> has a strict procedure and, without those procedures, all sorts of wonderful
> words about freedom, equality and brotherhood are simply slogans. But
> people like that don't exist in Russia and there is no place for them to come
> from.
>
> Sergei Kovalyov[1]

One is struck by the challenges Sergei Kovalyov faced as an individual. First
as a scientist and human rights activist living under a totalitarian regime,
and then as a public figure in the midst of Russia's struggle for democratic
institutions. One is convinced of his courage, resilience and dedication to the
cause of individual rights and liberties, and his vision for a more humane
and democratic politics in Russia.

What is interesting about Kovalyov's development was that he was forced to
recognize that human rights are political. Not as concepts in themselves, for
they are "inalienable", but political in so far as wise and benevolent politics are
integral to their success. Their implementation requires pressure from
numerous directions: government, civil society and prominent individuals.
Kovalyov was challenged more than his contemporaries on this score and he
pushed as far as he was capable to change the relationship between the Russian
government and the human rights community. And in that struggle, he was
criticised by his colleagues, vilified by the nationalist bloc and slowly sidelined
by Yeltsin and the presidential Administration. He was frequently in a position
of personal danger and once had his life publicly threatened on national television. Throughout all this he remained unnervingly committed.

Kovalyov was able, in a very real and public manner, to stage human
rights issues in the Russian press. He became a master spokesman, using
every opportunity to draw the media onto his side, to make the issues of
registration, refugees, military service, the judicial system and prison conditions a part of the Russian consciousness. Repeatedly and unashamedly, he
brought these issues to the forefront in an effort to evoke reflection, guilt
and action among Russian citizens. He removed the bandages of Russia's
wounds over and over again for examination. For this reason, his presence

often evoked feelings of bitterness and attacks of shame. In response, he became less sensitive to public opinion and sometimes reluctant to acknowledge the reality of economic concerns among the Russian population and their influence on the democratic vote.

After Andrei Sakharov's death, however, no other public figure in Russian politics made human rights their priority like Kovalyov. He and his colleagues ensured that "basic rights and liberties in conformity with the commonly recognized principles and norms of international law shall be recognized and guaranteed in the Russian Federation ... The basic rights and liberties of the human being shall be inalienable and shall belong to everyone from birth." These inspirational words are now an institutional component of Russian politics. They are the idealized words to which Russian society can aspire. He may not have succeeded in ensuring the implementation of the laws initiated by himself and his colleagues, but he succeeded in drawing attention to how they violated human rights, why they had to be reformed and what that could do for Russia's future. It might also be argued that his constant campaigning for clarification of the conflict between the right to self-determination and the territorial integrity of states might some day influence the world community to address this problem.

My focus has been upon Kovalyov's practical contributions. There were many positive sides to his work and the many lessons he learnt along the way. He openly acknowledged his managerial inexperience. He sometimes found it difficult to remove himself personally from events for the sake of a larger long-term goal. For some, especially the members of the Presidential Human Rights Commission, this was a disappointing personality trait. And one is left with the lingering question as to whether moral outrage is always the most constructive approach. In Russia's transition, the absolutism that characterized much of the action of the dissident movement during the Soviet era did not always work. Kovalyov knew this. He was far from uncompromising and always attempted to contact President Yeltsin personally to discuss issues of concern. But the first Chechen war challenged him on an unprecedented level, one that he felt unable to resolve. Others like him felt similar disgust. The tragedy is that the Chechen wars occurred at all. For the human rights community, they made its struggle harder and stretched its resources even further.

And what lessons has the Russian human rights community learned as a whole? Kovalyov showed that, ideally, civil society and government need to work together in countries undergoing transition. Western countries need to strengthen their commitment to providing managerial and administrative knowledge and technology to the Russian government and non-government agencies devoted to the defence of human rights. They need to continue sharing expertise, the exchange of information and mutual encouragement. In places like Russia, the non-government community needs political figures they can trust to voice their concerns and speak for their needs. Governments must recognize mistakes, civil society must apply pressure, and individuals must speak out. It is this constant give and take, pushing and pulling, that shapes new thinking. Many saw in Sergei Kovalyov the chance to bridge this gap.

Kovalyov found himself at the centre of the contradictions that defined the burgeoning Russian Federation and its struggling democratic transition. For that reason his experience is vital to our understanding of the place of human rights discourse in post-Soviet Russia. He tried, despite his own inexperience and the politically turbulent atmosphere, to structure a new vision for Russia and implement a political agenda. Of course, changing the law and changing the culture in which it is implemented are two different tasks. Did he, like a true liberal, place too much confidence in the rule of law and the formal structures of constitutions, parliaments and the office of the Human Rights Commissioner? Did he link a successful change in Russia's moral landscape too intimately with the rule of law? Quite simply, Kovalyov believed in the rule of law, not merely as an instrument that regulates human action, but as an educative tool with the potential to build and shape new behaviours, new attitudes and new perspectives. Restoring the lost faith between Russian society and its government structures was one of his long-term aims, and shaping the law to reflect that renewed faith was his personal strategy. He understood that it was one side of a multi-faceted problem.

One should consider these gains in the context of Soviet and Russian history. It took the freshness of resolve of this small group of human rights activists in the 1960s to build a civil society, to shift the discourse of injustice from the Soviet kitchen and private *kompanii* to make it a public issue. From here, with the easing of government oppression and the opening of political opportunities, many of them sought to institutionalize their ideals and aspirations. Kovalyov took the ideals of his closest contemporaries of the 1960s to their logical conclusion. From Valery Chalidze's Human Rights Committee of 1970 and Andrei Sakharov's attempts to meet with state bureaucrats in 1988, Kovalyov shifted the goal of cooperation from the dissident arena to the political arena. In choosing penal reform, states of emergency, freedom of movement and the office of the Human Rights Commissioner, he selected tasks he felt he could influence with the resources at hand. By December 1996, the law on the office of the Human Rights Commissioner had been passed and twenty other regional offices established. Their success is yet to be determined.

Given the circumstances, Kovalyov's efforts have undoubtedly contributed to the strengthening of civil and political rights in Russia, not only in the political, but also the civil sphere. There is growing recognition of the importance of social pressure as a tool that not only influences government policy, but functions as a mechanism of support independent of it. In this endeavour, Kovalyov is but one activist, one part of an expanding human rights landscape in Russia. We continue to witness the most admirable work of the Moscow Helsinki Group and its expansion to the regions, Memorial's Human Rights Centre, the Glasnost Defence Foundation, the Andrei Sakharov Museum and Public Centre, the Individual Council of Legal Expertise and the Inter-Regional Human Rights Centre.

Kovalyov and the human rights movement continue to face daily challenges from the arbitrary actions of the Russian government. Kovalyov remains the movement's public spokesman, while the human rights organizations carry on educating, providing legal advice and consultation, distributing information and monitoring human rights violations. Ludmilla Alekseeva actively promotes and encourages cooperation between government bodies in the centre and the regions in her capacity as President of the Moscow Helsinki Group. The movement's importance as a bulwark against arbitrariness remains as important as ever.

Kovalyov's return to civil society in 1996 happened at a time when Russia certainly needed his voice in public discourse as he led the campaign against the second Chechen war. He has the remarkable ability to see ahead, he links historical events with contemporary reality, he understands the motives that drive the Russian government and the weighty bureaucracy. Critics could accuse him of absolutism if only his fears were not justified. His position was by no means enviable. His speeches were rarely brimming with optimism and he could slice down the middle of an event or problem with razor sharp accuracy. This made his voice often abrasive in tone and his words pricked the conscience of his audience in their truth.

Kovalyov's role in Europe and the United States today is defined by a strange mixture of respect for his character and ideals, but a reluctance to act on his poignant speeches on topics like Chechnya. He recently matched his concern with the contradictions of self-determination with the search for a unified strategy in the face of massive human rights violations: a strategy, he argues, not motivated by political interests, but by individual liberties. He has repeatedly noted the paradox of a global discourse that acknowledges the universal problems of nuclear, chemical, ecological and economic concerns and a technology that promotes a "global village". But the idea, first espoused by the United Nations Universal Declaration of Human Rights in 1948 and later by the Helsinki Final Act of 1975, has a long struggle ahead in the area of human rights.[2]

In the international public arena, Kovalyov continues to fight against the claims of cultural imperialism. In a poignant statement, he claimed:

> ... accusations of cultural imperialism are the favourite weapon of African and Asian dictators. They are now part of the discourse of Russian, Ukrainian and Belorussian politicians. They clutch at this weapon every time the international community attempts to force them to live like human beings. They propose that we consider the torturous conditions of a prisoner, the belittling of human dignity, the death penalty, attacks on freedom of expression as "national traditions" ... And the saddest thing is that many European intellectuals are inclined to agree with this. That is: something is an unacceptable human rights violation in Austria or Denmark, but in the Republic of Togo, China or the Ukraine it is a structural component of the country's cultural inheritance. What is this exactly – a form of intellectual and cultural

spinelessness before the plurality of human societies? This is the way the supporters of this point of view love to explain it. But not one of them has ever sat in a Togo or Chinese prison in order to bear out their position. I suggest that this is simply a new variant of a common European arrogance, bordered with racism. Alas this arrogance is all still characteristic of even the best representatives of the Western European elite.[3]

Kovalyov recognizes the importance of the public intellectual as a spokesman of ideas and visions, not only in Russia but internationally. Without a trace of embarrassment, he has identified the Council of Europe as a model of a future world government capable of codifying a unified strategy to human rights violations. Despite the idealism, he is serious about this model. He doubts that the UN could assume this task, given its current structure as a forum for nation-states to trade on state interests rather than the rights of the individual. His idea of a world government consists of a parliament to completely revise and redraft a system of international laws, to wipe out "the chaos of inter-government treaties". He argues that the executive authorities would guarantee security once nation-states transferred part of their national sovereignty to the supranational organ. All states would maintain a small military force for internal security.[4]

From the outset, Sergei Kovalyov has sought to protect the individual from arbitrary state actions. As a scientist, he understood better than many of us that beyond race, religion or ideology we are all human beings, part of the one human community – a fact he encourages us not to forget. To predict the future of the human rights discourse that he did so much to promote is a hazardous task. For a brief moment in the history of the Russian Federation, he occupied centre stage and promoted a philosophy of the integrity of the individual as the supreme value. Political forces have changed in Russia and the human rights community is for the time being marginalized in the Putin regime. Compliant human rights officials may now occupy important posts, but it does not mean that structural change of the type promoted by Kovalyov will not have a role in the future. Kovalyov and the human rights community remain a strong, dedicated group of individuals who will continue to insist on that structural change. We can only hope that this pressure will one day be truly reflected in Russia's state institutions.

Notes

1 S. Kovalyov, "Helsinki Watch Meeting: New York March 9, 1996", Melbourne: Personal collection, E. Gilligan.
2 S. Kovalyov, "Na rubezhe dvukh tysyacheletii", in *Sergei Kovalyov: Pragmatika Politcheskogo Idealizma*, Moskva: Institut Prav Cheloveka, 1999, pp.44–50.
3 S. Kovalyov, "Ob otmene smertnoi kazni", *Sergei Kovalyov: Pragmatika Politcheskogo Idealizma*, Moskva: Institut Prav Cheloveka, 1999, pp. 82–3.
4 S. Kovalyov, "Na rubezhe dvukh tysyacheletii", in *Sergei Kovalyov: Pragmatika Politcheskogo Idealizma*, Moskva: Institut Prav Cheloveka, 1999, pp.44–50.

Appendix 1

PUBLIC DEFENCE OF THE RIGHTS OF THE INDIVIDUAL: RESOLUTION NO. 1

Resolution No. 1 recognizes that:

- human rights is one of the fundamental values of contemporary civilization;
- an entire complex of worldwide problems, including the questions of war and peace, confidence-building and cooperation between people, the preservation of the environment, revitalizing of the national economy and culture, political stability and other problems, are impossible to resolve effectively if human rights problems are ignored;
- the question of human rights is not the internal affair of any country, but has a universal significance for all humankind;
- activity in defence of human rights is fundamentally not a political opposition but a humanitarian movement based on the moral and legal principles of its participants.

And notes that:

- the human rights situation in the USSR in the course of the last year has improved to a certain degree; in particular, during this period, to our knowledge not a single trial on political charges has taken place and a significant number of political prisoners have been freed. Serious progress for the better has been made in the area of ideological censorship of the press.

Nevertheless, the human rights problem in the USSR remains severe. In particular:

- there is an ongoing concern for the release of political prisoners without imposed conditions;
- the judicial mechanisms for instigating criminal prosecution for exercizing freedom of opinion have not been eliminated;

- the government continues to maintain a monopoly over the press;
- the Crimean Tartar people, who were illegally exiled from the Crimea, are still violently deprived of their homeland; they are discriminated against in their right to choose their place of residence and are slandered in the government press;
- the Soviet Union continues its armed intervention in Afghanistan and the Soviet troops temporarily sent into Czechoslovakia in 1968 remain to this day and have not been withdrawn from the country;
- in the USSR, in violation of the UN Human Rights Declaration, restrictions are kept on one's free choice of country or place of residence within the country.

We emphasize that:

- progress in human rights is possible and desirable independent of the social and political system of a given country;
- the signatory governments of the Helsinki process are capable of substantially accelerating the process of bringing the human rights situation into accordance with international agreements;
- international public cooperation in the cause of human rights defence is desirable and imperative when, and the degree to which, it is exercized on a moral and legal basis.

We propose the following:

1 The publics of all countries that participate in the Helsinki process should unite their efforts in the cause of defending human rights. This unification should take place independent of political convictions, on a moral and legal basis. With this goal, the human rights activists of various countries should study the possibilities for creating international non-governmental organizations which would be involved in both the elaboration and the perfection of the concepts of human rights in the contemporary world, as well as the defence of these rights in the concrete instances of their violation. The proposal of LeRoy Moore (USA), a participant in the seminar, also deserves attention: that such organizations would take it upon themselves to work out agendas for the governmental conference on humanitarian problems which the Soviet government has proposed to hold in Moscow.

2 The international human rights movement should cooperate closely in its activity with other analogous citizen movements, like the ecological and anti-war movements and the movement to defend culture.

3 The governments of all countries that have signed the Helsinki act should cease viewing human rights activists as an internal political opposition and the question of human rights as a question of the internal politics of a given country.

4   Participants in the human rights movement, of course, can have definite political, philosophical and religious convictions and advocate them as they see fit. In their human rights activity, however, they should not introduce tendencies that oppose the universal nature of the struggle for human rights for all humankind.

5   We call on the government of all countries to do everything in their power to stop the violations of human rights in their countries. In particular, we call on the Soviet government to complete the release of all political prisoners in the shortest possible time without any preconditions, and also secure legislative guarantees that political persecution will not be allowed in the future. We also call for an end to the government monopoly over the press.

6   We consider it essential to continue persistent attempts to establish a dialogue between the human rights movement in the USSR and the authorities. We call on the broadest possible sectors of society to add their efforts to these attempts. In the framework of this dialogue, if it will take place, we, from our side, are prepared in all good faith to establish cooperation with the authorities at all levels. The final aim of such cooperation is envisioned by us to be a society in which human rights are not just declared but are successfully protected by the law, public opinion and executive authority. We do not consider such a goal unattainable.

7   We call on all governments also to be led in their activity first and foremost by the law. In that connection we support the slogan put forth by Jan Urban (Charter 77, Czechoslovakia), a participant in the seminar: "Peace Without Tanks!" This formula expresses our attitudes to armed intervention in the affairs of other nations as well as towards the use of violent methods in domestic policy.

December 14, 1987

Signed by seminar participants:
Ernst Orlovsky, Larisa Bogoraz, Iosif Dyadkin, Sergei Kovalyov, Igor Kalinchev, Ludmilla Kozhevnikova, Yury Chernyak, Aleksandr Vereshchagin, Aleksandr Lavut, Boris Rumshisky, Aleksei Smirnov, Aleksandr Daniel, Boris Smushkevich, Dmitry Leonov, Leonard Ternovsky.

Appendix 2

PUBLIC DEFENCE OF THE RIGHTS OF THE INDIVIDUAL: RESOLUTION NO. 2

Having reviewed the current situation regarding human rights problems in the USSR, the realities of the current *perestroika*, Party documents for the recent period (the leaders of the ruling party of the country – the Communist Party of the Soviet Union – have proclaimed *perestroika* and have not denied their personal responsibility for it), the laws of the USSR, and the economic situation in the country, we have come to the conclusion that the egregious violations of human rights in the USSR which we all see and sense are only a consequence of the legislatively, economically and psychologically entrenched non-recognition of the very idea of human rights in the USSR. We believe that this non-recognition is dictated by the very nature of our system and cannot be removed within its framework.

Therefore, we consider it essential to change the very essence of our social system, for which the following are characteristic:

- only one direction for future social development;
- a one-party political system;
- [the concept of] odiousness (censorship of subjects and judgements which reject the foundation of Soviet society).

A radical change must be expressed in the following actions and directions of society:

1 Do not resolve now, prematurely, the question of our future path, what type it will be, whether society will develop further in the socialist plan – the people themselves will decide after obtaining freedom of choice and complete information. We consider it necessary to allow complete free enterprise and to allocate land to those who wish it (particularly the peasants), not making *kolkhozes* and *sovkhozes* (collective and state farms) the only form of organizing the agricultural life of the village forever.

2 Completely abolish censorship, permit the activity of private publishing houses and printing shops; allow *samizdat* journals to obtain access to copying technology; provide credit for such initiatives; allow people to receive any book from abroad. The opposition should have the opportunity to use the mass media free of charge on an equal basis with the ruling groups. The ideological orientation of our culture should be eliminated, and all the best *samizdat* should be published in mass editions at the government's expense.

3 Ideological control over society should be completely removed; the Constitution should be de-ideologized, as should education and economics; the legalized intervention of the Communist Party in the economic and spiritual life of the country should be prohibited; the agencies of the KGB should be dismantled, since it has defiled itself by its monstrous crimes against humanity.

The consequences of such a reorientation of society would be:

- release and rehabilitation (exoneration) with moral and material compensation of all political prisoners;
- compliance by the Soviet Union with the international agreements it has signed;
- freedom of movement;
- cessation of Communist expansionism in the form of aggression and the colonization of seized territories (Afghanistan, the Warsaw bloc, the occupation of the Baltic States and so on);
- the abolition of the death penalty and the softening of the penitentiary regimen;
- the humanization of the entire life of society, the boosting of the economy, and a decent and free life for the entire country.

December 14, 1987

The resolution was signed by members of the Democracy and Humanism Seminar who are affiliated with the Group to Establish Trust Between East and West.

Appendix 3

RESULTS FROM THE JURIDICAL SECTION OF THE HUMAN
RIGHTS SEMINAR, DECEMBER 1988

This section considers that it is urgently necessary to publish normative
acts, preferably in the form of law, passed by the Supreme Soviet of the
USSR ... which would stipulate the following:

1 The Creation of a Constitutional Court or a Constitutional
   Council to make decisions on the constitutionality of laws or the
   granting of such powers to the Supreme Court of the USSR ...
2 A procedure for the application through the courts and other law-
   enforcement agencies of normative acts, by which the court upon
   demand from any of the sides is obligated to review the constitutionality of any law and the legality of any act under a law, subject
   to enforcement ...
3 The extension of the priority of international law over the domestic
   legislation of the USSR ...
4 Strict obligation to publicize all normative acts (except those having
   a strictly and exclusively narrow institutional nature and which
   concern only strictly specialized questions); a prohibition on the
   enforcement of unpublished normative acts.
5 A simple juridical procedure for the founding and activity of independent publishers and periodicals ...
6 Exact criteria for refusal of permission to conduct a rally or
   demonstration or to found a civic organization. To establish a court
   procedure for contesting such decisions.
7 Free access for all citizens and, in the first place, for media
   employees, to information on the work of government agencies and
   mass public organizations, except for types of information clearly
   defined in the law ...
8 Criteria and a procedure for the involuntary hospitalization of
   persons in psychiatric hospitals.
9 Bringing domestic legislation into complete compliance with the

International Covenants on Civil Rights and other conventions and agreements ratified by the USSR ...

10 The end of criminal liability for homosexuality among consenting adults.

11 Abolition of the death penalty.

12 Humanization of the penal system and, as a top priority, the removal of criminal liability for prisoners who violate the internal regimen in places of confinement (Art. 188–3) and criminal liability for passing materials to prisoners illegally (Art. 188–4); removal from corrective labour legislation of all types of punishment of prisoners connected to restriction on food as well as incarceration in punishment cells, solitary confinement, internal camp cells; the removal of restrictions on correspondence ...

13 Implementation of legislation on entry and exit from the USSR in compliance with Article 12 of the International Covenant on Civil and Political Rights ...

14 Removal of such forms of national discrimination, as for example the prohibition on the use of the languages of other republics in telegrams sent inside the RSFSR ...

15 The elimination of unjustified restrictions on the right to complaints through the courts of the actions of officials and state agencies ...

16 Prohibition of the dismissal of single mothers, mothers with many children, and disabled mothers, as a first step in improving labour legislation (in the event of dismissal for reasons of industrial necessity, a monetary compensation should be paid until a job placement is made).

17 Bringing into compliance with constitutional guarantees the inviolability of telephone conversations under Article 74 of the Communications Act which grants the City Telephone Network the right to shut down telephone services when used for purposes that contradict state interests.

We consider the following urgently necessary:

1 Recognition on the basis of reciprocity of the binding jurisdiction of the International Court of the United Nations.

2 Recognition as binding for the Soviet Union, Article 41 of the Convention on Civil and Political Liberties, that is, agreement to review reports about alleged violations in the USSR and reports by the USSR on alleged violations in other countries by the United Nations Human Rights Commission.

3 A comprehensive review and broad discussion on the question of signing the Optional Protocol of the Covenant which enables individual complaints to be lodged.

4   The adherence of the USSR to other international conventions:

1   Convention 105 of the International Labour Organization on forced labour.

2   The convention of the Universal Postal Union on subscription to foreign periodicals.

3   The conventions on the international right to refutation.

4   The UNESCO conventions on procedures for obtaining scientific, educational and cultural materials and the UNESCO coupon system.

5   For the purpose of guaranteeing a real right to housing, the section considers it advisable to overhaul radically the Soviet housing legislation ...

6   We consider it necessary to conduct a radical review of the passport regulations in force in the USSR ... The *propiska* should be abolished in the foreseeable future.[1]

Note

1   Resolutions and other documents of the Moscow Independent Seminar on Humanitarian Problems, December 10–15, 1987: A Helsinki Watch Report, August, 1988, Moscow: Memorial Archive. See also "O Professional'noi Dobrosovestnosti Yurista", *Referendum* No. 5, February 2 (1988): 10–14.

Bibliography

Archival sources

The Andrei Sakharov Archives. Moscow, Russian Federation.
The personal archive of Mr Edward Kline. New York, USA.
Arkhiv Samizdat. Memorial. Moscow, Russian Federation.
Fond 89 of the Center for the Preservation of Contemporary Documentation (Ts. Kh. S.D). Moscow, Russian Federation.
Emma Gilligan Personal Collection. Melbourne, Australia. (Tapes, letters and documents available.)

Newspapers and magazines

Ekspress Khronika
Express Chronicle
Izvestiya
Krasnaya Zvesda
Memorial Aspekt
Moscow News
Moscow Times
Moskovskii Komsomolets
Moskovskie Novosti
Moskovskaya Pravda
New Times
Novoe Vremya
Nezavisimaya Gazeta
Ogonek
Obshaya Gazeta
Pravda
Pravozashchitnik
Put'
Reuters
Ria-Novosti
Rossiiskaya Gazeta
Rossiiskie Vesti
Rysskaya Mysl'
Sevodnya

The New York Review of Books
The New York Times
The Times
The Washington Post
Trud

Selected works by Sergei Adamovich Kovalyov

"Dreams of a Political Idealist." *Capital's Eye/Reuters*, March, 2000: 5–9.
Sergei Kovalyov: Pragmatika Politicheskogo Idealizma. Moskva: Institut prav cheloveka, 1999.
"Andrei Sakharov: Otvetstvennost pered razumom." *Izvestiya*, May 21, 1998: 4.
Tvorchestvo i byt gulaga. Moskva: Zvenya, 1998: 6–7.
"Dissidenti o dissidentstve." *Znamya*, 9 (1997): 178–81.
Vospominaniia. Moscow: Memorial Archive, 1996.
"Speech at Human Rights Watch, New York." March 6, 1996. Melbourne: Personal Collection, E. Gilligan.
"A Letter of Resignation." *The New York Review of Books*, January 25, 1996: 30.
"On the New Russia." *The New York Review of Books*, April 18, 1996: 12.
"Nash edinstvennyi shans." *Memorial Aspekt*. June, 1995: 1, 4.
"Belaya vorona Rossiiskoi politiki," *Obshaya Gazeta*, February 3, 1995: 3.
"The Ruling Element and Society: Who Will Prevail?" *Moscow News*, No. 31, August 11–17, 1995: 1–2.
"Banket dissidentov: perestroika – intelligentsia i politika." *Nezavisimaya Gazeta*, March 16, 1995.
"Russia takes a detour on the road to the rule of law." *International Practioner's Notebook*, Issue 60, August (1995): 4–8.
"Missiya v Budyonnovsk: Kak eto bylo." *Novoe Vremya*, No. 26. July, 1995: 12–13.
"Vstat! Sud Idet," *Novoe Vremya*, No. 29, July, 1995: 8–11.
"Statement by Sergei Kovalyov, member of the Russian State Duma: Commission on Security and Cooperation in Europe. May 1, 1995." New York: Kline Archive, 1995.
"How the West shouldn't react to Events in Chechnya." *Demokratizatsiya: The Journal of Post-Soviet Democratization*, Vol. III, No. 4, (1995): 396–8.
"Pochemy neobkhodimo poddershat Ekspress-Khroniky?" *Ekspress Khronika*, No. 7, February 9–16, 1995: 1.
"Stenogramme of interview with Sergei Kovalyov. New York, October 22, 1995." New York: Kline Archive, unpublished. No author's name.
"Obrashenie predsedatel komiteta no prava cheloveka C.A. Kovalyova k grazh-danam Rossii, Okt, 1993." *Moskva Osen' – 93: Khronika protivostoyaniya.* Moskva: Respublika, 1995: 424.
"Odnazhdy propal prezidentskii ukaz." *New Times*, August 17, 1994 No. 33 (5513): 11.
"For Official Use Only: Scandal over Kovalev's Report." *New Times*, August 1994: 24.
"Ombudsmen znachit zastupnik: Inter'viu s Sergeem Kovalevym," *Rysskaya Mysl'*, No. 4057, December 15–21, 1994: 9.
Nauchno – prakticheskaya konferentsiya, posvyashchennaya 73–i godovshine so dnya rozhdeniya A. D. Sakharova, May 21, 1994. Moskva: Yuridicheskaya Literatura, 1994: 11–21.

Nauchno – prakticheskaya konferentsiya: Uroki avgusta 1991 goda: narod i vlast'. Moskva: Yuridicheskaya Literatura, 1994: 26–30.

"Odnazhdy propal prezidentskii ukaz," *Literaturnaya Gazeta*, August 17, 1994, No. 33 (5513): 11.

"Nasledie Sakharova. Idei i praktika." *Memorial Aspekt*, June 9, 1994: 2.

"Nashe Bydyshee – svobodnie grazhdane svobodnoi strani." *Rossiiskaya Gazeta*, August 9, 1994, No. 150 (1007): 4.

"Prezidentu Rossiiskoi Federatsii B. N. Eltsinu ob itogakh vsemirnoi konferentsii po pravam cheloveka." July 20, 1993, No. 16711. New York: Kline Archive.

Moskovskii Novosti, April 11, 1993: 11.

Cited in "Russian Parliament must be decent enough to resign, says reformer MP." *RIA-Novosti*, April 26, 1993.

"Ombudsmeni i sudebnie garantii zashchiti prav cheloveka," *Yuridicheskaya Zashchita Prav Cheloveka*. Moskva: Moskovskaya Khel'sinskaya Gruppa. February, (1993): 152–72.

"Deputaty trusyat pered referendumom." *Nezavisimaya Gazeta*, April 10, 1993, No. 68 (583): 4.

"Sergei Kovalyov's speech to the Council on Foreign Relations." December 20, 1993. New York: Kline Archive.

"Sergei Kovalyov's Speech to the Founding Congress of the Political Movement Russia's Choice." October 16, 1993. New York: Kline Archive.

"Khvatit li zdravogo smysla." *Vek XX i Mir*, 15 (1992): 2

"Parlament umer, da zdravstvuet parlament!" *Moskovskii Novosti*, October 3, 1992: 2.

"Vystuplenie Kovalyova v Konstitustionnom sude." July 28, 1992. Transcribed from video cassette. Available at the Andrei Sakharov Musuem & Public Centre, Moscow. Transcript: Melbourne: Personal Collection, E. Gilligan.

"Dissident s parlamentskim mandatom." *Referendum: Zhurnal Nezavisimikh Mnenii 1987–1990 No. 1–37*. Paris: Rysskaya Mysl', 1992.

"Sergei Kovalyov: ne vizhu smysla mstit." No. 2, 1992: 2. Title of newspaper unknown. New York: Kline Archive.

Chelovek i Pravo, No. 16, (1992): 529–30.

"Osleplenie Polifema ili O polze raznikh tochek zreniya." *Narodni Deputat*, No. 11, 1992 (574): 106–9.

Bogoraz, L and Goltsin, V. "Politecheskaya borba ili zashchita prav?" *Perestroika: Glasnost, Demokratiya, Sotsialism – Podrushenie v tryasiny*. Moscow: Progress, 1991: 501–45.

"Zakliuchennye osnovatelno podoshli k aktsii protesta." *Nezavisimaya Gazeta*, November 16, 1991, No. 145: 1.

"Pochemy v SSSR net pravozashchitnogo dvizheniya." *Vek XX I Mir*, 6 (1991): 9–11.

"Obshaya vina, obshaya otvetstvennost." *Moskovskii Novosti*, No. 5, January 31, 1991: 1, 2.

"Novgorodskoe veche v Moskve," *Novoe Vremya*, No. 32, 1991: 10–11.

"The wise state opens its borders," *New Times*, No. 39, 1991: 25–7.

"Popali pod ukaz." *Novoe Vremya*, No. 30, 1991: 9.

"Second speech at the Moscow Conference on the Human Dimension: OSCE." New York: Kline Archive, 1991.

"From discussions at the March 1991 Human Rights Conference: Introductory Speech by Sergei Kovalyov." New York: Kline Archive.

"Sergei Kovalyov za normalnii put razvitiya blagopoluchnoi strani – kogda ona stanet takoi!" *Put'*, February 25, 1990: 2–3.

"C.A. Kovalyov: Vse eti dela nado nepesmatrivat." *Ekspress-Khronika*, No. 34 (159), August 21, 1990: 8.

"Chelovesheskoe izmerenie nashei bedy." *Rysskaya Mysl'*, June 8, 1990: 2.

"Civic Action." *New Times*, No. 8, 1990: 25.

"Speech at the International Helsinki Federation Meeting." Moscow May 29 – June 5, 1990: 1–3. New York: Kline Archive.

"In Moscow, The Dissident Politician: Sergei Kovalyov, Keeping His Promise to Sakharov." *Washington Post*, March 7, 1990: B1.

"Time to Get Ready for Democracy." *Peace & the Twentieth Century*, 10 (1989): 7–11.

"Statement on Soviet Political Prisoners from Bogoraz, Kovalyov, Sakharov, Timofeev," October 23, 1988: 1. New York: Kline Archive.

"Without Barricades: Talks with Larisa Bogoraz and Sergei Kovalyov." *Peace & the Twentieth Century*, 9 (1988): 44–8.

"News from Helsinki Watch: Soviet Human Rights Leader Harassed After Reagan Reception." June 8, 1988.

"Pis'mo predsedatelu KGB Y. B. Andropov v svyazi s iz'yatiem y ego zhakomogo t. 2 knigi 'Arkhipelag Gulag' ". Moskva 17.10.78. Memorial Archive AC No. 1910.

"Ombudsmen upolmomochen zashchitit." *Obshaya Gazeta*, No. 20/45, year unknown: 4. New York: Kline Archive.

"Draft Speech by Sergei Kovalyov." New York: Kline Archive, undated, untitled.

"Stenogramme of interview with Sergei Kovalyov by David Remnick." Unpublished, undated. New York: Kline Archive.

"Tak Zhit v takom gosudarstve." *Karta*, Date unknown: 7–10. New York: Kline Archive.

Works cited

Adams, B. *The Politics of Punishment: Prison Reform in Russia 1863–1917*. Dekalb: Northern Illinois University Press, 1996.

Amnesty International, British section, Co-ordinating Group for Prisoners in the USSR. "The Trial of Sergei Kovalyov." New York: Kline Archive, 1974.

Amnesty International Annual Report 1990. London: Amnesty International, 1990.

Alexeyeva, Ludmilla. *Soviet Dissent*. Connecticut: Wesleyan University Press, 1995.

Arkhive Samizdat, A.S 5891. Moscow: Memorial Archive: 4.

Bacon, E. *The Gulag At War*. London: Macmillan, 1994.

Barry, D. "The Trial of the CPSU and the Principles of Nuremberg." *Review of Central and East European Law*, 3 (1996): 256.

Belaya Kniga Rossii: Mezhdunarodnaya Obshestvo Prav Cheloveka. Frankfurt: International Human Rights Society, 1994.

Bogoraz, Larisa. "Printsipi i metodi pravozashchitnoi raboty," Moskovskaya Khel'sinskaya Gruppa, Sbornik – 1992. Moskva: Moskovskaya Khel'sinskaya Gruppa, 1992.

Bogoraz, Larisa and Daniel, Alexander. "V poiskakh nesyshchestuyshchei nayki (Dissidentstvo kak istoricheskaya problema), *Sovremennaya Rossiya: Vsglyad Iznytri*. Moskva–Bremen: Forschungsstelle Osteuropa an der Universitat Bremen, 1992.

Boitsova, V. *Slyshba zashchiti prav cheloveka i grazhdanina: Mirovoi opit*. Moscow: Vek, 1996.

Boitsova, L., Boitsova, V. and Rudnev, V. "Upolnomochennii po delam nesovershen-noletnikh," *Sovetskaya Ustitsiya*, No. 19–20, October (1992): 10.

Bonner, Elena. *Dochki – Materi*. New York: Chekova, 1991.

Bukovsky, Vladimir. *Moskovskii Protsess*. Paris–Moscow: MIK, 1996.

Centre of Political-Geographical Investigations Bulletin, January 9, 1995. Moscow: Memorial Arkhiv.

Chalidze, Valery. *To Defend these Rights*. New York: Random House, 1974 .

—— *The Soviet Human Rights Movement: A Memoir*. New York: The American Jewish Committee, 1984.

—— *The Dawn of Legal Reform*. Vermont: Chalidze Publications, 1990.

—— Letter to Emma Gilligan, April 1997. Melbourne: Personal Collection, E. Gilligan.

Clearinghouse Report. "Kovalev's Contributions to Physiology", December (1981): 9.

Commission on Human Rights: Fifty-first session. Item 10 (a) of the provisional agenda – Report of the Special Rapporteur, Mr Nigel S. Rodley, submitted pursuant to Commission on Human Rights resolution 1994/37 Addendum. Visit by the Special Rapporteur to the Russian Federation.

"Constitution Watch: Russia". *East European Constitutional Review*, Vol. 1, No. 1 (1992): 6.

—— *East European Constitutional Review*, Vol. 4, No.1 (1995): 25.

Current Digest of the Post-Soviet Press. "Human Rights Organisations Talk About Cleansing in Accordance with the Ethnic Principle", Vol. XLV, No. 42 (1993): 10.

—— "The Curfew in Moscow – It's over and done with", Vol. XLV, No. 42 (1993): 11.

—— "Crime Leaves No Time for Reform of the Prosecutor's Office", Vol. XLVI, No. 25 (1994): 11.

—— "Operation Hurricane Sweeps through Moscow", Vol. XLVI, No. 25 (1994): 13.

Current Digest of the Soviet Press. "Law Governing States of Emergency April 3, 1990", Vol. XLII, No. 19 (1990).

Directory of Russian MPs. United Kingdom: Longman Group, 1992.

Dunlop, John. *The Rise of Russia and the Fall of the Soviet Empire*. Princeton: Princeton University Press, 1995.

"European Commission for Democracy through Law". *Judgement of the Constitutional Court of the Russian Federation of July 31, 1995*. Available Moscow: Lenin Library 15/96–4: 71–4.

"Federal'naya Programma Deistvii v oblasti prav cheloveka (proekt)." *Prava Cheloveka v Rossii*. Moskva: Prava Cheloveka, 1995.

Feldbrugge J. M. F. (ed.). *Encyclopedia of Soviet law*. Dobbs Ferry, N.Y.: Oceana Publications, 1973.

Feldbrugge, J. M. F. *Russian Law: the end of the Soviet system and the role of law*. Dordrecht/Boston: M. Nijhoff, 1993.

Feofanov, Yuri. "The Establishment of the Constitutional Court in Russia and the Communist Party Case". *Review of Central and East European Law*, 6 (1993): 629.

Filimonova. L. (ed.). *Vystuplenie Sergeia Adamovicha Kovaleva na zasedanii konstitutsionnogo suda*. Moskva: Evrazia, 1995.

Fitzpatrick, J. *Human Rights in Crisis: The International System for Protecting Rights During States of Emergency*. Pennsylvania: University of Pennsylvania Press, 1994.

Gilligan, Emma. (trans.). "Interview with Ilya Burmostrovitch." Moscow: Gilligan Collection, 1995.

—— (trans.). "Interview with Lydia Siomina 1." Moscow: Gilligan Collection, 1995.

—— (trans.). "Interview with Lydia Siomina 2." Moscow: Gilligan Collection, 1995.

—— (trans.). "Interview with Mikhail Aruntynov." Moscow: Gilligan Collection, 1995.

—— (trans.). "Interview with Valentin Petrovich." Moscow: Gilligan Collection, 1995.

—— (trans.). "Interview with Sergei Sirotkin." Moscow: Gilligan Collection, 1995.

—— "Interview with Edward Kline." New York: Gilligan Collection, 1996.

—— (trans.). "Interview with Aleksandr Daniel." Moscow: Gilligan Collection, 1998.

—— (trans.). "Interview with Aleksandr Lavut 1." Moscow: Gilligan Collection, 1998.

—— (trans.). "Interview with Lev Timofeev." Moscow: Gilligan Collection, 1998.

—— (trans.). "Interview with Ludmilla Alekseyeva." Moscow: Gilligan Collection, 1998.

—— (trans.). "Interview with Lydia Siomina 3." Moscow: Gilligan Collection, 1998.

—— (trans.). "Interview with Oleg Orlov 1." Moscow: Gilligan Collection, 1998.

—— (trans.). "Interview with Aleksandr Lavut 2." Moscow: Gillligan Collection, 1999.

—— (trans.). "Interview with Oleg Orlov 2." Moscow: Gilligan Collection, 1999.

Ginzburg, Aleksandr. *Belaya Kniga po delu Sinyavskogo i Danielya*. Frankfurt, 1967.

Golfand, Yuri. "Statement by Dr. Y. Golfand. Moscow, March 21, 1975," *Khronika Press: Information Bulletin*, No. 54. December 30, 1974. New York: Kline Archive.

Gooding, John. "Gorbachev and Democracy," *Soviet Studies*, Vol. 42. No. 2., April (1990): 195–231.

Gorbachev, Mikhail. *Selected Speeches and Writings*. Moscow, Progress Publishers, 1987.

—— "Declaration on the International Foundation for the Survival and Development of Humanity: Draft, 880923 Moscow." New York: Kline Archive.

Grigorenko, Pyotr. *Memoirs*. New York and London: W.W Norton and Company, 1982.

Hopkins, Mark. *Russia's Underground Press*. New York: Praeger, 1983.

"Human Rights Committee Meeting of The International Foundation for the Survival and Development of Humanity." September 24, 1988. New York: Kline Archive.

Human Rights Watch. *Prison Conditions in the Soviet Union*. New York: Human Rights Watch, 1991.

—— *Russia's War in Chechnya: Victims Speak Out*. New York: Human Rights Watch, 1995.

Huskey, Eugene. "A Framework for the Analysis of Soviet Law." *The Russian Review*, 50 (1991): 53–70.

"Information Bulletin No. 54: Sergei Adamovich Kovalyov." New York: Khronika Press, 1974.

Kartashkin, Vladimir. "International Relations and Human Rights." *International Affairs*, August (1977): 29–38.

—— "Human Rights and the Modern World." *International Affairs*, January (1979): 48–56.

—— "The Soviet Constitution and Human Rights." *International Affairs*, February (1979): 13–20.

Khronika Zashchiti Prav v SSSR, No. 12, 1974. New York: Khronika, 1975.

Kistiakovsky, Boris. "In Defense of Law: The Intelligentsia and Legal Consciousness," *Landmarks*. Marian Schwartz (trans.), Boris Shragin and Albert Todd (eds). New York: Karz Howard, 1977.

Kline, Edward. "Letter to Associates and Friends of Sergei Kovalyov." March 12, 1995: 1–2. (New York: Kline Archive).

—— *Narrative Report on the Russian–American Human Rights Group.* New York: Kline Archive, 1996.

—— *The International Foundation for the Survival and Development of Humanity: An Overview.* New York: Kline Archive, 1996.

Komarova, Valentina. "Zakonodatel'naya reglamentatsiya deyatel'nosti upol-nomochennogo po pravam cheloveka v Rossiiskoi Federatsii." *Pravozashchitnik*, 2 (1997): 63–73.

"Konets prezidentskoi komissii po pravam cheloveka," *Pravozashchitnik*, No. 3, July–September, 1995: 4–6.

Kononov, Anatoly. *Osoboe Mnenie*. Unpublished, 1995. Melbourne: Personal Collection, E. Gilligan.

Landa, Malva. "Eto nasha zhivaya istoriya i my – tak ili inache – ee uchastniki." *Rysskaya Mysl'*, December 7–8, 1991: 3.

—— "Sergei Kovalyov: fakty biografii." *Pravozashchitnik*, No. 2, April–June 1997: 79–85.

—— "Cooperation between Rights Defenders and the Authorities." *Express Chronicle: Human Rights Information Agency – English Weekly News Digest*, March 21, 1997: 15.

Letowska, Eva. "The Ombudman and Basic Rights." *East European Constitutional Review*, Winter, 4 (1995): 63–6.

Levitin-Krasnov, A. *Demokraticheskoe Dvizhenie, Vospominaniia Chast IV*. Frankfurt/Main: Possev-Verlag, 1981.

Liber, G. *Soviet Nationality Policy, Urban Growth and Identity Change in the Ukrainian SSR 1923–1934*. Cambridge: Cambridge University Press, 1992.

Libushe, Z. *Soviet prisons and concentration camps: an annotated bibliography*. Newtonville, Mass: Oriental Research Partners, 1980.

Litvinov, Pavel. "O dvizhenii za prava cheloveka v SSSR". *Samosoznanie: Sbornik Statei*. New York, 1976: 79.

Lubarsky, Kronid. *Vesti iz SSSR: Prava Cheloveka*, No. 1 (1978–1981), No 2 (1982–1984), No. 3 (1985–1986), No. 9 (1986), No. 4 (1987–1988). Munchen: Das Land Und Die Welt e. V.

McFaul, Michael. "Eurasia Letter: Russian Politics after Chechnya." *Foreign Policy*, Summer 1995: 149–65.

Materiali dela o proverke konstitutsionnosti ukazov Presidenta RF, kasayshikhsya deyatel'nosti KPSS i KP RSFSR, a takshe o proverke konstitutsionnosti CPSU i CP RSFSR. Moskva: Spark, 1996.

Medvedev, Zhores. *The Rise & Fall of T.D. Lysenko*. New York: Columbia University Press, 1969.

Meerson-Aksenov, M. and Shragin, B. (eds). *The Political, Social and Religious Thought of Russian Samizdat – An Anthology*. Massachusetts: Nordland Company Press, 1977.

Memorial Human Rights Centre. *Two Years After the War: Problem of Displaced Persons in the Zone of the Ossetian-Ingush Conflict*. Moscow: Memorial Human Rights Centre, 1994.

"Minutes from the Board of Directors meeting, Moscow, January 13, 1988." New York: Kline Archive.

"Minutes from the Executive Committee meeting, Leningrad, June 1988." New York: Kline Archive.

"Minutes from the Human Rights Committee meeting of The International Foundation for the Survival and Development of Humanity, Moscow, September 24, 1988." New York: Kline Archive.

Mironov, Oleg. *Geroi Dnya*, May 22, 1998: *NTV*, 7.30 p.m.

Mulin, S. "Pravozashchitniki predchuvstvuyut plokhie vremena." *Nezavisimaya Gazeta*, February 7, 1996: 2.

Nikolaev, Yuri (ed.). *Chechenskaya Tragediya: Kto Vinovat.* Moskva: Novosti. 1995.

Novodvorskaya, Valeriya. "Chem otlichaetsya politichskaya bor'ba ot pravozashchitnoi deyatel'notsi, ili sektantu li my?" *DS Bulleten'*, No. 2–3 (1988).

—— *Po Tu Storonu otchayaniya.* Moscow: Novosti, 1993.

"O sobliudenii prav cheloveka i grazhdanina v Rossiiskoi Federatsii za 1993 god: Doklad o soblydenii prav cheloveka i grazhdanina v Rossiiskoi Federatsii za 1993 god". Moskva: *Prava Cheloveka v Rossii, Vypusk 1*, 1995.

"On the Observance of the Rights of Man and the Citizen in the Russian Federation (1994–1995): Report of the President's Commission on Human Rights." Catherine A. Fitzpatrick (trans.) for the Human Rights Project Group, March 1996. New York: Kline Archive.

Orlova, Raisa and Kopelev, Lev. *My Zhili v Moskve, 1956–1980.* Moskva: Kniga, 1990.

Orlov, Yuri. *Before & After Glasnost.* New York: American Jewish Committee, 1989.

Orlov, Yuri, Velikhanova, Tatyana and Lavut, Alexander. *Delo Kovalyova.* New York: Khronika, 1976.

Ostrow, Joel. *Comparing Post-Soviet Legislatures: A Theory of Institutional Design and Political Conflict.* Columbus: Ohio State University Press, 2000.

Obrazhenie o sozdanii funda kluba "Glasnost". *Referendum: Zhurnal Nezavisimikh Mnenii* No. 2, December 1987: 10.

Obshestvo Memorial. "Rossiya – Chechnya: tsep' oshibok i prestuplenii." Moskva: Zven'ya, 1998.

Ontogenez 2, (1971): 512.

Ontogonez 3, (1972): 208–11.

Otchet Komiteta Verkhovnogo Soveta Rossiiskoi Federatsii po pravam cheloveka. Moscow: Memorial Archiv, 1993.

Pogany, Ivan (ed.). *Human Rights in Eastern Europe.* Aldershot: Edward Elgar Publishing, 1995.

Pohl, J. *The Stalinist Penal System: A Statistical History of Soviet Repressions & Terror 1930–53.* Jefferson, NC: McFarland & Company, 1997.

"Polozhenie o Komissii po pravam cheloveka pri Presidente Rossiiskoi Federatsii." Melbourne: Personal Collection, E. Gilligan.

Posev, No. 11, 1970: 8–9.

Rachinskii, Yan. "Posmertnaya pravota kommunisticheskoi propagandi, ili Kratkie zametki o tom, kak vazhno ne putat formu i soderzhanie." *Nezavisimaya Gazeta*, October 19, 1993, No. 199: 5.

Reddaway, Peter. *Uncensored Russia: The Human Rights Movement in the Soviet Union.* London: Jonathan Cape, 1972.

"Report on Russia's request for membership in the light of the situation in Chechnya." Council of Europe, Parliamentary Assembly, January 31, 1995. Doc. 7230.

Resolutions and other documents of the Moscow Independent Seminar on Humaniutarian Problems, December 10–15, 1987: A Helsinki Watch Report, "Appeal: To international and national non-governmental organisations and private citizens interested in the development of the Helsinki Process in the area of Humanitarian Problems and to the governments of the participating states of the Conference on Security and Cooperation in Europe (CSCE)," August, 1988: 11. Moscow: Memorial Archive.

Robertson, Geoffrey. *Crimes Against Humanity: The Struggle for Global Justice*. London: Penguin Books, 2000.

Romanuk, Svetlana. "Presidenty R.F. Eltsiny B.N, August 19, 1994." Melbourne: Personal Collection, E. Gilligan.

—— "Tekst vystypleniya zayavitelya – S.V. Romanuk na otkritikh slyshaniyakh v kommissii po pravam cheloveka 28.04.94 po povody raboti shkoli internat-eksternat Feniks." Melbourne: Personal Collection, E. Gilligan.

Rossiiskii biulleten' no pravam cheloveka 1994. "Pasportnaya Sistema i Sistema Propiski v Rossii." Moskva: Proektnaya gruppa po pravam cheloveka (1994): 14–16.

Sakharov, Andrei. Forum speech in *Andrei Sakharov: Mir, Progress i Prava Cheloveka*. Leningrad: Sovetskii Pisatel', 1990.

—— *Memoirs*. New York: Alfred Knopf, 1990.

—— *Moscow and Beyond*. New York: Alfred Knopf, 1991.

Sakwa, Richard. *Gorbachev and His Reforms*. Englewood Cliffs, NJ: Prentice Hall, 1991.

—— *Russian Politics and Society*, London and New York: Routledge, 1993.

Science: American Association for the Advancement of Science,"Sergei Kovalyov: Biologist Denied Due Process and Medical Care", Vol. 194, No. 4265, November 5, 1976.

"Seminar Moskovskoi Khel'sinskoi Gruppy 'Prava Cheloveka' Moskva, 1–4 fevralya 1991". Published as *Iztoriya, filosofiya, printsipy i metody pravozashitnoi deyatel'nosti*. Moskva: Rossiskaya–Amerikanskaya proektnaya gruppa po pravam cheloveka, 1995.

Semonov, N. "Nekotorye voprosy o sotsiologii nauki" *Nauka i Zhizn*. Moskva: Pravda, No. 2 (1975): 16–22.

Shenshuchenko, Y. and Murashin, G. "Institut ombudsmena v sovremennom burshyaznom gosudarstve." *Sovetskoe Gosudarstvo i pravo*, 1 (1971): 139–44.

Shragin, Boris.*Challenge of the Spirit*. New York: Knopf, 1978.

Sinyansky, Andrei. "Vse eto uzhe bylo: Pochemy ya segodnya protiv Eltsina." *Nezavisimaya Gazeta*, No. 295, October 13, 1993: 5.

—— *The Russian Intelligentsia*. New York: Columbia University Press, 1997.

Siomina, Lydia. "Letter to Edward Kline." New York: Kline Archive, undated.

Sirotkin, Sergei. "Sotsialnie i ekonomicheskie prava v proekte Constitutsii RF." *Sotsialnie Problemi i Prava Cheloveka*. Moskva: Moscow Helsinki Group, 1993: 35–8.

Solzhenitsyn, Alexander. *The Gulag Archipelago*. London: Collins Harvill Press, 1974.

—— *The Oak and the Calf*. London: Collins Harvill Press, 1980.

Sovet Ministrov SSSR postanovlenie ot 5 oktyba, 1988, No. 1167 o deyatel'nosti na territorii SSR mezhdunarodnovo fonda. New York: Kline Archive.

Stone, Jeremy. "Bibliography of Dr Sergei Kovalev." February 12, 1975. New York: Kline Archive.

—— "Letter to the Honorable Alan Cranston, United States Senate from Jeremy Stone, Director, Federation of American Scientists." November 28, 1975. New York: Kline Archive.

Sulskis, M. "Letter to The Honorable Gerald Ford," April 22, 1976: New York: Kline Archive.

Tabakova, A. "V zone osobogo ravnodushiia." *Moskovskaya Pravda*, June 8, 1990: 4.

"The Price of Independence: The Office of Ombudsman and Human Rights in the Russian Federation." A Report of the Lawyers' Committee for Human Rights, New York: March 1995.

Tikos, L. and Peppard, M. *For Freedom of Imagination*. New York: Holt, Rinehart and Winston, 1971.

Tiwari, Rajiv. "RUSSIA – HUMAN RIGHTS: Zhirinovsky's Strasbourg Heckling Censured." Moscow, January 31. An Inter Press Service, 1995.

Ukaz prezidenta Rossiiskoi Federatsii ob obespechenii deyatel'nosti komissii po pravam cheloveka pri prezidente Rossiiskoi Federatsii, November 1, 1993, No. 1798. New York: Kline Archive.

Ulanovskaya, Nadezhda and Ulanovskaya, Maya. *Iztoriya Odnoi Sem'i.* Moskva: Vest VIMO, 1994.

Vedomosti – Sezd Narodnogo Deputata i Vekhovnogo Soveta RSFSR "O vnesenii izmenenii i dopolnenii v Ispravitelno-trudovoi kodeks RSFSR, Ugolovnii kodeks RSFSR i Ugolovno-protsessualnii kodeks RSFSR." No. 29, (992): 2086–101, 1992.

—— "Deklaratsiya Prav i Svobod Cheloveka i Grashdanina." No. 52, December: 2101–07, 1992.

Velikov, Evgeny. "Letter to Susan Eisenhower, September 11, 1991." New York: Kline Archive.

Waltz, S. *Human Rights and Reform*. Berkeley: University of California Press, 1995.

World Conference on Human Rights, Vienna Declaration and Programme of Action. Available online at http://www.unhchr.ch/html/menu5/wchr.htm.

Yakhimovich, I. "The Duty of a Communist" (October 30, 1964), *In Quest of Justice: Protest & Dissent in the Soviet Union Today*, Abraham Brumberg (ed.). New York: Praeger, 1970.

Yakobsen, Anatoly. *Pochva i Sud'ba*. Vilnius-Moskva: Vest, 1992.

"Zaklychenie Komissii po pravam cheloveka pri prezidente RF po resultatam spetsialnogo rassledovaniya faktov narysheniya prav detei v eksternoi shkole-internate Feniks Stypinskogo paiona Moskovskoi oblasti." Undated. Melbourne: Personal Collection, E. Gilligan.

Zolotukhin, Boris. "Moshet li Rossii vyiti iz konstitutsionnogo Krisisa?" *Rysskaya Mysl'*, No. 3981, May 28–June 3, 1993: 7.

Zile, Z. *Ideas and Forces in Soviet Legal History*. Oxford: Oxford University Press, 1992.

Index